Banneker

Banneker

The Afro-American Astronomer

Daniel Alexander Payne
Murray and Will W. Allen

MINT EDITIONS

Banneker: The Afro-American Astronomer features work first published between 1792–1921.

This edition published by Mint Editions 2023.

ISBN 9798888970140 | E-ISBN 9798888970294

Published by Mint Editions®

MINT
EDITIONS

minteditionbooks.com

Publishing Director: Katie Connolly
Design: Ponderosa Pine Design
Production and Project Management: Micaela Clark
Typesetting: Westchester Publishing Services

Contents

Introduction

The author, or to be more precise, the compiler of this work, while in Maryland, found in the house of Samuel H. Hopkins, of Howard county, a copy of a letter written by one Benjamin Banneker to Thomas Jefferson, Secretary of State.

He became interested on account of the beautiful language of this colored man's letter written in 1792, and at that time no doubt, Banneker was with a few exceptions the only colored man south of the Mason and Dixon Line who could read and write beyond the ordinary.

The compiler became enthused and started to find out all he could about this remarkable man. He deems it his duty to publish his findings and to place a copy in the home of every colored family in the United States.

Credit is given herein to:

Martha E. Tyson papers. compiled by her daughter, Anne T. Kirk.
Daniel Murray, an Assistant Librarian of the Library of Congress.
P. Lee Phillip, Esq., of the Columbia Historical Society.
Henry Proctor Slaughter, editor Odd Fellows Journal.
Henry E. Baker, in the Journal of Negro History.

And to the Maryland Historical Society. Feeling that the memory of this colored astronomer should be kept green, I place the accompanying facts in the hands of the public.

Will W. Allen.
September 15, 1921.

A Paper

Read Before the Banneker Association of Washington by Daniel Murray, *an Assistant Librarian of the Library of Congress.*

My Friends:

I am particularly gratified over the opportunity afforded me to recall to the attention of the living the virtues and intellectual powers of one of the illustrious dead. And it is all the more gratifying since your assembling here to do honor to your patron, to my mind, bespeaks the beginning of an era of intellectual progress, already too long delayed. I therefore heartily congratulate your Society on the advanced sentiment shown to encourage in vestigation into the lives of the many eminent men belonging to the Negro race, who are omitted in the histories by Caucasian authors and allowed to sleep the sleep of oblivion, by those who might rescue their memories and put on record the testimony of their deeds. It is not for me standing in this place, to criticize those who periodically appear before our Lyceums and discuss political topics. I do feel, however, that I am justified in urging that those who have the time and inclination should turn their attention to building up testimony to refute the charge of intellectual inferiority, which may easily be done, by putting in evidence the lives of our eminent men. For it is a truth, that allied by blood with the Negro race were some of the greatest men the world has produced. What follows is only a beginning of the flood of testimony furnished in almost every instance by Caucasian writers, which some day I hope to give to the world in extenso. Scientists and investigators in every line are crowding all the avenues of discovery, invention and literary research; they are surprising our credulity with the marvelous results of their investigations. Therefore, it is not amiss that something previously overlooked in regard to the colored man should come to light, and be marshalled as testimony in favor of his intellectual equality with the races of mankind, and further prove that he has always been equal to his opportunities. This investigation into the storehouse of literature particularly as it relates to colored authors, it will be seen, is a work of no little magnitude; it is both philosophical and profound. Something of its magnitude as a separate effort will appear from a consideration of the bibliographical fact, that it requires about thirty thousand volumes to contain even the names of the world's authors. and titles of their works, not estimating tracts, pamphlets or newspapers. Someone may inquire, "Why has not this in regard to the Colored race been brought forward before?" To this query Jefferson's answer to the Abbe Raynal in regard to Young America is quite appropriate.

When Raynal wondered why America has not produced celebrated men, Jefferson replied, "When we shall have existed as a nation as long as the Greeks before they produced a Homer, the Romans a Virgil, or the French a Racine, there will be room for astonishment." And what room would there be for astonishment if the people of Africa had not produced great men since the days when Sir John Hawkins commenced dealing in their living bodies, under authority of Queen Elizabeth. Would Lord Bacon have made himself the prince of philosophers if he had been brought to the Court of Elizabeth in chains from some tribe as savage as were his own ancestors at the time of the Roman invasion? If we were to find among the descendants of Africa, under all their present disadvantages, minds equal in genius and accomplishments to Bacon, Shakespeare, John Milton, or Sir Isaac Newton, might we not expect then, in a few hundred years, with equal advantages, to eclipse the glories of the Caucasian race? If literature is the measure of greatness, the answer, what has become of the literature of the ancient Britons, who were slaves at Rome in the time of Nero? We call upon the claimants of Caucasian superiority to bring it forward, and failing to do so, to abandon such an untenable claim.

In 1790, President Washington commenced the work of laying out the Federal City. For this work Major Peter Chas. L'Enfant was engaged. L'Enfant had been in the Army under Washington and was highly esteemed. Associated with him was Mr. Andrew Ellicott, who engaged Banneker to assist. L'Enfant was an eccentric and highly tempered genius, very difficult to get along with. He was constantly in hot water with the President and Jefferson, particularly with the latter, whom it seems recommended him to Washington. Several times he threatened to abandon the work of laying out the city, and Washington was constantly in dread that he would carry his threat into execution and yielded every demand. At last L'Enfant made a demand that could not be accorded and upon being convinced of this, true to his previous threats, in a fit of high dudgeon gathered all his plans and papers and unceremoniously left. It seems, Daniel Carroll, who was one of the Commissioners, and the owner of the famous Mansion "Duddington," had built it outside L'Enfant lines and he against Washington's protest, tore it down. An interesting story is told of the Duddingston House, North Carolina Avenue, Southeast. Daniel Carroll, the owner, who was one of the Commissioners to lay out the City, assumed against L'Enfant's protest, to build his house right in the center of what was intended for New Jersey Avenue. L'Enfant objected and explained the situation, but that not availing to stop the work he tore the house down. Washington was deeply offended at L'Enfant's act and ordered its restoration, but not, however, in the middle of New Jersey Avenue. The next largest proprietor was David Burns, a Scotchman, who owned the land south of the White House and including a part of the Mall. His daughter married Gen. John P. Van Ness, a member of Congress from New York, and at the death of her father became very rich. Van Ness was at one time Mayor of Washington and during his career lived in great style. He used to drive through the city in a fine carriage drawn by six white horses.

Through L'Enfant's unceremonious abandonment of his work, Washington was in despair, since it involved a defeat of all his cherished plans in regard to the "Federal City." This perturbation on his part was quickly ended, however, when it transpired that Banneker had daily for the purposes of calculation and practice, transcribed nearly all L'Enfant's field notes and through the assistance they afforded Mr. Andrew Ellicott, L'Enfant's assistant, Washington City was laid down very nearly on the original lines. It was while engaged in this work, 1791, that Banneker sent his Almanac to Jefferson.

L'Enfant took his plans as originally laid down for Washington, to Michigan and there sold them to Governor Woodward, and upon them the City of Detroit was laid out, Woodward Avenue corresponding to Pennsylvania Avenue in Washington. Those who are familiar with the plans of Detroit and Washington must have noticed the similarity which is quite remarkable. The original of both, however, being taken from Versailles, France, the Royal residence for many years of the Frency Kings. By this act the brain of the Afro-American is indissolubly linked with the Capital and nation. It is an indisputable evidence of the capacity of the colored man, though as Banneker was mixed blood, his grandmother being a white woman, his talents may be, and probably will be ascribed to his Caucasian reinforcement. He never married, being rather disposed to solitude and the contemplation of his problems which required absolute quiet, which quiet matrimony did not offer.

In 1843 the Conference of the A. M. E. Church, in session in Baltimore, appointed a committee of three with Daniel A. Payne (afterwards a Bishop in the connection) as chairman, to report upon the possibility of finding the grave of Banneker and erecting a monument over his remains. The Committee went to Ellicott's Mills and made diligent inquiry as to the spot. Many old people in the vicinity were consulted, but were only able to describe the spot as near a certain tree, which upon investigation was found to have disappeared, thus removing the only means of identification. Dr. Payne was obliged to report that the Committee was unable to carry out the order of the Conference to place a monument over the grave of Benjamin Banneker.

Banneker and his Times

In presenting Benjamin Banneker as proof of the intellectual capacity of the African and his descendants, we are not compelled to rest our case alone upon him, notwithstanding the fine showing that can be made with him.

The limits I have set myself, in marshalling the cases and testimony on the intellectual capacity of the African does not permit me to go outside the confines of the United States. Happily it is possible to find within its boundaries many intellectual giants that are entitled to rank with him. Immortals.

In this list I will name Thos. Fuller, the Mathematician: Booker T. Washington, Dr. James Derham, Briton and Jupiter Hammon, Alonzo Othello, Prince Hall, Capt. Paul Cuffee, John B. Russworm, Samuel E Cornisly, Gen. Moses Horton, Bishop Rich. Allen, Rev. Absalom Jones, Phillis Wheatley, Dr. Peter Williams, Harry Hozier, Bishop Christopher Rush, John Stewart, Catherine Ferguson, Crispers Attuck, Daniel Coker, Elijah Johnson, Rt. Rev. James Varick, Father (Peter) Spencer, Peter Ogden, Rt. Rev. Francis Asbury, Stephen Hill, John Fortie, William J. Watkins, Mary Ann Hall, Rev. John Gloucester, John Chavis, Mrs. Jarena Lee, Salem Poor, Denmark Vesey, Emanuel Perira, Moses Roper, Samuel Frances, Louis Pachieco, Pompay Lamb, Hero of Story Point, July 15th, 1779; David Walker, Noah Caldwell Cannon, Robt. Benjamin Lewis, author of *Light and Truth*, 1836.

I

Benjamin Banneker, the Afric-American astronomer, was born in 1731 at Ellicott Mills, near Baltimore, Maryland, the son of Robert and Mary Banneker. The first that is known of the name of Banneker is that it was borne by an African prince, who, being captured and brought to America as a slave, was purchased by Molly Welsh, an English woman, owning a small farm near the Patapsco river.

It was through the desire of his grandmother to have someone read to her from the Bible, that she taught her daughter's child to the extent of her own education, which joined to his natural powers, enabled him to become an expert mathematician. It was while working for George Ellicott, who erected the first mill in Baltimore county, that Banneker was induced to undertake the labor of calculating an almanac, which the Ellicotts had done some years ago and were going to discontinue. The immensity of the labor and mathematical knowledge required for the prosecution of such undertaking is in a measure brought to our comprehension by an examination of the: history of the Gregorian calendar.

It is to be regretted that no portrait of Banneker has come down to us. Oil painting and engraving on copper was the only means known to that date for transmitting a portrait. It is true the silhouette method was used but it was not satisfactory.

He is described by a gentleman who frequently met him at this time "as of a brown complexion, medium stature, of uncommonly soft, gentle manners, and of pleasing colloquial powers." Whatever others thought of him, the friendship of George Ellicott, the owner of the mills, himself a man of high literary attainments, never faltered. Ellicott's visits to Banneker were frequent. Finally he induced our timid star-gazer to venture such calculations as are set down in almanacs. But what was Ellicott's chagrin to find that his black friend's first prediction of an eclipse was false; an error had slipped into his calculations. Ellicott drew his attention to it. To his mingled surprise and delight, Banneker answered by letter, pointing out that he had been misled by a discrepancy between the two authors, Ferguson and Leadbeater. "Now, Mr. Ellicott," runs the letter, "two such learned gentlemen as the above-mentioned, one in direct opposition to the other, stagnate young beginners. But I hope that the stagnation will not be of long duration." In the same letter, speaking of the greatness of the task, he thus writes:

> It is an easy matter for us, when a diagram is laid down before us, to draw one in resemblance to it; but it is a hard matter for a young tyro in astronomy, when only the elements for the prediction are laid down for him, to draw his diagram with any degree of certainty.

Of the labor of his work few of those can form an idea who would nowadays attempt such a task with all the assistance afforded by accurate tables and well-digested rules. Banneker had no aid whatever from men or tables; and Mr. George Ellicott, who promised him some astronomical tables and took them to him, declares that he had advanced unaided far in the preparation of the logarithms necessary for his purposes. A memorandum of his calculations points out other errors of Ferguson and of Leadbeater, both of whom, no doubt, would have been an zed had they been informed that their elaborate works had been reviewed and corrected by a negro in the then unheard-of-valley of the Patapsco.

The first almanac prepared by Banneker for publication was for the year 1792 almanac-publishers of Baltimore gave a very flattering praise to the compiler.

Banneker himself was entirely conscious of the bearings of his case upon the position of his people; and, though remarkable for an habitual modesty, he solemnly claimed that his work had earned respect for the African race. In this spirit he wrote to Thomas Jefferson, then Secretary of State under Washington, transmitting a manuscript copy of his almanac. The letter a fervent appeal for the down trodden negro, and a protest against the in justice and inconsistency of his treatment by the people of the United States—is herewith given entire. I beg the reader as he peruses this letter to weigh its pleadings well, putting himself and our times in place of Jefferson and one hundred and twenty years ago.

Maryland, Baltimore County,
Near Ellicott's Lower Mills,
August 19th, 1791.

To Thomas Jefferson, Secretary of State, Philadelphia.

Sir,

I am fully sensible of the greatness of that freedom which I take on the present occasion; a liberty, which seemed to me scarcely allowable, when I reflected on that distinguished and honorable station in which you stand; and, the almost general prejudice and prepossession which is prevalent in the world, against those of my complexion.

I suppose it is a truth too well attested to you to need a proof here, that we are a race of beings who have long labored under the abuse and censure of the world, and that we have long been considered rather brutish, than as human, and scarcely capable of mental endowments.

Sir, I hope I may safely admit, in consequences of that report which hath reached me that you are a man far less inflexible in sentiments of this nature, than many others; that you are measurably friendly, and ready to lend your aid and assistance to our relief, from the many distresses and numerous calamities to which we are reduced. Now, Sir, if this is founded in truth, I apprehend you will embrace every opportunity to eradicate that train of absurd and false ideas and opinions, which so generally prevail with respect to us; and that your sentiments are concurrent with mine, which are—that one Universal Father hath given being to us all, and that He hath not only made us all of one flesh, but that He hath also,without partiality, afford us all the same sensations, and endued us all with the same faculties; and that, however variable we may be in Society and Religion, however diversified in situation and color, we are all of the:same family, and stand in the same relation to Him.

Sir, if these are sentiments of which you are fully persuaded, I hope you cannot but acknowledge that it is the indispensable duty of those who maintain for themselves the rights of human nature, and who profess the obligations of Christianity, to extend their power and influence to the relief of every part of the human race, from whatever burden or oppression they may unjustly labor under; and *this*, I apprehend, a full conviction of the truth, and obligations of these principles should lead all to.

Sir, I have long been convinced, that if your love for yourselves, and for those inestimable laws which preserve to you the rights of human nature, was founded on sincerity, you could not but be solicitous that every individual, of whatever rank or distinction, might with you equally enjoy the blessings thereof; neither could you rest satisfied, short of the most active diffusion of your exertions, in order to their promotion from any state of degration to which the unjustifiable cruelty and barbarism of men may have reduced them.

Sir, I freely and cheerfully acknowledge that I am of the African race; and, in that color which is natural to them, of the deepest dye; and it is under a sense of the most profound gratitude to the Supreme Ruler of the Universe, that I now confess to you that I am not under that state of tyrannical thraldom and inhuman captivity to which too many of my brethren are doomed; but that I have abundantly tasted of the fruition of those blessings, which proceed from that free and unequalled liberty with which you are favored, and which I hope you will willingly allow you have received from the immediate Hand of that Being from whom proceedeth "every good and perfect gift."

Sir, suffer me to recall to your mind that time in which the arms and tyranny of the British Crown were exerted with every powerful effort, in order to reduce you to a state of servitude. Look back, I entreat you, to the variety of dangers to which you were exposed; reflect on that time in which every human aid appeared unavailable, and in which even hope and fortitude wore the aspect of inability to the conflict; and you cannot but be led to a serious and grateful sense of your miraculous and providential preservation.

You cannot but acknowledge that the present freedom and tranquility which you enjoy you have mercifully received, and that it is the peculiar blessing of Heaven.

This, Sir, was a time in which you clearly saw into the injustice of a state of slavery, and in which you had just apprehensions of the horrors of its condition; it was now, Sir, that your abhorrence thereof was so excited that you publicly held forth this true and invaluable doctrine, which is worthy to be recorded and remembered in all succeeding ages, "We hold these truths to be self-evident, that all men are created equal, and that they are endowed by their Creator with certain inalienable rights, that amongst these are life, liberty, and the pursuit of happiness."

Here, Sir, was a time in which your tender feelings for yourselves engaged you thus to declare; you were then impressed with a proper idea of the just valuation of liberty, and the free possession of those blessings to which you were entitled by nature; but, Sir, how pitiable it is to reflect, that although you were so fully convinced of th: benevolence of the Father of mankind, and of his equal and impartial distribution of those rights and privileges which He had conferred upon them, that you should, at the same time, counteract his mercies, in detaining, by fraud and violence, so numerous a part of my brethren, under groaning captivity and oppression; that you should, at the same time, be found guilty of that most criminal act, which you professedly detested in others, with respect to yourselves.

Sir, I suppose that your knowledge of the situation of my brethren is too extensive to need a recital here; neither shall I presume to prescribe methods by which they may be relieved, otherwise than by recommending to you, and to all others, to wean yourselves from those narrow prejudices which you have imbibed with respect to them, and, as Job proposed to his friends, "Put your souls in their souls' stead." Thus shall your hearts be enlarged with kindness and benevolence towards them, and thus shall you need neither the direction of myself nor others in what manner to proceed therein.

And now, Sir, although my sympathy and affection for my brethren hath caused my enlargement thus far, I ardently hope that your candor and generosity will plead with you in my behalf, when I make known to you that it was not originally my design, but that, having taken up my pen in order to direct to you, as a present, a copy of an Almanac which I have calculated for the ensuing year, I was unexpectedly and unavoidably led thereto.

This calculation, Sir, is the production of my arduous study, in this my advanced stage of life; for having long had unbounded desires to become acquainted with the secrets of nature, I have had to gratify my curiosity herein, through my own assiduous application to astronomical study, in which I need not recount to you the many difficulties and disadvantages I have had to encounter.

And, although I had almost declined to make my calculation for the ensuing year, in consequence of the time which I had allotted there for being taken up at the Federal Territory, by the request of Mr. Andrew Ellicott; yet, finding myself under engagements to printers of this State, to whom I had communicated my design, on my return to my place of residence, I industriously applied myself thereto, which I hope I have accomplished with correctness and accuracy, a copy of which I have taken the liberty to direct to you, and which I humbly request you will favorably receive; and, although you may have the opportunity of perusing it after its publication, yet I chose to send it to you in manuscript previous thereto, that thereby you might not only have an earlier inspection, but that you might also view it in my own handwriting.

And now, Sir, I shall conclude, and subscribe myself with the most profound respect,

Your most obedient, humble servant,
B. Banneker

Mr. Thomas Jefferson, Secretary of State, Philadelphia.

N.B.—Any communication to me may be had by a direction to Mr. Elias Ellicott, Baltimore Town.

Thomas Jefferson's reply to the above letter:

PHILADELPHIA,
August 30th, 1791.

SIR,

I thank you sincerely for your letter of the 19th instant, and for the almanac it contained. Nobody wishes more than I do, to see such proofs as you exhibit that nature has given to our black brethren talents equal to the other colors of men, and that the appearance of a want of them is owing merely to the degraded condition of their existence, both in Africa and America. I can add, with truth, that nobody wishes more ardently to see a good system commenced for raising the condition, both of their body and mind, to what it ought to be, as fast as the imbecility of their present existence, and other circumstances which can not be neglected, will admit.

I have taken the liberty of sending your almanac to Monsieur de Condorcet, Secretary of the Academy of Sciences at Paris, and a member of the Philanthropic Society, because I considered it as a document to which your whole color had a right, for their justification against the doubts which have been entertained of them.

I am with great esteem, Sir,
Your most obedient, humble servant,
THOMAS JEFFERSON

MR. BENJAMIN BANNEKER,
Near Ellicott's Lower Mills, Baltimore Co.

II

This Molly Welsh, spoken of on a preceding page, was a person of exceedingly fair complexion and moderate mental powers, had been an involuntary emigrant to America.

When a servant on a cattle-farm in her native land, where milking formed a part of her duty, she was accused of stealing a bucket of milk, which a cow had kicked over. For this supposed offense, she was, by the stern laws of her country, sentenced to transportation, escaping a heavier penalty from the fact that she could read. On her arrival here she was, as was the custom, sold to defray the expenses of the voyage, for a term of seven years, and purchased by a tobacco planter on Patapsco river.

When her term of service had expired, land being of merely nominal value at that period. She was able to purchase the farm mentioned above. Here, needing assistance in her work, she bought in 1692 two negro men, on: being the "Banneker" of whom we have spoken. The other slave proved an industrious and valuable servant, while Banneker seemed to show his royal blood by a decided disinclination for work.

After a few years their owner set them free. The diligent worker had meanwhile embraced the Christian religion; but the prince remained loyal to the faith of his ancestors, and retained his African name, being simply "Banneker." He was a man of bright intelligence and fine temper, with a very agreeable presence, dignified manners and contemplative habits.

Banneker died early, leaving his wife with four young children. The family tradition tells us nothing further of her until she had a daughter grown to womanhood. Mary, her oldest daughter, married early a native African. He had been purchased from a slave ship by a planter living near her mother. His devotional turn of mind induced him early to become a member of the Church of England, and he received the name of Robert in baptism, upon which event his master gave him his freedom.

It was subsequent to his being a free man, that he married Mary Banneker and assumed his wife's surname.

We learn, however, that seven years subsequent to the latter event he purchased a farm.

This property was conveyed to him by deed, from Richard Gist, on the 10th of March, 1737. We thus learn indirectly that the parents of

Benjamin Banneker were married about the year 1730. For this land Roben Banneker (recorded as Banneky) paid seven thousand pounds of tobacco, that article being used instead of money in the colony.

Immediately upon being possessed of the farm, which contained one hundred acres, and was near that of his mother-in-law, Robert Banneker set about building a house, improving his land, and making a comfortable home for his family Benjamin Banneker was six years old when his father made the above purchase. The date of his birth is recorded in his own handwriting in a quarto Bible, now in possession of one of his relatives. The earliest specimen of his handwriting begins with a note of the purchase of the Bible, thus:

> "I bought this book of Honora Buchanan the 4th day of January, 1763. B. B."
>
> "Benjamin Banneker was born November the 9th, in the year of the Lord God, 1731."

It is unfortunate that he did not complete his family record, but only added the death of his father.

> "Robert Banneker departed this life July the 10th, 1759."

Few of the circumstances of the early life of the subject of our narrative are now known. According to the testimony of John Henden (a son of Banneker's oldest sister), his bright mind made him a great favorite with his grandmother, who found much pleasure in imparting to him all her small stock of knowledge in the department of letters. She much desired he should grow up a religious man, in furtherance of which view it was her delight to have him read to her from a large Bible which she had imported from England. After he had learned to read he attended a small school, where a few white and two or three colored children received together instruction from the same master.

III

It was in this school that his love of study first became apparent. Jacob Hall, who was a fellow-pupil with Banneker, and was intimately acquainted with him during his whole life, said that, as a boy, he was never fond of play or any light amusement; that, "all his delight was to dive into his books."

Benjamin Banneker's opportunities for study under a teacher were very limited, and of short duration. The school was only open during the winter season, and he ceased to attend it after he had grown large enough to assist his father in his labors of the farm; but, happily, his love of reading and desire to acquire knowledge remained with him.

After his youth was passed, he still continued to reside with his parents, and at the time of his father's death, which, we have seen, took place in 1759, he was twenty-eight years old.

Robert Banneker left to his widow and to his son, as joint heirs, the dwelling in which they lived and seventy-two acres of land. The remaining twenty-eight acres he divided between his three daughters.

Despite the studious habits of Benjamin Banneker, he was a good farmer, and very industrious in his work. He had a fine garden and well selected assortment of fruit trees. He kept two horses and several cows, and was very skillful in the management of his bees. All his work kept him closely engaged, except during the winter, leaving but scant time for his favorite studies, but from the fact that life was for him a school, and whether he was following the plow or reaping his grain, his contemplative mind found time for development.

In order to picture to ourselves the difficult circumstances through which Banneker's genius struggled, we must recall the wildness of the country, and the merely dawning civilization of the period. Although there were, in this section of the country, many settlers, there were still vast tracts of primeval forest, where the native animals found ample range.

Here would be found deer, wild turkeys, and other timid creatures, while close at hand lurked their destroyers, the wolf, the panther, and the wildcat, whose nightly cries disturbed the neighboring settlers. These animals had full possession of the valley where Ellicott City centers until the year 1772, at which period Banneker was forty-one years old.

When he was twenty-one years old there were only two sea-going vessels owned in Baltimore, and he was forty-two years old before any newspaper was published there. *The Maryland Gazette and Commercial Advertiser* issued its first number August 20th, 1773 Previous to this, "Green's Maryland Gazette," first issued in 1745, at Annapolis, was the sole advertising medium of the Province.

The one or two public stores to be found at that time in Baltimore, Joppa, and Annapolis, were so far out of reach of the planters of Elk Ridge, that they were accustomed to make their own importations. The size and luxury of these fluctuated with the London tobacco market. When this commodity commanded a good price, they indulged in large importations, purchasing much more than they needed for their own use. Each of these importing planters had a store-house, which received the varied result of the importation.

After selecting all that was required for home use, the surplus was disposed of to non-importing planters and small farmers.

It was the custom on large plantations to fire a cannon at sunrise, to summon all hands to the business of the day; but when this can non was fired at sunset, it was a notification that a supply of goods had arrived, which would be offered for sale or barter the next and following days.

It was on such stores as this that Banneker was compelled to depend during the earlier period of his life.

Every description of farming implement, from a plow to a rake, was purchased here; manufacturers being discouraged by the home government. Even shoes were thus procured. Rich and poor all met here to purchase, many hurrying to get a first choice of the products of the looms of Great Britain and India. Here, could be had brocades, embroideries, china, glassware, and mirrors, engravings, choice editions of classical writers, wines, and groceries.

Goods were sold at these private stores that would make a modern country store proprietor stand aghast at the thought of purchasing. Specimens of these early importations, still carefully preserved in some old families, do not suffer by comparison with the production of modern times.

When Banneker, as well as his neighbors. visited these private store-houses, designing to purchase any bulky commodities, they wo be accompanied by one or more pack-horse according to the proposed extent of their purchases. There were no roads over which even a wagon could travel, except that from Fred. erick to Baltimore, with a branch road to Annapolis. Carriages were a thing unseen and almost unheard of. There was a network of "bridle-roads," as they were termed; mere winding paths, connecting parts of the country together. From Frederick, such a road was used to communicate with Georgia.

"Rolling roads" were those over which tobacco was taken to its place of shipment. Their name suggests the manner in which the tobacco was propelled. After being packed in hogs heads and securely hooped, each hogshead was consigned to the care of two men, who rolled it over and over to the place of shipment. Elk Ridge Landing, on the Patapsco River, near the residents of "Elk Ridge," as that large section of country was called. Shipments to London, and importations, were generally through the port of Joppa, the tobacco sent from Elk Ridge Landing being reshipped at the latter place.

Joppa took precedence of Baltimore in commercial importance until the year 1773. It was the seat of the courts of Baltimore County, in which at that time Harford County was included. At the above date the county was divided, and the northern part named after the proprietary of the time. This change was fatal to the town of Joppa. On this spot, where there was a courthouse, four-story warehouses and many dwellings built of imported brick, there now remains but one dwelling. This is the property of Mr. James Murray, a large landed proprietor. When the tide of prosperity receded, Joppa was stranded, and from that time the buildings served as a quarry or brick yard, from which the neighboring farmers purchased material for building. Bricks were hought there as late as 1849, when the supply came to an end.

The only local evidence that this town ever existed is found in the graveyard, where we may read on marble brought from London:

IN MEMORY OF
DAVID MCCULLOH,

MERCHANT IN JOPPA,
WHO DIED THE 7TH DAY OF SEPT., 1766,
AGED 48 YEARS.

The former site of Joppa may be seen to the left, in traveling northward over the Gunpowder bridge, on the Philadelphia, Wilmington and Baltimore Railroad.

During this simple state of society, people learned much self-reliance. Until Banneker was forty-two years old, there were no workshops except of a private character, not even a blacksmith's shop. Each plantation and family had its own shop or shops. There, horses were shod with imported shoes, and farming implements mended; all sorts of repairs were made in these shops. The black smith, the cobbler, the tinker, the tailor, were all traveling artisans. Plying their trade in a considerable area of country, they became necessarily depositories of local news, for which they were nonetheless welcome, as they made their various trips.

We shall see presently how desirable it would have been for the young Banneker to have had some delicate tools fashioned to assist him in an intricate piece of mechanism: and it is hard to realize how he was able to attain so high a degree of scientific culture and skilled manipulation, as he manifested at this time, when he was seemingly without opportunity for study or observation, and even without tools to aid him. His genius, however, developed in combatting difficulties.

During his earlier manhood he found a great delight in mechanics, but had passed the meridian of life before astronomy became the one study to which all others yielded precedence.

When he had seen no timepieces but a sundial and a watch, he made himself clock which struck the hours, and was an admirable time-keeper. The works were of hardwood, cut out with a knife. In 1773, this clock had been running twenty years, and was naturally regarded as a great curiosity. When the clock was completed, Banneker was twenty-two years old. The fame of this achievement spread far and wide, and caused people to marvel much over this self-taught son of Africa, who was thus outstripping his neighbors of Anglo-Saxon parentage.

IV

In 1772, when Banneker was forty-one years old, a new field opened to his mental vision. It was the advent of the Ellicott family, who at this time moved from Pennsylvania and settled in Banneker's neighborhood. These were men of great force and foresight. Arriving by water at Elk Ridge Landing, they took their wagons apart, and carried them, a piece at a time, into the wilderness, where they proposed to erect flour mills. Here they cleared away the forest and built dams, and began to build mills (with a view to exporting flour) in a country where no grain was raised except for family use.

Their neighbors were not slow to visit this scene of action, most of them protesting against the folly of the work, as there never was any grain for sale in the neighborhood, the main product of the soil being tobacco.

These Ellicotts had examined the character of the country before deciding to settle there. They considered it peculiarly adapted to the growth of cereals, and they told their neighbors that "a demand would create a supply," and that there would be wheat to grind as soon as there was a mill to grind it. Meantime, they had set an example of what could be done, by planting crops upon their own land at the same time that their building operations were going on.

By the time that their first mill was ready to run, there was no lack of grain being offered for sale, but the first flour was made from the growth of their fields. In a few years, the agricultural system of the community was revolutionized, and the district became noted for its abundant crops of grain.

The fame of Banneker's clock had been the cause: of an early acquaintance between him and his miller neighbors. They found him and his mother living together in great comfort and plenty. The boarding-houses for the workmen who erected the mills, and other buildings for Ellicott & Co., were largely supplied with provisions from the farm of Banneker. His mother, Mary Banneker, attended to the marketing, bringing for sale poultry, vegetables, fruit, and honey.

The mother of Banneker was (her opportunities considered) a woman of uncommon intelligence. She had a knowledge of the properties and uses of herbs, which was often of advantage to her neighbors. Her appearance was imposing, her complexion a pale copper color, similar to that of the fairest Indian tribes, and she had an ample growth of long black hair, which never became gray. Her grandsons, the children of one of her daughters, used to speak with admiration of her many good qualities and her remarkable activity. They loved to relate that when she wished to prepare a basket of chickens for market, "she would run them down and catch them without assistance." This continued her practice when she was over seventy years of age.

The erection of the milling machinery was watched with great interest by Banneker, and he continued to make frequent visits to the mills after their operations had ceased to be a novelty.

A store had naturally grown up beside the mills, in an apartment of which, very soon, a post office was opened and a daily mail established. This store became a place of resort for the planters and others, to whom it served as an exchange, where, after selling or buying and receiving their mail, they tarried to discuss the news of the day.

The conversational powers of Banneker being of the first order, he was encouraged by the proprietors to make them frequent visits, and he was thus introduced to many strangers.

When he could be induced to lay aside the modest reserve for which he was conspicuous, all were pleased to listen to him. His mind was filled with volumes of traditionary lore, from which he would relate various anecdotes of the first occupation of the country by the emigrants: their disappointments and difficulties, and final successes; when, ceasing their fruitless search for gold, they settled down to the cultivation of the soil.

Occasionally, Banneker would allude to his own life, and his laborious pursuit of knowledge, unaided by the auxiliaries he then enjoyed through the kindness of the owners of the mills.

There was an especial sympathy between one of the younger members of the Ellicott family and Banneker. This was George Ellicott, the father of Martha Tyson.

He had been a mere youth when the family settled at Ellicott's Mills. That he had much energy and business capacity, we may know from the fact that the present road from Frederick to Baltimore was surveyed and laid out by him when he was seventeen years old. It is three miles shorter than the previous road. George Ellicott had a great love for the science of astronomy, in which he was well versed. Conceiving early a high estimate of Banneker's powers, he found pleasure in making him frequent visits, and furnishing him with such books and instruments as would aid him in his studies.

V

We find from the records of the Columbia Historical Society, Volume 20, 1917, as follows:

Benj. Banneker is known to the residents of the District of Columbia as connected with Ellicott in surveying the ten miles square. Little is known of his efforts in literature, astronomy and mathematics.

The following notes of Banneker are found first published in his Almanac, 1792, and republished with abridgement in 1793, from which we are making extracts.

It was written by Banneker's esteemed friend and admirer, James McHenry, who was after ward senator from the state of Maryland, and evidently a man who appreciated intellect, whether in the soul of the black or white, that at the time Banneker wrote his *Plea of Peace* in 1793, there existed wars between the United States and American Indians, between the British nation and Tuppar Saib, between the planters of St. Domingo and their African slaves, and also between the French nation and Germany. Banneker's *Plea of Peace* ends with the following lines: "The son of man came into the world not to destroy men's lives, but to save them."

The Georgetown weekly Ledger of March 12, 1791, speaks of the arrival at Georgetown of Ellicott and L'Enfant, who were attended by one Benj. Banneker, an Ethiopian, whose abilities as a surveyor and astronomer would be used in laying out the city of Washington. That his color did not affect his reputation is proven by the friendship of Washington, Jefferson and Ellicott and many distinguished scientists in Europe, who called him the "African American Astronomer."

All who had known his grandfather, the African prince, conceded that it was from *him* that the student grandson inherited the fine qualities of mind through which the name of Banneker became famous. His superiority over other men of his race made him an object of interest with all who knew him. They accepted his advancement in knowledge as a harbinger of better days for his people. His cottage came to be much frequented by strangers, as well as by the neighboring gentry. It was in this retired abode that Elizabeth Ellicott made him a visit in company with some of her friends in 1790. His door stood wide open, and so closely was his mind engaged that they entered without being seen. Immediately upon observing them he arose, and with much courtesy invited them to be seated. The large oval table at which Banneker sat was strewn with works on astronomy and with scientific appur tenances. He alluded to his love of the study of astronomy and mathematics as quite unsuited to a man of his class, and regretted his slow advancement in them, owing to the laborious nature of his agricultural engagements, which obliged him to spend the greater portion of his time in the fields.

Whilst they were engaged in conversation his clock struck the hour, and at their request he gave them an account of its construction. With his inferior tools, with no other model than a borrowed watch, it had cost him long and patient labor to perfect it. It required much study to produce a concert of correct action between the hour, minute, and second machinery, and to cause it to strike the hours. He acknowledged himself amply repaid for all his cares in its construction by the precision with which it marked the passing time. His mother had died previously to this, and he was the sole occupant of his dwelling. There had been a very strong affection between this mother and her gifted son.

Banneker was very assiduous in all his pursuits, and had much interest in agriculture, but finding his material occupations interfere so much with his design of devoting himself mor: closely to science, he sought out some plan by which he might obtain the coveted leisure, and hesitated long before deciding on an arrange. ment adapted to his condition. He finally determined to convey his land to Ellicott & Co., reserving to himself a life-estate in it. By this plan he received an annuity of £12 a year. Estimating this yearly payment by the probable duration of his life, he remarked to his as signees, "I believe I shall live fifteen years, and consider my land worth £180, Maryland currency. By receiving £12 a year for fifteen years, I shall, in the contemplated time, receive its full value; if, on the contrary, I die before that day, you will be at liberty to take possession." On making this change in his affairs, he deemed some explanation necessary as an apology for his apparent selfishness.

He referred to his desire to increase his knowledge on subjects to which his attention had been directed from his youth, and to his inability, from physical infirmities, to perform much laborious exercise; his land would thus be poorly cultivated, and poverty, an evil he much dreaded, increase upon him. Should he attempt to divide his small property, by will, among his nearest relatives, the parcels would be too small to be of service to any. If he gave it all to two or three, they would become objects of envy. Under the pressure of these conflicting views, he avowed that he felt excusable for making an arrangement exclusively for his own benefit.

Being now relieved from the necessity for constant toil, he revelled as never before in his astronomical studies. Banneker never married, nor can we learn that his mind was ever turned to the thought of such a possibility as marriage. He was possessed of a rare self-reliance. His "unbounded desires to become acquainted with the secrets of nature" caused him to need little society. His sisters, Minta Black and Molly Morton, lived near him, and cared for his necessities.

Having ceased a life of labor, he mostly passed the night, wrapped in his cloak and lying prostrate on the ground, in contemplation of the heavenly bodies.

At dawn he retired to rest, and spent a part of the day in repose, but does not seem to have required as much sleep as ordinary mortals. Still cultivating sufficient ground to give him needful exercise, he might often be seen hoeing his corn, cultivating his garden, or trimming his fruit trees. Sometimes he would be found watching the habits of his bees.

Occasionally, as a relaxation from his favorite studies, he would pass the twilight hour seated beneath a large chestnut tree, which grew on the hillside near his house, playing on the flute or violin. He loved music, and had some little skill in using either of these instruments.

One matter, personal to himself, gave him great pleasure in the retrospect that during his stay in Washington, *he had not tasted either wine or spirituous liquors*.

He had experienced the fact that it was unwise for him to indulge, ever so slightly, in stimulating drinks. On this occasion he said, "I feared to trust myself even with wine, lest it steal away the little sense I have." He was a noble example of what may be accomplished by a firm resolve.

Before entering upon his engagements with Major Ellicott, he had surmounted the difficuls alluded to in his letter to George Ellicott, of October, 1789. On his returning from his journey, he completed his first almanac, and ar ranged for its publication in the year 1792.

We subjoin, without abridgement, the very comprehensive title-page of the Afric-American astronomer's first almanac:

Benjamin Banneker's
Pennsylvania, Delaware, Maryland, and
Virginia

Almanac
and
Ephemris
for the Year of Our Lord
1792

Being Bissestile or Leap Year, and the sixteenth year of American Independence, which commenced July 4th, 1776. Containing the motions of the Sun and Moon, the true places and aspects of the Planets, the Rising and Setting of the Sun, and the Moon, etc., the Lunations. Conjunctions, Eclipses, Judgments of the Weather. Festivals, and other remarkable days. Days for holding the Supreme and Circuit courts of the United States, as also the usual courts in Pennsylvania, Delaware, Maryland, and Virginia; also several useful Tables and valuable Recipes: various selections from the common-place Book of the Kentucky Philosopher, an American sage; with interesting and entertaining Essays in Prose and Verse, the whole comprising a greater, more pleasing and useful variety than any work of the kind and price in North America.

We also give the printer's advertisement.

> Baltimore; Printed and sold Wholesale and Retail by William Goddard and James Angell, at their Printing-office in Market Street; sold also by Mr. Joseph Cruikshank, Printer in Market Street, and Mr. Daniel Humphreys, Printer in South Front Street, Philadelphia, and by Messrs. Hanson and Bond, Printers, Alexandria, Va.

Annexed to the title-page was a card from William Goddard and James Angell, from which we extract the following:

> "The editors of the Pennsylvania, Delaware, Maryland, and Virginia Almanac feel them selves gratified in the opportunity of presenting to the public, through the medium of their press, what must be considered an extraordinary effort of genius—a complete and accurate Ephemeris for the year 1792, calculated by sable descendant of Africa, who, by this speci a men of ingenuity, evinces to demonstration that mental powers and endowments are not the exclusive excellence of white people; but that the rays of science may alike illumine the minds of men of every clime,

however they may differ in the color of their skin, particularly those whom tyrant custom hath taught us to depreciate as a race inferior in intellectual capacity.

"They flatter themselves that a philanthropic public, in this enlightened era, will be induced to give their patronage and support to this work, not only on account of its intrinsic merit (it having met the approbation of several of the most distinguished astronomers in America, particularly the celebrated Mr. Rittenhouse), but from similar motive to those which induced the editors to give this calculation the preference—the desire of drawing modest merit from obscurity, and controverting the long established, illiberal prejudice against them.

"The editors of Banneker's Almanac have taken the liberty of annexing a letter from Mr. James McHenry, containing particulars respecting Benjamin, which it is presumed will prove more acceptable to the reader than anything further in the prefactory way.

BALTIMORE, *August 20th, 1791,*
MESSRS. GODDARD AND ANGELL.

****

Benjamin Banneker, a free negro, has calculated an almanac for the ensuing year, 1792, which, being desirous to dispose of to the best advantage, he has requested me to aid his ap plication to you for that purpose. Having fully satisfied myself with respect to his title to this kind of authorship, if you can agree with him for the price of his work, I may venture to assure you, it will do you credit as editors, while it will afford you the opportunity to encourage talents that have thus far surmounted the most discouraging circumstances and prejudices.

This man is about fifty-eight years of age. He was born in Baltimore Co.

His father and mother were enabled to send him to an obscure school, where he learned. when a boy, reading, writing, and arithmetic as far as double fractions, and to leave him at their deaths a few acres of land, upon which he has supported himself ever since by means of economy and constant labor, and preserved a fair reputation.

To struggle incessantly against want is no way favorable to improvement. What he learned, however, he did not forget; for as some hours of leisure will occur in the most toilsome life, he availed himself of them—not to read and acquire knowledge from writings of genius and discovery, for of such he had none, but to digest and apply, as occasion presented, the few principles of the few rules of arithmetic which he had been taught at school.

This kind of mental exercise formed his chief amusement, and soon gave him a facility in calculation that was often serviceable to his neighbors, and at length attracted the attention of the Messrs. Ellicott, a family remarkable for their ingenuity and turn for the use of mechanics.

It is about three years since Mr. George Ellicott lent him *Mayer's Tables*, *Ferguson's Astronomy*, *Leadbeater's Lunar Tables*, and some astronomic instruments.

These books and instruments, the first of the kind he had ever seen, opened a new world to Benjamin, and from thence forward he employed his leisure in astronomical researches. He now took up the idea of the calculations for an almanac, and actually completed an entire set for the last year, upon his original stock of arithmetic.

Encouraged by his first attempt, he entered upon his calculations for 1792, which he began and finished without the least information or assistance from any person or other books than those I have mentioned, so that whatever merit is attached to his present performance, it is peculiarly and exclusively his own.

I have been the more careful to investigate those particulars and to ascertain their reality, as they form an interesting fact in the history of man; and, as you may want them to gratify curiosity, I have no objection to your selecting them for your account of Benjamin.

I consider this negro as a fresh proof that the powers of the mind are disconnected with the color of the skin, or, in other words, a striking contradiction to Mr. Hume's doctrine, that "the negroes are naturally inferior to the whites, and unsusceptible of attainments in arts and sciences." In every civilized country, we shall find thousands of whites liberally educated, and who have enjoyed greater opportunities for instruction than this negro, his inferiors in those intellectual acquirements and capacities that form the most characteristic features in the human race.

But the system that would assign to those de graded blacks an origin different from the whites, if it is not ready to be deserted by philosophers, must be relinquished as similar. instances multiply; and that such must frequently happen, cannot well be doubted, *should no check impede the progress of humanity,* which, meliorating the condition of slavery, necessarily leads to its final extinction. Let, however, the issue be what it will, I cannot but wish on this occasion to see the public patronage keep pace with my black friend's merit.

I am, gentlemen, your most obedient servant,

James McHenry

James McHenry was one of the most prominent men of Baltimore, and was several times honored by his fellow-citizens with positions of trust and dignity. He was elected a Senator of Maryland in 1781, but resigned his seat in 1786. He was also one of the commissioners for framing the Constitution of the United States, and with his colleagues signed that instrument in 1787.

On the election of John Adams to the Presidency of the United States, in 1797, James McHenry, as Secretary of War, became a member of his cabinet.

VI

Banneker was an adept in the solution of difficult mathematical problems. They were in his day, much more than at present. the pastime of persons of culture.

Such questions were frequently sent to him by scholars in different parts of the country, who wished to test his capacity. He never failed to return a solution, sometimes accompanying it by questions in rhyme of his own composition.

Charles W. Dorsey, a planter of Elk Ridge, at one time a clerk in the store of Ellicott & Co., very kindly furnished the author, in November, 1852, with the following recollections of Banneker, and also with one of those rhymed questions to which we have alluded:

"In the year 1800 I commenced my engagements in the store at Ellicott's Mills, where my first acquaintance with Benjamin Banneker began. He often came to the store to purchase articles for his own use, and, after hearing him converse, I was always anxious to wait upon him. After making his purchases, he usually went to the part of the store where George Ellicott was in the habit of sitting, to converse with him about the affairs of our government, and other matters. He was very precise in conversation and exhibited deep reflection. His deportment, whenever I saw him, was perfectly upright and correct, and he seemed to be acquainted with everything of importance that was passing in the country.

"I recollect to have seen his almanacs in my father's house, and believe they were the only ones used in the neighborhood at the time. He was a large man and inclined to be fleshy. He was far advanced in years when I first saw him.

"I remember being once at his house, but do not recollect anything of the comforts of the establishment, nor of the old clock, about which you queried.

"He was fond of, and well qualified to work out, abstruse questions in arithmetic. I remember he brought to the store one which he had composed himself and presented to George Ellicott for solution. I had a copy, which I have since lost, but the character and deportment of the man were so wholly different from anything I had ever seen in one of his color; his question made so deep an impression on my mind that I have ever since retained a perfect recollection of it, except two lines, which do not alter the sense.

"I remember George Ellicott was engaged in making out the answer, and cannot now say how he succeeded, but have no doubt he did. I have thus briefly given you my recollections of Benjamin Banneker. I was young when he died, and doubtless many incidents, from the time which has since elapsed, have passed from my recollection."

The following is the question:

A cooper and vintner sat down for a talk,
Both being so groggy that neither could walk;
Says cooper to vintner, "I'm the first of my trade,
There's no kind of vessel but what I have made,
And of any shape, sir, just what you will,
And of any size, sir, from a tun to a gill."
"Then," says the vintner, "you're the man for me.
Make me a vessel, if we can agree.
The top and the bottom diameter define,
To bear that proportion as fifteen to nine,
Thirty-five inches are just what I crave,
No more and no less in the depth will I have;
Just thirty-nine gallons this vessel must hold,
Then I will reward you with silver or gold,—
Give me your promise, my honest old friend."
"I'll make it tomorrow, that you may depend!"
So, the next day, the cooper, his work to discharge,
Soon made the new vessel, but made it too large;
He took out some staves, which made it too small,
And then cursed the vessel, the vintner, and all.
He beat on his breast, "By the powers" he swore
He never would work at his trade anymore.
Now, my worthy friend, find out if you can,
The vessel's dimensions, and comfort the man!

BENJAMIN BANNEKER

Benj. Hallowell, of Alexandria, solved this problem: the greater diameter of Banneker's tub must be 24.745 inches; the less diameter, 14.8476.*

---

* See Maryland Historical Society Publication.

Banneker continued the publication of almanacs for ten years, after which declining health caused him to discontinue his calculations.

His time, during this later period of his life, was much taken up with the visitors whom his fame had attracted to his simple home.

Of all who visited him, we find in only one published work any account of an interview with this extraordinary man.

We extract from this work, long since out of print, *Memoir of Susannah Mason, by her daughter, R. Mason.*

"We found the venerable star-gazer under a wide-spreading pear tree laden with delicious fruit. He came forward to meet us, and bade us welcome to his lowly dwelling. It was built of logs, one story in height, and was surrounded by an orchard. In one corner of the room was a clock of his own construction, which was a true herald of departing hours. He took down from a shelf a little book, where in he registered the names of those by whose visits he felt particularly honored, and recorded my mother's name upon the list. He then diffidently, but very respectfully, requested her acceptance of one of his almanacs in manuscript."

In the course of a few days, this lady sent Banneker a rhymed letter, which afterwards circulated through the newspapers of the day. We copy it from the same work from whence the preceding was taken.

"An address to Benjamin Banneker, the African astronomer, who presented the author with a manuscript almanac in 1796.

"Transmitted on the wings of fame,
Thine eclat sounding with thy name,
Well pleased I heard, 'ere 'twas my lot,
To see thee in thy humble cot,
That Genius smiled upon thy birth,
And application called it forth;
That times and tides thou couldst presage,
And traverse the celestial stage,
Where shining orbs their circles run,
In swift rotation round the sun.

****

Some men, who private walks pursue,
Whom fame ne'er ushered into view,
May run their race, and few observe

To right or left, if they should swerve;
Their blemishes would not appear
Beyond their lines a single year.
But thou, a man exalted high,
Conspicuous in the world's keen eye,
On record now thy name's enrolled;
And future ages will be told
There lived a man named BANNEKER
An Africa Astronomer!
Thou need'st to have a special care,
Thy conduct with thy talent square,
That no contaminating vice
Obscure thy lustre in our eyes."

Sometime after receiving this communication, he sent to its author the following letter, which we copy literally:

August 26th, 1797

DEAR FEMALE FRIEND,

I have thought of you everyday since I saw you last, and of my promise in respect of composing some verses for your amusement, but I am very much in disposed, and have been, ever since that time. I have a constant pain in my head, a palpitation in my flesh, and, I may say, I am attended with a complication of disorders, at this present writing, so that I cannot with any pleasure or delight gratify your curiosity in that particular at this present time, yet I may say, my will is good to oblige you, if I had it in my power; because you gave me good advice, and edifying language, in that piece of poetry which you was pleased to present unto me; and I can but love and thank you for the same; and, if it should ever be in my power to be serviceable to you in any measure, your reasonable request shall be armed with the obedience of

Your sincere friend and well wisher,
BENJAMIN BANNEKER

MRS. SUSANNAH MASON.

N. B.—The above is mean writing done with trembling hands.

This letter was directed to the care of Casandra Ellicott, afterwards married to Joseph Thornburg, of the mercantile house of Thorn urg, Miller & Webster, Baltimore.

We give some of the old astronomer's notes, which are found in close proximity to his calculations of cclipses and other scientific work. We learn from some of these observations how fully he was alive to all that was beautiful or remarkable about him.

> Our distilled spirits are like unto the water of the river of Phrygia, which, if drank sparingly, purges the brains and cures madness, but otherwise it infects the brains and creates madness.
>
> 2 Kings, chapter 23d, verse 11, 'And he look away the horses that the kings of Judah had given to the sun.'
>
> August 27th, 1797. Standing by my door, I heard the discharge: of a gun, and in four or five seconds of time the small shot came rattling about me, one or two of which struck the house, which plainly demonstrates that the velocity of sound is greater than that of a cannon-bullet. B. Banneker.
>
> 22nd of Dec., 1790. About 3 o'clock A.M., I heard a sound, and felt the shock, like unto heavy thunder. I went out, but could not observe any cloud above the horizon. I therefore concluded it must be a great earthquake in some quarter of the globe.
>
> 1803, Feb. 3d. In the morning part of the day there arose a very dark cloud, followed by snow and hail, a flash of lightning and a loud thunder-crash, and then the storm abated until afternoon, when another cloud arose at the same point, viz., the northwest, with a beautiful shower of snow. But what beautified the snow was the brightness of the sun, which was near setting at the time.

He wrote the following account of the locust years of his time in 1800:

> The first great locust year that I remember was in 1749. I was then about seventeen years old, when thousands of them came and were creeping about the bushes. I then imagined they came to cat and destroy the fruit of the earth, and would occasion a famine in the land. I therefore began to kill and destroy them, but soon saw that the labor was in vain, and therefore gave over my pretension. Again, in the year 1766,

which is seventeen years after their first appearance to me, they made a second, and appeared to me as numerous as the first. I then being about thirty-four years of age had more sense than to endeavor to destroy them, knowing they were not so pernicious to the fruits of the earth as I did imagine they would be.

Again in the year 1783, which was seventeen years from their second appearance to me, they made their third, and may be expected again in 1800, which is seventeen years since their third appearance to me. So that I may venture to express it, their periodical return is seventeen years; but they, like the comets, make a short stay with us.

I like to forget to inform, that if their lives are short, they are merry. They begin to sing or make a noise from the first they come out of the earth till die.

On the subject of his bees, he writes as follows:

In the month of January, 1797, on a pleasant day for the season, I observed my honey lees, and they seemed to be very busy, all but one hive. Upon examination, I found all the lees had evacuated this hive, and left not a drop of honey behind them. On the 9th of February ensuing, I killed the neighboring hive of bees on a special occasion, and found a great quantity of honey, considering the season, which. I imagine, the stronger had violently taken from the weaker, and the weaker had pursued them to their home, resolved to be benefited by their labor or die in the contest.

The commonplace book of the old astronomer gives ample assurance that his love for science had not diminished his prudent regard for the common affairs of life.

We give some of his memoranda:

Sold on the 2d of April, 1795, to Butler, Edwards, and Kiddy, the right of an Almanac for the year 1796, for the sum of eighty dollars, equal to £30.

On the 30th of April, 1795, lent John Ford five dollars—£1 17s. 6d. 12th of December, 1797, bought a pound of candles, at 1s. 8d.

> Sold to John Collins two quarts dried peaches, 6d., one quart mead, 4d.
>
> On the 26th of March came Joshua Sanks with three or four bushels of turnips to feed the cows.
>
> On the 13th of April, 1803, planted peas and sowed cabbage seed.

These domestic mementos occupy a strange proximity with entries of a more dignified nature, being occasionally found on the same page with a notice of astronomical character.

Benjamin Banneker possessed a remarkably mild and philosophic temperament, which was often manifested by his forbearance to his ignorant neighbors, who trespassed on his private rights, and to the boys of his vicinity who were in the constant habit of robbing his orchard. All his fruit was of the best kind, and his cherries and pears were in high favor with the youthful population, which had grown to be quite a formidable body in the last years of his life.

They would call respectfully at his door, ask and obtain permission to partake of some of his fruit, and afterwards retire; then, when he was shut up in his house immersed in calculations, they would return and strip his trees; thus he was often deprived of his fruit, and sometimes even before it had reached maturity.

For this he has been heard to remonstrate with the young culprits, and offer them an allowance of one-half, if they would leave him in undisturbed possession of the other half; but all to no purpose.

To a friend who once visited him in summer, he expressed his regret that he had no fruit to present him worthy of acceptance, adding, "I have no influence with th: rising generation; all my arguments have failed to induce them to set bounds to their wants." He was not, however, left without a hope from the powerful influence of good examples sometimes at hand.

On this subject he remarked at the same time, "It has been said, 'Evil communications corrupt good manners:' I hope to live to hear that 'Good communications correct had manners,'" a sentiment we find noted down amongst his manuscripts.

The situation of the astronomer's dwelling was one which would be admired by every lover of nature. Aside from furnishing a fine field for the observation of celestial phenomena, it commanded a prospect of the near and distant hills of the Patapsco river, which have always been celebrated for their picturesque beauty. A never-failing spring gushed forth beneath a large golden willow tree: in the midst of his orchard.

The health of Banneker, as he approached the evening of his days, often suffered from complaints produced by his long patient astronomical observations, continued throughout all seasons of the year.

His last recorded observations were for the month of January, 1804, and are contained in his commonplace book. After that period his writing appears but once, when we find the name "Benjamin Banneker," with the date "1805," written by a trembling hand, on a torn and stitched leaf of his volume of manuscript almanacs. This is his last known penmanship.

VII

However unfavorable the circumstances over which Banneker's genius triumphed, he was not without advantages. He was born *free*, the son of a *free man*. His father, and his grandfather before him, had experienced for only a short period the mental influences of a state of dependence. Banneker understood and respected his privileges, not the least among which was the elective franchise. In his letter to Thomas Jefferson, he says, "I have abundantly tasted of the fruition of those blessings which proceed from that free and unequalled liberty with which you are favored." All *free men* stood upon equal footing as voters, in Maryland, during the greater part of Banneker's life. There was a property qualification requisite, which, with age and residence, gave the right of voting until 1802. Then the law was changed, and the elective franchise conferred solely upon white men, twenty-one years old, who should have resided a given time in the place of voting. By this change the venerable astronomer was deprived of the valued privilege of voting during the last four years of his life.

We have said that Benjamin Banneker never married, neither did he unite himself with any religious sect. His life was one of constant worship in the great temples of nature and science. In his early days, places of worship were rare. As they increased in number during his later years, he would occasionally visit those of the various denominations. He finally gave a decided preference for the doctrines and form of worship of the Society of Friends, whose meeting-house at Ellicott's Mills he frequently attended.

The author well remembers Banneker's appearance on these occasions, when he always sat on the form nearest the door. He presented a most dignified aspect as he leaned in quiet contemplation on a long staff, which he always carried after passing his seventieth year, "And he worshipped leaning on the top of his staff." His reverent deportment on these occasions added to the natural majesty of his appearance.

The countenance of Banneker had a most benign and thoughtful expression. A fine head of white hair surmounted his unusually broad and ample forehead, whilst the lower part of his face was slender and sloping towards the chin. His figure was perfectly erect, showing no inclination to stop as he advanced in years. His raiment was always scrupulously neat; that for summer wear, being of unbleached linen, was beautifully washed and ironed by his sisters, Minta Black and Molly Morton, who we have seen, lived near him, and looked after his domestic affairs. In cold weather he dressed in light colored cloth, a fine drab broadcloth constituting his attire when he designed appearing in his best style.

Being cut off from his favorite employments by reason of his infirmities, and his love of nature remaining ever with him, it so happened that when the great messenger, Death, called for him he was found out upon his favorite hills.

It was on the peaceful Sabbath morning of the 9th of October, 1806, that he strolled forth, as was his custom, to enjoy the air and the sunshine and the view. It was his last look on them with earthly vision. He met an acquaintance, with whom he conversed pleasantly for a while, when, suddenly complaining of feeling sick, they immediately turned to his cottage. He laid himself upon his couch and never spoke again. In a little while his mortal frame lay dead.

The following notice of his death is taken from the *Federal Gasette and Baltimore Daily Advertiser,* Tuesday morning, October 28, 1806:

> On Sunday, the 9th instant, departed this life, at his residence in Baltimore County, Mr. Benjamin Banneker, a black man, and immediate descendent of an African father. He was well known in his neighborhood for his quiet and peaceful demeanor, and, among scientific men, as an astronomer and mathematician.
>
> In early life he was instructed in the most common rules of arithmetic, and thereafter, with the assistance of different authors, he was enabled to acquire a perfect knowledge of all the higher branches of learning. Mr. Banneker was the calculator of several almanacs, published in this as well as several of the neighboring States; and, although of late years none of his almanacs have been published, yet he never failed to calculate one every year, and left them among his papers.
>
> Preferring solitude to mixing with society, he devoted the greater part of his time to reading and contemplation, and to no book was he more attached than the Scriptures.
>
> At his death, he bequeathed all his astronomical and philosophical books and papers to a friend.
>
> Mr. Banneker is a prominent instance to prove that a descendent of Africa is susceptible of as great mental improvement and deep knowledge of the mysteries of nature as that of any other nation.

VIII

Some years prior of Banneker's death, he had been extremely ill, and apprehending that he would not recover, he gave particular directions respecting the disposition of his personal property, but made no written bequests. He ordered that all the articles which had been presented to him by George Ellicott should be returned to him as soon as he was no more.

It was owing to the singular promptness in carrying out these directions that any souvenirs of this extraordinary man were preserved. On the same day on which he died, one of his nephews carried out his wishes to the letter. Being himself the messenger who conveyed to Ellicott's Mills the tidings of his uncle's death, he arrived at the house of George Ellicott driving a cart, in which was the oval table on which all Banneker's calculations were made; a large number of scientific instruments, and many books on varied topics. These were accompanied by a legacy, which Banneker requested his friend to accept in memory of his long-continued kindness to the giver. It was a large volume of his manuscript and his common-place book. The former volume contains Banneker's observations on various subjects and copies of all his almanacs, as well as copies of his letter to Thomas Jefferson, and the reply of that statesman. We have extracted freely from these books in the preceding pages.

Banneker left to his surviving sisters, Minta Black and Molly Morton, everything else that he died possessed of. The Bible in which he read seems to have been removed from the 1ouse with the same promptness as the legacy to George Ellicott, as it is still extant. His remains were interred two days subsequent to his decease, and whilst the last rites were being performed at his grave, his house took fire, and burned so rapidly that nothing was saved. His clock and all other evidences of his ingenuity and scholarship were consumed in the flames. Some months previous to his death he had given to one of his sisters a feather bed. All his other gifts to her sister and herself, except the Bible, having been destroyed, this bed was highly valued and carefully preserved. After a lapse of some years, she felt something hard among the feathers, which proved to be a purse of money. This simple fact is a pleasing evidence that, though the venerable sage was, through failing health, long hindered from lucrative employment, yet no shadow of poverty rested upon the evening of his honored life.

In Conclusion

We should in some way show honor to the memory. of this wonderful mind, this distinguished citizen, who notwithstanding race prejudice of the times, rose to eminence in scientific attainments. One has only to look at Banneker's picture, "photographed from the original wood-cut," to see a face of determination, "one of intelligence, a face of moral force," under different condition, and different times, a leader of men.

In proposing a National Banneker Memorial Association, I think it is due him, and. I will, in my limited way, use my best efforts to encourage same.

The Author

BENJAMIN BANNEKER'S
ASTRONOMICAL JOURNAL

BANNEKER.

[illegible] 8 [illegible] / [illegible]

[illegible] 4

Cost [illegible]

1790 December the 18 [illegible] [illegible] informed me that the said [illegible] Charles [illegible] Stole my horse and [illegible] Coat and that [illegible] [illegible] [illegible] me [illegible] [illegible] [illegible] and further gave me Caution to let no person in my house after Dark.

1790 December the 23rd about 3 O'Clock A.M. I heard a Sound and felt the Shock like unto heavy thunder, I went out but could not observe any Cloud above the Horizon, I therefore Conclude it must be a great Earth Quake in Some part of the Globe

When the Moon Changes in the Descending Node at the time of an Eclipse.

In Calculating the Moons place, we must observe to add 2°. 44 to the
Longitude ~~given~~ that is gaven by the Table, to Compensate for the
in the Meredians, as the Tables was Calculated to the Meredian of Gr

To find the Moons Rising

We must Subtract the Suns Right Ascension, from the Moons Oblique
then Enter the Table Shewing the time of the planets Setting when they have
Declination, and their rising when they South Declination - Enter this Table
the Moons Declination at the head and your Latitude in the Side Column
Common Angle is the Hours and minuses thats is to be added to the defference of
Suns and Moons Ascension if in be less than Six Hours, but Subtracted if more
the ~~Line~~ Sum or Defference is the time of rising - practical Navigator

The Moons Setting may be obtained by adding half the Lunar day to her Southing, when
S[illegible] Declination, and by Subtracting when the Declination is North

[illegible] Astronomy Explaind on Sr. Isaac Newtons principles
[illegible] Stands in the Same line with Easter Sun
[illegible] must Serve for the given year,

[illegible]	[illegible]	[illegible]	[illegible]	[illegible]
[illegible]	6 . 0 . 46 . 0	7 . [illegible]	6 . 5 . [illegible]	6 . [illegible]
[illegible]	Mercury Aphe	Mercury Node	- - - -	[illegible]
[illegible]	2 . 22 . 26 . 28	1 . 16 . 0 . 10		[illegible]
[illegible]	Venus Aphe	Venus Node		[illegible]
91 [illegible]	9 . 0 . 51 . 11	2 . 14 . 44 . 54	- -	
Mars Longitude	Mars Aphe	Mars Node	Moon Longitude [illegible] Anomally [illegible]	
91 10 . 9 . [illegible]	[illegible]	1 . 18 . 22 . 20	Longitude	Anomaly
Jupiter [illegible]	[illegible]	Jupiter Node	4 . 28 . 56 . 4	[illegible]
[illegible]	[illegible]	3 . 8 . 50 . 18	[illegible]	

[illegible] the Moon [illegible] because [illegible] that must [illegible] of Greenwich [illegible] Baltimore [illegible]

[illegible] Table [illegible] page 150

[illegible]

[illegible] for instance [illegible]

7 . 21
20 . 2
17 . 2[illegible]
5 . 19
0 . [illegible] . 22
2 . 45
[illegible] . 16 . [illegible]

In Correcting the Moons place, we must observe to add 2.4.5 to the Longitude ~~given~~ that is given by the Table, to Compensate for the [illegible] in the Meridians, as the Tables was Calculated to the Meridian of [illegible]

To find the Moons Rising

We must Subtract the Suns Right Ascension, from the Moons Oblique [illegible] then Enter the Table Shewing the time of the planets Setting when they have [illegible] Declination, and their rising when they South Declination. Enter this Table [illegible] the Moons Declination at the head and your Latitude in the Side Column [illegible] Common Angle is the Hours and minutes that is to be added to the Difference [illegible] Suns and Moons Ascension if it is less than Six Hours but Subtracted if [illegible] the ~~Sum~~ Sum or Difference is the time of rising [illegible] Nov 1 90 10

The Moons Setting may be obtained by adding that the Same way to her Southern Declination, and by Subtracting when the Declination is North

[illegible] Explains [illegible] [illegible] [illegible] [illegible] [illegible]
[illegible] [illegible] [illegible] [illegible] [illegible]
[illegible] [illegible] [illegible]

Reduced to the New Stile

	Suns Longitude	Suns Anomally	Moons Longit	Moons Anomal	Moons Node
	s ° ′ ″	s ° ′ ″	s ° ′ ″		
1791	9 .. 10 .. 5 .. 0 (12)	6 .. 0 .. 46 .. 0	7 .. 14 .. 51 .. 39	6 .. 5 .. 32 .. 24	6 .. 27 .. 13 .. 49
	Mercury' Longit	Mercury Anno	Mercury Node	- - - -	N.B. 12″ must be added to the Suns mean Longitude [illegible]
	s ° ′ ″	s ° ′ ″	s ° ′ ″		
1791	11 .. 6 .. 29 .. 38	2 .. 22 .. 26 .. 28	1 .. 16 .. 3 .. 10		
	Venus' Longit	Venus' Anno.	Venus' Node	- - - -	[illegible]
	s ° ′ ″	s ° ′ ″			
1791	9 .. 8 .. 48 .. 21	11 .. 0 .. 51 .. 11	2 .. 14 .. 44 .. 54	- - - -	- - -
	Mars's Longit	Mars's Anno	Mars's Node	Moons Longitude and Anomally for 11 Days	
	s ° ′ ″	s ° ′ ″	s ° ′ ″		
1791	10 .. 9 .. 56 .. 43	5 .. 7 .. 37 .. 15	1 .. 18 .. 22 .. 20	Longitude	Annomally
	Jupiters Longit	Jupiters Anno	Jupiters Node	s ° ′	s ° ′
	s ° ′ ″	s ° ′ ″	s ° ′ ″	4 .. 24 .. 56	4 .. 23 .. 43
	5 .. 19 .. 1 .. 15	11 .. 7 .. 38 .. 15	3 .. 8 .. 50 .. 0	N.B. 2′ 45″ must be added to the Moons Longitude because her orbit motion is that much between the Meridian of Greenwich and that of Baltimore	

1791 Mercury Aphelial Anomally 9 .. 22 .. 26

1791 Mercury perihelial Anomally 3 .. 22 .. 34

1791 Venus's Aphelial Annomally 0 .. 29 .. 9
Venus's Perihelial Annomally 6 .. 29 .. 9

1791 Mars's Aphelial Anomally 6 .. 22 .. 23
Mars's Perihelial Annomally 0 .. 22 .. 23

1791 Jupiters Aphelial Anomally 0 .. 22 .. 22
Jupiters Perihelial Annomally 6 .. 22 .. 22

Saturns Aphelial Annomally 8 .. 18 .. 41
Saturns Perihelial Annomally 2 .. 18 .. 41

To find the Mean Changes of the Moon, See practical Navigator, page 150,

In Leap Year, the Longitude of the Moon for the given Year Serves for the first day of the new year, for instance 1792 is Leap year

	s	°	′
the Moons Longitude	0	7	29
Apogee	2	20	2
Anomally	9	17	27
Equation		5	53
	0	13	22
Difference of Longit		2	45
Long first day of New y.	0	16	7

To gain the Moons First Quarter, first find the place of each Luminary day before the aspect, then Subtract the Suns place from that of the Moon and the Residue is the distance of the Moon from the Sun, and if it is less than the 90 degrees, take what it wants of 90 degree and apply it to the Table of Lunar Aspects, and take out the Hours and minutes, which added to the noon of the day, gives the time of the Moons first Quarter. But if the distance of the Moon from the Sun be above 90 degrees, take the Surpluss and apply it to the Table of Lunar Aspects, and take out the Hours and Minute which Subtracted from the noon of the day will also leave the time of the Moons First Quarter.

But to find the last Quarter of the Moon, if the distance of the Moon from the Sun be above 90 degrees, then apply the Surpluss to the Table of Lunar Aspects with the Surpluss or distance above 90 degrees to the left hand and the Diurnal Motion at the head of the Table and take out the Hours and Minutes from it which added to the Noon of the day, gives the time of the last Quarter—But if the distance of the Moon from the Sun, be less than 90 degrees, then take what it wants of 90 degrees and apply it to the aforesaid Table and take out the Hours and Minutes, which Subtracted from the Noon of the day will leave the time of the last Quarter; you must observe to Subtract the Moons place from that of the Sun to find their distance at the last Quarter

---

To obtain the Southing of a Star or planet, find the true Longitude of the Sun and also of the Star or planet, then with their Longitudes enter the Table of Right Ascension and take out their Right Ascensions and Subtract that of the Sun from that of the Star or planets, the residue is the time of their Southing near enough for Common practice

---

To find the Geocentric Latitude of a planet, we must Say as Sine Commutation is to Sine of Elongation, So is Tangent Inclination to Geocentric Lat. of the planet. But at the true time of Conjunction there is neither Commutation nor Elongation But we must with the Argument of Latitude take out of the proper Table, the Inclination or Heliocentric Latitude which answers the purpose of the Geocentric in Such cases

1791 September the 27th day there will be an Eclips of the Sun, invisible in our Hemisphere, But may be observed 6h..43m west Longitude from the Meridian of Baltimore

Beginning of the Eclips	5h..55m	}	P.M.	{ Apparent time
Greatest Obscuration	7..23			
End of the Eclips	8..43			

Digits Eclipsed 6 on the Suns South Limb, Sun from ♌ 11s..21°..38′, Suns Declination 1°..41′ South

1792 Suns Long according Leadbetter	1792 Logarithm of Suns distance from the Earth	D	1792 Suns Long According to Leadbetter	1792 Logar of Suns distance from the Earth
January S ° ′			July S ° ′	
9..11..26	4.992757	1	3..10..1	5.007134
9..17..34	4.992966	7	3..15..45	5.006943
9..23..40	4.993255	13	3..21..29	5.006681
9..29..46	4.993620	19	3..27..15	5.006408
10..5..51	4.994058	25	4..2..59	5.0060[illegible]
February 1792		D	August 1792	

1792 January 1st Day Saturn ♄ Occidental
♄ Oriental April 10th day
♄ Occidental October 21 day

1792 January 1st day Jupiter Orient[al]
April 16th day Jupiter Occident[al]
November 3d day Jupiter Orient[al]

1792 January 1st day Mars Orient[al]
March 15th day Mars Occidental

1792 January 1st ♀ Oriental
August 5th ♀ Occidental
and commences Evening Star

[illegible]		hard	7..18	4..42	2..28..41	18..6	11..3	13 [illegible]
A	1st Sunday past Epiphany		7..17	4..43	3..10..32	♂	11..49	14
2	Bulls Eye S..8..56	frosts	7..17	4..43	3..22..30	rises	12..38	15
3			7..16	4..44	4..4..34	6..32	13..24	16
4	Days 9..30	now	7..15	4..45	4..16..51	7..28	14..9	17
5			7..15	4..45	4..29..21	8..23	14..54	18
6	Sirius S..10..50	grows	7..14	4..46	5..12..8	9..25	15..42	19
7			7..13	4..47	5..25..15	10..26	16..29	20
A	2nd Sunday past Epiphany		7..13	4..47	6..8..39	11..33	17..20	21
2		more moderate	7..12	4..48	6..22..25	12..38	18..12	22
3			7..11	4..49	7..6..30	13..49	19..8	23
4	☌ ☉ ☿ Oriental	clouds	7..10	4..50	7..20..50	14..55	20..7	24
5			7..10	4..50	8..5..23	16..4	21..4	25
6	□ ☉ ♃ ☉ enters ♒		7..9	4..51	8..20..4	17..8	22..5	26
7		with	7..8	4..52	9..4..45	18..9	23..6	27
A	3d Sunday past Epiphany	wind	7..7	4..53	9..17..24	☌	☌	28
2	Arcturus rise 10..26		7..6	4..54	10..3..55	sets	0..3	☽
3		now expect	7..5	4..55	10..18..10	6..12	0..52	1
4	Conversion St paul		7..4	4..56	11..2..10	7..19	1..46	2
5	Days 9..54	snow	7..3	4..57	11..15..51	8..22	2..35	3
6			7..2	4..58	11..29..7	9..23	3..24	4
7			7..1	4..59	0..12..8	10..27	4..10	5
A	4th Sunday past Epiphany	or	7..0	5..0	0..24..49	11..23	4..56	6
2		Cold	6..59	5..1	1..7..15	12..22	5..44	7
3	Day increase 48 m.	rain	6..58	5..2	1..19..28	13..20	6..32	8

If the New year begins on Sunday, the Dominical is A
If on Monday G
If on Tueday F
If on Wednesday E
If on Thursday D
If on Fryday C
If on Saturday B

[illegible]

Common Notes and Movable Feasts for the year

Dominical Letter	G	Easter Sunday	April 8
Cycle of the Sun	9	Ascension Day	May. [illegible]
Golden Number	7	Whitsunday	May. [illegible]
Epact	6	Trinity Sunday	June [illegible]
Number of Direction	18	Advent Sunday	Decem[illegible]

It is to be observed that the Moon and the five primary planets [illegible] the Same Declination as the Sun has, when in the Same Sign and ~~the same Degree the Moon or planet is in at the given time~~

that of the Sun to, find their distance at the last Quarter

To obtain the Southing of a Star or planet, find the true Longitude of [the] Sun and also of the Star or planet, then with their Longitudes enter ~~in~~ the Table [of] Right Ascension and take out their Right Ascensions and Subtract that of the [Sun] from that of the Star or planets, the residue is the time of their Southing [near] enough for Common practice

To find the Geocentric Latitude of a planet, we must Say as Sine Commutation is to Sine of elongation, So is Tangent Inclination to Geocentric Lat. of the [planet]

But at the true time of Conjunction there is neither Commutation nor Elongation

But we must with ~~take~~ the Argument of Latitude take out of the proper Table, the [illegible] Inclination or Heliocentric Latitude which answers the purpose of the Geo[centric] in Such cases

1792

January. First Month hath 31 Days.

	D. H. M.
First ☽	1 .. 5 .. 23 Morn
Full ○	9 .. 4 .. 25 Morn
Last ☾	16 .. 6 .. 43 Aft
New ●	23 .. 0 .. 53 Aft
First ☽	30 .. 6 .. 34 Aft

☊ { 1, 11, 21 } ♎ { 8, 7, 7 } Deg.

Planets Places							
D	☉	♄	♃	♂	♀	☿	☽
	♑	♈	♎	♍	♏	♒	Lat
1	11	11	29	28	23	0	1 S
7	18	11	♏ 0	♎ 0	29	5	5 S
13	24	12	1	3	♐ 6	4	2 S
19	♒ 0	12	1	3	13	♑ 27	4 N
25	6	13	1	4	20	22	3 N

M D	W D	Remarkable Days Aspects weather &c		☉ rise	☉ Set	☽ Long	☽ Sets	☽ South	☽ Age
1	A	Circumcision □ ☉ ♄	Clear	7 .. 20	4 .. 40	S. D. 0 .. 16 .. 8	0 .. 35 Morn	6 .. 25	7
2	2	Days 9 . 20	(♀ great Elong	7 .. 20	4 .. 40	0 .. 28 .. 39	13 .. 41	7 .. 10	8
3	3		and	7 .. 20	4 .. 40	1 .. 10 .. 57	14 .. 36	7 .. 55	9
4	4	Days increase 5 m.	Cold	7 .. 19	4 .. 41	1 .. 23 .. 1	15 .. 34	8 .. 42	10
5	5			7 .. 19	4 .. 41	2 .. 5 .. 0	16 .. 29	9 .. [illegible]	11
6	6	Epiphany	very	7 .. 18	4 .. 42	2 .. 16 .. 51	17 .. 20	10 .. 17	12
7	7	pleades S 8 .. 16	hard	7 .. 18	4 .. 42	2 .. 28 .. 41	18 .. 6	11 .. 3	13
	A	1st Sunday past Epiphany		7 .. 17	4 .. 43	3 .. 10 .. 32	☍	11 .. 49	14
	2	Bulls Eye S 8 . 56	frosts	7 .. 17	4 .. 43	3 .. 22 .. 30	rises	12 .. 38	15
	3			7 .. 16	4 .. 44	4 .. 4 .. 34	6 .. 32	13 .. 24	16
	4	Days 9 .. 30	now	7 .. 15	4 .. 45	4 .. 16 .. 51	7 .. 28	14 .. 9	17
	5			7 .. 15	4 .. 45	4 .. 29 .. 21	8 . 23	14 . 54	18
	6	Sirius S 10 .. 50	grows	7 .. 14	4 .. 46	5 .. 12 .. 8	9 .. 25	15 .. 42	19
	7			7 .. 13	4 .. 47	5 .. 25 .. 15	10 .. 26	16 .. 29	20
	A	2nd Sunday past Epiphany		7 .. 13	4 .. 47	6 .. 8 .. 39	11 .. 33	17 .. 20	21
	2		more moderate	7 .. 12	4 .. 48	6 .. 22 .. 25	12 .. 38	18 .. 12	22
	3			7 .. 11	4 .. 49	7 .. 6 .. 30	13 .. 49	19 .. 8	23
	4	☌ ☉ ☿ Oriental	Clouds	7 .. 10	4 .. 50	7 .. 20 .. 50	14 .. 55	20 .. 7	24
	5			7 .. 10	4 .. 50	8 .. 5 .. 23	16 .. 4	21 .. 4	25
	6	□ ☉ ♃	☉ enters ♒	7 .. 9	4 .. 51	8 .. 20 .. 4	17 .. 8	22 .. 5	26
	7		with	7 .. 8	4 .. 52	9 .. 4 .. 45	18 .. 9	23 .. 6	27
	A	3d Sunday past Epiphany	wind	7 .. 7	4 .. 53	9 .. 19 .. 24	☌	☌	28
	2	Arcturus rise 10 .. 26		7 .. 6	4 .. 54	10 .. 3 .. 55	Sets	0 .. 3	☽
	3		now expect	7 .. 5	4 .. 55	10 .. 18 .. 10	6 .. 12	0 .. 52	1
	4	Conversion St. paul		7 .. 4	4 .. 56	11 .. 2 .. 10	7 .. 19	1 .. 46	2
	5	Days 9 .. 54	snow	7 .. 3	4 .. 57	11 .. 15 .. 51	8 .. 22	2 .. 35	3
	6			7 .. 2	4 .. 58	11 .. 29 .. 7	9 .. 23	3 .. 24	4
	7			7 .. 1	4 .. 59	0 .. 12 .. 8	10 .. 27	4 .. 10	5
	A	4th Sunday past Epiphany	or	7 .. 0	5 .. 0	0 .. 24 .. 49	11 .. 23	4 .. 56	6
	2		Cold	6 .. 59	5 .. 1	1 .. 7 .. 15	12 .. 22	5 .. 44	7
	3	Day increase 48 m.	rain	6 .. 58	5 .. 2	1 .. 19 .. 28	13 .. 20	6 .. 32	8

	D H m
March 1792 True time of New Moon	22..1..4
	° '
Semidiameter of the Earths Disc — —	58
Suns Distance from the nearest Solstice viz. ♋	87..12
Suns Declination North — —	1
Moons Latitude North Descending — —	1
Moons Horary Motion — —	' " 29..55
Angle of the Moons visible path with the Ecliptic — — —	5..35
Suns Semidiameter — — —	
Moons Semidiameter	
Semidiameter of the penumbra — — — —	

Question by Hopkins

When fleecy Skies had Cloth'd the ground
With a white mantle all around
Then with a grey hound Snowy fair
In milk white fields we Cours'd a Hare
Just in the midst of a Champaign
We set her up, away She ran,
The Hound I think was from her then
Just thirty leaps or three times ten
Oh it was pleasant for ~~me~~ to See
How the Hare did run So timorously
But yet so very Swift that I
Did think She did not run but fly
When the Dog was almost at her heels
She ~~made~~ quickly turn'd, and down the fields
She ran again with full Carear
And 'gain she turn'd to the place she were
At every turn she gain'd of ground
As many yards as the greyhound
Could leap at three, and She did make,
Just Six, if I do not mistake
Four times She leap'd for the Dogs three
But two of the Dogs leaps did agree
With three of hers, now pray declare
How many leaps he took to Catch the Hare

Answer

Just Seventy two I did Suppose
An answer false from thence aro[se]
I Doubled the Sum of Seventy tw[o]
But still I found that would no[t do]
I mix'd the Numbers of them bot[h]
Which Shew'd so plain that I'll [...]
Eight hundred leaps the Dog did m[ake]
And Sixty four, the Hare to take

4 : 72 :: 48
48
576
288
4)3456
864 ans.

February Second Month hath 29 Days

1792

	D	H	M	
Full ☉	7	10	31	Aft
Last ☾	15	4	26	Morn
New ☽	22	0	34	Morn
First ☾	29	2	3	Aft

{1, 11, 21} ♎ {6, 6, 5} Deg.

Planets Places

D	☉	♄	♃	♂	♀	☿	☽ Lat
	♒	♈	♏	♎	♐	♑	
1	13	13	2	4	28	19	4 S
7	19	14	2	4	♑ 5	24	4 S
13	25	14	2	4	12	29	2 N
19	♓ 1	15	2	3	19	♒ 7	5 N
25	7	16	2	1	26	14	1 S

M D	W D	Remarkable Days, Aspects, weather &c.		☉ rise	☉ Set	☽ Long. S ° '	☽ Sets	☽ South	☽ Age
	4	✶ ☉ ♄	now	6..57	5..3	2..1..28	14..13	7..17	9
	5	purification V. M	grows	6..56	5..4	2..13..24	15..11	8..4	10
	6	Arturus rise 9..41		6..55	5..5	2..25..14	15..54	8..51	11
	7		mild	6..54	5..6	3..7..3	16..41	9..38	12
	A	Septuagesima		6..53	5..7	3..18..57	17..26	10..26	13
	2	□ ♂ ♀	for the	6..52	5..8	4..0..57	☍	11..13	14
	3	pleades Sets 1..33	Season	6..51	5..9	4..13..6	rises	11..59	15
	4			6..50	5..10	4..25..27	6..11	12..45	16
	5	Spica ♍ rises 10..16	but	6..49	5..11	5..8..6	7..7	13..31	17
	6		soon	6..48	5..12	5..20..59	8..11	14..18	18
	7	Sirius Sets 1..56		6..46	5..14	6..4..12	9..14	15..7	19
	A		Changes	6..45	5..15	6..17..49	10..17	15..57	20
	2	☿ great elong. 26..8		6..44	5..16	7..1..42	11..23	16..49	21
	3	Valentine	to	6..43	5..17	7..15..54	12..31	17..43	22
	4		Cold	6..42	5..18	8..0..20	13..42	18..46	23
	5	Days increase 1..24		6..40	5..20	8..14..57	14..52	19..49	24
	6		and	6..39	5..21	8..29..38	15..52	20..49	25
	7	☉ enters ♓	windy	6..38	5..22	9..14..22	16..51	21..48	26
	A	Quinquagesima		6..36	5..24	9..28..57	17..40	22..44	27
	2		weather	6..35	5..25	10..13..21	18..24	23..39	28
	3	Shrove Tuesday		6..34	5..26	10..27..31	☌	☌	29
	4	Ash Wednesday		6..33	5..27	11..11..20	[illegible]	0..30	☽
	5	Sirius South 8..9	rain	6..32	5..28	11..21..51	7..11	1..14	1
	6		or Snow	6..31	5..29	0..8..2	8..13	2..3	2
	7	♃ South 3..25		6..30	5..30	0..20..52	9..15	2..51	3
	G	1st Sunday in Lent	now	6..28	5..32	1..3..28	10..12	3..38	4
	2	pleades Sets 12..15	Clear	6..27	5..33	1..15..45	11..13	4..25	5
	3		and	6..26	5..34	1..27..55	12..8	5..12	6
	4	Days 11..12	Cold	6..24	5..36	2..9..51	13..0	6..0	7

Question by Elicott Geographer Genral

Divide 60 into four such parts, that the first being increased by 4, the second de-creased by 4, the third multiplyd by 4, and the fourth part divided by 4, that the Sum, the difference, the product, and the Qutient, Shall be one and the Same Num[ber]

Ans. first part	5.6	increased by 4	is	9.6
Second part	13.6	decreased by 4		9.6
third part	2.4	multiplyd by 4		9.6
fourth part	38.4	divided by 4		9.6
	60.0			

May the 4th: 1792. In a Squall from the N. W. I observed the Lower region [of] Clouds to move Swiftly before the wind, and the upper region Slowly against

March Third Month hath 31 Days

1792

	D	H	M	
Full ○	8	1	59	Aft
Last ☾	15	2	2	Aft
New ☽	22	1	4	Aft
First ☾	30	7	31	Morn

☊ {1 ♎ 5, 11 ♎ 4, 21 ♎ 4} Deg.

Planets Places

D	☉	♄	♃	♂	♀	☿	☽
	♓	♈	♏	♍	♒	♒	Lat
1	12	16	1	29	2	22	5 S
7	18	17	1	27	9	♓ 0	3 S
13	24	18	0	20	16	10	4 N
19	♈ 0	19	0	23	23	21	3 N
25	6	19	♎ 29	21	♓ 0	♈ 3	3 S

W D	Remarkable Days Aspects weather &c		☉ rise	☉ Sets	☽ Long	☽ Sets	☽ South	☽ Age
5	St. David	flying	6..24	5..36	2..21..44	13..51	6..48	8
6	pegasi Algenib Sets 7..57		6..23	5..37	3..3..35	14..37	7..34	9
7		Clouds	6..22	5..38	3..15..26	15..23	8..20	10
G	2nd. Sunday in Lent	with	6..21	5..39	3..27..23	16..4	9..8	11
2	pegasi Markab South 1..50		6..19	5..41	4..9..25	16..43	9..55	12
3		high	6..17	5..43	4..21..39	17..15	10..41	13
4	Days 11..28		6..16	5..44	5..4..7	[illegible]	11..28	14
5	♃ South 2..37	wind	6..14	5..46	5..16..49	rises	12..15	15
6	Days increase 2..18		6..13	5..47	5..29..56	7..4	13..4	16
7		Some	6..12	5..48	6..13..18	8..7	13..54	17
G	3d. Sunday in Lent		6..11	5..49	6..27..0	9..18	14..47	18
2	Gregory	appearance	6..9	5..51	7..11..7	10..23	15..42	19
3	pleades Sets 11..24	of	6..8	5..52	7..25..21	11..33	16..41	20
4			6..7	5..53	8..9..55	12..40	17..40	21
5	☍ ☉ ♂ Occident.	Snow	6..6	5..54	8..24..35	13..42	18..39	22
6		or	6..4	5..56	9..9..17	14..42	19..38	23
7			6..3	5..57	9..23..56	15..33	20..37	24
G	4th. Sunday in Lent	Cold	6..2	5..58	10..8..28	16..22	21..34	25
2	Equal Day and Night	rain	6..0	6..0	10..22..46	17..6	22..28	26
3	☉ enters ♈		5..59	6..1	11..6..46	17..40	23..16	27
4	Benedict		5..58	6..2	11..20..32	☌	☌	28
5	☉ eclipsed	now grow	5..57	6..3	0..3..49	Sets	0..5	☽
6		temperate	5..55	6..5	0..16..48	6..53	0..50	1
7	☌ ☉ ☿ Occidental	for	5..54	6..6	0..29..35	7..43	1..36	2
G	5th. Sunday in Lent	the	5..53	6..7	1..12..3	8..34	2..24	3
2		Season	5..52	6..8	1..24..26	9..26	3..13	4
3	Algol South 2..30		5..50	6..10	2..6..19	10..15	4..2	5
4		Cool	5..49	6..11	2..18..10	11..8	4..51	6
5	Bulls eye Sets 10..47		5..48	6..12	3..0..5	11..56	5..36	7
6		westerly	5..46	6..14	3..11..54	12..47	6..23	8
7	Days increase 2..14	winds	5..45	6..15	3..23..47	13..35	7..8	9

Sun Eclipsed 22 d..1 h..4 m Aft being 5 s..29°..39′ Distant from the Moons North Node

NB the Node is Equated

Required the Lengths of the Sides of an Equaliteral Triangle inscribed in a Circle … ter is 200 perches, with a general Theorim for all shuch Questions

Solution of the above problem

10.00 . . . . 3.142 . . . 200

200

1000) 628 | 400

Lenght of the periphery	628.400
1/3 of the lenght of the periphery	209.466
1/3 of 1/3 of the periphery	69.822
2/3 of 1/3 of the periphery	139.644
Length of the Sides required	349.110

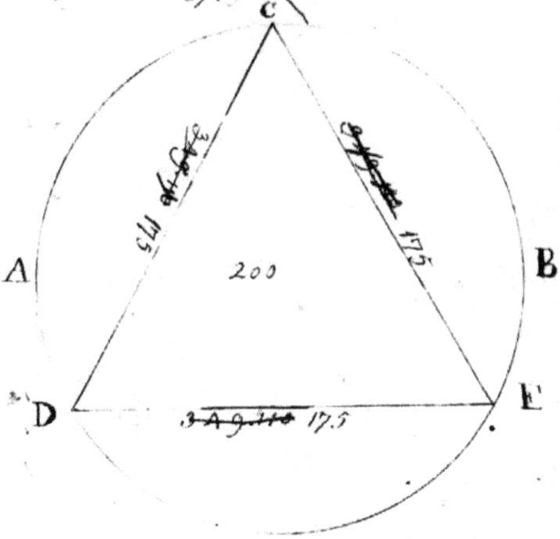

Fifth Month hath 30 Days

	D	☉	♄	♃	♂	♀	☿	☽ Lat.
[illegible]								
First Q. 29 .. 1 . 37 Morn	7	18	21	28	18	17	♉ 0	2 N
	13	24	22	27	17	25	6	5 N
{1, 11, 21} ♎ {3, 3, 2} Deg.	19	♉ 0	23	26	17	♈ 2	19	1 S
	25	6	24	25	17	9	24	5 S

W D	Remarkable Days Aspects weather &c		☉ rise	☉ Sets	☽ Long.	☽ Sets	☽ South	☽ Age
G	Palm Sunday	now expect	5 .. 44	6 .. 16	4 .. 5 .. 46	14 .. 51	7 .. 59	10
2		Clouds	5 .. 43	6 .. 17	4 .. 17 .. 54	15 .. 25	8 .. 44	11
3	Arctus Sets 8 . 24	and	5 .. 41	6 .. 19	5 .. 0 .. 15	16 .. 2	9 .. 31	12
4	Spica ♍ South 12 . 21		5 .. 40	6 .. 20	5 .. 12 .. 51	16 .. 35	10 .. 18	13
5		rainy	5 .. 39	6 .. 21	5 .. 25 .. 41	17 .. 10	11 .. 7	14
6	Good Fryday	weather	5 .. 38	6 .. 22	6 .. 8 .. 57	☍	11 .. 56	15
7	♃ South 12 . 59		5 .. 36	6 .. 24	6 .. 22 . 27	rises	12 .. 48	16
G	Easter Sunday	moderate	5 .. 35	6 .. 25	7 .. 6 .. 18	8 . 18	13 . 40	17
2			5 .. 34	6 .. 26	7 .. 20 .. 28	9 .. 25	14 .. 37	18
3	☌ ☉ ☿ Oriental	Clear and	5 .. 33	6 .. 27	8 .. 4 .. 52	10 .. 31	15 . 35	19
4	Pleades Sets 9 . 38		5 .. 32	6 .. 28	8 .. 19 .. 30	11 .. 49	16 . 46	20
5		pleasant	5 .. 30	6 .. 30	9 .. 4 .. 12	12 .. 40	17 .. 37	21
6	♃ South 12 .. 14	and	5 .. 29	6 .. 31	9 .. 18 .. 53	13 . 35	18 .. 35	22
7		fine	5 .. 28	6 .. 32	10 .. 3 . 31	14 .. 19	19 .. 31	23
G	1st Sunday after Easter	growing	5 .. 27	6 .. 33	10 .. 17 . 56	15 .. 7	20 .. 26	24
2	☍ ☉ ♃ Occidental		5 .. 26	6 .. 34	11 .. 2 .. 7	15 .. 45	21 .. 18	25
3	Arcturus South 12 .. 23	weather	5 .. 25	6 .. 35	11 .. 15 .. 59	16 .. 20	22 .. 7	26
4			5 .. 23	6 .. 37	11 .. 29 .. 34	16 .. 58	22 .. 55	27
5	☿ great elong 19 .. 14	☉ enters ♉	5 .. 22	6 .. 38	0 .. 12 .. 43	17 .. 30	23 .. 43	28
6			5 .. 21	6 .. 39	0 .. 25 .. 38	☌	☌	29
7	Days 13 .. 20	perhaps	5 .. 20	6 .. 40	1 .. 8 .. 15	Sets	0 .. 30	☽
G	2nd Sunday after Easter	a	5 .. 18	6 .. 42	1 .. 20 .. 33	8 .. 2	1 .. 14	1
2		thunder	5 .. 17	6 .. 43	2 .. 2 .. 44	9 .. 0	2 .. 0	2
3	Days increase 4 .. 12	Gust	5 .. 16	6 .. 44	2 .. 14 .. 43	9 .. 53	2 .. 50	3
4	Capella South 2 .. 49	with	5 .. 15	6 .. 45	2 .. 26 . 36	10 .. 40	3 .. 37	4
5		rain	5 .. 14	6 .. 46	3 .. 8 .. 26	11 .. 28	4 .. 25	5
6	Cassiopea South 10 .. 9	toward	5 .. 13	6 .. 47	3 . 20 . 16	12 .. 13	5 .. 13	6
7		the	5 .. 12	6 .. 48	4 .. 2 . 12	12 .. 50	5 .. 58	7
G	3d Sunday after Easter	end of	5 .. 11	6 .. 49	4 .. 14 . 13	13 . 31	6 .. 46	8
2	Days 13 .. 40	the month	5 .. 10	6 .. 50	4 .. 26 . 26	14 .. 4	7 . 30	9

Required the Lengths of the Sides of an Equaliteral Triangle inscribed in a Circle [...] ter is 200 perches, with a general Theorim for all such Questions

Solution of the above problem

10.00 ...... 3.142 200

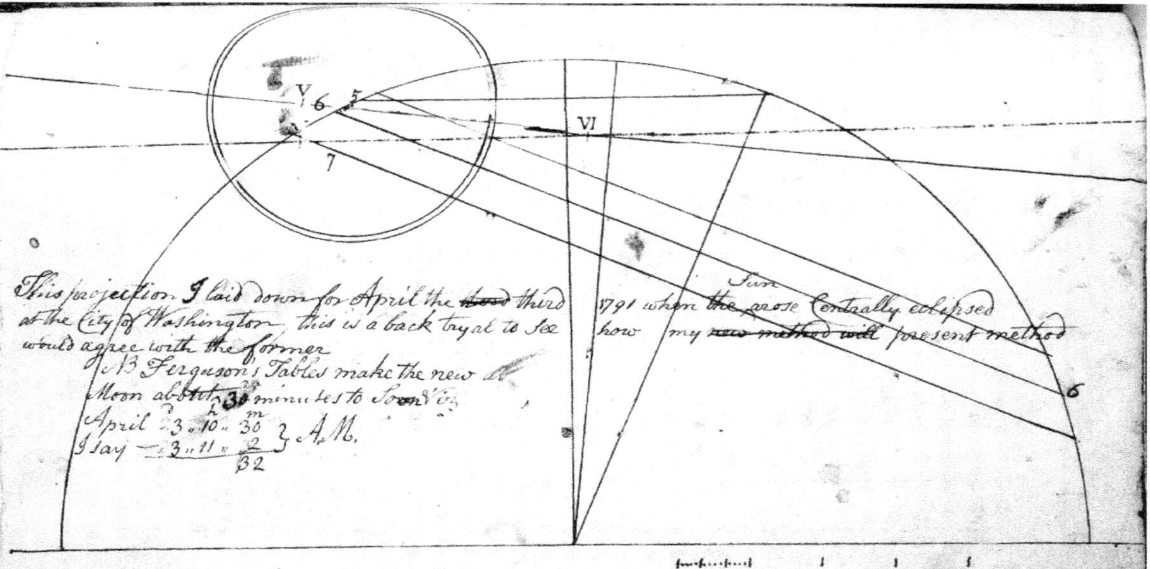

This projection I laid down for April the ~~moon~~ third 1791 when the Sun rose Centrally eclipsed at the City of Washington this is a back tryal to see how my ~~new method will~~ present method would agree with the former

N B Ferguson's Tables make the new Moon about 30 minutes to soon &c

	d	h	m	
April	3	10	30	A.M.
I say	3	11	2	A.M.
			32	

Fifth Month hath 31 Days

			Planets Places					
[illegible]		[illegible]	♄	♃	♂	♀	☿	☽ Lat
[illegible] 4 Aft		♉	[illegible]	[illegible]	[illegible]	[illegible]	♊	
10 . 3 . 34 [illegible]						18	0	2 S
[illegible] 2 . 8 Aft	1	12	24	24	14	26 ☌	26	4 S
[illegible] 4 . 24 Aft	7	18	[illegible]	24	15	[illegible]	[illegible]	[illegible]
	7	22	24	23	[illegible]	1	26	3 N
[illegible] } Days	13	[illegible]	[illegible]	[illegible]	[illegible]	8	24	4 S
[illegible] }	20	[illegible]	[illegible]	[illegible]		[illegible]	21	3 S
	25	♊ [illegible]	[illegible]	[illegible]				

Month's Days, weather &c.	☉ rise	☉ sets	☽ Longs	☽ Lat	☽ South	☽ Age
[illegible] warm	4 . [illegible]	6 . 41	5 . 3 . 54	4 . 36	3 . 16	15 r
[illegible] agreeable	[illegible]	6 . 52	[illegible]	15	[illegible]	11 r
[illegible] weather	[illegible]	6 . 53	[illegible]	[illegible]	[illegible] 41	12 r
	[illegible] 5	6 . 55	6 . 18 [illegible]	[illegible]	[illegible] 12	13 r
[illegible] cloudy	[illegible]	6 . 56	7 . 1 . [illegible]	[illegible]	[illegible]	14
[illegible] St. John Evang.	[illegible]	[illegible]	[illegible]	[illegible]	[illegible]	[illegible]
	[illegible]	[illegible]	[illegible]	[illegible]	[illegible]	[illegible]
and	[illegible]	[illegible]	8 . 14 . [illegible]	[illegible]	[illegible]	[illegible]
like	[illegible]	7 . [illegible]	[illegible]	[illegible]	[illegible]	[illegible]
for a	4 . 59	[illegible]	[illegible]	[illegible]	[illegible]	[illegible]
warm	[illegible] 58	7 . 2	[illegible]	12	[illegible]	20 r
[illegible]	4 . 58	7 . 2	[illegible]	[illegible]	[illegible]	21 r
	4 . 57	7 . 3	[illegible]	[illegible]	[illegible]	22
[illegible]	4 . [illegible]	7 . 3	[illegible]	14	[illegible]	23 r
[illegible]	[illegible]	[illegible]	[illegible]	[illegible]	[illegible]	23
[illegible]	4 . [illegible]	[illegible]	[illegible]	[illegible]	[illegible]	[illegible]
[illegible]	4 . [illegible]	7 . [illegible]	[illegible]	16	[illegible]	[illegible]
[illegible]	[illegible]	[illegible]	[illegible]	16	[illegible]	[illegible]
	4 . [illegible]	[illegible]	[illegible]	[illegible]	[illegible]	[illegible]
[illegible]	[illegible]	[illegible]	[illegible]	[illegible]	[illegible]	[illegible]
[illegible]	4 . 51	7 . 9	[illegible]	[illegible]	[illegible]	[illegible]
[illegible]	4 . [illegible]	7 . 10	[illegible]	[illegible]	[illegible]	2
[illegible]	4 . [illegible]	7 . [illegible]	[illegible]	[illegible]	[illegible]	3
[illegible]	4 . [illegible]	[illegible]	[illegible]	[illegible]	[illegible]	4
	4 . [illegible]	[illegible]	[illegible]	[illegible]	[illegible]	5
[illegible]	4 . [illegible]	[illegible]	[illegible]	[illegible]	[illegible]	6
[illegible]	4 . [illegible]	[illegible]	[illegible]	[illegible]	[illegible]	[illegible]
	4 . [illegible]	[illegible] 15	[illegible]	[illegible]	[illegible]	8
[illegible]	4 . [illegible]	[illegible]	[illegible]	[illegible]	[illegible]	[illegible]
[illegible]	4 . [illegible]	7 . [illegible]	[illegible]	[illegible]	[illegible]	[illegible]
[illegible]	4 . [illegible]	[illegible]	6 . 13 . [illegible]	4 . [illegible]	[illegible]	[illegible]

Solution of the above problem

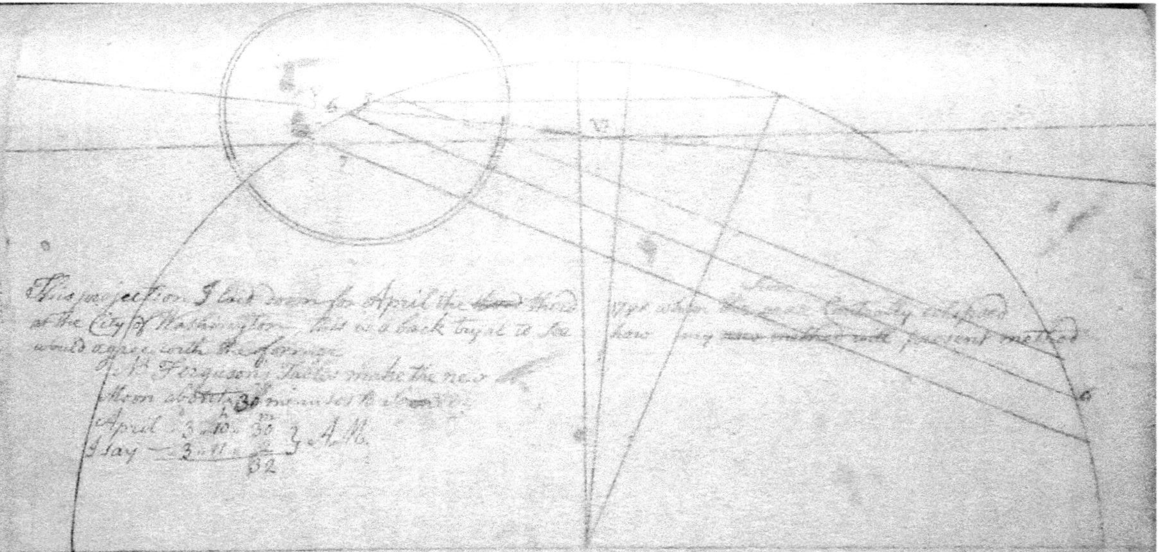

This projection I laid down for April the ~~[illegible]~~ third [illegible] when the Sun is Centrally eclipsed at the City of Washington, this is a back tryal to see how my new method with present method would agree with the former

Mr Ferguson's Tables make the new Moon about 30 minutes to [illegible]

April 3 10 30 } A.M.

May 3 11 2 }

32

May Fifth Month hath 31 Days 1792

	D	H	M	
Full ○	6	0	4	Aft
Last ☾	13	3	54	Morn
New ☽	20	2	8	Aft
First ☽	28	5	34	Aft

{1, 11, 21} ♎ {2, 1, 0} Deg.

Planets Places

D	☉ ♉	♄ ♈	♃ ♎	♂ ♍	♀ ♈	☿ ♊	☽ Lat
1	12	24	24	14	17	0	2 S
7	18	25	24	15	24	♉ 28	4 N
13	23	26	23	18	♉ 1	26	3 N
19	29	27	23	19	8	24	4 S
25	♊ 5	27	22	21	15	21	5 S

W D	Remarkable Days Aspects weather &c		☉ rise	☉ Sets	☽ Longe	☽ Sets	☽ South	☽ Age
3	☍ ♄ ♃	warm	5..9	6..51	5..8..54	14..36	8..16	10 r
4		agreeable	5..8	6..52	5..21..32	15..9	9..2	11 r
5	♃ South 10..48	weather	5..7	6..53	6..4..38	15..44	9..51	12 r
6			5..5	6..55	6..18..3	16..25	10..42	13 r
7	Spica ♍ South 10..25	Cloudy	5..4	6..56	7..1..38	☍	11..32	14
G	4th Sunday after Easter	St. John Evan	5..3	6..57	7..15..40	rises	12..28	15
2	☍ ♃ ♀		5..2	6..58	7..29..56	8..22	13..26	16 r
3	[illegible]	and	5..1	6..59	8..14..27	9..28	14..25	17 r
4	Lyra South 3..28	like	5..0	7..0	8..29..6	10..28	15..25	18 r
5		for a	4..59	7..1	9..13..48	11..29	16..26	19 r
6	Days 14..4	warm	4..58	7..2	9..28..30	12..18	17..22	20 r
7	♃ Sets 4..45	rain	4..58	7..2	10..13..1	13..3	18..18	21 r
G	Rogation Sunday		4..57	7..3	10..27..24	13..48	19..14	22 r
2		now	4..56	7..4	11..11..22	14..25	20..5	23 r
3	Days increase 4..54	Clear	4..55	7..5	11..25..12	15..3	20..56	24 r
4	☌ ☉ ☿ orient		4..54	7..6	0..8..32	15..30	21..40	25 r
5	Ascension Day	with	4..53	7..7	0..21..32	16..5	22..29	26 r
6		some	4..52	7..8	1..4..24	16..43	23..17	27 r
7	Days 14..16		4..52	7..8	1..16..49	[illegible]	☌	28 r
G		Cool	4..51	7..9	1..29..5	☽ Sets	0..4	☽
2	☉ enters ♊	breezes	4..51	7..9	2..11..5	7..46	0..46	1 r
3	Lyra South 2..37		4..50	7..10	2..23..4	8..35	1..32	2 r
4	pegasi Algenib South 8..6	followed	4..49	7..11	3..4..54	9..17	2..21	3 r
5		with	4..48	7..12	3..16..46	10..10	[illegible]..10	4 r
6	△ ♂ ☿		4..47	7..13	3..28..29	10..52	[illegible]..56	5 r
7		thunder and	4..46	7..14	4..10..35	11..25	4..40	6 r
G	Whitsunday	rain	4..46	7..14	4..22..41	12..1	5..23	7 r
2			4..45	7..15	5..5..2	12..38	6..11	8 r
3	procyon Sets 9..29	now Clear	4..44	7..16	5..17..35	13..9	6..56	9 r
4	Arcturus South 9..36	and	4..44	7..16	6..0..24	13..48	[illegible]..46	10 r
5		warm	4..43	7..17	6..13..38	14..23	8..40	11

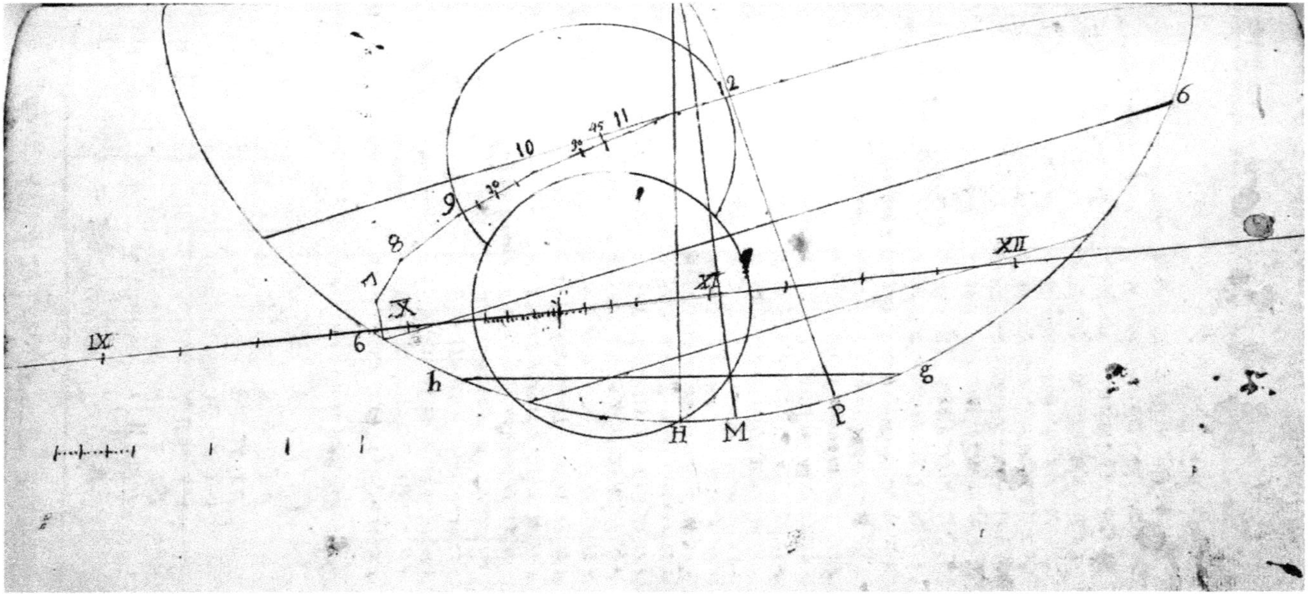

IX
X
XI
XII
6
7
8
9
10
11
12
6
h
g
H
M
P

June Sixth Month hath 30 Days

		D	H	M	
Full	○	4	7	55	Aft
Last	☾	11	1	10	Aft
New	●	19	7	49	Morn
First	☽	27	5	10	Morn

♄ { 1 ♍ 30 / 11 29 / 21 29 } Deg.

	Planets Places						
D	☉	♄	♃	♂	♀	☿	☽'s
	♊	♈	♎	♍	♉	♉	Lat
1	11	28	22	24	24	19	2 N
7	17	29	22	26	♊ 1	25	5 N
13	23	♉ 0	22	29	8	♊ 0	2 S
19	29	1	22	♎ 0	16	9	5 S
25	♋ 4	1	22	2	24	17	1 S

W D	Remarkable Days Aspects weather &c		☉ rise	☉ Sets	☽ Long?	☽ Sets	☽ South	☽ Age
6	△ ♂ ♀	warm	4..43	7..17	6..27.6	14..37	9..28	12
7		weather	4..42	7..18	7..10.56	15..39	10..20	13
G	Trinity Sunday		4..42	7..18	7..25.4	☍	11..17	14
2		Some	4..41	7..19	8..9..25	rises	12..16	15
3	Spica ♍ Sets 1..47	appearance	4..41	7..19	8..24.2	8..18	13..15	16
4		rain	4..41	7..19	9..8..46	9..17	14..[illegible]	17
5			4..40	7..20	9..23..26	10..12	15..12	18
6	△ ♂ ☿	Sultry	4..40	7..20	10..8..2	10..56	16..8	19
7		hot	4..40	7..20	10..22.31	11..40	17..2	20
G	1st Sunday after Trinity	weather	4..39	7..21	11..6..45	12..18	17..54	21
2	St Barnabas		4..39	7..21	11..20.39	12..49	18..42	22
3	△ ☉ ♃	Moderate	4..39	7..21	0..4..15	13..23	19..30	23
4	☿ great elongation 22..53	gentle	4..39	7..21	0..17..26	14..1	20..18	24
5		breezes	4..39	7..21	1..0.22	14..35	21..6	25
6	pegasi Markab rise 10..32		4..38	7..22	1..13..1	15..8	21..53	26
7			4..38	7..22	1..25.24	15..48	22..40	27
G	2nd Sunday after Trinity St Alban		4..38	7..22	2..7..32	16..27	23..27	28
2			4..38	7..22	2..19.30	☌	☌	29
3	Days 14..44	Cloudy	4..38	7..22	3..1..24	Sets	0..14	☽
4	☉ enters ♋	and like	4..38	7..22	3..13..15	7..58	0..55	1
5	Longest Day	for	4..38	7..22	3..25..4	8..40	1..44	2
6		rain	4..38	7..22	4..7..0	9..30	2..38	3
7	△ ♃ ♀		4..38	7..22	4..19..2	10..6	3..25	4
G	3d Sunday after Trinity St John Bap		4..38	7..22	5..1..13	10..36	4..5	5
2			4..38	7..22	5..13..39	11..7	4..50	6
3		thunder	4..38	7..22	5..26..19	11..41	5..34	7
4	♃ Sets 1..2	gusts	4..38	7..22	6..9..20	12..12	6..22	8
5		and rain	4..38	7..22	6..22..40	12..48	7..12	9
6	St peter and paul	toward	4..39	7..21	7..6..[illegible]	13..22	8..3	10
7	Days decrease 2 m	the end	4..39	7..21	7..20..16	14..10	8..55	11

1792

July Seventh Month hath 31 Days.

		D	H	M	
Full	○	4	2	38	Morn
Last	☾	10	10	30	Aft
New	☽	18	11	15	Aft
First	☽	26	4	21	Aft

{ 1		28	}	Deg.
11	♍	28		
21		27		

Planets Places

☽	☉	♄	♃	♂	♀	☿	☽ Lat
	♋	♉	♎	♎	♋	♊	
1	10	1	22	5	0	29	5 N
7	16	1	22	9	7	♋ 12	2 N
13	21	2	23	12	15	25	4 S
19	27	2	23	16	22	♌ 7	4 S
25	♌ 3	2	24	19	♌ 0	13	2 N

W D	Remarkable Days Aspects weather &c		☉ rise	☉ Sets	☽ Long.	☽ Sets	☽ South	☽ Age
G	4th Sunday after Trinity		4..39	7..21	8..4..31	14..58	9..54	12
2	Visitation of V. Mary		4..40	7..20	8..19..2	15..51	10..54	13
3		very warm	4..40	7..20	9..3..39	☍	11..54	14
4	St. Martin	dry	4..40	7..20	9..18..23	rises	12..56	15
5		weather	4..41	7..19	10..3..3	8..47	13..51	16
6	Lyra South 11..29		4..41	7..19	10..17..37	9..30	14..45	17
7		followed	4..42	7..18	11..1..58	10..9	15..38	18
G	5th Sunday after Trinity	with	4..42	7..18	11..16..1	10..48	16..31	19
2		thunder	4..43	7..17	11..29..48	11..19	17..19	20
3	☌ ☉ ☿ Occident	gusts	4..43	7..17	0..13..15	11..52	18..5	21
4		Expect	4..44	7..16	0..26..19	12..24	18..51	22
5	Days 14..32	a very	4..44	7..16	1..9..5	12..59	19..40	23
6		warm	4..45	7..15	1..21..35	13..44	20..32	24
7	♃ Sets 11..42	harvest	4..45	7..15	2..3..52	14..26	21..22	25
G	6th Sunday after Trinity		4..46	7..14	2..15..56	15..5	22..11	26
2	□ ☉ ♃	Cloudy	4..47	7..13	2..27..53	15..52	22..55	27
3		Some	4..47	7..13	3..9..44	16..36	23..39	28
4	Days decrease 20 m.	appearance	4..48	7..12	3..21..34	☌	☌	☽
5		of	4..49	7..11	4..3..27	Set	0..23	1
6	Margaret	rain	4..49	7..11	4..15..24	7..52	1..7	2
7			4..50	7..10	4..27..29	8..29	1..51	3
G	7th Sunday after Trinity		4..51	7..9	5..9..49	9..1	2..37	4
2	☉ enters ♌	gusty	4..52	7..8	5..22..19	9..35	3..25	5
3		afternoons	4..53	7..7	6..5..7	10..10	4..13	6
4	St. James	with	4..54	7..6	6..18..19	10..44	5..1	7
5	St. Anne	frequent	4..54	7..6	7..1..46	11..19	5..50	8
6		shower of	4..55	7..5	7..15..34	11..58	6..43	9
7			4..56	7..4	7..29..39	12..46	7..38	10
G	8th Sunday after Trinity	rain	4..57	7..3	8..14..2	13..33	8..36	11
2		in many	4..58	7..2	8..28..36	14..34	9..37	12
3		places	4..59	7..1	9..13..20	15..34	10..37	13

August Eighth Month hath 31 Days

	D. H. M.		
Full ○	2..9..35	Morn	
Last ☾	9..10..1	Morn	
New ☽	17..2..0	Aft	
First ☽	25..0..12	Morn	
Full ○	31..5..42	Aft	
1	27	Deg.	
11	♍ 26	Deg.	
21	26	Deg.	

Planets Places

D	☉	♄	♃	♂	♀	☿	☽
	♌	♉	♎	♎	♌	♌	Lat
1	10	2	24	24	8	29	4 N
7	15	2	25	26	16	♍ 10	2 S
13	21	2	26	29	25	17	5 S
19	27	2	27	♏ 4	♍ 2	24	1 S
25	♍ 3	2	28	9	8	♎ 0	5 N

W D	Remarkable Days Aspects weather &c	☉ rise	☉ Sets	☽ Long.	☽ Sets	☽ South	☽ Age
4	☌ ♃ ♂ Lamas Day	5..0	7..0	9..28..1	☍	11..35	14
5		5..1	6..59	10..12..40	rises	12..32	15
6	♄ Stationary	5..2	6..58	10..27..9	8..4	13..26	16
7		5..3	6..57	11..11..23	8..42	14..18	17
G	9th Sunday after Trinity	5..4	6..56	11..25..15	[illegible]	15..9	18
2	Transfiguration ☌ ☉ ♀ occident	5..5	6..55	0..8..56	9..48	15..58	19
3		5..6	6..54	0..22..9	10..21	16..45	20
4	Bulls eye rise 12..15	5..7	6..53	1..5..6	10..57	17..31	21
5		5..8	6..52	1..17..45	11..36	18..21	22
6	St Lawrence	5..9	6..51	2..0..10	12..22	19..14	23
7		5..10	6..50	2..12..20	13..2	20..2	24
G	10th Sunday after Trinity	5..11	6..49	2..24..20	13..48	20..51	25
2		5..12	6..48	3..6..13	14..34	21..37	26
3	pleiades rise 10..36	5..13	6..47	3..18..6	15..22	22..22	27
4		5..14	6..46	3..29..54	16..11	23..7	28
5	Days 13..15	5..15	6..45	4..11..48	☌	23..55	29
6	Spica ♍ Sets 8..5	5..16	6..44	4..23..49	Sets	☌	☽
7		5..18	6..42	5..5..59	7..13	0..36	1
G	11th Sunday after Trinity	5..19	6..41	5..18..23	7..30	1..17	2
2		5..20	6..40	6..1..3	8..6	2..6	3
3	Sirius rise 3..33	5..21	6..39	6..14..2	8..44	2..57	4
4	Days decrease 1..18	5..22	6..38	6..27..20	9..19	3..46	5
5	☉ enters ♍	5..23	6..37	7..10..56	9..59	4..37	6
6	△ ☉ ♄ St Bartholomew	5..24	6..36	7..24..53	10..44	5..32	7
7	☿ great elongation 27°						
G	12th Sunday after Trinity	5..26	6..34	8..9..7	11..29	6..29	8
2		5..27	6..33	8..23..37	12..25	7..28	9
3	St Augustine	5..28	6..32	9..8..15	13..24	8..27	10
4	St John beheaded	5..29	6..31	9..22..58	14..29	9..29	11
5		5..30	6..30	10..7..39	15..38	10..26	12
6	Sirius rise 2..53	5..32	6..28	10..22..13	☍	11..21	13
		5..33	6..27	11..6..35	rises	12..16	14

	D	H
True time of New Moon in September 1792	16 .	4
Semidiameter of the Earths Disc		
		°
Sun from the Nearest Solstice		56
Suns Declination North	84 .	[illegible]
Moons Latitude South Ascending	2 .	2[illegible]
Moons Horary Motion		
Angle of the Moons visible path with the Ecliptic		2
Suns Semidiameter	5 .	[illegible]
Moons Semidiameter		
Semidiameter of the penumbra		

1792

September Ninth Month hath 30 Days

	D	H	M	
ast ☾	8	1	41	Morn
New ☽	16	4	12	Morn
irst ☽	23	7	18	Morn
ull ○	30	5	42	Aft

1, 11, 21 — ♍ 25, 24, 24 Deg.

Planets Places

☽	☉	♄	♃	♂	♀	☿	☽ Lat
	♍	♉	♎	♏	♍	♎	Lat
1	10	2	29	14	16	3	0 N
7	16	2	♏ 0	17	24	4	5 S
13	21	2	1	19	♎ 2	♍ 29	3 S
19	27	1	2	25	9	23	3 N
25	♎ 3	1	4	29	16	19	4 N

	W D	Remarkable Days Aspects weather &c	☉ rise	☉ Sets	☽ Long.	☽ rises	☽ South	☽ Age
	7	♄ South 3..21	5..34	6..26	11..20..4	7..21	13..8	15
	G	13th Sunday after Trinity	5..35	6..25	0..4..28	7..47	13..54	16
	2		5..36	6..24	0..17..56	8..24	14..44	17
	3	Pleiades rise 9..19	5..38	6..22	1..1..2	9..0	15..34	18
	4		5..39	6..21	1..13..51	9..37	16..22	19
	5	Days 12..40	5..40	6..20	1..26..22	10..17	17..9	20
	6		5..41	6..19	2..8..40	11..0	18..0	21
	7	✶ ☉ ♂ Nativity V. Mary	5..43	6..17	2..20..46	11..45	18..48	22
	G	14 Sunday after Trinity	5..44	6..16	3..2..43	12..31	19..34	23
	2		5..45	6..15	3..14..34	13..17	20..20	24
	3	Days decrease 2..16	5..46	6..14	3..26..23	14..8	21..8	25
2	4		5..48	6..12	4..8..15	15..8	21..56	26
3	5	Bulls eye rise 10..2	5..49	6..11	4..20..[illegible]	16..4	22..45	27
4	6		5..5[illegible]	6..10	5..2..16	17..3	23..34	28
5	7	♄ South 2..29	5..52	6..8	5..14..34	☌	☌	29
6	G	15th Sunday after Trinity	5..53	6..7	5..27..4	Sets	0..13	☽
7	2	☌ ☉ ☿ Orient.	5..54	6..6	6..9..50	6..46	0..56	1
8	3		5..55	6..5	6..23..0	7..18	1..42	2
9	4	Sirius rise 1..48	5..56	6..4	7..6..25	7..57	2..35	3
0	5		5..58	6..2	7..20..12	8..52	3..30	4
1	6	St. Matthew	5..59	6..1	8..4..17	9..32	4..28	5
2	7	Equal Day and Night	6..0	6..0	8..18..38	10..23	5..26	6
3	G	16th Sunday after Trinity	6..2	5..58	9..3..11	11..23	6..26	7
4	2	☉ enters ♎	6..3	5..57	9..17..52	12..26	7..26	8
5	3		6..4	5..56	10..2..34	13..30	8..26	9
6	4	St. Cyprian	6..5	5..55	10..17..14	14..37	9..22	10
7	5		6..7	5..53	11..1..44	15..47	10..18	11
8	6		6..8	5..52	11..15..58	16..52	11..9	12
9	7	St. Michael	6..9	5..51	11..29..56	☍	11..59	13
0	G	17th Sunday after Trinity	6..11	5..49	0..13..34	rises	12..50	14

New Moon Sep 16..4..12 Morn Sun Eclipsed ⟶ his [illegible] Distance from the [illegible] Ascending Node being 11..29..35

a copy

Maryland. Baltimore County - Near Ellicotts Lower Mills Augt. 19th 1791

Thomas Jefferson Secretary of State

Sir

I am fully Sensible of the greatness of that freedom which I take with you
sent occasion; a liberty which seemed to me Scarcely allowable, when I reflected on that di
and dignified station in which you Stand, and the almost general prejudice and prepo
is so prevalent in the world against those of my complexion.
I suppose it is a truth too well attested to you, to need a proof here, that we are a race
who have long laboured under the abuse and censure of the world, that we have long been
rather as brutish than human, and Scarcely capable of mental endowments.

Sir I hope I may Safely admit, in consequence of that report which hath r
that you are a man far less inflexible in Sentiments of this nature, than many othe
are measureably friendly and well disposed toward us, and that you are willing and
lend your aid and assistance to our relief from those many distresses and numerous
to which we are reduced.

Now Sir, if this is founded in truth, I apprehend you will readily em
opportunity, to eradicate that train of absurd and false ideas and oppinion
generally prevails with respect to us, and that your Sentiments are concurrent
which are that one universal Father hath given Being to us all, and that he hath
made us all of one flesh, but that he hath also without partiality afforded us all the sa
and endued us all with the same faculties, and that however variable we may be
or religion, however diversified in Situation or colour, we are all of the same f
and Stand in the same relation to him.

Sir, if these are sentiments of which you are fully persuaded, I hope you
but acknowledge, that it is the indispensible duty of those who maintain for them
rights of human nature and who profess the obligations of christianity, to exte
power and influence to the relief of every part of the human race, from whatev
or oppression they may unjustly labour under, and this I apprehend a full con
the truth and obligation of these principles should lead all to.

Sir, I have long been convinced, that if your love for yourselves
and for those inesteemable laws which preserve to you the rights of huma
was founded on Sincerity, you could not but be Solicitous that every indiv
whatever rank or distinction, might with you equally enjoy the blessings
neither could you rest satisfied, short of the most active diffusion of your e
order to their promotion from any State of degradation, to which the unjustifiab
barbarism of men may have reduced them.

Sir, I freely and chearfully acknowledge, that I am of the African ra
that colour which is natural to them of the deepest dye, and it is under a Sense
profound gratitude to the Supreme Ruler of the universe, that I now conf
I am not under that State of tyrannical thraldom, and inhuman captivity
too many of my brethren are doomed; but that I have abundantly tast
ition of those blessings, which proceed from that free and unequalled libe
which you are favoured, and which I hope you will willingly allow

October Tenth Month hath 31 Days

		D	H	M	
Last	☾	7	7	48	Aft
New	☽	15	5	31	Aft
First	☽	22	4	5	Aft
Full	○	29	4	53	Aft

☊ { 1 ♍ 23, 11 ♍ 23, 21 ♍ 22 } Deg.

Planets Places

D	☉	♄	♃	♂	♀	☿	☽s
	♎	♉	♏	♐	♎	♍	Lat
1	9	0	5	3	24	20	3 S
7	15	r 0	6	8	♏ 2	29	5 S
13	21	29	7	12	9	♎ 17	0 S
19	27	29	9	16	17	10	5 N
25	♏ 3	28	10	20	24	28	1 N

W D	Remarkable Days Aspects weather &c	☉ rise	☉ Sets	☽ Long.	☽ rises	☽ South	☽ Age
2	☿ great elongation 18..45	6..12	5..48	0..26..51	7..6	13..33	15
3		6..13	5..47	1..9..52	7..42	14..23	16
4	Pleiades South 2..57	6..14	5..46	1..22..31	8..24	15..16	17
5		6..15	5..45	2..4..56	9..9	16..5	18
6	Sirius rise 12..45	6..17	5..43	2..17..7	9..51	16..54	19
7	Days 11..24	6..18	5..42	2..29..9	10..39	17..42	20
G	18th Sunday after Trinity	6..19	5..41	3..11..3	11..25	18..28	21
2		6..20	5..40	3..22..54	12..13	19..13	22
3	Days decrease 3..28	6..22	5..38	4..4..45	13..8	20..0	23
4		6..23	5..37	4..16..38	14..2	20..47	24
5	[illegible]	6..24	5..36	4..28..38	14..57	21..31	25
6		6..25	5..35	5..10..27	15..51	22..15	26
7	♄ South 12..40	6..27	5..33	5..23..10	16..50	23..0	27
G	19th Sunday after Trinity	6..28	5..32	6..5..49	☌	23..48	28
2		6..29	5..31	6..18..44	Sets	☌	☽
3		6..30	5..30	7..1..59	6..5	0..36	1
4		6..32	5..28	7..15..34	6..39	1..24	2
5	St. Luke	6..33	5..27	7..29..30	7..30	2..22	3
6		6..34	5..26	8..13..42	8..18	3..21	4
7		6..35	5..25	8..28..11	9..17	4..20	5
G	20th Sunday after Trinity	6..36	5..24	9..12..49	10..16	5..19	6
2	☍ ☉ ♄ Occident }	6..38	5..22	9..27..30	11..18	6..18	7
3	☉ enters ♏	6..39	5..21	10..12..12	12..29	7..17	8
4		6..40	5..20	10..26..46	13..29	8..7	9
5	☌ ♄ ☿ Crispin	6..41	5..19	11..11..11	14..40	9..4	10
6		6..42	5..18	11..25..18	15..48	9..58	11
7		6..44	5..16	0..9..7	16..55	10..48	12
G	21st Sunday after Trinity	6..45	5..15	0..22..38	☍	11..37	13
2	(St. Simon and Jude	6..46	5..14	1..5..46	rises	12..24	14
3		6..47	5..13	1..18..36	6..23	13..11	15
4	Days 10..24	6..48	5..12	2..1..9	7..4	13..58	16

received from the immediate hand of that Being, from whom proceedeth every per
fect gift.

Sir, Suffer me to recall to your mind that time, in which the Arms and tyranny of the
Crown were exerted with every powerful effort in order to reduce you to a State
look back I entreat you on the variety of dangers to which you were expos
that time in which every human aid appeared unavailable, and in which
and fortitude wore the aspect of inability to the conflict, and you cannot
to a Serious and ~~gratful~~ grateful sense of your miraculous and providential
tion; you cannot but acknowledge, that the present freedom and tranquility
enjoy you have mercifully received, and that it is the peculiar blessing of

This Sir, was a time in which you clearly saw into the injustice of a
Slavery, and in which you had just apprehensions of the horrors of its condition
Sir, that your abhorrence thereof was so excited, that you publickly held forth
and valuable doctrine, which is worthy to be recorded and remembered in
ing ages. "We hold these truths to be self evident, that all men are crea
and that they are endowed by their creator with certain unalienable righ
among these are life, liberty, and the pursuit of happiness."

Here Sir, was a time in which your tender feelings for your selves had
you thus to declare, you were then impressed with proper Ideas of the great
of liberty, and the free possession of those blessings to which you were intitled by
but Sir, how pitiable is it to reflect that altho you were so fully convinced of
lence of the Father of mankind, and of his equal and impartial distribution of
and privileges which he had conferred upon them, that you should at the
counteract his mercies, in detaining by fraud and violence so numerous a
brethren under groaning captivity and cruel oppression, that you should
time be found guilty of that most criminal act which you professedly detested
with respect to your selves.

Sir, I suppose that your knowledge of the Situation of my brethren is too
to need a recital here; neither shall I presume to prescribe methods by
which they may be relieved, otherwise than by recommending to you and all
your selves from those narrow prejudices which you have imbibed with respect
and as Job proposed to his friends "Put your Souls in their Souls stead," thus sh
hearts be enlarged with kindness and benevolence toward them, and thus shall
neither the direction of my self or others in what manner to proceed herein.

And now Sir, altho my Sympathy and affection for my brethren hath caused
ment thus far, I ardently hope that your candour and generosity will plead wi
behalf, when I make known to you, that it was not originally my design; but
taken up my pen in order to direct to you as a present, a copy of an Almanac
calculated for the Succeeding year, I was unexpectedly and unavoidably led

This calculation Sir, is the production of my arduous Study in this my
stage of life; for having long had unbounded desires to become acquainted
the Secrets of nature, I have had to gratify my curiosity herein thro
assiduous application to Astronomical Study, in which I need not

1792 Month

November Eleventh hath 30 Days.

	D	H	M	
Last ☾	6	3	55	Aft
New ☽	14	5	57	Mom
First ☾	21	0	12	Mom
Full ○	28	8	55	Mom
☊	1 ♍ 22	11 ♍ 21	21 ♍ 21	Deg.

Planets Places

D.	☉	♄	♃	♂	♀	☿	☽
	♏	♓	♏	♐	♐	♏	Lat.
1	10	27	12	25	3	10	5 S
7	16	27	13	♑ 0	10	19	2 S
13	22	26	14	4	18	♐ 5	4 N
19	28	25	15	9	25	8	4 N
25	♐ 4	25	17	14	♑ 3	17	4 S

M D	W D	Remarkable Days Aspects weather &c	☉ rise	☉ Set	☽ Long.	☽ rises	☽ South	☽ Age
1	5	All Saints	6..49	5..11	2..13..38	7..48	14..46	17
2	6	☌ ☉ ♀ Occidental	6..51	5..9	2..25..35	8..37	15..40	18
3	7	☌ ☉ ♃ Oriental	6..52	5..8	3..7..32	9..26	16..29	19
4	G	22nd Sunday after Trinity	6..53	5..7	3..19..25	10..14	17..14	20
5	2		6..54	5..6	4..1..14	11..3	17..59	21
6	3	♄ South 10..58	6..55	5..5	4..13..5	11..56	18..44	22
7	4	Sirius rise 10..41	6..56	5..4	4..25..2	12..51	19..29	23
8	5		6..57	5..3	5..7..6	13..49	20..16	24
9	6	Bull's eye South 1..29	6..58	5..2	5..19..11	14..46	20..59	25
10	7		6..59	5..1	6..1..50	15..40	21..43	26
11	G	23d Sunday after Trinity	7..0	5..0	6..14..36	16..45	22..32	27
12	2	St Martin	7..1	4..59	6..27..41	17..51	23..24	28
13	3		7..2	4..58	7..11..4	☌	☌	29
14	4	Days 9..54	7..3	4..57	7..24..48	Sets	0..17	☽
15	5	pleades South 12..12	7..4	4..56	8..8..51	6..10	1..10	1
16	6	Days decrease 4..54	7..5	4..55	8..23..11	7..2	2..5	2
17	7		7..6	4..54	9..7..43	8..1	3..5	3
18	G	24th Sunday after Trinity	7..7	4..53	9..22..25	9..5	4..5	4
19	2		7..8	4..52	10..7..7	10..11	5..3	5
20	3	♄ South 9..50	7..8	4..52	10..21..46	11..20	5..58	6
21	4		7..9	4..51	11..6..17	12..25	6..52	7
22	5	☉ enters ♐	7..10	4..50	11..20..32	13..32	7..45	8
23	6	St Clement	7..11	4..49	0..4..34	14..36	8..30	9
24	7		7..12	4..48	0..18..14	15..37	9..24	10
25	G	25th Sunday after Trinity	7..12	4..48	1..1..34	16..39	10..12	11
26	2		7..13	4..47	1..14..36	17..45	11..0	12
27	3		7..14	4..46	1..27..18	☍	11..48	13
28	4	Sirius South 2..22	7..15	4..45	2..9..46	rises	12..36	14
29	5		7..15	4..45	2..21..58	6..24	13..27	15
30	6	St Andrew	7..16	4..44	3..4..0	7..10	14..13	16

to you the many difficulties and disadvantages which I have had to encounter. And altho I had almost declined to make my calculation for the ensuing year, in consequence of that time which I had allotted therefor being taken up at the Federal Territory, by the request of Mr. Andrew Ellicott, yet finding myself under several engagements to printers of this state to whom I had communicated my design, on my return to my place of residence, I industriously applyed myself thereto, which I hope I have accomplished with correctness and accuracy, a copy of which I have taken the liberty to direct to you, and which I humbly request you will favourably receive, and altho you may have the opportunity of perusing it after its publication, yet I chose to send it to you in manuscript previous thereto, that thereby you might not only have an earlier inspection, but that you might also view it in my own hand writing

and now Sir, I shall conclude
and Subscribe my Self with the most profound respect
your most obedient humble Servant

B. Banneker

To Thomas Jefferson
Secretary of State
Philadelphia

N.B. any communication to me may be had by a direction to Mr. Elias Ellicott merchant in Baltimore Town

B. B.

Mr. Jeffersons answer to the above Letter.

Philadelphia Augt. 30: 1791

Sir

I thank you sincerely for your letter of the 19th. instant and for the Almanac it contained. no body wishes more than I do to see such proofs as you exhibit, that nature has given to our black Brethren, talents equal to those of the other colours of men, & that the appearance of a want of them is owing merely to the degraded condition of their existence both in Africa and America. I can add with truth that no body wishes more ardently to see a good System commenced for raising the condition both of their body and mind to what it ought to be, as fast as the imbecility of their present existence, and other circumstances which cannot be neglected will admit. I have taken the liberty of sending your Almanac to monsieur de Condorcet, Secretary of the Academy of Sciences at paris, and Member of the Philanthropic Society because I considered it as a document to which your whole colour had a right for their justification against the doubts which have been entertained of them. I am with great esteem Sir,

Your most obedt. humble Servt.

Tho Jefferson

Mr. Benjamin Banneker
near Ellicotts lower mills Baltimore County.

1792

December Twelfth Month hath 31 Days

	D	H	M	
Last Q.	6	9	30	Morn
New ☽	13	5	31	Aft
First Q.	21	10	18	Morn
Full ○	28	3	32	Morn

☊			
1		20	Deg.
11	♍	20	
21		19	

Planets Places

D	☉	♄	♃	♂	♀	☿	☽
	♐	♈	♏	♑	♑	♐	Lat
1	11	25	18	18	10	26	5 S
7	17	24	19	23	18	♑ 4	1 N
13	23	24	21	28	25	14	5 N
19	29	24	22	♒ 2	♒ 2	16	0 N
25	♑ 5	24	23	7	10	19	5 S

M D	W D	Remarkable Days Aspects weather &c	☉ rise	☉ Set	☽ Long.	☽ rises	☽ South	☽ Age
1	7	⚹ ♃ ♂	7..16	4..44	3..15..55	7..55	14..58	17
2	G	Advent Sunday	7..17	4..43	3..27..45	8..43	15..43	18
3	2		7..18	4..42	4..9..36	9..38	16..30	19
4	3	Sirius rise 8..48	7..18	4..42	4..21..29	10..30	17..15	20
5	4		7..19	4..41	5..3..28	11..25	17..59	21
6	5	pleades South 10..42	7..19	4..41	5..15..37	12..23	18..43	22
7	6		7..20	4..40	5..27..58	13..21	19..28	23
8	7	⚹ ♃ ♀ Conception of V. Mary	7..20	4..40	6..10..34	14..24	20..14	24
9	G	2nd Sunday in Advent	7..20	4..40	6..23..26	15..23	21..3	25
10	2		7..21	4..39	7..6..40	16..29	21..55	26
11	3	Arcturus rise 1..44	7..21	4..39	7..20..12	17..35	22..47	27
12	4		7..21	4..39	8..4..5[illegible]	[illegible]	23..45	28
13	5	☿ great elongation 20..39	7..21	4..39	8..18..[illegible]	Sets	☌	☽
14	6	△ ☉ ♄	7..22	4..38	9..2..40	5..41	0..44	1
15	7		7..22	4..38	9..17..19	6..36	1..39	2
16	G	3d Sunday in Advent	7..22	4..38	10..2..0	7..38	2..38	3
17	2	Days 9..16	7..22	4..38	10..16..42	8..39	3..37	4
18	3		7..22	4..38	11..1..19	9..53	4..27	5
19	4	☌ ♂ ♀	7..22	4..38	11..15..44	11..5	5..25	6
20	5	Shortest Day	7..22	4..38	11..29..54	12..13	6..16	7
21	6	St. Thomas, ☉ enters ♑	7..22	4..38	0..13..45	13..22	7..5	8
22	7		7..2[illegible]	4..38	0..27..19	14..23	7..52	9
23	G	4th Sunday in Advent	7..22	4..38	1..10..17	15..20	8..42	10
24	2		7..22	4..38	1..23..22	16..19	9..31	11
25	3	Christmas Day	7..22	4..38	2..5..57	17..15	10..19	12
26	4	St. Stephen	7..22	4..38	2..18..17	18..9	11..6	13
27	5	St. John	7..22	4..38	3..0..26	☍	11..54	14
28	6	Innocents	7..21	4..39	3..12..24	rises	12..42	15
29	7		7..21	4..39	3..24..18	6..30	13..30	16
30	G	1st Sunday past Christmas	7..21	4..39	4..6..8	7..18	14..14	17
31	2	Silvester	7..20	4..40	4..17..59	8..10	14..58	18

1793 January the first day at noon, ~~that~~ we find the Suns Longitude at Meredian of Greenwich to be 9ˢ. 11°. 39′ and as his mean motion is 59.8 ... Difference between the Meredian of Greenwich and that of the Federal District ... 5 hours west Longitude, we must say by trigonometry As 24 hours in time is to 59.8 ... to 12 7/24 minutes motion which must be added to the Greenwich ~~time to me it agree~~ Longitude, to make it right at the Federal district

1793 Suns Long January	Logarithm of Suns distance from Earth
1 — 9ˢ. 11°. 50′	4.992593
7 — 9 . 17 . 59	4.992663
13 — 9 . 24 . 6	4.992818
19 — 10 . 0 . 13	4.993055
25 — 10 . 6 . 18	4.993369
February	Logarithm
1 — 10 . 13 . 24	4.993831
7 — 10 . 19 . 29	4.994302
13 — 10 . 25 . 33	4.994836
19 — 11 . 1 . 36	4.995427
25 — 11 . 7 . 38	4.995959
March	Logarithm
1 — 11 . 11 . 38	4.996405
7 — 11 . 17 . 38	4.997106
13 — 11 . 23 . 37	4.997837
19 — 11 . 29 . 35	4.998590
25 — 0 . 3 . 32	4.999354
April	Logarithm
1 — 0 . 12 . 26	5.000252
7 — 0 . 18 . 19	5.001016
13 — 0 . 24 . 12	5.001767
19 — 1 . 0 . 3	5.002495
25 — 1 . 5 . 52	5.003194
May	Logarithm
1 — 1 . 11 . 44	5.003749
7 — 1 . 17 . 32	5.004377
13 — 1 . 23 . 18	5.004956
19 — 1 . 29 . 5	5.005480
25 — 2 . 4 . 50	5.005946
June	Logarithm
1 — 2 . 11 . 32	5.006408
7 — 2 . 17 . 17	5.006730
13 — 2 . 23 . 0	5.006980
19 — 2 . 28 . 44	5.007158
25 — 3 . 4 . 6	5.007260

1793 Suns Long. July	Logarithm sun from Earth
1 — 3 . 10 . 12	5.007285
7 — 3 . 15 . 52	5.007235
13 — 3 . 21 . 37	5.007134
19 — 3 . 27 . 21	5.006943
25 — 4 . 3 . 5	5.006681
August	Logarithm
1 — 4 . 9 . 46	5.006284
7 — 4 . 15 . 30	5.005872
13 — 4 . 21 . 16	5.005397
19 — 4 . 27 . 2	5.004863
25 — 5 . 2 . 50	5.004275
Septemb.	Logarithm
1 — 5 . 9 . 36	5.003531
7 — 5 . 15 . 26	5.002849
13 — 5 . 21 . 17	5.002134
19 — 5 . 27 . 8	5.001518
25 — 6 . 3 . 1	5.000762
October	Logarithm
1 — 6 . 8 . 56	4.999995
7 — 6 . 14 . 51	4.999227
13 — 6 . 20 . 48	4.998463
19 — 6 . 26 . 46	4.997714
25 — 7 . 2 . 45	4.996987
November	Logarithm
1 — 7 . 9 . 45	4.996180
7 — 7 . 15 . 47	4.995531
13 — 7 . 21 . 50	4.994932
19 — 7 . 27 . 54	4.994387
25 — 8 . 3 . 59	4.993904
December	Logarithm
1 — 8 . 10 . 3	4.993555
7 — 8 . 16 . 8	4.993201
13 — 8 . 22 . 14	4.992926
19 — 8 . 28 . 21	4.992731
25 — 9 . 4 . 29	4.992618

1793 April 24th ♄ be... Orient, the Anomally ... mutation being less than ... ☌ ☉ ♄.

November 3d ☍ ☉ ♄ ... the Anomally of Comm... being more than 6 Sig...

1793 May 18th ☍ ☉ ... the Anomally of Com... at that time arising ... that 6 Signs

December 4th Day ... Oriental, the Anom... of Commutation ... than 6ˢ = 180°

1793 May 13 ☌ ☉ ... the Anomally of Com... m be found less than 6ˢ = ...

1793 May 28 ☌ ☉ ♀ ... the Anomally of Co... tion being greater ... 6ˢ = 180°

NB ♀ greatest elonga... Feb. 22, and in the ... Character or Quadrant

♀ greatest elongation ... 5th in the oriental ...

1793 January 1st ... Oriental, the Anom... mutation being gr... 6ˢ = 180°

♀ greatest elongation ... ary 22d. day, in the ... Quadrant

93 January First Month 31 Days

	D	H	M	
Last ☾	5	6	0	Morn
New ☽	12	4	29	Morn
First ☽	18	11	4	Aft
Full ○	26	11	4	Aft

☊ { 1, 11, 21 } ♍ { 19, 18, 17 } Deg.

Planets Places

D	☉	♄	♃	♂	♀	☿	☽
	♑	♈	♏	♒	♒	♑	Lat.
1	12	24	25	12	18	12	2 S.
7	18	24	26	17	25	4	4 N
13	24	24	27	22	♓ 3	4	3 N
19	♒ 0	25	28	27	10	6	4 S
25	6	25	29	♓ 1	17	12	4 S

M D	W D	Remarkable Days, Aspects, weather, &c	☉ rise	☉ Set	☽ Long	☽ rise	☽ South	☽ Age
1	3	Circumcision ☌ ☉ ☿ Orient	7 20	4 40	5 0 28	8 58	15 44	19
2	4	Days increase 4 m.	7 20	4 40	5 11 56	9 55	16 27	20
3	5	♄ Stationary	7 20	4 40	5 24 6	10 53	17 12	21
4	6	pleiades South 8 33	7 19	4 41	6 6 29	11 48	17 57	22
5	7		7 19	4 41	6 19 20	12 48	18 43	23
6	F	Epiphany	7 18	4 42	7 2 22	13 48	19 33	24
7	2		7 18	4 42	7 15 29	15 0	20 25	25
8	3	Sirius South 11 16	7 17	4 43	7 29 25	16 5	21 23	26
9	4		7 17	4 43	8 13 25	17 7	22 17	27
10	5	Arcturus rise 11 26	7 16	4 44	8 26 53	18 8	23 15	28
11	6	Spica ♍ rise 12 16	7 15	4 45	9 12 14			29
12	7		7 15	4 45	9 26 54	sets	☌ 12	☽
13	F	1st Sund. past Epiphany	7 14	4 46	10 11 36	6 32	1 10	1
14	2		7 13	4 47	10 26 32	7 42	2 10	2
15	3	Bulls eye South 8 34	7 13	4 47	11 10 48	8 54	3 4	3
16	4	Days 9 36	7 12	4 48	11 25 6	9 57	3 55	4
17	5		7 11	4 49	0 9 9	11 6	4 47	5
18	6	pleiades South 7 32	7 10	4 50	0 22 52	12 8	5 36	6
19	7	□ ♃ ♂	7 10	4 50	1 6 15	13 13	6 26	7
20	F	2d Sun. past Epiphany ☉ enters ♒	7 9	4 51	1 19 20	14 13	7 15	8
21	2	Agnes	7 8	4 52	2 2 5	15 13	8 3	9
22	3	☿ great Elong.	7 7	4 53	2 14 34	16 10	8 53	10
23	4		7 6	4 54	2 26 49	17 0	9 43	11
24	5	Days increase 34 min.	7 5	4 55	3 8 48	17 47	10 30	12
25	6	Conver: St. paul	7 4	4 56	3 20 45		11 15	13
26	7	Spica ♍ rise 11 11	7 3	4 57	4 2 36	rises	12 3	14
27	F	Septuagesima Sunday	7 2	4 58	4 15 20	5 49	12 48	15
28	2		7 1	4 59	4 26 19	6 40	13 31	16
29	3	Arcturus rise 10 5	7 0	5 0	5 8 18	7 34	14 13	17
30	4		6 59	5 1	5 20 25	8 30	14 59	18
31	5	Sirius South 9 39	6 58	5 2	6 2 29	9 25	15 40	19

1793 March 11th Day ☌ ☉ ☿ Occident the Annomally of Commutation
April 7 day ☿ great Elong in the occident Quadrant
Less than 6s. or 180° ^ April 25 ☌ ☉ ☿ Oriental, the Annomally of Comm
being greater than 6s or 180°. May 25th day is ☿ greatest elongation in the
Quadrant. (N.B. that on the 25th of April at the conjunction the Sun is distant
Mercury's ☿ ascending Node 8°)

1793 June 25 day ☌ ☉ ☿ Occidental, the Anomally of Commutation being
6s or 180°. August 1st day is ☿ greatest elongation in the Occidental Quadrant
August 31st day, ☌ ☉ ☿ Oriental the Annomally of Commutation being
6s or 180°. September the 16th day, ☿ greatest elongation in the Oriental Quadrant
1793 October 13th day ☌ ☉ ☿ occident, the Anomally of Commutation being
6s or 180°. November the 26th day is ☿ greatest elongation in the Occidental

---

Common Notes and moveable feasts for year of our Lord 1793

Dominical Letter	F	Easter Sunday	March 31
Cycle of the Sun	10	Ascension Day	May 9
Golden Number	8	Whitsunday	May 19
Epact	17	Trinity Sunday	May 26
Number of Direction	10	Advent Sunday	December 1

1793 The first Eclipse is of the moon Feb 25 at 55 min. past 5 Aft
The Second is of the Sun March 12 at 8 min past [illegible]
Third is of the moon August 21 ~~st~~ ~~afternoon~~ at 9? past [illegible]
The fourth is of the Sun September 5th at 49 min. ~~past~~ past 6 m

---

The Elements for Constructing an Eclipse of the moon February 1793

True time of full Moon in February 1793	D H M 25 .. 5 .. 55 P.M.	
	° ′ ″	
Moons Horizontal paralax	0 .. 54 .. 55	The Suns true [illegible]
Sun's Semidiameter	0 .. 16 .. 21	☊ is 5s [illegible]
Moon's Semidiameter	0 .. 14 .. 59	And by the [illegible]
Semidiameter of the Earths Shadow at the Moon	0 .. 38 .. 44	6 Signs [illegible] Moons distance [illegible]
Moons true Latitude S. Ascending	0 .. 39 .. 32	☊ Viz 11 [illegible]
Angle of her visible path with Ecliptic	5 .. 35 .. 0	
Her true horary Motion from the Sun	0 .. 28 .. 2	

The above requisites for a visible Eclipse of the Moon Feb 25 1793

	H M	
Beginning of the Eclipse	4 .. 41	P.M.
Middle of the Eclipse	5 .. 59	
End of the Eclipse	7 .. 17	the Moon rises Eclipsed [illegible]

Digits Eclipsed 5 4/6 from the South Side of the Earths Showdow

Duration 2 .. 36

3 February Second Month hath 28 Days

	D	H	M	
Last ☾	3	6	51	Aft
New ☽	10	2	58	Aft
First ☽	17	2	41	Aft
Full ○	25	5	55	Aft

☊ { 1, 11, 21 } ♍ { 17, 16, 16 } Deg.

Planets Places

☽	☉	♄	♃	♂	♀	☿	☽
	♒	♈	♏	♓	♓	♑	Lat
1	13	25	29	7	26	20	2 N
7	19	26	♐ 0	12	♈ 3	28	5 N
13	26	26	1	16	10	♒ 6	1 S
19	♓ 2	27	1	21	17	16	5 S
25	8	28	2	26	21	26	1 S

M D	W D	Remarkable Days Aspects weather &c.	☉ rise	☉ set	☽ Long.	☽ rise	☽ South	☽ Age
1	6	pleiades Sets 2..1	6..57	5..3	6..15..19	10..18	16..30	20
2	7	purification V. Mary	6..56	5..4	6..28..9	11..25	17..20	21
3	F	Arcturus rise 9..45	6..55	5..5	7..11..20	12..35	18..13	22
4	2		6..54	5..6	7..24..49	13..44	19..6	23
5	3	□ ♄ ☿	6..53	5..7	8..8..38	14..50	20..0	24
6	4	Days 10..16	6..52	5..8	8..22..46	15..52	20..59	25
7	5	Spica ♍ rise 10..27	6..51	5..9	9..7..9	16..35	22..2	26
8	6		6..50	5..10	9..21..44	17..32	22..59	27
9	7	Days increase 1..6	6..49	5..11	10..6..31		23..56	28
10	F	Quinquagesima	6..48	5..12	10..21..32	sets	☌	☽
11	2		6..46	5..14	11..5..48	6..34	0..50	1
12	3	Shrove Tuesday	6..45	5..15	11..20..16	7..37	1..38	2
13	4	Ash wednesday, ✶ ☉ ♄	6..44	5..16	0..4..28	8..42	2..31	3
14	5	Valentine	6..43	5..17	0..18..22	9..49	3..20	4
15	6		6..42	5..18	1..1..57	10..54	4..10	5
16	7	Sirius South 8..35	6..40	5..20	1..15..11	12..1	5..2	6
17	F	♀ Sets 9..11	6..39	5..21	1..28..6	12..58	5..52	7
18	2		6..38	5..22	2..10..45	13..55	6..41	8
19	3	☉ enters ♓	6..36	5..24	2..23..7	14..49	7..32	9
20	4	pleiades Sets 12..42	6..35	5..25	3..5..17	15..40	8..18	10
21	5		6..34	5..26	3..17..16	16..25	9..8	11
22	6	♀ great Elong.	6..33	5..27	3..29..3	17..3	9..53	12
23	7		6..32	5..28	4..11..2	17..41	10..39	13
24	F	St. Matthias	6..31	5..29	4..22..49		11..27	14
25	2	~~✶ ♄ ☿~~ ☽ Eclipsed visible	6..30	5..30	5..4..45	rise	12..9	15
26	3	✶ ♄ ☿	6..28	5..32	5..16..46	6..23	12..52	16
27	4		6..27	5..33	5..28..58	7..27	13..39	17
28	5	Days 11..8	6..26	5..34	6..11..23	8..31	14..23	18

Venus (♀) Will be evening Star untill the Twenty eighth day of May and morning Star from that time untill the end of the year

On the night of the fifth of December 1791, Being a deep Sleep, I dreamed that [illegible]
public Company, one of them demanded of me the Limits Rasannah Crandophs Soul [illegible]
play itself in, after it departed from her Body and taken its flight. In answer [illegible]
that he shew me the place of Beginning "thinking it like making a Survey on [illegible]
plyd I cannot inform you but there is a man about three days Jorney from [illegible]
Satisfy your demand, I forthwith went to the man and requested of him to inform me [illegible]
of the Limits that Rasannah Crandophs Soul had to display its self in, after the Separ[illegible]
her Body; who gave me for answer, the Vernal Equinox,
When I returned I found the Company together and I was able to Solve their Doubt [illegible]
them the following answer Quincunx..

Fergusons Arts and Sciences page 27

In the Calculation of New and full moons this to be observed that when the [illegible]
from the Ambibazon or North Node of the moon's obit, is more than 11 Signs, 18 degre[illegible]
time the Sun will be Eclipsed at that time. And when the Sun's distance fro[illegible]
is less than 0 Signs, 12 degrees ~~to~~ or anything between 5 Signs 18 degrees, and [illegible]
12 degrees, at the time of full moon, the moon will be Eclipsed at that time

---

The Elements for Constructing an Eclips of the Sun March 1793

	D H M	
True time of New Moon in March 1793	12 .. 1 .. 6	Morn
Semidiameter of the Earths Disc	0 .. 60 .. 36	
Suns Distance from the nearest Solstice	82 .. 0 .. 0	
Suns Declination South	3 .. 11 .. 0	
Moons Latitude South Descending	0 .. 39 .. 25	
Moons Horary motion from the Sun	0 .. 34 .. 57	
Angle of the Moons visible path with Eclip	5 .. 35 .. 0	
Suns Semidiameter	0 .. 16 .. 19	
Moons Semidiameter	0 .. 16 .. 38	
Semidiameter of the penumbra	0 .. 32 .. 57	

Those [illegible]
taken [illegible]
Suns [illegible]
& Eclip[illegible]

13 March Third Month hath 31 Days

	D	H	M	
Last ☾	5	5	8	Morn
New ☽	12	1	8	Morn
First ☽	19	6	0	Morn
Full ○	27	10	32	Morn

☊ { 1 ♍ 15; 11 ♍ 15; 21 ♍ 14 } Deg.

Planets Places

D	☉	♄	♃	♂	♀	☿	☽
	♓	♈	♐	♓	♈	♓	Lat
1	12	28	2	29	25	3	3 N
7	18	29	2	♈ 3	♉ 2	14	4 N
13	24	29	2	8	8	26	2 S
19	♈ 0	♉ 0	2	13	14	♈ 7	5 S
25	6	1	2	17	20	20	0 N

M D	W D	Remarkable Days Aspects weather &c.	☉ rise	☉ set	☽ Long.	☽ rise	☽ South	☽ Age
1	6	St. David	6..24	5..36	6..24..3	9..33	15..9	19
2	7	pleiades Sets 12..0	6..23	5..37	7..7..4	10..35	16..2	20
3	F	pegasi Alge. Sets 7..53	6..22	5..38	7..20..22	11..37	16..55	21
4	2		6..21	5..39	8..4..1	12..39	17..48	22
5	3	Days increase 2..6	6..19	5..41	8..17..59	13..41	18..48	23
6	4	△ ♃ ♂	6..17	5..43	9..2..14	14..40	19..47	24
7	5		6..16	5..44	9..16..29	15..40	20..45	25
8	6	Days 11..32	6..14	5..46	10..1..21	16..34	21..44	26
9	7		6..13	5..47	10..16..4	17..21	22..43	27
10	F	♃ rise 11..53	6..12	5..48	11..0..45	18..0	23..36	28
11	2	☌ ☉ ☿ Occident.	6..11	5..49	11..15..20			29
12	3	☉ eclipsed invisible. St. Gregery	6..9	5..51	11..29..29	Sets	☌ 29	☽
13	4	Sirius Sets 12..6	6..8	5..52	0..13..29	7..39	1..17	1
14	5		6..7	5..53	0..27..27	8..49	2..10	2
15	6	♃ Stationary	6..6	5..54	1..11..0	9..52	3..1	3
16	7		6..4	5..56	1..24..3	10..53	3..51	4
17	F	St. patrick	6..3	5..57	2..6..49	11..52	4..39	5
18	2		6..2	5..58	2..19..32	12..47	5..30	6
19	3	☉ enters ♈ Equal Day and Night	6..0	6..0	3..1..37	13..38	6..21	7
20	4		5..59	6..1	3..13..41	14..25	7..7	8
21	5	Benedict	5..58	6..2	3..25..39	15..8	7..58	9
22	6	Bulls eye Sets 11..13	5..57	6..3	4..7..31	15..49	8..43	10
23	7		5..55	6..5	4..19..21	16..27	9..28	11
24	F	Days 12..12	5..54	6..6	5..1..12	16..59	10..12	12
25	2	Annunciation of V. Mary	5..53	6..7	5..13..10	17..31	10..58	13
26	3		5..52	6..8	5..26..16		11..43	14
27	4	Algol South 2..30	5..50	6..10	6..7..32	rise	12..26	15
28	5		5..49	6..11	6..20..4	7..47	13..12	16
29	6	~~Arietis Sets 8..42~~ Good Fryday	5..48	6..12	7..2..53	8..18	13..58	17
30	7	Arietis Sets 8..46	5..46	6..14	7..16..1	9..26	14..51	18
31	F	Easter Sunday	5..45	6..15	7..29..27	10..32	15..50	19

The lines Drawn on each side the axes of the Ecliptic Shew how to lay the Axes of the Moon in its four different positions, on each side the axes of the Ecliptic

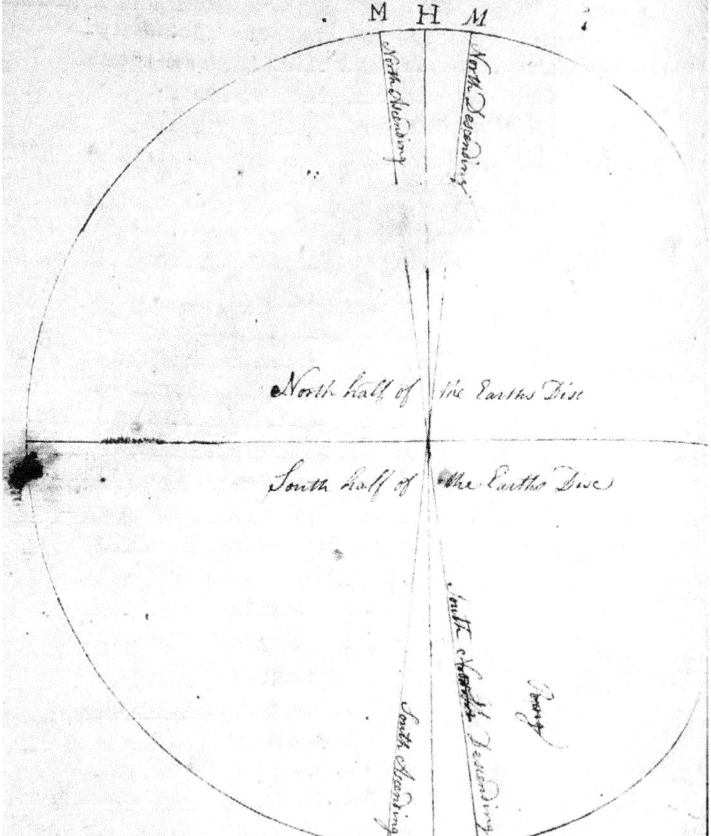

1793 April Fourth Month hath 30 Days

	D	H	M	
Last ☾	3	4	48	Aft
New ☽	10	11	26	Morn
First ☽	18	0	0	Morn
Full ○	26	0	9	Morn

☊ { 1 ♍ 14; 11 ♍ 13; 21 13 } Deg.

Planets Places

D	☉ ♈	♄ ♉	♃ ♐	♂ ♈	♀ ♉	☿ ♉	☽ Lat.
1	12	2	2	22	27	0	4 N
7	18	2	1	26	♊ 2	8	0 S
13	24	3	1	♉ 1	6	10	5 S
19	♉ 0	4	0	5	10	10	2 S
25	6	5	0	10	13	6	4 N

M D	W D	Remarkable Days Aspects weather &c	☉ rise	☉ set	☽ Long.	☽ rise	☽ South	☽ Age
1	2	Days 12..32 m.	5..44	6..16	8..13..17	11..37	16..47	20
2	3		5..43	6..17	8..27..23	12..39	17..46	21
3	4	pleiades Sets 10..7	5..41	6..19	9..11..28	13..37	18..44	22
4	5	St Ambrose	5..40	6..20	9..26..20	14..32	19..46	23
5	6		5..39	6..21	10..11..0	15..24	20..42	24
6	7	Days increase 3..4	5..38	6..22	10..25..42	16..4	21..36	25
7	F	☿ great Elong	5..36	6..24	11..10..31	16..43	22..32	26
8	2		5..35	6..25	11..24..48	17..20	23..23	27
9	3	Regulus South 8..43	5..34	6..26	0..9..3			28
10	4		5..33	6..27	0..22..59	Sets	8..14	☽
11	5	Spica ♍ South 11..55	5..32	6..28	1..6..36	7..49	1..2	1
12	6		5..30	6..30	1..19..54	8..52	1..54	2
13	7	Eagle rise 11..43	5..29	6..31	2..2..52	9..53	2..43	3
14	F	Days 13..4	5..28	6..32	2..15..31	10..50	3..33	4
15	2		5..27	6..33	2..27..55	11..41	4..24	5
16	3	♃ South 2..21	5..26	6..34	3..10..6	12..31	5..14	6
17	4	pegasi Markab rise 2..26	5..25	6..35	3..22..7	13..18	6..1	7
18	5		5..23	6..37	4..4..1	13..58	6..16	8
19	6		5..22	6..38	4..15..50	14..36	7..35	[illegible]
20	7	☉ enters ♉	5..21	6..39	4..27..40	15..10	8..19	[illegible]
21	F	Days increase 4..4	5..20	6..40	5..9..35	15..[illegible]	9..2	[illegible]
22	2		5..18	6..42	5..21..35	16..9	9..44	12
23	3	St George	5..17	6..43	6..3..46	16..41	10..29	13
24	4	☌ ☉ ♄ Orient.	5..16	6..44	6..16..10	17..30	11..15	14
25	5	☌ ☉ ☿ Orient. St Mark	5..15	6..45	6..28..49		12..1	15
26	6		5..14	6..46	7..11..46	rise	12..52	16
27	7		5..13	6..47	7..25..2	8..23	13..45	17
28	F	Bulls Eye Sets 8..57	5..12	6..48	8..8..39	9..30	14..40	18
29	2		5..11	6..49	8..22..34	10..31	15..38	19
30	3	pegasi Algenib rise 2..48	5..10	6..50	9..6..48	11..30	16..37	20

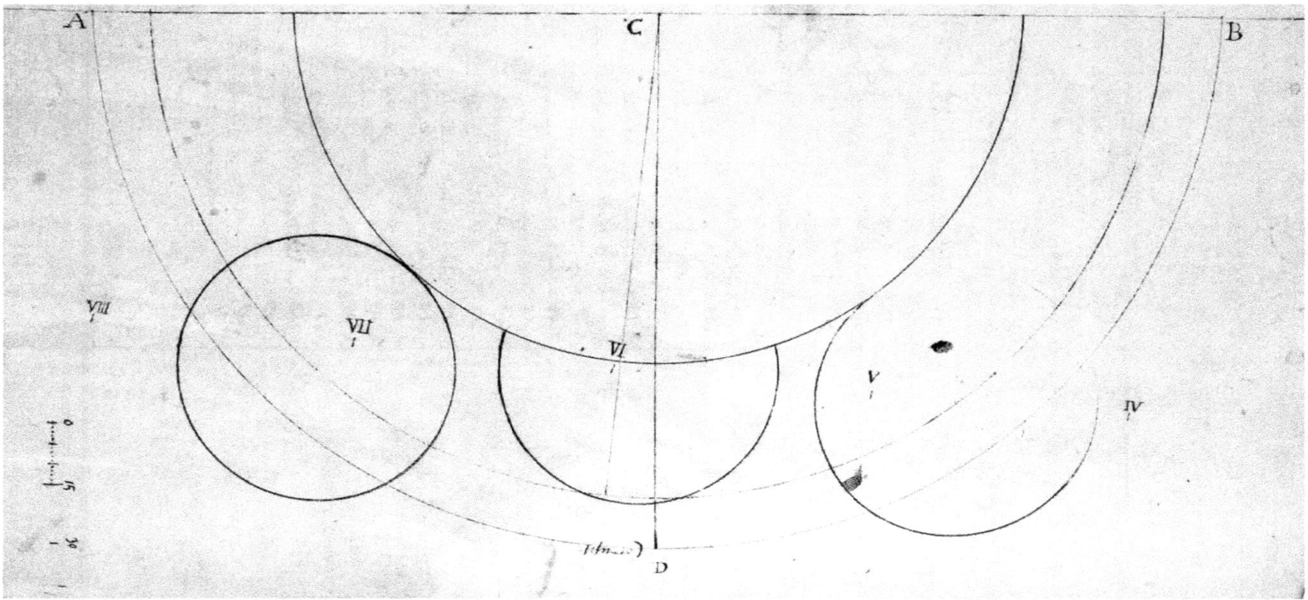
A
C
B
VIII
VII
VI
V
IV
D
0
15
30

May Fifth Month hath 31 Days

	D	H	M	
Last Q.	2	11	12	Aft
New ☽	9	10	22	Aft
First Q.	17	6	0	Aftn
Full ○	25	10	56	Morn

☊			
1		12	
11	♍	12	Deg.
21		11	

Planets Places							
D	☉	♄	♃	♂	♀	☿	☽
	♉	♉	♏	♉	♊	♉	Lat.
1	12	6	29	15	15	2	4 N
7	18	7	28	19	15	1	3 S
13	23	7	28	23	15	2	5 S
19	29	8	27	27	12	3	1 N
25	♊ 5	9	26	♊ 2	9	9	5 N

M D	W D	Remarkable Days Aspects weather &c	☉ rise	☉ Set	☽ Long.	☽ rise	☽ South	☽ Age
1	4	St. philip and James	5 . 9	6 . 51	9 . 21 . 17	12 . 28	17 . 35	21
2	5	♀ Sets 9 . 40	5 . 8	6 . 52	10 . 5 . 54	13 . 18	18 . 32	22
3	6	Spica ♍ South 10 . 33	5 . 7	6 . 53	10 . 20 . 36	14 . 6	19 . 31	23
4	7	♀ Stationary	5 . 5	6 . 55	11 . 5 . 32	14 . 45	20 . 23	24
5	F	Rogation Sunday	5 . 4	6 . 56	11 . 19 . 54	15 . 21	21 . 15	25
6	2	St. John Evangelist	5 . 3	6 . 57	0 . 4 . 17	15 . 46	22 . 8	26
7	3	pleiades Sets 7 . 57	5 . 2	6 . 58	0 . 18 . 22	16 . 36	23 . 1	27
8	4		5 . 1	6 . 59	1 . 2 . 10		23 . 53	28
9	5	Ascension Day	5 . 0	7 . 0	1 . 15 . 38	Sets	☌	☽
10	6		4 . 59	7 . 1	1 . 28 . 47	7 . 48	0 . 42	1
11	7	Days 14 . 4	4 . 58	7 . 2	2 . 11 . 36	8 . 45	1 . 31	2
12	F		4 . 58	7 . 2	2 . 24 . 7	9 . 39	2 . 22	3
13	2	☌ ☉ ♂ Orient.	4 . 57	7 . 3	3 . 6 . 26	10 . 29	3 . 12	4
14	3		4 . 56	7 . 4	3 . 18 . 29	11 . 17	4 . 0	5
15	4	Days increase 4 . 34	4 . 55	7 . 5	4 . 0 . 29	11 . 57	4 . 47	6
16	5	Arcturus South 10 . 32	4 . 54	7 . 6	4 . 12 . 20	12 . 33	5 . 31	7
17	6		4 . 53	7 . 7	4 . 24 . 10	13 . 10	6 . 15	8
18	7	☍ ☉ ♃ Occident	4 . 52	7 . 8	5 . 6 . 1	13 . 40	7 . 0	9
19	F	Whitsunday. ☍ ♃ ♂	4 . 52	7 . 8	5 . 17 . 58	14 . 10	7 . 45	10
20	2	☉ enters ♊	4 . 51	7 . 9	6 . 0 . 3	14 . 42	8 . 27	11
21	3	Alphard Sets 10 . 58	4 . 50	7 . 10	6 . 12 . 19	15 . 17	9 . 12	12
22	4	Ceti rise 4 . 49	4 . 49	7 . 11	6 . 24 . 50	15 . 50	9 . 58	13
23	5		4 . 48	7 . 12	7 . 7 . 36	16 . 22	10 . 43	14
24	6	Lyra South 2 . 29	4 . 48	7 . 12	7 . 20 . 42		11 . 36	15
25	7	☌ ♄ ☿	4 . 47	7 . 13	8 . 4 . 8	rise	12 . 29	16
26	F	Trinity Sunday	4 . 46	7 . 14	8 . 17 . 52	8 . 21	13 . 28	17
27	2		4 . 46	7 . 14	9 . 1 . 59	9 . 14	14 . 21	18
28	3	☌ ☉ ♀ Orient	4 . 45	7 . 15	9 . 16 . 12	10 . 14	15 . 21	19
29	4		4 . 44	7 . 16	10 . 0 . 44	11 . 11	16 . 21	20
30	5	Procyon Sets 9 . 18	4 . 44	7 . 16	10 . 15 . 33	11 . 55	17 . 17	21
31	6	Arcturus South 9 . 32	4 . 43	7 . 17	11 . 0 . 31	12 . 35	18 . 11	22

1793 There will be four Eclipses this Year, to wit two of the Sun and two of the

The first is of the Moon partly visible February the 25th. in the afternoon

	H	M	
Beginning of the Eclips	4 ..	42	P.M
Greatest obscuration	5 ..	59	
End of the Eclips	7 ..	18	Digits eclipsed $5\frac{2}{3}$ from the South
Total Duration	2 ..	36	Side of the Earths Shadow

NB The Moon rises $4\frac{3}{4}$ Digits Eclipsed

The Second is an Eclips of the Sun March the 12th at 8 minute past 10 (in

Morning invisible in our part of the globe

The third is of the Moon August 21st. at 57 minutes past 9 in Morning invis

---

The fourth is of the Sun Septr. 5th in the Morning this Eclips is visible at Que

a very Small portion can be Seen by us; the western of the Moon abandons the

of the Sun 7 minute after Sun rise

June Sixth Month hath 30 Days

	☽	H	M	
Last Q.	1	5	8	Morn
New ☽	8	10	26	Morn
First Q.	16	10	0	Morn
Full ○	23	7	26	Aft
Last Q.	29	8	10	Aft

☊ { 1 ♍ 11, 11 10, 21 9 } Deg.

		Planets Places					
D	☉	♄	♃	♂	♀	☿	☽
	♊	♉	♏	♊	♊	♉	Lat.
1	12	10	25	7	5	18	0 N
7	17	10	25	11	2	28	5 S
13	23	11	24	15	0	♊ 16	2 S
19	29	11	24	19	♉ 0	22	4 N
25	♋ 4	12	23	23	0	♋ 5	3 N

W D	Remarkable Days Aspects weather &c.	☉ rise	☉ Set	☽ Long	☽ rise	☽ South	☽ Age
7	Days 14..34	4..43	7..17	11..14..55	13..13	19..4	23
F	1st Sund. past Trin.	4..42	7..18	11..29..25	13..47	19..56	24
2	Days increase 5..20	4..42	7..18	0..13..29	14..26	20..48	25
3		4..41	7..19	0..27..29	15..0	21..39	26
4	☍ ♃ ☿	4..41	7..19	1..11..20	15..41	22..32	27
5	Spica ♍ Sets 1..44	4..41	7..19	1..24..36	16..23	23..23	28
6	Arcturus South 9..3	4..40	7..20	2..7..36			29
7		4..40	7..20	2..20..33	Sets	☌ 19	☽
F	2d Sunday past Trin.	4..40	7..20	3..2..43	8..18	1..1	1
2		4..39	7..21	3..14..53	9..13	1..32	2
3	St Barnabas	4..39	7..21	3..26..52	9..50	2..36	3
4	pegasi Markab ~~rise~~ rise 10..44	4..39	7..21	4..8..50	10..29	3..23	4
5		4..39	7..21	4..20..40	11..9	4..10	5
6	Arietis rise 1..6	4..39	7..21	5..2..31	11..44	4..57	6
7		4..38	7..22	5..14..23	12..6	5..34	7
F	3d Sund. past Trin.	4..38	7..22	5..26..23	12..37	6..15	8
2	St. Alban	4..38	7..22	6..8..29	13..13	7..0	9
3		4..38	7..22	6..20..29	13..40	7..46	10
4	♀ Stationary	4..38	7..22	7..3..13	14..12	8..32	11
5	☉ enters ♋	4..38	7..22	7..16..28	14..51	9..22	12
6	Longest Day	4..38	7..22	7..29..29	15..30	10..12	13
7		4..38	7..22	8..13..16		11..9	14
F	4th Sund. past Trin	4..38	7..22	8..27..14	rise	12..4	15
2	St. John Baptist	4..38	7..22	9..11..25	8..0	13..7	16
3	☌ ☉ ☿ Occident	4..38	7..22	9..25..52	8..57	14..7	17
4		4..38	7..22	10..10..32	9..51	15..5	18
5	Bulls eye rise 3..7	4..38	7..22	10..25..31	10..31	16..0	19
6		4..38	7..22	11..9..56	11..8	16..52	20
7	St. peter	4..39	7..21	11..24..29	11..43	17..45	21
F	5th Sund past Trin	4..39	7..21	0..8..54	12..27	18..39	22

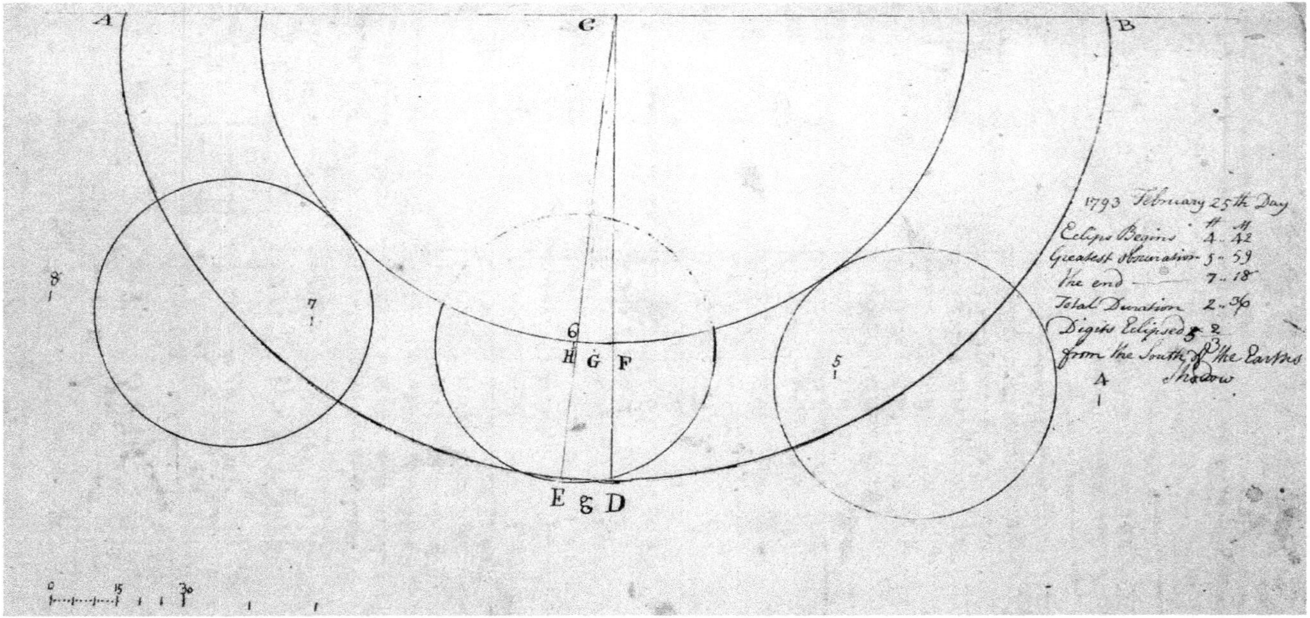
A
C
B
8
7
6
H G F
E & D
5
4
1793 February 25th Day
Eclipse Begins 4 . 42
Greatest Obscuration 5 . 59
The end 7 . 18
Total Duration 2 . 36
Digits Eclipsed 5 2
from the South of the Earths Shadow
0 15 30

13 July Seventh Month hath 31 Days

	D	H	M		
New ☽	8	0	3	Morn	
First ☾	16	2	0	Morn	
Full ○	23	2	47	Morn	
Last ☾	29	6	51	Aft	
☊	1 / 11 / 21	♍	9 / 8 / 8	Deg.	

Planets Places

☽	☉	♄	♃	♂	♀	☿	☽
	♋	♉	♏	♊	♊	♋	Lat.
1	10	13	23	27	3	18	4 S
7	16	14	23	♋ 1	6	29	4 S
13	22	14	23	5	9	♌ 9	1 N
19	27	14	23	9	14	19	5 N
25	♌ 3	14	23	13	19	28	0 N

M D	W D	Remarkable Days Aspects weather &c.	☉ rise	☉ set	☽ Long	☽ rise	☽ South	☽ Age
1	2	Days Decrease 2 m.	4..39	7..21	0..23..0	12..59	19..28	23
2	3	Visitation of V. Mary	4..40	7..20	1..6..50	13..32	20..19	24
3	4		4..40	7..20	1..20..19	14..10	21..12	25
4	5	St. Martin	4..40	7..20	2..3..29	14..51	22..1	26
5	6	⚹ ☉ ♄	4..41	7..19	2..16..21	15..39	22..56	27
6	7		4..41	7..19	2..28..53	16..24	23..41	28
7	F	6th Sund. past Trin.	4..42	7..18	3..11..13			29
8	2		4..42	7..18	3..23..18	Sets	8 27	☽
9	3	Lyra South 11..15	4..43	7..17	4..5..17	8..27	1..17	1
10	4		4..43	7..17	4..17..10	9..2	2..1	2
11	5	Days 14..32	4..44	7..16	4..29..0	9..36	2..45	3
12	6	♃ Stationary	4..44	7..16	5..10..50	10..6	3..30	4
13	7	⚹ ♀ ☿	4..45	7..15	5..22..46	10..37	4..12	5
14	F	7th Sund. past Trin	4..45	7..15	6..4..50	11..8	4..48	6
15	2		4..46	7..14	6..17..5	11..39	5..34	7
16	3	Spica ♍ set 10..58	4..47	7..13	6..29..29	12..12	6..25	8
17	4		4..47	7..13	7..12..20	12..46	7..12	9
18	5	Arcturus Sets 1..25	4..48	7..12	7..25..24	13..26	8..4	10
19	6		4..49	7..11	8..8..48	14..10	8..57	11
20	7	Margaret	4..49	7..11	8..22..31	14..56	9..52	12
21	F	8th Sund. past Trin	4..50	7..10	9..6..35	15..44	10..51	13
22	2	Magdalene	4..51	7..9	9..20..55		11..49	14
23	3	☉ enters ♌	4..52	7..8	10..5..26	rise	12..45	15
24	4	~~Dog Days begins~~	4..53	7..7	10..20..7	8..20	13..45	16
25	5	St. James	4..54	7..6	11..4..48	9..4	14..40	17
26	6	St. Anne	4..54	7..6	11..19..32	9..39	15..33	18
27	7		4..55	7..5	0..4..0	10..14	16..26	19
28	F	9th Sund past Trin	4..56	7..4	0..18..18	10..49	17..14	20
29	2	Days 14..6	4..57	7..3	1..2..17	11..27	18..9	21
30	3	~~Days 14..4~~ Dog Days begins	4..58	7..2	1..15..58	12..5	18..58	22
31	4	Days Decrease 42 m.	4..59	7..1	1..29..18	12..44	19..50	23

July 30 is the true time the Dog Days begins
for that morning that star rises with the Sun
Sept. 5 the Dog Days end

The Elements for the Construction of an Eclips of the Moon August 1793

	D	H	M	
True time of full Moon in August 1793	21	9	58	Morn
	°	′	″	
Moons Horizontal paralax	0	60	45	
Suns Semidiameter	0	15	56	
Moons Semidiameter	0	16	39	
Semidiameter of the Earths Shadow at the Moon	0	44	59	
Moons true Latitude North Descending	0	32	13	
Angle of her visible path with the Ecliptic	5	35	0	
Her true Horary Motion from the Sun	0	35	15	

93c August Eighth Month hath 31 Days

	D	H	M	
New ☽	6	2	53	Aft
First ☾	14	1	50	Aft
Full ○	21	9	57	Morn
Last ☾	28	6	28	Morn

1		7	
11	♍	7	Deg.
21		6	

Planets Places

D	☉	♄	♃	♂	♀	☿	☽
	♌	♉	♏	♋	♊	♍	Lat.
1	10	15	23	18	24	7	5 S
7	16	15	23	22	29	12	1 S
13	21	16	24	26	♋ 6	15	5 N
19	27	16	24	♌ 0	12	17	3 N
25	♍ 3	16	25	4	18	15	4 S

	W D	Remarkable Days Aspects weather &c.	☉ rise	☉ set	☽ Long.	☽ rise	☽ South	☽ Age
	5	Lammas Day, ☿ great Elong.	5..0	7..0	2..12..19	13..31	20..45	24
	6		5..1	6..59	2..25..2	14..18	21..35	25
	7		5..2	6..58	3..7..32	15..4	22..22	26
	F	10th Sund. past Trin.	5..3	6..57	3..19..40	15..50	23..7	27
	2	☿ great Elong.	5..4	6..56	4..1..43		23..56	28
	3	□ ☉ ♄ Transfiguration	5..5	6..55	4..13..38	Sets	6	☽
	4		5..6	6..54	4..25..32	7..34	0..40	1
	5	△ ♃ ♂	5..7	6..53	5..7..19	8..5	1..21	2
	6		5..8	6..52	5..19..8	8..36	2..3	3
	7	St. Laurence	5..9	6..51	6..1..8	9..10	2..46	4
	F	11th Sund. past Trin.	5..10	6..50	6..13..19	9..45	3..30	5
2	2		5..11	6..49	6..25..29	10..21	4..16	6
3	3	Arietis rise 9..5	5..12	6..48	7..8..17	10..58	5..5	7
4	4		5..13	6..47	7..21..11	11..36	5..54	8
5	5	Bulls eye rise 11..48	5..14	6..46	8..4..24	12..15	6..47	9
6	6	Days 13..30	5..15	6..45	8..17..56	12..58	7..41	10
7	7		5..16	6..44	9..1..51	13..47	8..40	11
8	F	12th Sund. past Trin.	5..18	6..42	9..16..1	14..42	9..[illegible]	12
9	2		5..19	6..41	10..0..27	15..47	10..37	13
0	3	Days Decrease 1..24	5..20	6..40	10..15..3		11..34	14
1	4	☽ Eclipsed	5..21	6..39	10..29..29	rise	12..28	15
2	5		5..22	6..38	11..14..28	7..35	13..24	16
3	6	☉ enters ♍	5..23	6..37	11..29..3	8..14	14..19	17
4	7	St. Bartholomew	5..24	6..36	0..13..32	8..52	15..10	18
5	F	13th Sund. past Trin.	5..26	6..34	0..27..39	9..28	16..4	19
6	2		5..27	6..33	1..11..32	10..3	16..50	20
7	3		5..28	6..32	1..25..2	10..42	17..49	21
8	4	St. Augustine	5..29	6..31	2..8..12	11..21	18..30	22
9	5	St. John Bapt. Beheaded	5..30	6..30	2..21..5	12..5	19..33	23
0	6		5..32	6..28	3..3..40	13..0	20..28	24
1	7	☌ ☉ ☿ Orient.	5..33	6..27	3..16..1	13..54	21..11	25

The Elements for the Construction of an Eclips of the Sun September 1793

True time of New Moon in September 1793 - - - - - - -	D H M 5 " 6. 49 Morn	
Semidiameter of the Earths Disc	0 " 54 " 37 -	
Suns Distance from the nearest Solstice	73 " 17 - 0 -	
Suns Declination North - - - - - - - -	6 " 11 - 0	
Moons Latitude North Ascending - - - -	40 " 27	
Moons Horary Motion from the Sun - - -	0 - 27 " 51	
Angle of the Moons visible path with ye Ecliptic	5 " 35 - 0	
Suns Semidiameter - - - - - -	0 " 15 " 59	
Moons Semidiameter - - - - - - -	0 " 14 " 57	
Semidiameter of the penumbra - - -	0 " 30 " 56	

The fourth is an Eclips of the Sun Sepr 5th in the morning

	H M	
Beginning of this Eclips	4 " 12	A M
Greatest obscuration - - -	5 " 0	
End of the Eclips	5 " 46	
Total Duration - - -	1 " 34	
Digits Eclipsed 5 1/3 on Suns N. Limb		

A very Small portion to this Eclips is Seen here the Eclips end 17 minutes after Sun rise

These ... are take... Annu...

13 September Ninth Month hath 30 Days

	D	H	M	
New ☽	5	6	49	Morn
First Q.	13	0	0	Morn
Full ○	19	5	54	Aft
Last Q.	26	8	0	Aft

Q.	1	♍	6	Deg.
	11		5	
	21		5	

Planets Places

☽	☉	♄	♃	♂	♀	☿	☽
	♍	♉	♏	♌	♋	♍	Lat.
1	10	16	25	8	26	8	3 S
7	15	16	26	11	♌ 3	4	3 N
13	21	16	27	15	10	4	5 N
19	27	15	28	19	16	9	2 S
25	♎ 3	15	29	23	23	20	5 S

M D.	W D.	Remarkable Days Aspects weather &c.	☉ rise	☉ set	☽ Long.	☽ rise	☽ South	☽ Age
1	F	14th Sund. past Trin.	5..34	6..26	3..28..0	14..39	21..56	26
2	2		5..35	6..25	4..10..5	15..31	22..41	27
3	3	Dog Days end	5..36	6..24	4..21..59	16..30	23..28	28
4	4		5..38	6..22	5..3..48			29
5	5	Sun Eclipsed.	5..39	6..21	5..15..41	sets	0..11	☽.
6	6	pleiades rise 9..11	5..40	6..20	5..27..36	7..17	0..55	1
7	7		5..41	6..19	6..9..35	7..52	1..37	2
8	F	15th Sund. past Trin. △ ☉ ♄	5..43	6..17	6..21..51	8..17	2..23	3
9	2	Nativity V. Mary	5..44	6..16	7..4..19	8..48	3..8	4
10	3		5..45	6..15	7..17..4	9..25	3..56	5
11	4	Bulls eye rise 10..9	5..46	6..14	8..0..6	10..6	4..48	6
12	5		5..48	6..12	8..13..28	10..53	5..43	7
13	6		5..49	6..11	8..27..9	11..44	6..37	8
14	7	□ ♄ ♂	5..50	6..10	9..11..11	12..40	7..37	9
15	F	16th Sund. past Trin.	5..52	6..8	9..25..28	13..43	8..36	10
16	2	☿ great Elong.	5..53	6..7	10..10..1	14..47	9..33	11
17	3		5..54	6..6	10..24..39	15..58	10..29	12
18	4	Days 12..10	5..55	6..5	11..9..33		11..22	13
19	5		5..56	6..4	11..24..4	rise	12..18	14
20	6	✶ ☉ ♃	5..58	6..2	0..8..29	6..59	13..11	15
21	7	St. Matthew	5..59	6..1	0..22..53	7..36	14..5	16
22	F	17th Sund. past Trin. Eq. Day Night	6..0	6..0	1..6..57	8..16	15..0	[illegible]
23	2	☉ enters ♎	6..2	5..58	1..20..38	8..57	15..48	18
24	3		6..3	5..57	2..4..0	9..39	16..42	19
25	4	☌ ♂ ♀	6..4	5..56	2..17..2	10..22	17..37	20
26	5	St. Cyprian	6..5	5..55	2..29..47	11..6	18..25	21
27	6		6..7	5..53	3..12..16	11..53	19..14	22
28	7		6..8	5..52	3..24..29	12..43	20..2	23
29	F	18th Sund. past Trin. St. Michael	6..9	5..51	4..6..29	13..35	20..49	24
30	2	Days Decrease 3..6	6..11	5..49	4..18..27	14..31	21..33	25

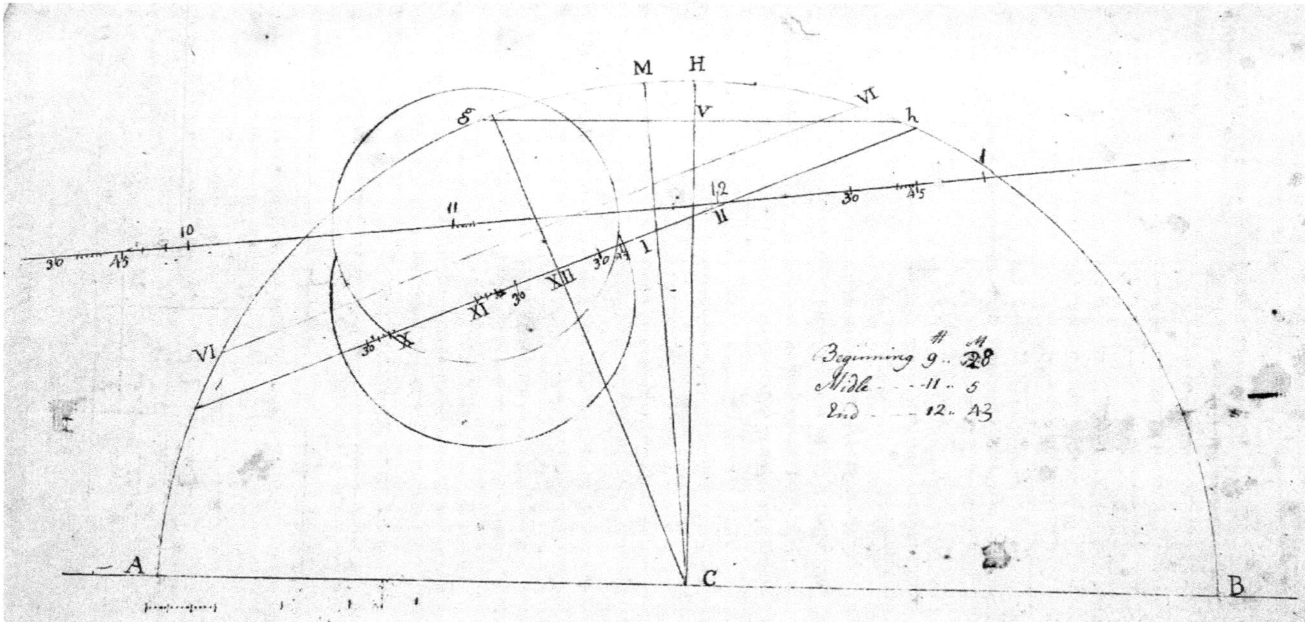

M
H
V
g
h
VI
VI
A
C
B
Beginning 9 .. 28
Midle .. 11 .. 5
End .. 12 .. 43

October Tenth Month hath 31 Days

	D	H	M	
New ☽	4	11	16	Aft
First ☾	12	8	34	Morn
Full ○	19	3	28	Morn
Last ☾	26	2	0	Aft

☊				
	1		4	Deg.
	11	♍	4	
	21		3	

Planets Places

D	☉	♄	♃	♂	♀	☿	☽
	♎	♉	♐	♌	♍	♍	Lat
1	9	15	0	27	0	29	0 S
7	15	14	1	♍ 1	7	♎ 10	5 N
13	21	14	2	4	15	20	3 N
19	27	13	3	7	22	♏ 1	4 S
25	♏ 3	13	4	10	♎ 1	10	4 S

M D	W D	Remarkable Days Aspects weather &c	☉ rise	☉ Set	☽ Long.	☽ rise	☽ South	☽ Age
1	3	□ ♃ ♀.	6..12	5..48	5..0..19	15..27	22..17	26
2	4	♃ Sets 8..7	6..13	5..47	5..12..9	16..23	23..3	27
3	5		6..14	5..46	5..24..1		23..45	28
4	6	Sirius rise 12..50	6..15	5..45	6..6..1	sets	☌	☽
5	7		6..17	5..43	6..18..8	6..29	0..27	1
6	F	19th Sund. past Trin.	6..18	5..42	7..0..28	6..55	1..11	2
7	2	□ ♃ ♂	6..19	5..41	7..13..1	7..29	1..57	3
8	3		6..20	5..40	7..25..54	8..7	2..45	4
9	4	Days 11..16	6..22	5..38	8..9..5	8..48	3..38	5
10	5	pleiades South 3..35	6..23	5..37	8..22..36	9..41	4..34	6
11	6		6..24	5..36	9..6..32	10..39	5..32	7
12	7	[illegible] South 12..45	6..25	5..35	9..20..36	11..39	6..27	8
13	F	20th Sund. past Trin. ☌ ☉ ☿ Occident	6..27	5..34	10..5..0	12..43	7..26	9
14	2		6..28	5..32	10..19..36	13..52	8..23	10
15	3	Days Decrease 3..42	6..29	5..31	11..4..32	15..1	9..17	11
16	4		6..30	5..30	11..19..1	16..13	10..11	12
17	5	Arcturus Sets 7..46	6..32	5..28	0..3..43	17..19	11..7	13
18	6	St. Luke	6..33	5..27	0..18..4		12..1	14
19	7		6..34	5..26	1..2..15	rise	12..55	15
20	F	21st Sund. past Trin.	6..35	5..25	1..16..7	6..54	13..48	16
21	2		6..36	5..24	1..29..42	7..34	14..40	17
22	3	Days 10..44	6..38	5..22	2..12..55	8..16	15..30	18
23	4	☉ enters ♏	6..39	5..21	2..25..49	9..0	16..26	19
24	5		6..40	5..20	3..8..35	9..46	17..12	20
25	6	Crispin	6..41	5..19	3..20..47	10..36	18..2	21
26	7		6..42	5..18	4..2..57	11..33	18..47	22
27	F	22d Sund. past Trin	6..44	5..16	4..14..56	12..33	19..35	23
28	2	St. Simon and Jude	6..45	5..15	4..26..50	13..29	20..18	24
29	3		6..46	5..14	5..[illegible]..40	14..25	21..2	25
30	4	pleiades South 1..20	6..47	5..13	5..20..31	15..19	21..42	26
31	5	Days Decrease 4..20	6..48	5..12	6..2..26	16..9	22..29	27

True time of Moons Southing in Greenwich 1793

January	☽ South	☽ rise	Feb	☽ South	rise	March	☽ South	rise	April	☽ South	rise
1 ♌ 27	15..32	8.6	1 ♎ 12	16..18	10.18	1 ♎ 21	14..54	9..34	1 ♐ — 10	16..30	12.[illegible]
2 ♍ 9	16..15	9.37	2 25	17..5	11.55	2 ♏ 4	15..47	10..53	2 — 24	17..29	13..3?
3 — 21	16..58	10.26	3 ♏ 8	17..57	13.9	3 — 17	16..43	12..12	3 ♑ 8	18..28?	14..34
4 ♎ 3	17..43	11.3?	4 22	18..54	14.29	4 ♐ 1	17..36	13..23	4 — 23	19..28	15..28
5 — 16	18..24		5 ♐ 6	19..48	15.41	5 — 15	18..36	14..42	5 ♒ 8	20..27	16..27
6 — 29	[illegible]..17		6 — 20	20..46	16.52	6 — 29	19..34	15..40	6 — 23	21..27	16..39
7 ♏ 12	20..20		7 ♑ 4	21..46	17.52	7 ♑ 13	20..33	16..39	7 ♓ 8	22..21	17..6
8 — 26	21..6		8 — 19	22..47	18.47	8 — 28	21..30	17..23	8 — 22	23..12	17..27
9 ♐ 10	22..4		9 ♒ 4	23..48		9 ♒ 13	22..29	17..58	9 ♈ 6	23..57	
10 — 24	23..9		10 — 19	☌	set	10 — 28	23..27	18..28	10 — 20	☌ —	set
11 ♑ 9			11 ♓ 3	0..41	5.51	11 ♓ 12			11 ♉ 4	0..50	7..56
12 — 24	☌ 4		12 — 17	1..34	7..6	12 — 26	☌ 0..11	sets	12 — 17	1..44	9..13
13 ♒ 9	0..58		13 ♈ 1	2..16	8..16	13 ♈ 10	1..2	7..22	13 ♊ 0	2..31	10..18
14 — 24	1..58		14 — 15	3..9	9..39	14 — 24	1..54	8..39	14 — 13	3..21	11..18
15 ♓ 8	2..53		15 — 29	3..58	10..54	15 ♉ 8	2..46	9..58	15 — 25	4..12	12..18
16 — 22	3..44		16 ♉ 12	4..50	12..7	16 — 21	3..39	11..14	16 ♋ 7	5..0	13..6
17 ♈ 6	4..36		17 25	5..40	13..21	17 ♊ 4	4..27	12..20	17 — 19	5..48	13..48
18 — 20	5..25		18 ♊ 8	6..29	14..29	18 — 17	5..19	13..25	18 ♌ 1	6..34	14..21
19 ♉ 3	6..11		19 20	7..19	15..25	19 — 29	6..8	14..14	19 — 13	7..21	14..31?
20 — 16	7..3		20 ♋ 2	8..5	16..11	20 ♋ 11	6..55	15..1	20 — 25	8..8	15..14
21 — 29	7..51		21 14	8..51	16..57	21 — 23	7..42	15..42	21 ♍ 7	8..51	15..36
22 ♊ 12	8..40		22 26	9..41	17..34	22 ♌ 5	8..31	16..12	22 — 19	9..37	15..57
23 24	9..31		23 ♌ 8	10..27	18..2	23 — 16	9..16	16..39	23 ♎ 1	10..18	16..18
24 ♋ 6	10..17		24 20	11..11		24 — 28	10..0	17..1	24 — 13	11..2	16..37
25 — 18	11..7		25 ♍ 2	11..58	rise	25 ♍ 10	10..43	17..23	25 — 26	11..50	
26 ♌ 0	11..51		26 14	12..41	6..11	26 23	11..32		26 ♏ 9	12..41	rise
27 12	12..36		27 26	13..23	7..13	27 ♎ 5	12..15	rise	27 — 22	13..33	9..8
28 23	13..20		28 ♎ 8	14..8	8..23	28 — 17	13..0	7..35	28 ♐ 6	14..27	10..20
29 ♍ 5	14..2					29 ♏ 0	13..48	8..46	29 — 20	15..26	11..32
30 17	14..44					30 — 13	14..40	10..3	30 ♑ 4	16..22	12..28
31 29	15..29					31 — 26	15..32	11..13			

179[illegible] November Eleventh Month hath 30 Days

	D	H	M	
New ☽	3	3	9	Aft
First ☾	10	8	0	Aft
Full ○	17	3	24	Aft
Last ☾	25	8	0	Morn

	1		2	
☊	11	♍	2	Deg.
	21		1	

Planets Places

D	☉	♄	♃	♂	♀	☿	☽
	♏	♉	♐	♍	♎	♏	Lat.
1	10	12	6	14	8	21	3 N
7	16	12	7	18	15	♐ 0	4 N
13	21	11	9	21	21	9	2 S
19	28	10	10	25	29	18	5 S
25	♐ 4	10	11	28	♏ 6	25	0 N

M D	W D	Remarkable Days Aspects weather &c	☉ rise	☉ Set	☽ Long	☽ rise	☽ South	☽ Age
1	6	All Saints	6 .. 49	5 .. 11	6 .. 14 .. 27	16 .. 56	23 .. 11	28
2	7		6 .. 51	5 .. 9	6 .. 26 .. 29		23 .. 58	29
3	F	23d Sund. past Trin. ☌ ☉ ♄ Occident	6 .. 52	5 .. 8	7 .. 9 .. 5	Sets	☌	☽
4	2		6 .. 53	5 .. 7	7 .. 21 .. 48	6 .. 13	0 .. 48	1
5	3	pleiades South 12 .. 52	6 .. 54	5 .. 6	8 .. 4 .. 48	6 .. 48	1 .. 34	2
6	4		6 .. 55	5 .. 5	8 .. 18 .. 7	7 .. 31	2 .. 24	3
7	5	Days 10 .. 8	6 .. 56	5 .. 4	9 .. 1 .. 49	8 .. 24	3 .. 21	4
8	6	Days Decrease 4 .. 38	6 .. 57	5 .. 3	9 .. 15 .. 48	9 .. 25	4 .. 18	5
9	7		6 .. 58	5 .. 2	10 .. 0 .. 5	10 .. 26	5 .. 16	6
10	F	24th Sund. past Trin.	6 .. 59	5 .. 1	10 .. 14 .. 29	11 .. 31	6 .. 13	7
11	2	St. Martin	7 .. 0	5 .. 0	10 .. 29 .. 14	12 .. 42	7 .. 10	8
12	3		7 .. 1	4 .. 59	11 .. 13 .. 55	13 .. 54	8 .. 7	9
13	4	✶ ☉ ♂	7 .. 2	4 .. 58	11 .. 28 .. 36	15 .. 9	9 .. 4	10
14	5	Capella South 1 .. 46	7 .. 3	4 .. 57	0 .. 13 .. 9	16 .. 16	9 .. 57	11
15	6		7 .. 4	4 .. 5[illegible]	0 .. 27 .. 28	17 .. 26	10 .. 50	12
16	7	Sirius rise 10 .. 4	7 .. 5	4 .. 55	1 .. 11 .. 29		11 .. 42	13
17	F	25th Sund. past Trin.	7 .. 6	4 .. 54	1 .. 25 .. 16	rise	12 .. 38	14
18	2	Bulls eye South 12 .. 48	7 .. 7	4 .. 53	2 .. 8 .. 42	6 .. 12	13 .. 26	15
19	3		7 .. 8	4 .. 52	2 .. 21 .. 48	7 .. 2	14 .. 19	16
20	4	Days Decrease 5 .. 0	7 .. 8	4 .. 52	3 .. 4 .. 33	7 .. 52	15 .. 6	17
21	5		7 .. 9	4 .. 51	3 .. 17 .. 2	8 .. 41	15 .. 54	18
22	6	☉ enters ♐	7 .. 10	4 .. 50	3 .. 29 .. 18	9 .. 29	16 .. 43	19
23	7	St. Clement	7 .. 11	4 .. 49	4 .. 11 .. 23	10 .. 17	17 .. 27	20
24	F	26th Sund. past Trin.	7 .. 12	4 .. 48	4 .. 23 .. 20	11 .. 11	18 .. 10	21
25	2		7 .. 12	4 .. 48	5 .. 5 .. 8	12 .. 10	18 .. 57	22
26	3	☿ great Elong.	7 .. 13	4 .. 47	5 .. 17 .. 0	13 .. 7	19 .. 39	23
27	4		7 .. 14	4 .. 46	5 .. 28 .. 52	14 .. 1	20 .. 20	24
28	5	Days 9 .. 30	7 .. 15	4 .. 45	6 .. 10 .. 50	14 .. 55	21 .. 2	25
29	6		7 .. 15	4 .. 45	6 .. 22 .. 56	15 .. 53	21 .. 47	26
30	7	St. Andrew	7 .. 16	4 .. 44	7 .. 5 .. 15	16 .. 51	22 .. 35	27

1793 May	☽ South	☽ rise	1793 June	☽ South	☽ rise	1793 July	☽ South	☽ rise	1793 August	☽ South	☽ rise	1793 Septem.
1 ♑ 18	17..21	13.21	1 ♓ 12	18..52	13.27	1 ♈ 20	19..17	12.37	1 ♊ 9	20.28	12..28	1 ♋ 2
2 ♒ 3	18..21	14..8	2 — 26	19..43	13.53	2 ♉ 4	20..8	13.2	2 — 22	21..21	13..15	2 ♌ 7
3 — 18	19..20	14.38	3 ♈ 10	20..33	14..13	3 — 17	20..56	13.27	3 ♋ 5	22..9	14..3	3 — 19
4 ♓ 3	20..13	15..3	4 — 24	21..24	14.39	4 ♊ 0	21..49	14..2	4 — 17	22.56	14.56	4 ♍ 1
5 — 17	21..4	15.39	5 ♉ 8	22..18	15..6	5 — 13	22..40	14..40	5 — 29	23..44	15..57	5 13
6 ♈ 1	21..57	15.57	6 22	23..11	15.36	6 — 26	23..29	15.23	6 ♌ 11	☌	Sets	6 25
7 — 15	22..46	16..16	7 ♊ 5	23..58		7 ♋ 8	0		7 — 23	0..29	7..41	7 ♎ 7
8 — 29	23..41	16..45	8 — 18	☌	Sets	8 — 20	☌..15	Sets	8 ♍ 4	1..7	7..57	8 — 19
9 ♉ 13			9 ♋ 0	0..48	8..54	9 ♌ 2	0..58	8..45	9 — 16	1..52	8..11	9 ♏ 1
10 — 26	☌..30	Sets	10 — 12	1..34	9..40	10 — 14	1..42	9..11	10 — 28	2..35	8..40	10 — 14
11 ♊ 9	1..18	9..18	11 — 24	2..24	10..17	11 — 26	2..26	9.32	11 ♎ 10	3..19	8..59	11 — 27
12 — 21	2..8	10..14	12 ♌ 6	3..11	10.52	12 ♍ 8	3..11	9.56	12 — 22	4..2	9.17	12 ♐ 10
13 ♋ 3	2..55	11..1	13 — 18	3..58	11..15	13 — 20	3..57	10..17	13 ♏ 5	4..53	9..47	13 — 24
14 — 15	3..46	11..52	14 ♍ 0	4..40	11..33	14 ♎ 2	4..43	10..43	14 18	5..42	10..13	14 ♑ 8
15 — 27	4..32	12..25	15 — 11	5..21	11..56	15 — 14	5..29	10..59	15 ♐ 1	6..34	10..47	15 — 22
16 ♌ 9	5..17	12..52	16 — 23	6..4	12..19	16 — 26	6..15	11..25	16 — 15	7..29	11..23	16 ♒ 7
17 — 21	6..5	13..22	17 ♎ 5	6..46	12..36	17 ♏ 9	7..4	11..41	17 — 29	8..28	12..22	17 — 22
18 ♍ 3	6..57	13..42	18 — 17	7..29	12..54	18 — 22	7..50	12..15	18 ♑ 13	9..23	13..17	18 ♓ 7
19 — 15	7..34	14..4	19 ♏ 0	8..16	13..18	19 ♐ 6	8..45	12..52	19 27	10..21	14..28	19 — 21
20 — 27	8..16	14..21	20 — 13	9..8	13..45	20 20	9..42	13..36	20 ♒ 12	11..21		20 ♈ 5
21 ♎ 9	9..0	14..40	21 — 26	9..56	14..15	21 ♑ 4	10..38	14..32	21 26	12..15	rise	21 — 20
22 — 22	9..45	15..0	22 ♐ 10	10..48	14..48	22 18	11..38		22 ♓ 11	13..13	7..48	22 ♉ 4
23 ♏ 5	10..35	15..29	23 — 24	11..48		23 ♒ 2	12..35	rise	23 26	14..9	8..16	23 — 18
24 — 18	11..24		24 ♑ 8	12..50	rise	24 — 17	13..31	8..54	24 ♈ 11	15..2	8..42	24 ♊ 1
25 ♐ 1	12..16	rise	25 23	13..52	9..52	25 ♓ 2	14..29	9..25	25 25	16..0	9..10	25 — 14
26 — 15	13..12	9..18	26 ♒ 8	14..50	10..25	26 — 17	15..22	9..47	26 ♉ 9	16..44	9..30	26 — 27
27 — 29	14..8	10..14	27 — 23	15..44	10..56	27 ♈ 1	16..11	10..11	27 22	17..35	10..0	27 ♋ 9
28 ♑ 13	15..8	11..14	28 ♓ 7	16..39	11..24	28 — 15	17..3	10.3[illegible]	28 ♊ 5	18..26	10..33	28 — 21
29 28	16..8	12..1	29 — 21	17..32	11..52	29 — 29	17..54	10..58	29 18	19..17	11..11	29 ♌ 3
30 ♒ 13	17..10	12..39	30 ♈ 6	18..28	12..28	30 ♉ 13	18..46	11..23	30 ♋ 1	20..7	12..1	30 — 15
31 28	18..2	13..3	3-			31 26	19..36	11..55	31 13	20..56	12..50	

December Twelfth Month hath 31 Days

	D	H	M	
New ☽	3	5	55	Morn
First ☾	9	5	34	Aft
Full ○	17	6	1	Morn
Last ☾	23	4	0	Morn

☊ { 1, 11, 21 } ♍ { 0, 0, 0 } Deg.

Planets Places

D	☉	♄	♃	♂	♀	☿	☽
	♐	♉	♐	♎	♏	♑	Lat.
1	10	9	12	2	14	0	5 N
7	16	9	13	5	21	4	2 N
13	22	9	14	9	29	0	5 S
19	28	8	16	12	♐ 6	♐ 22	3 S
25	♑ 4	8	18	15	14	16	3 N

M D	W D	Remarkable Days Aspects weather &c.	☉ rise	☉ set	☽ Long.	☽ rise	☽ South	☽ Age
1	F	Advent Sunday	7 . 16	4 . 44	7 . 17 . 48	17 . 51	23 . 23	28
2	2		7 . 17	4 . 43	8 . 0 . 37			29
3	3	Sirius rise 8 . 52	7 . 18	4 . 42	8 . 13 . 46	set	0 . 15	☽
4	4	☌ ☉ ♃ Orient	7 . 18	4 . 42	8 . 27 . 14	6 . 13	1 . 6	1
5	5		7 . 19	4 . 41	9 . 11 . 3	7 . 7	2 . 0	2
6	6	St. Nicholas	7 . 19	4 . 41	9 . 25 . 10	8 . 6	2 . 59	3
7	7	Arcturus rise 2 . 1	7 . 20	4 . 40	10 . 9 . 28	9 . 11	3 . 57	4
8	F	Conception of V. Mary	7 . 20	4 . 40	10 . 24 . 7	10 . 18	4 . 53	5
9	2		7 . 20	4 . 40	11 . 8 . 48	11 . 25	5 . 51	6
10	3	Pleiades South 10 . 25	7 . 21	4 . 39	11 . 23 . 34	12 . 32	6 . 44	7
11	4		7 . 21	4 . 39	0 . 8 . 11	13 . 45	7 . 33	8
12	5	Capella South 11 . 42	7 . 21	4 . 39	0 . 22 . 38	14 . 57	8 . 28	9
13	6		7 . 21	4 . 39	1 . 6 . 52	16 . 6	9 . 19	10
14	7	Spica ♍ rise 2 . 25	7 . 22	4 . 38	1 . 20 . 46	17 . 10	10 . 11	11
15	F	Cassiopea South 6 . 57	7 . 22	4 . 38	2 . 4 . 23	18 . 12	11 . 2	12
16	2		7 . 22	4 . 38	2 . 17 . 28		11 . 57	13
17	3	Days Decrease 5.28	7 . 22	4 . 38	3 . 0 . 29	rise	12 . 47	14
18	4	Days 9 . 16	7 . 22	4 . 38	3 . 13 . 15	6 . 25	13 . 42	15
19	5		7 . 22	4 . 38	3 . 25 . 38	7 . 13	14 . 27	16
20	6	Shortest Day	7 . 22	4 . 38	4 . 7 . 49	8 . 1	15 . 12	17
21	7	St. Thomas	7 . 22	4 . 38	4 . 19 . 49	8 . 50	15 . 59	18
22	F	☉ enters ♑	7 . 22	4 . 38	5 . 1 . 42	9 . 42	16 . 42	19
23	2		7 . 22	4 . 38	5 . 13 . 34	10 . 40	17 . 23	20
24	3	~~Christmas~~	7 . 22	4 . 38	5 . 25 . 22	11 . 39	18 . 5	21
25	4	~~St. Stephen~~ Christmas	7 . 22	4 . 38	6 . 7 . 17	12 . 38	18 . 50	22
26	5	~~St. John~~ St. Stephen	7 . 22	4 . 38	6 . 19 . 18	13 . 36	19 . 31	23
27	6	~~Innocents~~ St. John	7 . 22	4 . 38	7 . 1 . 29	14 . 36	20 . 18	24
28	7	Innocents	7 . 21	4 . 39	7 . 13 . 52	15 . 36	21 . 5	25
29	F	1st. Sunday past Christmas	7 . 21	4 . 39	7 . 26 . 33	16 . 38	21 . 53	26
30	2		7 . 21	4 . 39	8 . 9 . 31	17 . 40	22 . 47	27
31	3	Silvester	7 . 20	4 . 40	8 . 22 . 48		23 . 41	28

1794
Lat.
January

1	4 N
	3 N
	2 N
	1 N
	0 S
	1 S
	2 S
	3 S
	4 S
10	5 S
	5 S
	5 S
	5 S
	4 S
	3 S
	2 S
	1 S
	0 N 4
	1 N
	2 N
21	3 N
22	4 N
23	5 N
24	5 N
25	5 N
26	5 N
27	5 N
28	4 N
29	3 N
30	2 N
31	1 N

By Subtracting the Longitude of the North Node of the Moon from her we obtain her Distance from the Said Node, but not the Moon's Longitude ~~the Node~~ that of the Node

1793 October	☽ South	☽ rise	1793 Novemb	☽ South	☽ rise	1793 Decemb	☽ South	☽ rise
1 ♌ 27	22.6	15.7	1 ♎ 11	22.58	17.23	1 ♏ 15	23.13	18.36
2 ♍ 9	22.50	16.10	2 — 23	23.42	[illegible]	2 — 28	23.59	
3 — 21	23.34	17.17	3 ♏ 6	☌	Sets	3 ♐ 11	☌ —	Sets
4 ♎ 3			4 — 19	0.30	4.58	4 — 24	0.49	4.43
5 — 15	☌ 16	Sets	5 ♐ 2	1.20	5.30	5 ♑ 8	1.47	5.41
6 — 27	0.55	6.5	6 — 15	2.11	6.8	6 — 22	2.44	6.44
7 ♏ 10	1.46	6.29	7 — 29	3.10	7.4	7 ♒ 6	3.41	8.0
8 — 23	2.33	6.58	8 ♑ 13	4.6	8.0	8 — 21	4.41	9.27
9 ♐ 6	3.25	7.32	9 — 27	5.5	9.12	9 ♓ 6	5.38	10.53
10 — 20	4.22	8.16	10 ♒ 11	6.1	10.29	10 — 21	6.33	12.16
11 ♑ 4	5.19	9.13	11 — 26	6.58	11.52	11 ♈ 5	7.24	13.34
12 — 18	6.16	10.16	12 ♓ 11	7.56	13.21	12 — 20	8.18	14.58
13 ♒ 2	7.14	11.36	13 — 26	8.51	14.44	13 ♉ 4	9.8	15.14
14 — 17	8.13	12.50	14 ♈ 10	9.44	16.4	14 — 18	9.59	17.31
15 ♓ 2	9.8	14.12	15 — 24	10.35	17.20	15 ♊ 1	10.50	18.37
16 — 16	10.3	15.36	16 ♉ 8	11.28		16 — 14	11.40	[illegible]
17 ♈ 1	10.56	16.56	17 22	12.22	rise	17 27	12.34	rise
18 — 15	11.50		18 ♊ 6	13.14	5.21	18 ♋ 10	13.26	5.20
19 — 29	12.40	rise	19 — 19	14.7	6.1	19 — 23	14.15	6.19
20 ♉ 13	13.36	6.13	20 ♋ 2	14.59	6.53	20 ♌ 5	15.3	7.22
21 27	14.28	6.44	21 — 14	15.45	7.39	21 — 17	15.48	8.25
22 ♊ 10	15.18	7.18	22 — 26	16.31	8.38	22 — 29	16.31	9.36
23 — 23	16.11	8.5	23 ♌ 8	17.13	9.38	23 ♍ 11	17.14	10.39
24 ♋ 6	17.2	8.56	24 — 20	17.59	10.42	24 — 22	17.54	11.39
25 — 18	17.50	9.50	25 ♍ 2	18.46	11.51	25 ♎ 4	18.36	12.43
26 ♌ 0	18.35	10.48	26 — 14	19.28	12.58	26 — 16	19.19	13.49
27 — 12	19.22	11.53	27 — 26	20.9	14.2	27 — 28	20.3	14.59
28 — 24	20.7	12.58	28 ♎ 8	20.52	15.7	28 ♏ 11	20.53	16.10
29 ♍ 6	20.51	14.6	29 — 20	21.[illegible]	16.16	29 — 24	21.45	17.26
30 — 18	21.35	15.10	30 ♏ 2	[illegible]	[illegible] 20	30 ♐ 7	[illegible] 35	18.31
31 — 29	22.16	16.16				31 — 20	23.27	19.33

1794 ♄ Long 1..18..36 (s ° ′)
his Anom. 4..17..58

January	February	March	April	May	June	July	August	[illegible]
1 ♄ ♉ 8	1 ♄ ♉ 8	1 ♄ ♉ 10	1 ♄ ♉ 14	1 ♄ ♉ 18	1 ♄ ♉ 22	1 ♄ ♉ 25	1 ♄ 28	1 ♄
7 ♄ ♉ 8	7 ♄ ♉ 8	7 ♄ ♉ 11	7 ♄ ♉ 14	7 ♄ ♉ 19	7 ♄ ♉ 22	7 ♄ ♉ 26	7 ♄ 28	7 ♄
13 ♄ ♉ 8	13 ♄ ♉ 9	13 ♄ ♉ 11	13 ♄ ♉ 15	13 ♄ ♉ 19	13 ♄ ♉ 23	13 ♄ ♉ 27	13 ♄ 29	13 ♄
19 ♄ ♉ 8	19 ♄ ♉ 9	19 ♄ ♉ 12	19 ♄ ♉ 16	19 ♄ ♉ 20	19 ♄ ♉ 24	19 ♄ ♉ 28	19 ♄ 29	19 ♄
25 ♄ ♉ 8	25 ♄ ♉ 10	25 ♄ ♉ 13	25 ♄ ♉ 17	25 ♄ ♉ 21	25 ♄ ♉ 25	25 ♄ ♉ 28	25 ♄ 29	25 ♄

January First Month hath 31 Days

	D	H	M	
New ☽	1	7	9	Aft
First ☾	8	1	43	Aft
Full ○	15	10	56	Aft
Last ☾	23	11	55	Aft
New ☽	31	6	51	Morn

☊ { 1 ♌ 29 / 11 ♌ 29 / 21 ♌ 28 } Day.

Planets Places

d	☉	♄	♃	♂	♀	☿	☽'s Lat.
	♑	♉	♐	♎	♐	♐	Lat.
1	12	8	20	19	23	19	4 N.
7	18	8	21	21	♑ 0	24	2 S.
13	24	8	22	24	8	♑ 1	5 S.
19	♒ 0	8	23	27	15	9	1 N.
25	6	9	25	♏ 0	23	18	5 N.

One Magnus a Shepherd first discovered the wonderful power of the Lead Stone. See practical Navigator page 176

M D	W D	Remarkable Days Aspects weather &c.	☉ rise	☉ set	☽ Long.	☽ sets	☽	☽ South	☽'s Age
1	4	Circumcision	7.20	4.40	9.6.22	sets		6 Aft.	☽
2	5	♄ Stationary	7.20	4.40	9.20.29	5.33		0.40	1 One mag-
3	6	~~2nd Sund past Chris.~~	7.20	4.40	10.4.59	6.34		1.34	2 nus a Shep-
4	7	Days increase 6 min.	7.19	4.41	10.19.36	7.41		2.29	3 herd
5	E	2nd. Sund. past Chris.	7.19	4.41	11.4.17	8.51		3.25	4
6	2	Epiphany ☿ great elong.	7.18	4.42	11.18.55	10.3		4.20	5
7	3	⚹ ♃ ♂	7.18	4.42	0.3.26	11.14		5.14	6
8	4		7.17	4.43	0.17.43	12.24		6.6	7
9	5	Bullseye So. 9.0	7.17	4.43	1.1.50	13.29		6.57	8
10	6		7.16	4.44	1.15.43	14.31		7.48	9
11	7		7.15	4.45	1.29.21	15.31		8.39	10
12	E	1st. Sund. past Epip.	7.15	4.45	2.12.48	16.31		9.31	11
13	2	□ ☉ ♂	7.14	4.46	2.25.59	17.27		10.23	12
14	3		7.13	4.47	3.8.57	~~18.22~~		11.15	13
15	4	Sirius So. 10.46	7.13	4.47	3.21.43	~~19.12~~	rise	12.7	14
16	5		7.12	4.48	4.4.14	~~19.58~~	5.55	12.58	15
17	6		7.11	4.49	4.16.34	~~20.36~~	6.49	13.43	16
18	7	△ ♄ ☿	7.10	4.50	4.28.42	~~21.12~~	7.44	14.28	17
19	E	2nd Sund. past Epip	7.10	4.50	5.10.40	~~21.46~~	8.39	15.9	18
20	2	☉ enters ♒	7.9	4.51	5.22.32	~~22.14~~	9.34	15.49	19
21	3	pleiades So. 7.20	7.8	4.52	6.4.19	~~22.44~~	10.30	16.35	20
22	4		7.7	4.53	6.16.9	~~23.16~~	11.28	17.18	21
23	5	Days increase 32 min.	7.6	4.54	6.28.1	~~23.52~~	12.26	18.1	22
24	6		7.5	4.55	7.10.6		13.24	18.40	23
25	7	Convers. St paul	7.4	4.56	7.22.3	~~0.32~~	14.23	19.32	24
26	E	3d. Sund. past Epip	7.3	4.57	8.4.56	~~1.22~~	15.23	20.23	25
27	2	Bulls eye So 7.43	7.2	4.58	8.17.55	~~2.14~~	16.23	21.17	26
28	3		7.1	4.59	9.1.20	~~3.6~~	17.23	22.13	27
29	4	Days 10.	7.0	5.0	9.15.6	~~4.1~~	18.23	23.12	28
30	5		6.59	5.1	9.29.29				29
31	6	~~Pleiades So. 6.38~~ ☉ eclip. invis	6.58	5.2	10.14.3	~~sets~~	Sets	6.10	☽

As 24 hours is to the Moons Diurnal motion So is the Semidiurnal ark of the moon to the time to be added to the said Semidiurnal ark, to find the true time of her rising & setting

1794 ☽'s Lat. February	
1	0 S
2	2 S
3	3 S
4	4 S
5	5 S
6	5 S
7	5 S
8	5 S
9	5 S
10	4 S
11	3 S
12	2 S
13	1 S
14	0 S
15	1 N
16	2 N
17	3 N
18	4 N
19	4 N
20	5 N
21	5 N
22	5 N
23	5 N
24	5 N
25	4 N
26	3 N
27	2 N
28	0 N

January 1794 ☉ Long. ♉ ° ′	Logarithm ☉ from ⊕	July 1794 ☉ Long	Logarithm ☉ from ⊕
1 — 9 . 11 . 36	4.992593	1 — 3 . 9 . 54	5.007285
7 — 9 . 17 . 44	4.992663	7 — 3 . 15 . 39	5.007249
13 — 9 . 23 . 51	4.992818	13 — 3 . 21 . 22	5.007134
19 — 9 . 29 . 58	4.993055	19 — 3 . 27 . 6	5.006943
25 — 10 . 6 . 3	4.993364	25 — 4 . 2 . 50	5.006681

February ☉ Long.	Logarithm ☉ from ⊕	August ☉ Long.	Logarithm ☉ from ⊕
1 — 10 . 13 . 8	4.993759	1 — 4 . 9 . 31	5.006284
7 — 10 . 19 . 13	4.994219	7 — 4 . 15 . 13	5.005872
13 — 10 . 25 . 17	4.994743	13 — 4 . 21 . 1	5.005312
19 — 11 . 1 . 20	4.995325	19 — 4 . 26 . 47	5.004863
25 — 11 . 7 . 23	4.995959	25 — 5 . 2 . 35	5.004275

March ☉ Long.	Logarithm ☉ from ⊕	September ☉ Long.	Logarithm ☉ from ⊕
1 — 11 . 11 . 23	4.996405	1 — 5 . 9 . 21	5.003531
7 — 11 . 17 . 23	4.997106	7 — 5 . 15 . 11	5.002849
13 — 11 . 23 . 22	4.997837	13 — 5 . 21 . 2	5.002254
19 — 11 . 29 . 20	4.998590	19 — 5 . 26 . 53	5.001518
25 — 0 . 5 . 17	4.999354	25 — 6 . 2 . 47	5.000762

April ☉ Long.	Logarithm ☉ from ⊕	October ☉ Long	Logarithm ☉ from ⊕
1 — 0 . 12 . 11	5.000252	1 — 6 . 8 . 41	4.999995
7 — 0 . 18 . 4	5.001016	7 — 6 . 14 . 36	4.999227
13 — 0 . 23 . 57	5.001653	13 — 6 . 20 . 33	4.998463
19 — 0 . 29 . 49	5.002375	19 — 6 . 26 . 31	4.997714
25 — 1 . 5 . 39	5.003080	25 — 7 . 2 . 30	4.996987

May ☉ Long.	Logarithm ☉ from ⊕	November ☉ Long.	Logarithm ☉ from ⊕
1 — 1 . 11 . 29	5.003749	1 — 7 . 9 . 30	4.996180
7 — 1 . 17 . 17	5.004377	7 — 7 . 15 . 32	4.995531
13 — 1 . 23 . 3	5.004956	13 — 7 . 21 . 35	4.994932
19 — 1 . 28 . 50	5.005486	19 — 7 . 27 . 39	4.994387
25 — 2 . 4 . 35	5.005946	25 — 8 . 3 . 42	4.993982

June ☉ Long.	Logarithm ☉ from ⊕	December ☉ Long.	Logarithm ☉ from ⊕
1 — 2 . 11 . 17	5.006408	1 — 8 . 9 . 48	4.993555
7 — 2 . 17 . 2	5.006730	7 — 8 . 15 . 53	4.993201
13 — 2 . 22 . 45	5.006980	13 — 8 . 21 . 59	4.992926
19 — 2 . 28 . 29	5.007158	19 — 8 . 28 . 6	4.992731
25 — 3 . 4 . 11	5.007260	25 — 9 . 4 . 14	4.992618

October 1794 ♄ Long. ♉	November 1794 ♄ Long. ♉	December ♄ Long. ♉
1 — 29	1 — 28	1 — 24
7 — 29	7 — 27	7 — 24
13 — 29	13 — 27	13 — 23
[illegible]	19 — 26	19 — 23
[illegible]	25 — 25	25 — 22

Errors that ~~my~~ … corrected in my … Tables are these viz … page 204. when ♄ … 15° 4 - 30 the equation … ~~with~~ ought to have …

In ♂ equation … the Logarithm of … tance from ☉ … been as thus … place from the … of 7. ~~that~~ is from the … that his Annomali… untill it is 4 …

In ☿ Note Novem… ~~46~~ 66 read 46

1794 February Second Month hath 28 Days

		☽	☉	♄	♃	♂	♀	☿	☽
				Planets Places					
First ☾	D. H. M. 6..11..4 Aft		♒	♉	♐	♏	♒	♑	Lat.
Full ○	14..5..28 Aft	1	13	9	26	2	2	29	0 S.
Last ☾	22..5..32 Aft	7	19	9	27	5	9	♒ 8	5 S.
		13	25	9	28	7	17	18	1 S.
☊ { 1 / 11 / 21	♌ { 28 / 27 / 27 } Deg.	19	♓ 1	10	29	8	24	29	4 N.
		25	7	10	♑ 0	10	♓ 2	♓ 10	4 N.

M D	W D	Remarkable days Aspects weather &c	☉ rise	☉ Set	☽ Longt.	☽ Sets	☽ South	☽ Age
1	7	□ ♂ ♀	6..57	5..3	10..28..30	6..22	1..3	1
2	E	4th Sund past Epip.	6..56	5..4	11..13..49	7..34	2..2	2
3	2	Day increase 54 min.	6 55	5..5	11..28..38	8..45	2..58	3
4	3		6..54	5..6	0..13..13	9..55	3..52	4
5	4	pleiades Sets 1..41	6..53	5..7	0..27..34	11..3	4..44	5
6	5		6..52	5..8	1..11..30	12..4	5..36	6
7	6	□ ♄ ♀	6..51	5..9	1..25..18	13..13	6..28	7
8	7		6..50	5..10	2..8..42	14..13	7..20	8
9	E	5th Sund. past Epip.	6..49	5..11	2..21..50	15..11	8..12	9
10	2	Sirius South 8..59	6..48	5..12	3..4..45	16..8	9..3	10
11	3		6..46	5..14	3..17..26	17..1	9..54	11
12	4	☌ ♀ ☿	6..45	5..15	3..29..58	17..47	10..44	12
13	5		6..44	5..16	4..12..20	[illegible]	11..32	13
14	6	Valentine, ☽ eclip. vis.	6..43	5..17	4..[illegible]..39	rise	12..19	14
15	7	~~Spica ♍ rise 9..52~~	6..42	5..18	5..6..15	6..33	13..4	15
16	E	Septuagesima Sund.	6..40	5..20	5..18..47	7..27	13..47	16
17	2	Arcturus rise 8..49	6..39	5..21	6..0..49	8..23	14..30	17
18	3		6..38	5..22	6..12..45	9..19	15..13	18
19	4	✶ ♃ ☿, ☉ enters ♓	6..36	5..24	6..24..40	10..15	15..57	19
20	5		6..35	5..25	7..6..49	11..12	16..41	20
21	6		6..34	5..26	7..19..2	12..12	17..27	21
22	7	☌ ☉ ☿ Occident	6..33	5..27	8..1..27	13..11	18..15	22
23	E	Sund. past Septu.	6..32	5..28	8..14..9	14..9	19..6	23
24	2	☌ ☽ ♃	6..31	5..29	8..27..9	15..6	20..0	24
25	3	☍ ♄ ♂, ✶ ♄ ☿, △ ♂ ☿	6..30	5..30	9..10..33	16..3	20..56	25
26	4		6..28	5..32	9..24..22	16..57	21..54	26
27	5		6..27	5..33	10..8..36	17..49	22..53	27
28	6	Days 11..8	6..26	5..34	10..23..18		23..52	28

As 24 hours is to 48 minutes, the moons motion in that time so is the moons semidiurnal arc to the time that must be added to the said arc to find the true time of rising and setting of the moon.

♀ Venus will be morning Star till the 19th day of March, & is evening Star from that time untill the end of the Year.

1794 ☽ Lat March	
1	1 S
2	2 S
3	3 S
4	4 S
5	5 S
6	5 S
7	6 S
8	5 S
9	4 S
10	4 S
11	3 S
12	2 S
13	1 S
14	1 N
15	2 N
16	3 N
17	3 N
18	4 N
19	5 N
20	5 N
21	5 N
22	5 N
23	5 N
24	4 N
25	3 N
26	2 N
27	1 N
28	1 S
29	2 S
30	3 S
31	4 S

Common Notes and moveable Feasts for the Year

Dominical Letter	E	Easter Sunday	Ap
Cycle of the Sun	11	Ascension Day	Ma
Golden Number	9	Whitsunday	
Epact	29	Trinity Sunday	Ju
Number of Direction	30	Advent Sunday	

The Elements for an eclipse of the Sun January 31st 1794

True time of New Moon in January 1794 } D H M 31 . 6 . 51

Semidiameter of the Earths Disc — 0

Suns Distance from the nearest Solstice — 1 .

Suns Declination South — 41 . 33

Moons Latitude North Descending — 17 . 11

Moons Horary motion — 1 . 2

Angle of the Moons visible path with the Ecliptic

Suns Semidiameter — 5

Moons Semidiameter

Semidiameter of the penumbra

The Elements for an eclipse of the Moon in February 1794

True time of Full Moon in February, 1794 } D H M 14 . 5 . 28 Aft.

Moons Horizontal paralax

Suns Semidiameter

Moons Semidiameter

Semidiameter of the Earths Shadow at the Moon

Moon true Latitude South Ascending

Angle of the Moons visible path with the ecliptic

Moons Horary Motion from the Sun

The Elements for an Eclipse of the Sun March 1794

True time of New Moon in March 1794 } D H M 1 . 5 . 3 Aft

Semidiameter of the Earths disc

Suns distance from the Nearest Solstice VP; VS — 71

Suns declination South — 7

Moons Latitude South Descending — 1

Moons Horary Motion

Angle of the Moons visible path with the Ecliptic

Suns Semidiameter

Moons Semidiameter

Semidiameter of the penumbra

1794 March Third Month hath 31 Days

	D	H	M	
New ☽	1..	5..	6	Aft
First ☽	8..	0..	0	Noon
Full ○	16	.11	-51	Morn
Last ☾	24	5	-8	Morn
New ☽	31..	2	.16	Morn

☊ { 1 / 11 / 21 } ♌ { 26 / 26 / 25 } Deg.

Planets Places	☉	♄	♃	♂	♀	☿	☽'s
	♓	♉	♑	♏	♓	♓	Lat.
1	11	11	1	11	7	18	1 S.
7	17	11	2	11	14	29	5 S.
13	23	12	2	12	22	♈ 10	1 S.
19	29	12	3	12	29	18	5 N.
25	♈ 5	13	3	12	♈ 7	22	3 N.

M D	W D	Remarkable Days Aspects weather &c	☉ rise	☉ Set	☽ Long.	☽ Sets	☽ south	☽ Age
1	7	☉ eclip. invis. ✶ ☉ ♄, □ ☉ ♂, St. David	6..24	5..36	11..8..8	Sets	☌	☽
2	E	Quinquagesima Sund.	6..23	5..37	11..23.6	6..38	0..48	1
3	2	~~Sirius Set 12..42~~	6..22	5..38	0..8..1	7..50	1..42	2
4	3	Shrove Tuesday	6..21	5..39	0.22..46	9..2	2..36	3
5	4	Ash wednesday	6..19	5..41	1..7..12	10..14	3..29	4
6	5		6..17	5..43	1..21..15	11..25	4..22	5
7	6	Sirius Sets 12..28	6..16	5..44	2..4..32	12..30	5..15	6
8	7		6..14	5..46	2..18..7	13..30	6..7	7
9	E	1st Sund. in Lent.	6..13	5..47	3..0..33	14..22	6..59	8
10	2		6..12	5..48	3..13..40	15..10	7..50	9
11	3	pleiades Sets..11..31	6..11	5..49	3..26..7	15..54	8..39	10
12	4		6..9	5..51	4..8..9	16..32	9..27	11
13	5	Days increase 2..28	6..8	5..52	4..20..18	17..7	10..15	12
14	6		6..7	5..53	5..2..24	17..39	11..1	13
15	7		6..6	5..54	5..14..26		11..46	14
16	E	2nd. Sund. in Lent	6..4	5..56	5..26..31	rise	12..31	15
17	2	St. patrick	6..3	5..57	6..8..36	7..28	13..15	16
18	3		6..2	5..58	6..20..46	8..28	14..0	17
19	4	☌ ☉ ♀ Occident, E.D.&N.	6..0	6..0	7..[illegible]	9..28	14..46	18
20	5	☉ enters ♈ (☿ great elong.	5..59	6..1	7..15..20	10..28	15..32	19
21	6	Spica ♍ So. 1..11	5..58	6..2	7..27..50	11..28	16..19	20
22	7		5..57	6..3	8..10..28	12..28	17..9	21
23	E	3d. Sund. in Lent	5..55	6..5	8..23..25	13..26	18..3	22
24	2	☌ ☽ ♃	5..54	6..6	9..6..39	14..18	18..57	23
25	3	Annunciation V. M	5..53	6..7	9..20..11	15..8	19..53	24
26	4	Pleiades Sets 10..36	5..52	6..8	10..4..5	15..56	20..49	25
27	5		5..50	6..10	10..18..21	16..38	21..45	26
28	6	Days 12..22	5..49	6..11	11..2..56	17..18	22..43	27
29	7		5..48	6..12	11..17..47	17..57	23..40	28
30	E	4th Sunday in Lent	5..46	6..14	0..2..43		☌	29
31	2		5..45	6..15	0..17..38	sets	0..35	☽

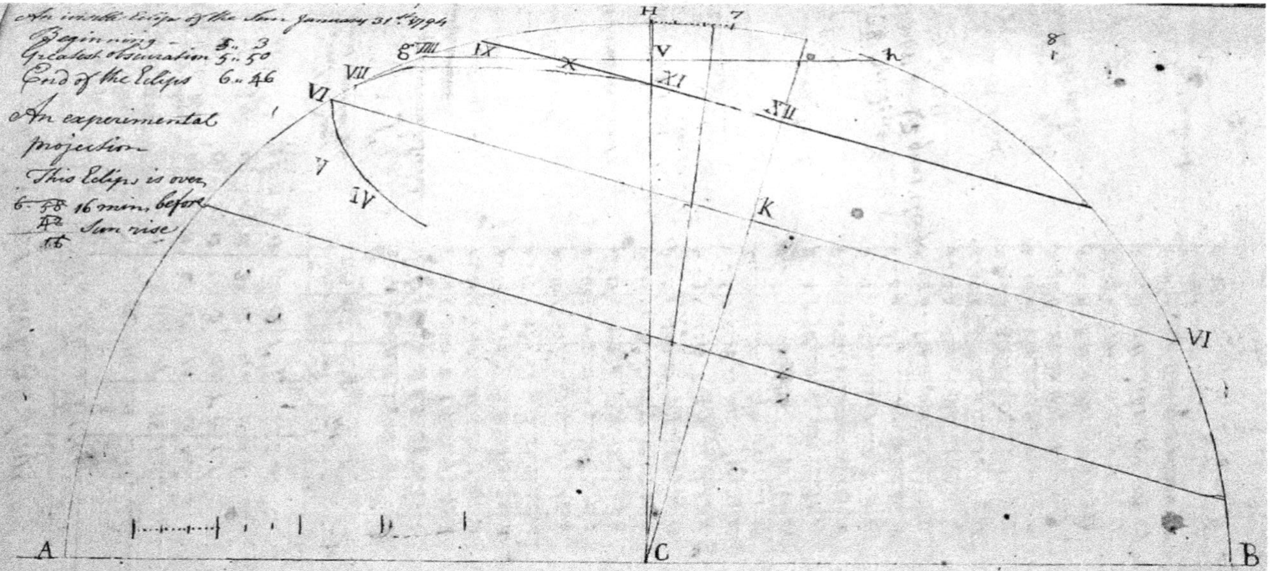

1794

D's Lat

April

1	5 S
2	5 S
3	5 S
4	5 S
5	4 S
6	3 S
7	2 S
8	2 S
9	1 S
10	0 N
11	1 N
12	2 N
13	3 N
14	4 N
15	5 N
16	5 N
17	5 N
18	5 N
19	4 N
20	4 N
21	3 N
22	2 N
23	1 N
24	0 S
25	2 S
26	3 S
27	4 S
28	5 S
29	5 S
30	5 S

1794 April Fourth Month hath 30 Days

First ☽ . 7 .. 0 .. 55 Morn
Full ○ . 15 .. 4 .. 58 Morn
Last ☾ . 22 .. 5 .. 9 Aft
New ☽ . 29 .. 10 .. 57 Morn

☊ { 1, 11, 21 } ♌ { 24, 24, 23 } Deg.

	Planets Places						
D	☉	♄	♃	♂	♀	☿	☽
	♈	♉	♑	♍	♈	♈	Lat
1	12	14	4	10	15	21	5 S.
7	18	14	4	9	22	17	2 S.
13	24	15	4	8	♉ 0	13	3 N.
19	♉ 0	16	5	6	7	11	4 N.
25	6	17	5	3	15	12	2 S.

M D	W D	Remarkable Days Aspects weather &c.	☉ rise	☉ Set	☽ Long.	☽ Sets	☽ South	☽ Age
1	3	Days increase 3 .. 16	5 .. 44	6 .. 16	1 .. 2 .. 21	8 .. 6	1 .. 25	1
2	4		5 .. 43	6 .. 17	1 .. 16 .. 45	9 .. 14	2 .. 17	2
3	5	pleiades Sets 10 .. 7	5 .. 41	6 .. 19	2 .. 0 .. 43	10 .. 20	3 .. 11	3
4	6	St. Ambrose	5 .. 40	6 .. 20	2 .. 14 .. 16	11 .. 24	4 .. 7	4
5	7		5 .. 39	6 .. 21	2 .. 27 .. 22	12 .. 24	5 .. 1	5
6	E	5th Sund. in Lent	5 .. 38	6 .. 22	3 .. 10 .. 7	13 .. 14	5 .. 53	6
7	2	☌ ☉ ♀ Orient	5 .. 36	6 .. 24	3 .. 22 .. 32	14 .. 2	6 .. 45	7
8	3		5 .. 35	6 .. 25	4 .. 4 .. 42	14 .. 42	7 .. 33	8
9	4		5 .. 34	6 .. 26	4 .. 16 .. 44	15 .. 18	8 .. 19	9
10	5	Spica ♍ So. 11 .. 59	5 .. 33	6 .. 27	4 .. 28 .. 38	15 .. 48	9 .. 4	10
11	6		5 .. 32	6 .. 28	5 .. 10 .. 32	16 .. 14	9 .. 47	11
12	7		5 .. 30	6 .. 30	5 .. 22 .. 28	16 .. 40	10 .. 30	12
13	E	Palm Sund.	5 .. 29	6 .. 31	6 .. 4 .. 28	17 .. 7	11 14	13
14	2		5 .. 28	6 .. 32	6 .. 16 .. 35	/	11 .. 59	14
15	3	♃ rise 12 .. 10	5 .. 27	6 .. 33	6 .. 28 .. 49	rise	12 .. 46	15
16	4		5 .. 26	6 .. 34	7 .. 11 .. 13	8 .. 24	13 .. 34	16
17	5		5 .. 25	6 .. 35	7 .. 23 .. 47	9 .. 30	14 .. 23	17
18	6	Good Fryday	5 .. 23	6 .. 37	8 .. 6 .. 35	10 .. 28	15 .. 13	18
19	7		5 .. 22	6 .. 38	8 .. 19 .. 33	11 .. 24	16 .. 4	19
20	E	Easter Sunday; ☌ ☽ ♃	5 .. 21	6 .. 39	9 .. 2 .. 43	12 .. 18	16 .. 57	20
21	2	☉ enters ♉	5 .. 20	6 .. 40	9 .. 16 .. 11	13 .. 12	17 .. 53	21
22	3		5 .. 18	6 .. 42	9 .. 29 .. 52	14 .. 2	18 .. 51	22
23	4	St. George	5 .. 17	6 .. 43	10 .. 13 .. 48	14 .. 46	19 .. 45	23
24	5	☍ ☉ ♂ Occident. △ ☉ ♃	5 .. 16	6 .. 44	10 .. 28 .. 5	15 .. 22	20 .. 37	24
25	6		5 .. 15	6 .. 45	11 .. 12 .. 27	15 .. 57	21 .. 33	25
26	7	Bullseye Sets 9 .. 4	5 .. 14	6 .. 46	11 .. 27 .. 15	16 .. 32	22 .. 29	26
27	E	1st Sund. past Easter	5 .. 13	6 .. 47	0 .. 12 .. 2	17 .. 7	23 .. 24	27
28	2	Day 13 .. 36	5 .. 12	6 .. 48	0 .. 26 .. 50			28
29	3		5 .. 11	6 .. 49	1 .. 11 .. 27	Sets	0 .. 17	☽
30	4	Lyra So. 9 .. 55	5 .. 10	6 .. 50	1 .. 25 .. 48	8 .. 16	1 .. 9	1

Eclipses for the Year 1794

The first is of the Sun January 31st invisible to us for the Eclipse is over twelve min. before Sun rise

1794 D.s	Lat Magt
1	5 S
2	4 S
3	4 S
4	3 S
5	2 S
6	1 S
7	0 N
8	1 N
9	2 N
10	3 N
11	4 N
12	4 N
13	5 N
14	5 N
15	5 N
16	5 N
17	4 N
18	3 N
19	2 N
20	1 N
21	0 S
22	1 S
23	2 S
24	3 S
25	4 S
26	5 S
27	5 S
28	5 S
29	5 S
30	4 S
31	3 S

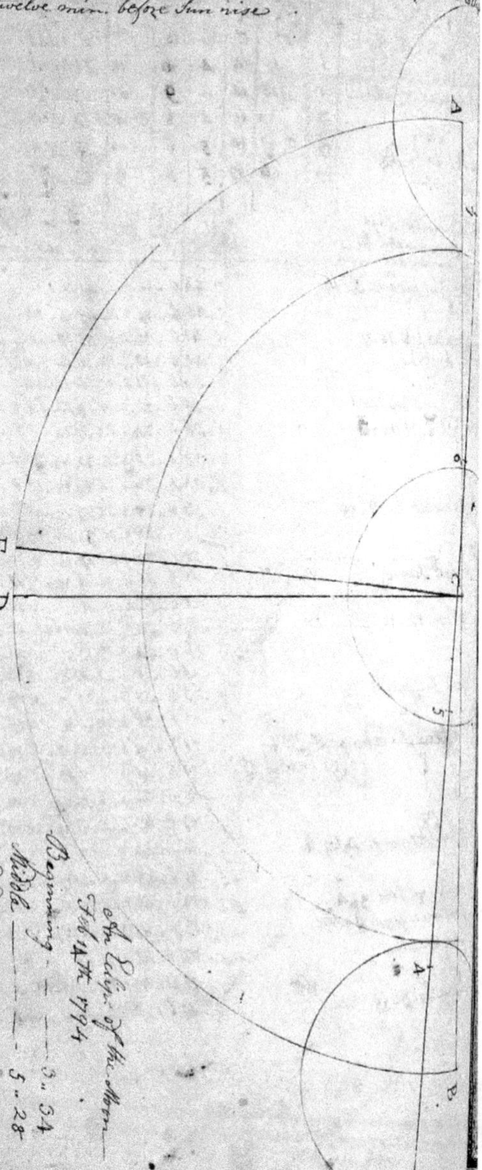

An Eclipse of the Moon Feb 14th 1794

Beginning — 3..54
Middle — 5..28
End — 7..20
Duration — 3..46
Digits Eclips:d 21½

1794 May Fifth Month hath 31 Days.

		D	H	M	
First	Q.	6	4	0	Aft
Full	○	14	7	42	Aft
Last	Q.	22	12	0	Morn
New	☽	28	7	42	Aft

☊ { 1, 11, 21 } ♌ { 23, 22, 22 } Deg.

Planets Places

☽	☉	♄	♃	♂	♀	☿	☽ Lat.
	♉	♉	♑	♏	♉	♈	Lat.
1	11	18	4	1	23	15	5 S.
7	17	19	4	♎ 29	♊ 0	21	0 N.
13	23	19	4	27	7	28	5 N.
19	29	20	3	26	15	♉ 7	2 N.
25	♊ 5	21	3	25	22	18	4 S.

M D	W D	Remarkable Days Aspects weather &c–	☉ rise	☉ Set	☽ Long.	☽ Sets	☽ South	☽ Age
1	5	St. philip and James	5..9	6..51	2..9..49	9..21	2..2	2
2	6		5..8	6..52	2..23..22	10..14	2..58	3
3	7		5..7	6..53	3..6..29	11..4	3..52	4
4	E	☿ great elong. 2nd Sund. p. East	5..5	6..55	3..19..11	11..52	4..43	5
5	2		5..4	6..56	4..1..33	12..38	5..33	6
6	3	St John Evang.	5..3	6..57	4..13..38	13..18	6..20	7
7	4		5..2	6..58	4..25..28	13..50	7..5	8
8	5		5..1	6..59	5..7..14	14..20	7..49	9
9	6	☌ ☉ ♄ Orient	5..0	7..0	5..18..56	14..48	8..32	10
10	7		4..59	7..1	6..0..42	15..14	9..14	11
11	E	3d Sund. past East	4..58	7..2	6..12..34	15..40	9..57	12
12	2	☍ ♂ ☿	4..58	7..2	6..24..38	16..7	10..41	13
13	3		4..57	7..3	7..6..53		11..27	14
14	4	Arcturus So. 10..40	4..56	7..4	7..19..23	rise	12..15	15
15	5		4..55	7..5	8..2..8	8..20	13..5	16
16	6	Days 14..12	4..54	7..6	8..15..8	9..16	13..57	17
17	7	☌ ☽ ♃	4..53	7..7	8..28..24	10..10	14..51	18
18	E	4th Sund. past East	4..52	7..8	9..11..55	11..4	15..47	19
19	2		4..52	7..8	9..25..38	11..56	16..45	20
20	3	☉ enters ♊	4..51	7..9	10..9..35	12..44	17..42	21
21	4		4..50	7..10	10..23..40	13..26	18..37	22
22	5	Spica ♍ So. 9..42	4..49	7..11	11..7..56	13..58	19..27	23
23	6		4..48	7..12	11..22..28	14..30	20..20	24
24	7		4..48	7..12	0..6..56	15..4	21..14	25
25	E	Rogation Sund.	4..47	7..13	0..21..32	15..38	22..8	26
26	2		4..46	7..14	1..6..5	16..13	23..2	27
27	3	Days increase 5..12	4..46	7..14	1..20..31		23..56	28
28	4		4..45	7..15	2..4..44	Sets		☽
29	5	Ascension Day	4..44	7..16	2..18..38	8..13	0..50	1
30	6		4..44	7..16	3..2..10	9..7	1..44	2
31	7	procyon Sets 9..14	4..43	7..17	3..15..18	10..0	2..38	3

An Eclips of the Moon Feb 14th
1794

Beginning	3 .. 33
Middle	5 .. 28
End	7 .. 19
Digits Eclipsd	21 ½
Duration	3 .. 46

D. Lat.

June	
1	2 S
2	1 S
3	0 N
4	1 N
[illegible]	2 N
[illegible]	3 N
7	4 N
8	5 N
9	5 N
10	5 N
11	5 N
12	5 N
13	4 N
14	3 N
15	2 N
16	1 N
17	0 N
18	1 S
19	2 S
20	3 S
21	4 S
22	5 S
23	5 S
24	5 S
25	5 S
26	4 S
27	3 S
28	2 S
29	1 S
30	0 S

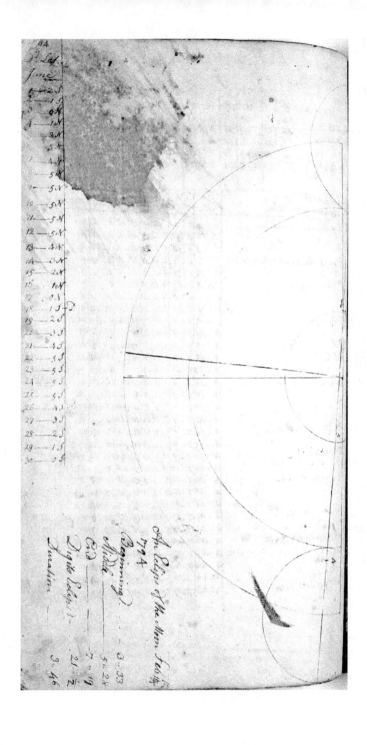

1794 June Sixth Month hath 30 Days

D. H. M.								
	Planets Places							
	D	☉ ♊	♄ ♉	♃ ♑	♂ ♎	♀ ♋	☿ ♊	☽'s Lat.
First ☽. 5..8..0 Morn	1	11	22	2	25	1	1	2 S.
Full ○ 13..7..27 Morn	7	17	22	1	25	8	14	4 N.
Last ☾. 20..5..9 Morn	13	23	23	0	25	15	27	4 N.
New ☽ 27..5..36 Morn	19	28	24	0	26	22	♋ 10	2 S.
☊ {1 ♌ 21, 11 ♌ 21, 21 ♌ 20} Deg.	25	♋ 4	25	♐ 29	28	♌ 0	21	5 S.

M D	W D	Remarkable Days Aspects weather &c	☉ rise	☉ Set	☽ Long.	☽ Sets	☽ South	☽ Age
1	E	Sund. past Ascen.	4..43	7..17	3..28..1	10..43	3..28	4
2	2		4..42	7..18	4..10..21	11..19	4..15	5
3	3	Days increase. 5..20	4..42	7..18	4..22..26	11..50	5..1	6
4	4		4..41	7..19	5..4..14	12..20	5..46	7
5	5	Spica ♍ Sets 1..47	4..41	7..19	5..15..56	12..48	6..30	8
6	6		4..41	7..19	5..27..54	13..14	7..12	9
7	7		4..40	7..20	6..9..13	13..38	7..51	10
8	E	Whitsunday	4..40	7..20	6..21..17	14..8	8..33	11
9	2		4..40	7..20	7..2..55	14..39	9..17	12
10	3	☌ ☉ ☿ Occident.	4..39	7..21	7..15..8	15..10	10..4	13
11	4	St. Barnabas	4..39	7..21	7..27..38	15..42	10..53	14
12	5		4..39	7..21	8..10..29		11..43	15
13	6	Arcturus So. 8..38	4..39	7..21	8..23..38	rises	12..36	16
14	7		4..39	7..21	9..7..9	8..50	13..31	17
15	E	~~[illegible]~~ Trinity Sund. △ ☉ ♂ ☌ ☽ ♃	4..38	7..22	9..20..56	9..34	14..28	18
16	2		4..38	7..22	10..5..0	10..17	15..24	19
17	3		4..38	7..22	10..19..11	10..59	16..19	20
18	4	Days 14..44	4..38	7..22	11..3..31	11..39	17..13	21
19	5		4..38	7..22	11..17..54	12..18	18..6	22
20	6	☉ enters ♋ Longest day	4..38	7..22	0..2..20	12..56	18..58	23
21	7	☍ ☉ ♃ Occident. ~~Longest day~~	4..38	7..22	0..16..45	13..30	19..51	24
22	E	1st Sund. past Trin.	4..38	7..22	1..1..10	14..4	20..45	25
23	2		4..38	7..22	1..15..29	14..42	21..40	26
24	3	St. John Baptist	4..38	7..22	1..29..39	15..24	22..36	27
25	4		4..38	7..22	2..13..37	16..6	23..29	28
26	5	Lyra So. 12..9	4..38	7..22	2..27..19		☌	29
27	6		4..38	7..22	3..10..46	Sets.	0..21	☽
28	7		4..38	7..22	3..23..50	8..26	1..11	1
29	E	2nd Sund. past Trin.	4..39	7..21	4..6..33	9..6	1..59	2
30	2	St. peter & paul	4..39	7..21	4..18..58	9..44	2..46	3

1794

July	D's Lat.	D's Mean Distance from ☊ s °
1	1N	0 : 11
2	2N	0 : 23
3	3N	1 .. 4
4	4N	1 .. 16
5	4N	1 .. 28
6	5N	2 .. 10
7	5N	2 .. 22
8	5N	3 .. 4
9	5N	3 .. 16
10	5N	3 .. 28
11	4N	4 .. 13
12	3N	4 .. 27
13	2N	5 .. 11
14	0N	5 .. 25
15	1S	6 .. 10
16	2S	6 .. 24
17	3S	7 .. 9
18	4S	7 .. 23
19	5S	8 .. 8
20	5S	8 .. 22
21	5S	9 .. 6
22	5S	9 .. 20
23	5S	10 .. 4
24	4S	10 .. 17
25	3S	11 .. 0
26	2S	11 .. 13
27	0S	11 .. 26
28	1N	0 .. 8
29	2N	0 .. 20
30	3N	1 .. 2
31	4N	1 .. 14

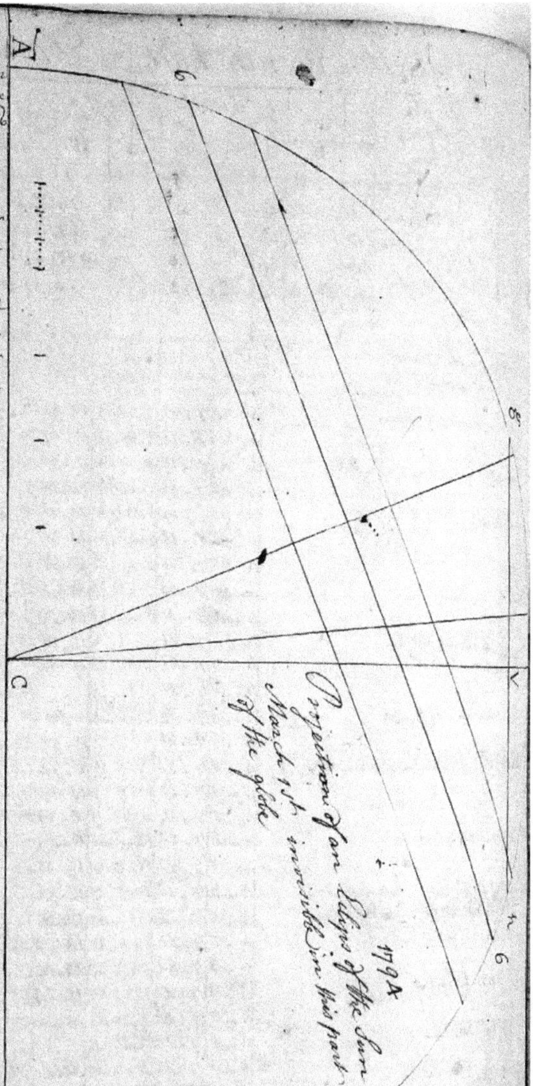

1794 July Seventh Month hath 31 Days

	D	☉	♄	♃	♂	♀	☿	☽ ☋
First Q. 4 .. 8 .. 0 Aft.		♋	♉	♐	♎	♌	♌	Lat
Full ○ 12 .. 5 .. 59 Aft.	1	10	25	29	29	7	1	1 N.
Last Q. 19 .. 10 .. 24 Morn	7	16	26	28	♏ 1	14	11	5 N.
New ☽ 26 .. 5 .. 24 Aft	13	21	26	28	4	21	18	2 N.
☊ {1 ♌ 20; 11 19; 21 19} Deg.	19	27	27	27	7	28	24	5 S.
	25	♌ 3	27	26	9	♍ 6	27	3 S.

Planets Places

M D	W D	Remarkable Days Aspects weather &c.	☉ rise	☉ sets	☽ Long.	☽ Sets	☽ South	☽ Age
1	3	✶ ♃ ♂	4 .. 39	7 .. 21	5 .. 1 .. 2	10 .. 18	3 .. 32	4
2	4	Visitation V. Mary	4 .. 40	7 .. 20	5 .. 12 .. 55	10 .. 48	4 .. 18	5
3	5		4 .. 40	7 .. 20	5 .. 24 .. 19	11 .. 14	5 .. 2	6
4	6	Translation of St. Martin	4 .. 40	7 .. 20	6 .. 6 .. 11	11 .. 39	5 .. 45	7
5	7		4 .. 41	7 .. 19	6 .. 17 .. 55	12 .. 4	6 .. 27	8
6	E	3d. Sund. past Trin.	4 .. 41	7 .. 19	6 .. 29 .. 36	12 .. 31	7 .. 10	9
7	2		4 .. 42	7 .. 18	7 .. 11 .. 30	13 .. 1	7 .. 53	10
8	3	♃ So. 10 .. 43	4 .. 42	7 .. 18	7 .. 23 .. 39	13 .. 33	8 .. 38	11
9	4		4 .. 43	7 .. 17	8 .. 6 .. 9	14 .. 11	9 .. 26	12
10	5	☌ ☽ ♃	4 .. 43	7 .. 17	8 .. 19 .. 0	14 .. 54	10 .. 17	13
11	6	Lyra So. 11 .. 7	4 .. 44	7 .. 16	9 .. 2 .. 13		11 .. 42	14
12	7		4 .. 44	7 .. 16	9 .. 15 .. 52	rise	12 .. 9	15
13	E	4th Sund. past Trin.	4 .. 45	7 .. 15	9 .. 29 .. 51	8 .. 18	13 .. 7	16
14	2		4 .. 45	7 .. 15	10 .. 14 .. 12	9 .. 6	14 .. 6	17
15	3		4 .. 46	7 .. 14	10 .. 28 .. 39	9 .. 46	15 .. 2	18
16	4	☿ great elong.	4 .. 47	7 .. 13	11 .. 13 .. 14	10 .. 24	15 .. 56	19
17	5		4 .. 47	7 .. 13	11 .. 27 .. 49	10 .. 58	16 .. 48	20
18	6	□ ♃ ♀	4 .. 48	7 .. 12	0 .. 12 .. 18	11 .. 28	17 .. 40	21
19	7	✶ ☉ ♄	4 .. 49	7 .. 11	0 .. 26 .. 41	11 .. 58	18 .. 32	22
20	E	5th Sund. past Trin.	4 .. 49	7 .. 11	1 .. 10 .. 56	12 .. 32	19 .. 25	23
21	2		4 .. 50	7 .. 10	1 .. 25 .. 2	13 .. 11	20 .. 19	24
22	3		4 .. 51	7 .. 9	2 .. 8 .. 55	13 .. 54	21 .. 13	25
23	4	☉ enters ♌	4 .. 52	7 .. 8	2 .. 22 .. 34	14 .. 44	22 .. 7	26
24	5		4 .. 53	7 .. 7	3 .. 6 .. 1	15 .. 38	23 .. 1	27
25	6	□ ♄ ☿	4 .. 54	7 .. 6	3 .. 19 .. 3		23 .. 55	28
26	7	☉ Eclip. invis	4 .. 54	7 .. 6	4 .. 2 .. 14	Sets		☽
27	E	6th Sund. past Trin.	4 .. 55	7 .. 5	4 .. 14 .. 59	7 .. 47	0 .. 46	1
28	2		4 .. 56	7 .. 4	4 .. 27 .. 15	8 .. 17	1 .. 32	2
29	3	Spica ♍ Sets, 10 .. 6	4 .. 57	7 .. 3	5 .. 9 .. 24	8 .. 46	2 .. 15	3
30	4	Dog Days begins	4 .. 58	7 .. 2	5 .. 21 .. 22	9 .. 14	2 .. 58	4
31	5	Days decrease. 42 min.	4 .. 59	7 .. 1	6 .. 3 .. 11	9 .. 40	3 .. 41	5

1794

D.	Lat
August	
1	4 N
2	5 N
3	5 N
4	5 N
5	5 N
6	5 N
7	4 N
8	3 N
9	2 N
10	1 N
11	0 S ☊
12	2 S
13	3 S
14	4 S
15	5 S
16	5 S
17	5 S
18	5 S
19	5 S
20	4 S
21	3 S
22	2 S
23	1 S
24	0 N ☋
25	2 N
26	3 N
27	4 N
28	4 N
29	5 N
30	5 N
31	5 N

True time of new Moon in July 1794 } D 26 .. H 5 .. M 18 P.M.

Semidiameter of the Earths disc

Suns distance from the nearest Solstice — 54

Suns declination North — 34.

Moons Latitude South Ascending — 19.

Moons Horary Motion from the Sun —

Angle of the Moons visible path with the Ecliptic —

Suns Semidiameter — — — — —

Moons Semidiameter — — — —

Semidiameter of the penumbra — — —

True time of Full Moon in August 1794 } D 11 .. H 2 .. M 35 A.M

Moons Horizontal parallax —

Suns Semidiameter —

Moons Semidiameter —

Semidiameter of the Earths Shadow at the Moon

Moons Latitude South descending —

Angle of the Moons visible path with the Ecliptic —

Moons Horary Motion from the Sun —

~~True Time of New Moon in August 1794~~ } ~~D 25 .. H 7 .. M 21 A.M~~

~~Moons Horizontal paralax~~

~~Suns Semidiameter~~

~~Moons Semidiameter~~

~~Semidiameter of the Earths Shadow at the Moon~~

~~Moons Latitude North Ascending~~

~~Angle of the moons visible path with the Ecliptic~~

~~Moons Horary Motion~~

This Eclips ~~a Con~~ ~~cannot be seen here, the Moon having a North Latitude~~

True time of New Moon in August 1794 } D 25 .. H 7 .. M 20

Semidiameter of the Earths disc

Suns distance from the nearest Solstice — 63

Suns declination North — 11

Moons Latitude North Ascending —

Moons Horary Motion from the Sun —

Angle of the Moons visible path with the Ecliptic — —

Suns Semidiameter —

Moons Semidiameter —

Semidiameter of the penumbra —

1794 August Eighth Month hath 31 Days

		Planets Places							
First ☽ 3 .. 6 .. 30 Aft.	☽	☉	♄	♃	♂	♀	☿	☽'s
Full ○ 11 .. 2 .. 35 Morn.		♌	♉	♐	♏	♍	♌	Lat.
Last ☾ 17 .. 6 .. 51 Aft.	1	10	28	25	12	14	29	4 N.
New ☽ 25 7 .. 23 Morn.	7	15	28	25	16	21	26	4 N.
	13	21	29	25	19	28	22	3 S.
☊ { 1 ♌ 18 } Deg.	19	27	29	25	22	♎ 5	17	5 S.
☊ { 11 ♌ 17 } Deg.	25	♍ 3	29	25	26	12	16	2 N.
☊ { 21 ♌ 17 } Deg.								

M D	W D	Remarkable Days Aspects weather &c.	☉ rise	☉ sets	☽ Long.	☽ Sets	☽ South	☽ Age
1	6	Lammas Day	5 .. 0	7 .. 0	6 .. 14 .. 55	10 .. 6	4 .. 24	6
2	7		5 .. 1	6 .. 59	6 .. 26 .. 37	10 .. 32	5 .. 6	7
3	E	7th Sund. past Trin.	5 .. 2	6 .. 58	7 .. 8 .. 24	11 .. 0	5 .. 48	8
4	2		5 .. 3	6 .. 57	7 .. 20 .. 20	11 .. 29	6 .. 30	9
5	3		5 .. 4	6 .. 56	8 .. 2 .. 27	12 .. 3	7 .. 18	10
6	4	Transfiguration	5 .. 5	6 .. 55	8 .. 14 .. 55	12 .. 45	8 .. 10	11
7	5	☌ ☽ ♃	5 .. 6	6 .. 54	8 .. 27 .. 44	13 .. 35	9 .. 2	12
8	6	♃ Sationary	5 .. 7	6 .. 53	9 .. 10 .. 58	14 .. 33	9 .. 56	13
9	7		5 .. 8	6 .. 52	9 .. 24 .. 39	15 .. 34	10 .. 52	14
10	E	□ ☉ ♂, 8th Sund. past. Trin.	5 .. 9	6 .. 51	10 .. 8 .. 47		11 .. 49	15
11	2	☽ eclip. vis. (St. Lawrence	5 .. 10	6 .. 50	10 .. 23 .. 14	rise	12 .. 46	16
12	3	Bulls rise, 11 .. 59	5 .. 11	6 .. 49	11 .. 7 .. 58	8 .. 14	13 .. 43	17
13	4		5 .. 12	6 .. 48	11 .. 22 .. 46	8 .. 49	14 .. 39	18
14	5	☌ ☉ ☿ Orient.	5 .. 13	6 .. 47	0 .. 7 .. 29	9 .. 24	15 .. 33	19
15	6		5 .. 14	6 .. 46	0 .. 22 .. 12	9 .. 59	16 .. 27	20
16	7		5 .. 15	6 .. 45	1 .. 6 .. 36	10 .. 35	17 .. 21	21
17	E	9th Sund. past Trin.	5 .. 16	6 .. 44	1 .. 20 .. 47	11 .. 12	18 .. 15	22
18	2		5 .. 18	6 .. 42	2 .. 4 .. 39	11 .. 53	19 .. 8	23
19	3	Pleiades rise 10 .. 17	5 .. 19	6 .. 41	2 .. 18 .. 17	12 .. 38	20 .. 1	24
20	4		5 .. 20	6 .. 40	3 .. 0 .. 40	13 .. 28	20 .. 54	25
21	5	□ ☉ ♄	5 .. 21	6 .. 39	3 .. 14 .. 49	14 .. 23	21 .. 46	26
22	6		5 .. 22	6 .. 38	3 .. 27 .. 44	15 .. 21	22 .. 36	27
23	7	☉ enters ♍	5 .. 23	6 .. 37	4 .. 10 .. 26	16 .. 22	23 .. 25	28
24	E	10th Sund. past Trin. St. Bar.	5 .. 24	6 .. 36	4 .. 23 .. 0			29
25	2		5 .. 26	6 .. 34	5 .. 5 .. 20	Sets	0 .. 12	☽
26	3	♃ Sets 11 .. 58	5 .. 27	6 .. 33	5 .. 17 .. 31	7 .. 15	0 .. 58	1
27	4		5 .. 28	6 .. 32	5 .. 29 .. 36	7 .. 43	1 .. 43	2
28	5	St. Augustine	5 .. 29	6 .. 31	6 .. 11 .. 31	8 .. 11	2 .. 27	3
29	6	St. John Baptist beheaded	5 .. 30	6 .. 30	6 .. 23 .. 25	8 .. 39	3 .. 7	4
30	7		5 .. 32	6 .. 28	7 .. 5 .. 18	9 .. 8	3 .. 49	5
31	E	☿ great. elong. 11th Sund. p. Trin.	5 .. 33	6 .. 27	7 .. 17 .. 15	9 .. 37	4 .. 33	6

1794
D. Lat.
September

1	5 N
2	5 N
3	4 N
4	3 N
5	2 N
6	1 N
7	0 N
8	0 S
9	1 S
10	2 S
11	3 S
12	4 S
13	5 S
14	5 S
15	5 S
16	4 S
17	3 S
18	2 S
19	1 S
20	0 N
21	1 N
22	2 N
23	3 N
24	4 N
25	5 N
26	5 N
27	5 N
28	5 N
29	5 N
30	4 N

An Eclips of the Sun
July 26 . 5 . 18 P.M.
Appears to be invisible
On acct. of the Moons great
South Latitude

1 — Semid. of penumbra — 1

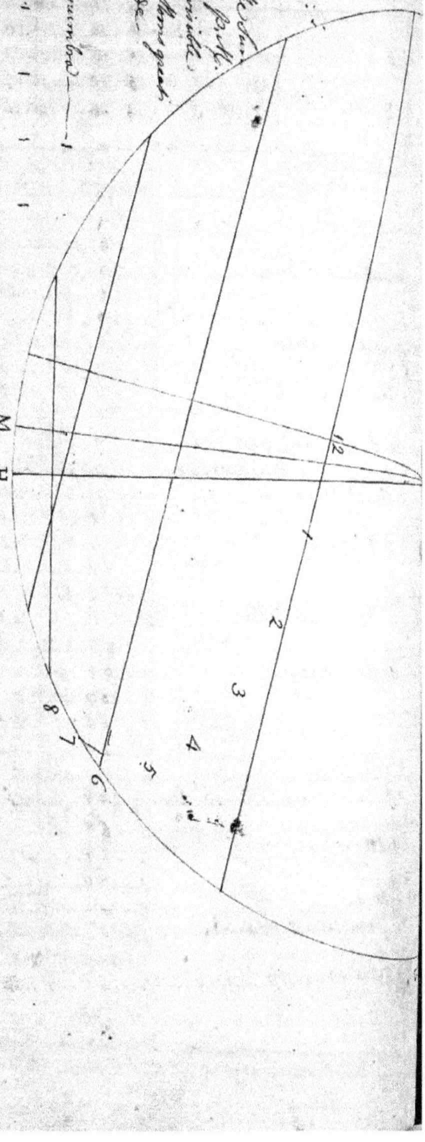

1794 September Ninth Month hath 30 Days

	D	H	M	
First ☽	2	8	0	Morn
Full ○	9	10	37	Morn
Last ☾	16	3	26	Morn
New ●	23	11	40	Aft.

☊ { 1 — 16; 11 ♌ 16; 21 — 15 } Deg.

Planets Places

☽	☉	♄	♃	♂	♀	☿	☽'s
	♍	♉	♐	♐	♎	♌	Lat.
1	9	29	25	0	20	21	5 N.
7	15	29	25	4	27	♍ 0	0 N.
13	21	29	26	8	♏ 4	10	5 S.
19	27	29	26	12	11	21	1 S.
25	♎ 3	29	27	16	♐ 18	♎ 2	5 N.

M D	W D	Remarkable Days Aspects weather &c.	☉ rise	☉ sets	☽ Long.	☽ Sets	☽ South	☽ Age
1	2	Days 12..52	5..34	6..26	7..29..10	10..9	5..19	7
2	3		5..35	6..25	8..11..26	10..48	6..7	8
3	4	☌ ☽ ♃ Dog Days ends	5..36	6..24	8..23..57	11..35	7..0	9
4	5		5..38	6..22	9..6..47	12..30	7..54	10
5	6	Pleïades rise 9..15	5..39	6..21	9..20..2	13..30	8..49	11
6	7	□ ♄ ☿	5..40	6..20	10..3..44	14..35	9..44	12
7	E	12th Sund. past Trin.	5..41	6..19	10..17..50	15..47	10..39	13
8	2	Nativity V. Mary	5..43	6..17	11..2..23		11..34	14
9	3		5..44	6..16	11..17..12	rise	12..29	15
10	4	Sirius rise 2..15	5..45	6..15	0..2..8	7..22	13..25	16
11	5		5..46	6..14	0..17..4	7..58	14..21	17
12	6	Bulls eye rise 10..6	5..48	6..12	1..1..51	8..36	15..17	18
13	7		5..49	6..11	1..16..19	9..16	16..13	19
14	E	13th Sund. past Trin.	5..50	6..10	2..0..29	9..58	17..9	20
15	2		5..52	6..8	2..14..19	10..42	18..4	21
16	3	Arcturus Sets 9..39	5..53	6..7	2..27..45	11..32	18..57	22
17	4		5..54	6..6	3..10..53	12..27	19..[illegible]	23
18	5	□ ☉ ♃	5..55	6..5	3..23..44	13..25	20..42	24
19	6	Regulus rise 3..24	5..56	6..4	4..6..23	14..25	21..31	25
20	7		5..58	6..2	4..18..52	15..25	22..17	26
21	E	△ ☉ ♄, 14th Sund. past Trin.	5..59	6..1	5..1..10	16..25	23..2	27
22	2	Equal day and night, (St. Mat	6..0	6..0	5..13..23		23..47	28
23	3	(☉ enters ♎	6..2	5..58	5..25..31	Sets	–	☽
24	4		6..3	5..57	6..7..35	6..22	0..32	1
25	5	☌ ☉ ☿, Occident. ~~☉ enters ♎~~	6..4	5..56	6..19..38	6..51	1..16	2
26	6	St. Cyprian	6..5	5..55	7..1..39	7..21	2..0	3
27	7		6..7	5..53	7..13..47	7..52	2..44	4
28	E	15th Sund. past Trin.	6..8	5..52	7..25..51	8..24	3..27	5
29	2	St. Michael	6..9	5..51	8..8..[illegible]	8..59	4..12	6
30	3	☌ ☽ ♃	6..11	5..49	8..20..29	9..42	5..0	7

1794

D's Lat

October

1	4 N
2	3 N
3	2 N
4	0 N
5	1 S
6	2 S
7	3 S
8	4 S
9	5 S
10	5 S
11	5 S
12	5 S
13	4 S
14	3 S
15	2 S
16	1 S
17	0 S
18	1 N
19	2 N
20	3 N
21	4 N
22	4 N
23	5 N
24	5 N
25	5 N
26	5 N
27	4 N
28	4 N
29	3 N
30	2 N
31	0 N

August 11th 1794 4 M

This Eclipse Begins 0 .. 50

Middle ___ 2 .. 35

End ___ 4 .. 19 } A.M

Duration 3 .. 29

Digits Eclipsed 17 .. 1/4

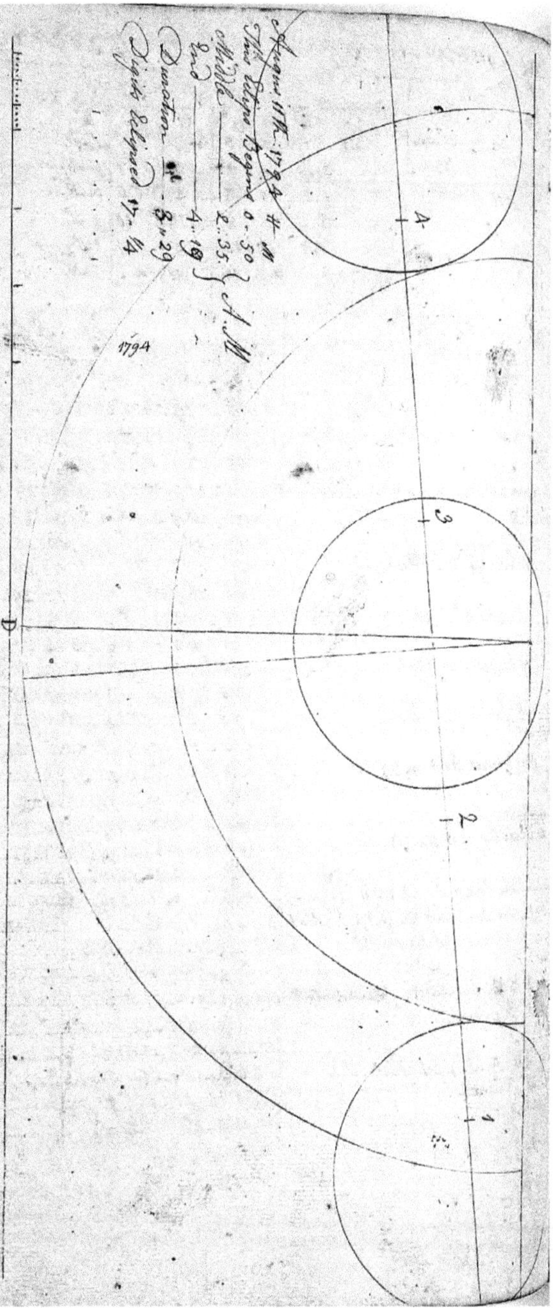

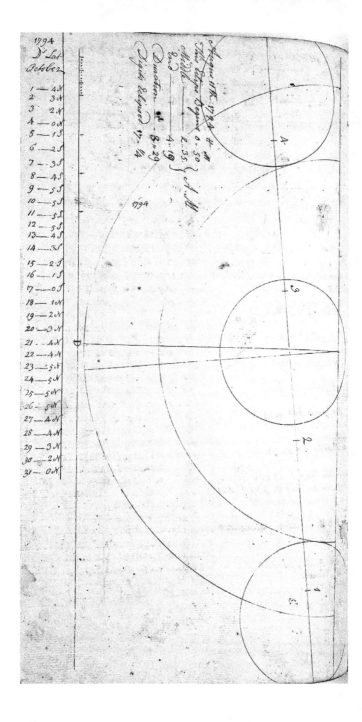

1791 October Tenth Month hath 31 Days

	☽	☉	♄	♃	♂	♀	☿	☽
First ☽ 1..11..5 Aft				Planets Places				
Full ○ 8..7..6 Aft		♎	♉	♐	♐	♏	♎	Lat.
Last ☾ 15..5..32 Aft								
New ☽ 23..5..16 Aft	1	9	29	27	20	24	13	4 N.
First ☽ 31..0..0 Noon	7	15	29	28	24	♐ 1	22	3 S.
☊ {1, 11, 21} ♌ {15, 15, 14} Deg.	13	21	28	29	28	7	♏ 2	4 S.
	19	27	28	♑ 0	♑ 3	13	12	2 N.
	25	♏ 3	28	1	8	19	20	5 N.

M D	W D	Remarkable Days Aspects weather &c	☉ rise	☉ sets	☽ Long.	☽ Sets	☽ South	☽ Age
1	4	Days decrease 3..8	6..12	5..48	9..3..9	10..31	5..54	8
2	5		6..13	5..47	9..16..6	11..26	6..45	9
3	6	pleiades rise 7..34	6..14	5..46	9..29..5	12..27	7..37	10
4	7		6..15	5..45	10..13..3	13..33	8..31	11
5	E	16th Sund. past Trin.	6..17	5..43	10..27..9	14..45	9..27	12
6	2	Sirius rise. 12..43	6..18	5..42	11..11..38	16..0	10..25	13
7	3		6..19	5..41	11..26..24		11..22	14
8	4	procyon rise 12..11	6..20	5..40	0..11..22	rise	12..18	15
9	5		6..22	5..38	0..26..22	6..40	13..14	16
10	6	Bulls eye so. 4..24	6..23	5..37	1..11..15	7..18	14..10	17
11	7		6..24	5..36	1..25..49	7..59	15..6	18
12	E	17th Sund. past Trin.	6..25	5..35	2..10..2	8..43	16..2	19
13	2		6..27	5..33	2..23..50	9..35	16..58	20
14	3	☌ ♃ ♂	6..28	5..32	3..7..14	10..29	17..52	21
15	4		6..29	5..31	3..20..12	11..25	18..44	22
16	5	♀ Sets 7..53	6..30	5..30	4..2..51	12..25	19..34	23
17	6		6..32	5..28	4..15..15	13..25	20..22	24
18	7	St. Luke	6..33	5..27	4..27..27	14..25	21..8	25
19	E	18th Sund. past Trin.	6..34	5..26	5..9..32	15..24	21..52	26
20	2		6..35	5..25	5..21..33	16..24	22..34	27
21	3		6..36	5..24	6..3..33	17..21	23..14	28
22	4	♀ great elong.	6..38	5..22	6..15..34		23..54	29
23	5	☉ enters ♏	6..39	5..21	6..27..36	Sets	–	☽
24	6		6..40	5..20	7..9..45	5..46	0..38	1
25	7	Crispin	6..41	5..19	7..22..0	6..21	1..24	2
26	E	19th Sund. past Trin.	6..42	5..18	8..4..20	6..59	2..12	3
27	2		6..44	5..16	8..16..49	7..41	3..4	4
28	3	☌ ☽ ♃. St. Simon & Jude	6..45	5..15	8..29..31	8..29	3..56	5
29	4		6..46	5..14	9..12..23	9..25	4..48	6
30	5	pleiades So. 1..20	6..47	5..13	9..25..33	10..27	5..42	7
31	6	Days 10..24	6..48	5..12	10..8..57	11..33	6..36	8

1794 Ds Novemb	Lat
1	1 S
2	2 S
3	3 S
4	4 S
5	5 S
6	5 S
7	5 S
8	5 S
9	4 S
10	3 S
11	2 S
12	1 S
13	0 S
14	1 N
15	2 N
16	3 N
17	4 N
18	5 N
19	5 N
20	5 N
21	5 N
22	5 N
23	4 N
24	4 N
25	3 N
26	2 N
27	1 N
28	1 S
29	2 S
30	3 S

There will be Six Eclipses for the year 1794 Viz four of the Sun two of the Moon

First of the Sun January 31st. 51. min. past 6 in the morning the Eclips being over about 12 min before Sun rise

The Second is a partly ~~visible~~ ~~and~~ total & ~~central~~ Eclips of the Moon partly visible February 15th in the ...

Beginning — 3.34
Middle — 5.28
End — 7.20
Duration — 3.46 } P.M. Digits Eclipsed 21½

NB The Moon rises totally Eclipsed

The third of the Sun March 1st. 3 min. past 5. P.M. invisible, the Moon having great South Latitude

The fourth of the Sun July 26th. 18 min. past 5 in the Evening but the Moons Latitude is too far South to afford any part of it to be Seen in this part of the globe

The fifth is a total and visible Eclipse of the Moon ~~of the Moon August 11th~~ A.M Augt. 11th A.M

	h m
Beginning	0..50
Middle	2.35
End	4.19
Duration	3..29

} A.M Digits Eclipsed 17¾

~~The Sixth and last is of the Sun July 26th. 18 min past 5 in afternoon invisible~~

The Sixth and last is of the Sun August 25th, 23 min. past 7 in Morning invisible, the Moon having great ~~South~~ North Latitude

1794 November Eleventh Month hath 30 Days

		D	H	M	
Full	○	7	4	22	Morn
Last	☾	14	8	0	Morn
New	☽	22	11	20	Morn
First	☾	29	8	7	Aft.

☊ { 1 ♌ 13; 11 13; 21 12 } Deg.

Planets Places

D	☉	♄	♃	♂	♀	☿	☽'s
	♏	♉	♑	♑	♐	♐	Lat.
1	10	28	2	13	26	0	1 S.
7	16	27	3	18	♑ 2	8	5 S.
13	22	27	4	22	7	14	0 S.
19	28	26	6	27	11	17	5 N.
25	♐ 4	25	7	♒ 1	15	16	3 N.

M D	W D	Remarkable Days Aspects weather &c.	☉ rise	☉ Sets	☽ Long.	☽ Sets	☽ South	☽ Age
1	7	All Saints.	6 . 49	5 . 11	10 . 22 . 41	12 . 43	7 . 31	9
2	E	20th Sund. past Trin.	6 . 51	5 . 9	11 . 6 . 45	13 . 55	8 . 26	10
3	2		6 . 52	5 . 8	11 . 21 . 7	15 . 8	9 . 21	11
4	3	pleiades So. 12 . 56	6 . 53	5 . 7	0 . 5 . 47	16 . 23	10 . 16	12
5	4		6 . 54	5 . 6	0 . 20 . 38	17 . 38	11 . 11	13
6	5	Sirius rise 10 . 45	6 . 55	5 . 5	1 . 5 . 35		12 . 6	14
7	6		6 . 56	5 . 4	1 . 20 . 24	rise	13 . 1	15
8	7	♀ Sets 7 . 56	6 . 57	5 . 3	2 . 5 . 0	6 . 41	13 . 56	16
9	E	21st Sund. past Trin.	6 . 58	5 . 2	2 . 19 . 16	7 . 28	14 . 51	17
10	2		6 . 59	5 . 1	3 . 3 . 3	8 . 18	15 . 45	18
11	3	☿ great. elong. St. Martin	7 . 0	5 . 0	3 . 16 . 27	9 . 12	16 . 37	19
12	4		7 . 1	4 . 59	3 . 29 . 23	10 . 10	17 . 27	20
13	5	Days 9 . 56	7 . 2	4 . 58	4 . 11 . 57	11 . 12	18 . 15	21
14	6		7 . 3	4 . 57	4 . 24 . 17	12 . 14	19 . 2	22
15	7		7 . 4	4 . 56	5 . 6 . 16	13 . 16	19 . 48	23
16	E	22nd. Sunday past Trin.	7 . 5	4 . 55	5 . 18 . 9	14 . 16	20 . 32	24
17	2		7 . 6	4 . 54	5 . 29 . 52	15 . 16	21 . 15	25
18	3	☍ ☉ ♄ Occident.	7 . 7	4 . 53	6 . 11 . 45	16 . 16	21 . 58	26
19	4		7 . 8	4 . 52	6 . 23 . 38	17 . 14	22 . 41	27
20	5	Days decrease 5 . 0	7 . 8	4 . 52	7 . 5 . 37	18 . 12	23 . 24	28
21	6		7 . 9	4 . 51	7 . 17 . 46			29
22	7	☉ enters ♐	7 . 10	4 . 50	8 . 0 . 7	Sets	0 . 7	☽
23	E	23d. Sund. past Trin.	7 . 11	4 . 49	8 . 12 . 37	5 . 32	0 . 51	1
24	2		7 . 12	4 . 48	8 . 25 . 21	6 . 14	1 . 37	2
25	3	☌ ☽ ♃	7 . 12	4 . 48	9 . 8 . 19	7 . 4	2 . 27	3
26	4		7 . 13	4 . 47	9 . 21 . 30	8 . 2	3 . 21	4
27	5	pleiades So. 11 . 21	7 . 14	4 . 46	10 . 4 . 54	9 . 8	4 . 17	5
28	6		7 . 15	4 . 45	10 . 18 . 33	10 . 21	5 . 13	6
29	7		7 . 15	4 . 45	11 . 2 . 25	11 . 35	6 . 9	7
30	E	Advent Sund.	7 . 16	4 . 44	11 . 16 . 31	12 . 48	7 . 5	8

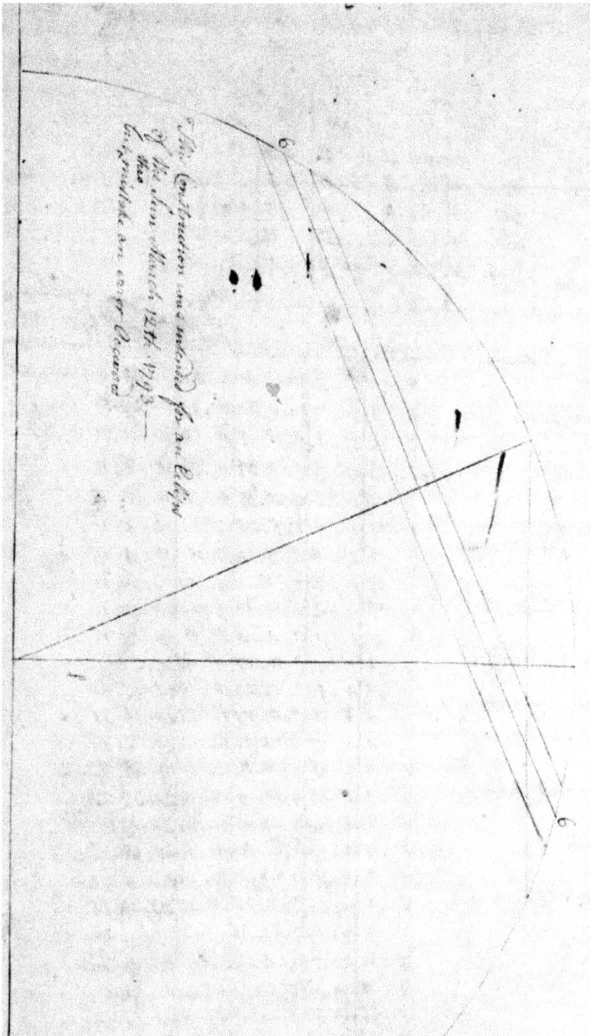

1794

Dr Lat.

Decemb

1	4 S
2	5 S
3	5 S
4	5 S
5	5 S
6	4 S
7	3 S
8	2 S
9	1 S
10	0 S
11	1 N
12	2 N
13	3 N
14	4 N
15	4 N
16	5 N
17	5 N
18	5 N
19	5 N
20	4 N
21	4 N
22	3 N
23	2 N
24	1 N
25	0 S
26	2 S
27	3 S
28	4 S
29	5 S
30	5 S
31	5 S

1794 December Twelfth Month hath 31 Days

	D	H	M	
Full ○	6	3	31	Aft
Last ☾	13	2	0	Morn
New ☽	22	4	24	Morn
First ☽	30	5	36	Morn

☊ { 1 ♌ 12 ; 11 ♌ 11 ; 21 ♌ 10 } Deg.

Planets Places

☽	☉	♄	♃	♂	♀	☿	☽
	♐	♉	♑	♒	♑	♐	Lat.
1	10	25	8	6	17	9	4 S.
7	16	24	9	10	19	2	3 S.
13	22	24	11	15	20	2	3 N.
19	28	23	12	19	19	6	5 N.
25	♑ 4	23	13	24	17	13	0 S.

M D	W D		☉ rise	☉ Sets	☽ Long.	☽ Sets	☽ South	☽ Age
1	2	☌ ☉ ☿ Orient	7..16	4..44	0..0..51	14..1	7..59	9
2	3		7..17	4..43	0..15..23	15..12	8..52	10
3	4	♀ Sets 7..12	7..18	4..42	1..0..4	16..24	9..46	11
4	5	Days 9..24	7..18	4..42	1..14..49	17..36	10..40	12
5	6		7..19	4..41	1..29..32		11..35	13
6	7	St. Nicholas	7..19	4..41	2..14..1	rise	12..30	14
7	E	2nd Sund. in Advent	7..20	4..40	2..28..11	6..1	13..24	15
8	2	Concept. V. Mary	7..20	4..40	3..12..1	7..0	14..18	16
9	3		7..20	4..40	3..25..24	8..0	15..11	17
10	4	Sirius rise 8..22	7..21	4..39	4..8..22	9..1	16..3	18
11	5		7..21	4..39	4..20..56	10..3	16..53	19
12	6	pleiades So. 10..16	7..21	4..39	5..3..10	11..5	17..39	20
13	7		7..21	4..39	5..15..7	12..3	18..21	21
14	E	~~Bulls eye So. 10..50~~ 3d. Sund. in	7..22	4..38	5..26..54	13..1	19..3	22
15	2	Advent	7..22	4..38	6..8..35	13..59	19..45	23
16	3	Days Decrease 5..28	7..22	4..38	6..20..18	14..56	20..27	24
17	4		7..22	4..38	7..2..0	15..53	21..10	25
18	5	Days 9..16	7..22	4..38	7..13..53	16..50	21..55	26
19	6		7..22	4..38	7..25..57	17..48	22..41	27
20	7	☿ great elong. Short Day	7..22	4..38	8..8..17	18..47	23..28	28
21	E	St. Thomas, 4th Sund. in Advent	7..22	4..38	8..20..52			29
22	2	☉ enters ♑, ☌ ☽ ♃	7..22	4..38	9..3..46	Sets	0..16	☽
23	3		7..22	4..38	9..16..58	5..47	1..6	1
24	4		7..22	4..38	10..0..26	6..47	1..58	2
25	5	Christmas	7..22	4..38	10..14..9	7..53	2..52	3
26	6	St. Stephen	7..22	4..38	10..28..4	9..5	3..48	4
27	7	St. John	7..22	4..38	11..12..29	10..19	4..43	5
28	E	Innocent. 1st Sund. past Chris.	7..21	4..39	11..26..25	11..31	5..37	6
29	2		7..21	4..39	0..10..45	12..43	6..30	7
30	3		7..21	4..39	0..25..13	13..56	7..22	8
31	4	Silvester	7..20	4..40	1..9..44	15..4	8..12	9

1793
may 15 Due Docr. Hulse
Cash paid him £3 .. 18 .. 9

Longitude ♄	Amomally ♄	Longitude ♀	Anomally ♀	Longitude ☿	An
S ° ′	S ° ′	S .. ° .. ′	S ° .. ′	S ° ′	S
1795 2 .. 0 .. 50	5 .. 0 .. 10	3 .. 9 .. 34	5 .. 1 .. 34	6 .. 15 .. 27	10 ..

As the Moons Diurnal motion in Degrees and minutes, is to that motion turned into time, So is 2° .. 44 the Moons obit motion between the Meridian of [Green]wich and that of Baltimore to a fourth proportional number which [must] be added to the moons apparant Southing to reduce it to the mean time [of] Southing)
NB The above must be farther examined before I can pass it [for] the truth —

As the Moons ~~moon~~ Diurnal motion turned into time is to 24 hours so is 5 hours, [the dif]ference between the meridian of Greenwich and that of Baltime, to a fourth proportional number which must be added to the moon Southing on the [meri]dian of Greenwich to reduce it to meridian of Baltimore

When the Moons Diurnal motion is 11°, add to her Southing	Min 9
When 12° add	10
When 13° add	11
When 14 add	12
When 15 add	13

Common Notes and Moveable Feasts for the Year 1795 —

Dominical Letter	D	Easter Sunday,	April
Cycle of the Sun	12	Ascension Day,	May
Golden Number	10	Whitsunday,	May
Epact	9	Trinity Sunday,	May
Number of Direction	15	Advent Sunday,	November

Four Eclipses for the Year 1795. Vizt. two of each Luminary —
First of the Sun January 20th. invisible in the united State of Am[erica] ☌ at 7h. 20m. P.M. ☉ true place ♒ 1°. 2′ ☉ is centrally eclipsed on the [meridian] at 7h. 26m. in Longitude 111° ½ west from the Meridian of Baltimore and 25 ¼ North —

Second is a visibe eclips of the Moon Feb. 3d. at 7h. 46 min. P.[M.]

	h m		
Beginning	6 .. 31	P. M.	
Greatest obscuration	7 .. 49	digits eclipsed 7 ¼	
End	9 .. 7	on her South Limb	
Whole duration	2 .. 36.		

For the other two Eclipses turn over —

1795 January First Month hath 31 Days.

	D. H. M.	
Full ○	5..4..39	Morn.
Last ☾	12..10..59	aft.
New ☽	20..7..20	Aft.
First ☽	27..4..16	aft.

(Equation added)

☊ { 1 ♌ 10; 11 ♌ 9; 21 ♌ 9 } deg.

D	☉	♄	♃	♂	♀	☿	☽'s Lat.
	♑	♉	♑	♒	♑	♐	Lat.
1	11	23	14	29	12	22	5 S.
7	17	23	16	♓ 4	9	♑ 1	0 N.
13	24	23	17	9	6	10	5 N.
19	♒ 0	23	19	13	4	19	2 N.
25	6	23	20	18	4	29	4 S.

M D	W D	Remarkable Days Aspects weather &c.		☉ rise	☉ sets	☽'s place	☽ Sets	☽ South	☽ age
1	5	Circumcision	wind	7..20	4..40	♉ 23	4..36	9..3	10
2	6	☌ ☉ ♀ Orient	with	7..20	4..40	♊ 9	6..33	9..59	11
3	7		flying	7..20	4..40	21	[illegible]..51	10..56	12
4	D	2nd. Sund past Chris.	Clouds	7..19	4..41	♋ 5	4..53	11..54	13
5	2	☌ ☉ ♃ Orient		7..19	4..41	19	rise	12..51	14
6	3	Epiphany	rain	7..18	4..42	♌ 2	6..29	13..46	15
7	4		or	7..18	4..42	16	7..28	14..35	16
8	5	pleiades So. 8..15	Snow	7..17	4..43	29	8..27	15..23	17
9	6			7..17	4..43	♍ 11	9..25	16..8	18
10	7	Days increase 12 min.		7..16	4..44	24	10..22	16..50	19
11	D	1st. Sund. past Epip	Cold	7..15	4..45	♎ 6	11..19	17..33	20
12	2	△ ☉ ♄		7..15	4..45	18	12..16	18..13	21
13	3		freezing	7..14	4..46	29	13..13	18..57	22
14	4	Days 9..34		7..13	4..47	♏ 11	14..10	19..40	23
15	5			7..13	4..47	23	15..7	20..25	24
16	6	Sirius So. 10..41	weather	7..12	4..48	♐ 5	16..4	21..14	25
17	7			7..11	4..49	18	17..2	22..6	26
18	D	2nd. Sund. past Epip.	Snow	7..10	4..50	♑ 1	18..1	22..59	27
19	2	☌ ♃ ☿, ☌ ☽ ♃, ☉ enters ♒		7..10	4..50	14		23..53	28
20	3	☉ eclipsed invis	with	7..9	4..51	27	sets	0	☽
21	4			7..8	4..52	♒ 11	5..35	0..49	1
22	5	♀ Stationary	wind,	7..7	4..53	24	6..41	1..44	2
23	6	♄ Stationary		7..6	4..54	♓ 8	7..48	2..39	3
24	7			7..5	4..55	22	8..55	3..32	4
25	D	3d. Sund. past Epip	Cloudy	7..4	4..56	♈ 7	10..3	4..23	5
26	2			7..3	4..57	21	11..11	5..13	6
27	3	pleiades Sets 2..14	and	7..2	4..58	♉ 5	12..19	6..7	7
28	4		cold,	7..1	4..59	20	13..27	6..56	8
29	5	Days increase 44 min.		7..0	5..0	♊ 4	14..34	7..53	9
30	6		Snow	6..59	5..1	18	15..40	8..47	10
31	7	Sirius So 9..38	or rain	6..58	5..2	♋ 1	16..43	9..42	11

The rising, setting, and Southing of the Moon in this page is corrupt therefore turn over ——

1795 January ~~Second~~ Mo

	D Sets	D South
1	15..40	8..59
2	16..52	9..54
3	17..58	10..51
4		11..48
5	rise	12..45
6	6..33	13..39
7	7..32	14..28
8	8..31	15..15
9	9..29	16..0
10	10..26	16..43
11	11..22	17..24
12	12..18	18..5
13	13..13	18..47
14	14..9	19..30
15	15..5	20..15
16	16..4	21..3
17	17..3	21..55
18	18..2	22..48
19	Sets	23..42
20	Sets	☌
21	5..31	0..37
22	6..39	1..32
23	7..47	2..27
24	8..55	3..19
25	10..3	4..10
26	11..10	5..1
27	12..19	5..53
28	13..26	6..45
29	14..33	7..39
30	15..38	8..34
31	16..40	9..29

according to common reckoning
D Sets 3..44 January 2d.
Sets 3..38 January 31st
Feb 1 D Sets 4..40
Feb 28 Sets 2..36

The Elements for an Eclips of the Sun January 20th

True time of New Moon in ~~January~~ January 1795 } H. M. 20..7..20 P.M.
Semidiameter of the Earths Disc
Sun from nearest Solstice
Suns Declination South
Moons Latitude North Descending
Moons Horary motion from the Sun
Angle of the Moons visible path with the Ecliptic
Suns Semidiameter
Moons Semidiameter
Semidiameter of the penumbra

The Elements for an Eclipse of the moon February 3

True time of Full Moon in February 1795 }
Moons Horizontal paralax
Suns Semidiameter
Moons Semidiameter
Semidiameter of the Earths Shadow at the Moon
Moons true Latitude North Ascending
Angle of her visible path with the Ecliptic
Her true horary motion from the Sun

The third Eclipse for the year 1795, is of the Sun July 16th invisible in the united States of America, ☌ at 2h. 37m. in Long 3s..23°..38, ☉ is centrally Eclipsed on the Meridian 2h. 41 m. in Longitude 139° ½ east from the Meridian of and Lat 10¾ South.

Fourth and last is of the Moon July 31st. at 59 minutes past 0 clock in the after noon, invisible in these States; the ... sed 2½ digits on her North Limb at Greenwich —

1795 February Second Month hath 28 Days

	D	H	M	
Full ○	3	7	46	Aft.
Last ☾	11	9	23	aft.
New ☽	19	8	19	morn
First ☽	26	0	16	morn

(Equation added)

☊ {1, 11, 21} ♌ {8, 8, 7} deg.

Planets Places

D	☉	♄	♃	♂	♀	☿	☽'s
	♒	♉	♑	♓	♑	♒	Lat.
1	13	23	22	23	6	11	2 S.
7	19	23	23	28	9	21	4 N.
13	25	23	24	♈ 2	12	♓ 2	4 N.
19	♓ 1	23	26	7	17	13	2 S.
25	7	24	27	11	22	23	5 S.

M D	W D	Remarkable Days Aspects weather &c.		☉ rise	☉ sets	☽'s place	☽ sets	☽ south	☽'s age
1	D	Septuagesima Sund. ✶♄♂		6..57	5..3	♋ 15	~~17..41~~	~~10..28~~	12
2	2	purification V. Mary		6..56	5..4	28		~~11..21~~	13
3	3	☽ eclip. vis.	high	6..55	5..5	♌ 11	rise	~~12..14~~	14
4	4	☌ ☉ ☿ Occident,		6..54	5..6	24	~~6..14~~	12..3	15
5	5		wind	6..53	5..7	♍ 7	~~7..14~~	13..49	16
6	6		with	6..52	5..8	19	8..14	14..35	17
7	7	△♄♃		6..51	5..9	♎ 1	9..11	15..18	18
8	D	Sexagesima Sund. □♄☿		6..50	5..10	13	10..7	16..0	19
9	2		snow	6..49	5..11	25	11..1	16..41	20
10	3	Days 10..24		6..48	5..12	♏ 7	11..58	17..24	21
11	4	□☉♄	flying	6..46	5..14	19	12..55	18..8	22
12	5		clouds	6..45	5..15	♐ 1	13..53	18..35	23
13	6			6..44	5..16	13	14..50	19..44	24
14	7	Valentine	cold	6..43	5..17	26	15..46	20..35	25
15	D	Quinqua. Sund.		6..42	5..18	♑ 8	16..42	21..29	26
16	2	☌☽♃	with	6..40	5..20	21	17..34	22..23	27
17	3	Shrove Tuesday		6..39	5..21	♒ 5	18..22	23..19	28
18	4	Ash wednesday, ☉ enters ♓		6..38	5..22	19		0	29
19	5		hard	6..36	5..24	♓ 3	sets	af. 15	☽
20	6	pleiades sets 12..41		6..35	5..25	18	6..38	1..9	1
21	7		frost	6..34	5..26	♈ 2	7..50	2..3	2
22	D	1st Sund. in Lent		6..33	5..27	17	9..1	2..56	3
23	2			6..32	5..28	♉ 2	10..11	3..50	4
24	3	St. Matthias	with	6..31	5..29	16	11..21	4..43	5
25	4	✶♀☿	snow	6..30	5..30	♊ 0	12..27	5..36	6
26	5		more	6..28	5..32	14	13..33	6..30	7
27	6			6..27	5..33	28	14..37	7..27	8
28	7	Days increase 1..52	moderate	6..26	5..34	♋ 12	15..36	8..23	9

The rising, Setting, and Southing of the Moon in the above page is corrupt, therefore turn over.

♀ Will be evening Star until the Second day of January, and then morning Star untill the 16th day of October, and then evening Star untill the end of the year

1795

	February ☽ Sets	☽ South	March ☽ Sets	☽ South
1	17..38	10..25	16..26	9..14
2		11..18	17..12	10..6
3	rise	12..11	17..54	10..56
4	6..12	13..0		11..43
5	7..11	13..46	rise	12..29
6	8..9	14..30	7..1	13..13
7	9..6	15..13	7..57	13..54
8	10..2	15..55	8..53	14..36
9	10..56	16..36	9..50	15..19
10	11..53	17..19	10..46	16..3
11	12..51	18..3	11..42	16..48
12	13..50	18..50	12..39	17..35
13	14..46	19..39	13..35	18..24
14	15..41	20..30	14..30	19..16
15	16..36	21..24	15..23	20..10
16	17..31	22..20	16..13	21..6
17	18..20	23..17	17..00	22..2
18		☌	17..42	22..57
19	Sets	0..13		23..52
20	6..35	1..8	Sets	☌
21	7..49	2..2	6..45	0..48
22	8..59	2..55	7..58	1..43
23	10..9	3..48	9..12	2..39
24	11..19	4..41	10..23	3..35
25	12..27	5..35	11..32	4..31
26	13..32	6..29	12..37	5..28
27	14..36	7..26	13..37	6..24
28	15..36	8..22	14..32	7..19
29			15..19	8..11
30			16..2	9..2
31			16..38	9..50

The Elements for an Eclips of the Moon

True time of Full Moon in February 1795 } D 9 H 7 M 46

Moons Horizontal paralax — 55

Sun's Semidiameter — 01

Moons Semidiameter — 0

Semidiameter of the Earths Shadow at ☽

Moons Latitude North Ascending

Moons visible path with the Ecliptic

Her true Horary motion from the Sun

1795 March Third Month hath 31 Days.

	D	H	M	
Full ○	5	0	18	Aft.
Last ☾	13	4	29	Aft.
New ☽	20	6	49	Aft.
First ☽	27	9	27	morn.

equation added

☊ { 1 — 7; 11 ♌ 6; 21 — 6 } deg.

Planets Places

☽	☉	♄	♃	♂	♀		☽'s
	♓	♉	♑	♈	♑	♓	Lat.
1	11	24	28	14	25	♒ 29	1 S.
7	17	24	29	19	♒ 1	♈ 4	4 N.
13	23	25	♒ 0	23	6	3	4 N.
19	29	25	1	28	12	♓ 29	3 S.
25	♈ 5	26	2	♉ 2	19	24	4 S.

M D	W D	Remarkable Days Aspects weather &c.	☉ rise	☉ sets	☽'s place	☽ sets	☽ south	☽'s age
1	D	2d. Sund. in Lent, St. David	6..24	5..36	♋ 25	16..26	9..14	10
2	2	high	6..23	5..37	♌ 8	17..12	10..6	11
3	3	pleiades Sets 12..0	6..22	5..38	20	17..54	10..56	12
4	4	wind	6..21	5..39	♍ 3		11..43	13
5	5	Days increase 2..6	6..19	5..41	15	rise	12..29	14
6	6	with	6..17	5..43	28	7..1	13..13	15
7	7	snow	6..16	5..44	♎ 10	7..57	13..54	16
8	D	3d. Sund. in Lent	6..14	5..46	22	8..53	14..36	17
9	2	Days 11..34 or	6..13	5..47	♏ 4	9..50	15..19	18
10	3	rain	6..12	5..48	15	10..46	16..3	19
11	4		6..11	5..49	27	11..42	16..48	20
12	5	Gregory, ☿ great elong. clear	6..9	5..51	♐ 9	12..39	17..35	21
13	6	and	6..8	5..52	21	13..35	18..24	22
14	7		6..7	5..53	♑ 4	14..30	19..16	23
15	D	⚹ ☉ ♄. 4th Sund. in Lent	6..6	5..54	16	15..23	20..10	24
16	2	☌ ☽ ♃ cold	6..4	5..56	29	16..13	21..6	25
17	3	St. patrick with	6..3	5..57	♒ 13	17..0	22..2	26
18	4		6..2	5..58	27	17..42	22..57	27
19	5	☌ ☉ ☿ Orient. ☉ enters ♈	6..0	6..0	♓ 11		23..52	28
20	6	(equal day & night	5..59	6..1	20	sets	☌	☽
21	7	flying	5..58	6..2	♈ 11	6..45	0..48	1
22	D	5th Sund. in Lent.	5..57	6..3	26	7..58	1..43	2
23	2	Clouds	5..55	6..5	♉ 11	9..12	2..39	3
24	3	with rain	5..54	6..6	26	10..23	3..35	4
25	4	□ ♃ ♂. Annunciation V. Mary	5..53	6..7	♊ 10	11..32	4..31	5
26	5	moderate	5..52	6..8	25	12..37	5..28	6
27	6	Bulls eye Sets 10..54 for	5..50	6..10	♋ 8	13..38	6..24	7
28	7	the	5..49	6..11	22	14..32	7..19	8
29	D	6th. Sund. in Lent, palm Sund.	5..48	6..12	♌ 5	15..19	8..11	9
30	2	season	5..46	6..14	17	16..2	9..2	10
31	3	Spica ♍ South 12..34	5..45	6..15	♍ 0	16..38	9..50	11

1795
April

☽ Days	☽ Setts	☽ Souths
1	17..9	10..33
2	17..40	11..18
3		12..1
4	rise	12..42
5	7..52	13..24
6	8..48	14..7
7	9..44	14..52
8	10..42	15..39
9	11..37	16..27
10	12..31	17..17
11	13..23	18..8
12	14..13	19..2
13	14..58	19..55
14	15..39	20..48
15	16..20	21..43
16	16..57	22..37
17	17..34	23..33
18		6
19	Sets	0..29
20	8..8	1..27
21	9..22	2..25
22	10..31	3..24
23	11..36	4..22
24	12..34	5..19
25	13..24	6..13
26	14..8	7..5
27	14..46	7..54
28	15..20	8..39
29	15..50	9..23
30	16..18	10..6

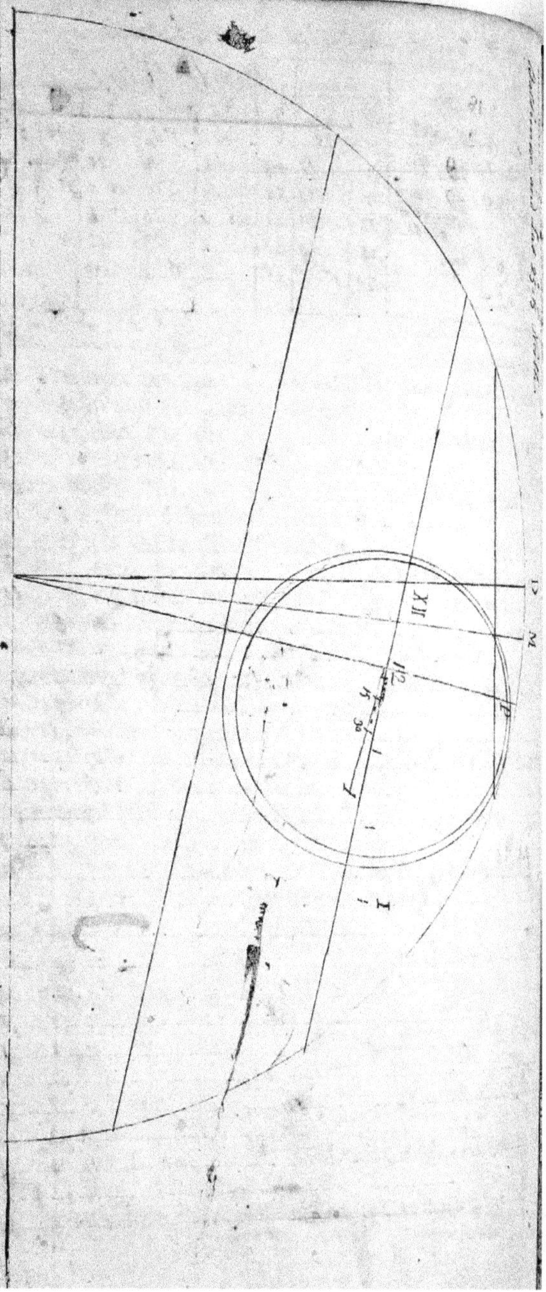

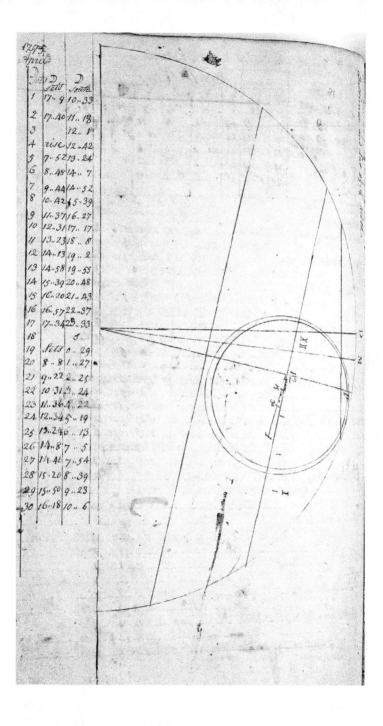

1795 April Fourth Month hath 30 Days

	D	H	M	
Full ○	4	5	13	morn.
Last ☾	12	8	4	morn.
New ☽	19	3	14	morn.
First ☽	25	8	27	after.

~~equation added~~

☊ { 1 ♌ 5 / 11 5 / 21 4 } deg.

		Planets Places					
☽	☉	♄	♃	♂	♀	☿	☽'s
	♈	♉	♒	♉	♒	♓	Lat.
1	12	27	3	7	26	21	3 N.
7	18	27	4	11	♓ 3	23	5 N.
13	24	28	5	16	9	26	0 S.
19	♉ 0	29	5	20	16	♈ 2	5 S.
25	♉ 5	29	6	24	23	10	0 S.

M D	W D	Remarkable Days Aspects weather &c.		☉ rise	☉ sets	☽'s place	☽ sets	☽ south	☽'s Age
1	4	Days 12-32	wind	5..44	6..16	♍ 12	7..3	10..27	12
2	5	□ ♄ ♀	with	5..43	6..17	24	17..38	11..11	13
3	6	Good Fryday	flying	5..41	6..19	♎ 6	[illegible]	11..53	14
4	7	St. Ambrose		5..40	6..20	18	rise	12..35	15
5	D	Easter Sund.	Clouds	5..39	6..21	♏ 0	7..32	13..17	16
6	2	Easter Mond.		5..38	6..22	12	8..39	13..59	17
7	3	Easter Tues.	followed	5..36	6..24	24	9..36	14..44	18
8	4		by	5..35	6..25	♐ 6	10..33	15..31	19
9	5	Days 12..52	rain,	5..34	6..26	18	11..29	16..19	20
10	6			5..33	6..27	♑ 0	12..22	17..8	21
11	7		pleasant	5..32	6..28	12	13..14	17..59	22
12	D	1st. Sund. past Easter		5..30	6..30	25	14..3	18..52	23
13	2	☌ ☽ ♃	weather	5..29	6..31	♒ 8	14..48	19..45	24
14	3		expect	5..28	6..32	21	15..29	20..38	25
15	4	✶ ♄ ☿	rain	5..27	6..33	♓ 5	16..8	21..31	26
16	5	☿ Great Elong.		5..26	6..34	19	16..45	22..25	27
17	6	pleiades Sets 9..15	clear	5..25	6..35	♈ 4	17..22	23..21	28
18	7			5..23	6..37	19		0	29
19	D	2d. Sund. past Easter, ☉ enters ♉,		5..22	6..38	♉ 4	Sets	0..17	☽
20	2		and	5..21	6..39	20	7..56	1..14	2
21	3	procyon sets 11..43	warm	5..20	6..40	♊ 5	9..10	2..13	3
22	4		for	5..18	6..42	20	10..20	3..13	4
23	5	St. George	the	5..17	6..43	♋ 4	11..26	4..12	5
24	6			5..16	6..44	18	12..24	5..9	6
25	7	St. Mark	season	5..15	6..45	♌ 1	13..15	6..4	7
26	D	3d. Sund. past Easter, □ ☉ ♃,		5..14	6..46	14	13..59	6..56	8
27	2			5..13	6..47	27	14..38	7..46	9
28	3	Days increase 4..20	now	5..12	6..48	♍ 9	15..12	8..32	10
29	4		expect	5..11	6..49	21	15..42	9..16	11
30	5	pleiades Sets 8..26	rain	5..10	6..50	♎ 3	16..11	9..59	12

The moons rising, Setting, and Southing is Corrupt in this page, therefore See left hand page

Delineated for an eclips of the Moon Feb. 3d. 1795

	h	m
Beginning	6 ..	34
greatest obscuration	7 ..	50
end of the Eclips	9 ..	5
Duration	2 ..	31

Digits Eclipsed 7 ½ on the Moons South Limb

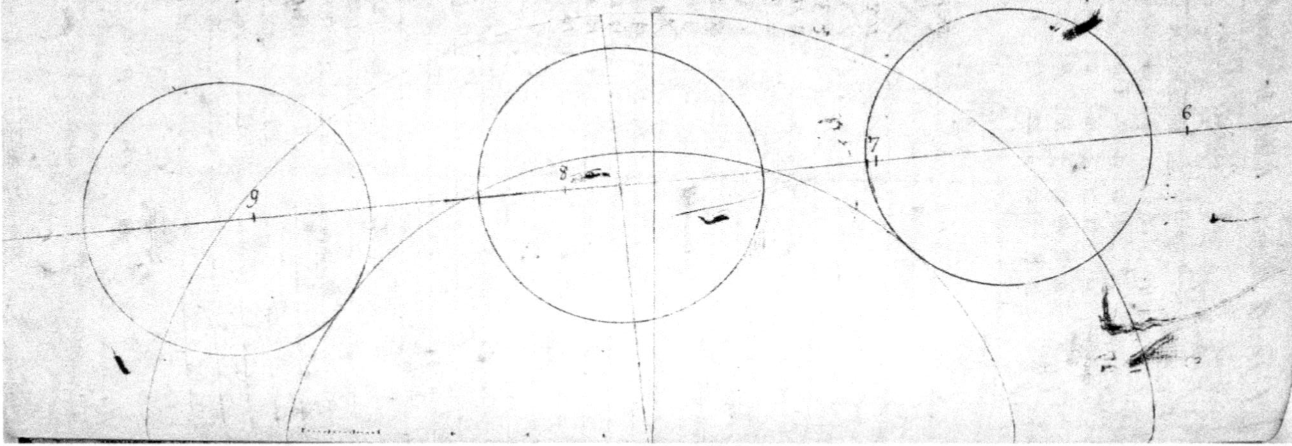

1795 May Fifth Month hath 31 Days

	D	H	M	
Full ☉	3	9	40	aft.
Last Q.	11	7	44	aft.
New ☽	18	10	41	morn.
First Q.	25	9	30	morn.

~~equation subtract~~

☊ { 1 ♌ 4 ; 11 ♌ 3 ; 21 ♌ 2 } deg.

Planets Places							
D	☉	♄	♃	♂	♀	☿	☽
	♉	♊	♒	♉	♈	♈	Lat.
1	11	0	7	28	0	18	5 N.
7	17	1	7	♊ 3	7	28	3 N.
13	23	2	7	7	14	♉ 9	3 S.
19	29	2	7	11	21	22	4 S.
25	♊ 4	3	7	15	28	♊ 5	3 N.

M D	W D	Remarkable Days Aspects weather &c.		☉ rise	☉ sets	☽'s place	☽ sets	☽ south	☽ Age
1	6	St. philip and James ✶ ♄ ♀		5..9	6..51	♎ 15	16..46	10..48	13
2	7	♃ Stationary	pleasant	5..8	6..52	27	[illegible]	11..29	14
3	D	4th. Sund. past Easter		5..7	6..53	♏ 9	rises	12..16	15
4	2		weather	5..5	6..55	21	7..44	12..55	16
5	3			5..4	6..56	♐ 3	8..42	13..41	17
6	4	St. John Evang.	followed	5..3	6..57	15	9..37	14..28	18
7	5	✶ ♃ ♀ south	by	5..2	6..58	27	10..32	15..18	19
8	6	Spica ♍ 10..13	Showers	5..1	6..59	♑ 9	11..24	16..9	20
9	7		of	5..0	7..0	21	12..13	17..0	21
10	D	Rogation Sund. ☌ ☽ ♃	rain,	4..59	7..1	♒ 4	12..59	17..52	22
11	2		& fine	4..58	7..2	17	13..40	18..44	23
12	3	Days 14..4		4..58	7..2	♓ 0	14..19	19..36	24
13	4	△ ♃ ♂	growing	4..57	7..3	14	14..55	20..28	25
14	5	Ascen. day Holy Thursday		4..56	7..4	28	15..31	21..21	26
15	6		weather	4..55	7..5	♈ 13	16..7	22..15	27
16	7		warm &	4..54	7..6	27	16..43	23..11	28
17	D	Sund. after Ascen.		4..53	7..7	♉ 13		[illegible]	29
18	2		and	4..52	7..8	28	sets	0..8	☽
19	3	Days increase 5..0		4..52	7..8	♊ 13	8..11	1..8	2
20	4		pleasant	4..51	7..9	28	9..20	2..8	3
21	5	Arcturus South 10..12, ☉ enters ♊		4..50	7..10	♋ 12	10..24	3..8	4
22	6	Lyra South 2..37	followed	4..49	7..11	26	11..20	4..6	5
23	7		by	4..48	7..12	♌ 10	12..7	5..0	6
24	D	Whitsunday ☌ ☉ ♄ Orient.	rain	4..48	7..12	23	12..47	5..50	7
25	2	Whitmonday, ☌ ☉ ☿ Occident.	and	4..47	7..13	♍ 6	13..23	6..38	8
26	3	Whit. Tuesday	south	4..46	7..14	18	13..53	7..22	9
27	4		wind	4..46	7..14	♎ 0	14..21	8..4	10
28	5	Procyon Sets 9..26		4..45	7..15	12	14..47	8..46	11
29	6	Spica ♍ Sets 2..20	thunder	4..44	7..16	24	15..15	9..28	12
30	7		gusts	4..44	7..16	♏ 6	15..43	10..10	13
31	D	Trin. Sund.	and rain	4..43	7..17	18	16..12	10..52	14

T 0

A

1795 June Sixth Month hath 30 Days.

	D	H	M	
Full ○	2	0	59	aft.
Last ☾	10	3	49	morn
New ☽	16	6	8	aft.
First ☾	24	0	27	Morn

Equation added

	1	2	
☊	11 ♌	1	deg.
	21	1	

Planets Places

D	☉	♄	♃	♂	♀	☿	☽
	♊	♊	♒	♊	♉	♊	Lat.
1	11	4	7	20	6	20	5 N.
7	17	5	7	24	13	♋ 2	1 S.
13	23	6	7	28	20	12	5 S.
19	28	6	7	♋ 2	27	22	0 N.
25	♋ 4	7	6	6	♊ 4	29	5 N.

M D	W D	Remarkable Days Aspects weather &c.		☉ rise	☉ sets	☽'s place	☽ sets	☽ south	☽'s Age
1	2	~~Days 14..34~~ ☌ ♂ ☿	windy	4..43	7..17	♐ 0		11..37	15
2	3		and	4..42	7..18	12	rise	12..24	16
3	4	Days increase 5..20.	warm	4..42	7..18	24	7..50	13..13	17
4	5		with	4..41	7..19	♑ 6	8..52	14..3	18
5	6			4..41	7..19	19	9..57	14..56	19
6	7	☌ ☽ ♃	flying	4..41	7..19	♒ 1	10..57	15..48	20
7	D	1st. Sund. past Trin.		4..40	7..20	14	11..53	16..39	21
8	2		Clouds	4..40	7..20	27	12..44	17..29	22
9	3	Arcturus South 8..54		4..40	7..20	♓ 10	13..32	18..19	23
10	4		followed	4..39	7..21	24	14..17	19..10	24
11	5	St. Barnabas	with	4..39	7..21	♈ 8	14..58	20..2	25
12	6		thunder	4..39	7..21	22	15..37	20..54	26
13	7		gust	4..39	7..21	♉ 7	16..16	21..49	27
14	D	2d. Sund. past Trin		4..39	7..21	22	16..55	22..46	28
15	2		and	4..38	7..22	♊ 7		23..45	29
16	3		rain	4..38	7..22	22	sets	☌	☽
17	4	St. Alban		4..38	7..22	♋ 6	8..1	0..46	1
18	5		Clear	4..38	7..22	21	9..2	1..46	2
19	6	Spica ♍ Sets 12..48		4..38	7..22	♌ 5	9..52	2..41	3
20	7		and	4..38	7..22	18	10..38	3..36	4
21	D	3d. Sund. past Trin. ☉ enters ♋.		4..38	7..22	♍ 1	11..15	4..26	5
22	2	△ ♄ ♃	(Longest Days	4..38	7..22	14	11..48	5..12	6
23	3		very	4..38	7..22	26	12..18	5..57	7
24	4	St. John Bap.	warm	4..38	7..22	♎ 9	12..46	6..39	8
25	5		with	4..38	7..22	21	13..11	7..19	9
26	6	Days 14..44		4..38	7..22	♏ 3	13..39	8..1	10
27	7			4..38	7..22	14	14..7	8..43	11
28	D	4th Sund. past Trin. ☿ Great Elong		4..38	7..22	26	14..40	9..28	12
29	2	St. peter and paul	thunder	4..39	7..21	♐ 8	15..14	10..14	13
30	3	Days decreas 2 min.	rain	4..39	7..21	20	15..53	11..2	14

True time of New moon in July 1795 } D H M 16 . 2 . 37 A. M

	° ′ ″
Semidiameter of the Earths disc	0 .. 59 .. 54
Suns distance from nearest Solstice	24 .. 0 .. 0
Suns declination North	21 .. 22 .. 0
Moons Latitude South Ascending	0 .. 30 .. 45
Moons Horary motion from the Sun	0 .. 34 .. 7
Angle of the Moons visible path with eclip^c	5 .. 35 .. 0
Suns Semidiameter	0 .. 15 .. 50
Moons Semidiameter	0 .. 16 .. 26
Semidiameter of the penumbra	0 .. 32 .. 16

True time of full moon in July 1795 } D H M 31 .. 2 .. 59 P. M.

	° ′ ″
Moons Horizontal paralax	0 .. 57 .. 0
Suns Semidiameter	0 .. 15 .. 51
Moons Semidiameter	0 .. 15 .. 36
Semidiamter of the Earths Shadow at D	0 .. 41 .. 19
Moons true Latitude South Ascending	0 .. 29 .. 32
Angle of Moons visible path with the eclip^c	5 .. 35 .. 0
Her true Horary motion from the Sun	0 .. 30 .. 48

1795 July Seventh Month hath 31 Days

	D	H	M	
Full ○	2	2	47	morn.
Last ☾	9	9	23	morn.
New ☽	16	2	37	morn.
First ☾	23	4	51	aft.
Full ○	31	2	59	aft. (equation added)

☊ { 1 ... 0 / 11 ♌ 0 / 21 ♋ 29 } deg.

Planets Places

☽	☉	♄	♃	♂	♀	☿	☽'s
	♋	♊	♒	♋	♊	♌	Lat.
1	10	8	5	10	12	5	3 N.
7	15	9	5	14	19	9	4 S.
13	21	9	4	18	26	10	4 S.
19	27	10	3	22	♋ 3	8	3 N.
25	♌ 3	10	3	25	11	4	5 N.

M D	W D	Remarkable Days Aspects weather &c.		☉ rise	☉ sets	☽'s place	☽ set	☽ south	☽'s Age
1	4	☌ ☉ ♂ Orient.	hot	4..39	7..21	♑ 3		11..53	15
2	5	Visitation of B.V. Mary	and	4..40	7..20	15	rise	12..46	16
3	6		sultry	4..40	7..20	28	8..49	13..38	17
4	7	Translation of St. Martin ☌ ☽ ♃		4..40	7..20	♒ 11	9..33	14..30	18
5	D	5th. Sund. past Trin.		4..41	7..19	24	10..11	15..21	19
6	2		weather	4..41	7..19	♓ 7	10..47	16..11	20
7	3	⚹ ♄ ☿	with	4..42	7..18	21	11..21	17..1	21
8	4		thunder	4..42	7..18	♈ 5	11..55	17..51	22
9	5	Spica ♍ Sets 11..26	gusts	4..43	7..17	19	12..28	18..42	23
10	6	Lyra South 11..11	and	4..43	7..17	♉ 3	13..3	19..34	24
11	7		rain	4..44	7..16	17	13..41	20..28	25
12	D	6th. Sund. past Trin. ☿ Stationary		4..44	7..16	♊ 2	14..26	21..26	26
13	2		warm	4..45	7..15	16	15..15	22..25	27
14	3	Days 14..30	winds	4..45	7..15	♋ 1	16..10	23..25	28
15	4		from	4..46	7..14	15		☌	29
16	5	☉ eclipsed. invis		4..47	7..13	29	sets	0..22	☽
17	6		the	4..47	7..13	♌ 13	8..23	1..17	2
18	7		South	4..48	7..12	26	9..5	2..10	3
19	D	7th. Sund. past Trin.		4..49	7..11	♍ 9	9..40	2..59	4
20	2	Margaret	with	4..49	7..11	22	10..12	3..45	5
21	3		flying	4..50	7..10	♎ 5	10..41	4..29	6
22	4	Magdalen. ☉ enters ♌		4..51	7..9	17	11..7	5..10	7
23	5		clouds	4..52	7..8	29	11..35	5..52	8
24	6		and ~~with~~ rain	4..53	7..7	♏ 11	12..3	6..35	9
25	7	☍ ☉ ♃, St. James		4..54	7..6	23	12..34	7..19	10
26	D	8th Sund. past Trin. St. Anne		4..54	7..6	♐ 5	13..8	8..4	11
27	2	(☌ ☉ ☿ Orient.		4..55	7..5	17	13..46	8..52	12
28	3		followed by	4..56	7..4	29	14..29	9..42	13
29	4		thunder	4..57	7..3	♑ 11	15..18	10..34	14
30	5	Dog days begins	gusts	4..58	7..2	24	[illegible]..13	11..28	15
31	6	☌ ☽ ♃. ☽ eclips invis	and wind	4..59	7..1	♒ 7	rise	12..22	16.

1795 July 13th. the Sun will be totally eclipsed at 14h. 37'. on the meridian in Long. 139°3/4 east from the meridian of Baltimore, and Lat. 10 1/4 South

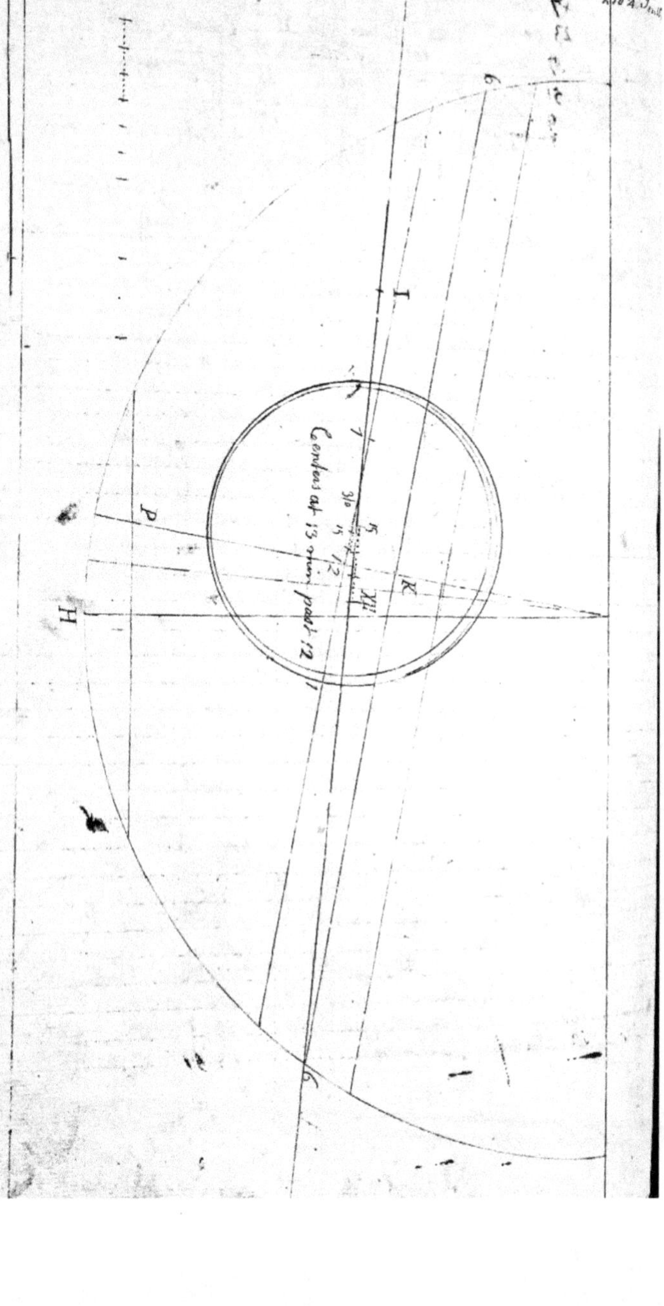

1795 August Eighth Month hath 31 Days

	☽	☉	♄	♃	♂	♀	☿	☽'s
		♌	♊	♒	♌	♋	♌	Lat.
	1	9	11	2	0	19	0	2 S.
	7	15	12	1	4	26	♋ 29	5 S.
	13	21	12	0	8	♌ 4	♌ 2	1 N.
	19	27	12	♑ 0	11	11	9	5 N.
	25	♍ 2	13	29	15	19	19	2 N.

Planets Places.

D. H. M.
Last ☾ 7..1..52 aft.
New ☽ 14..0..57 aft.
First ☽ 22..10..29 morn
Full ○ 30..1..37 morn.
~~equation added~~

☊ {1 29 / 11 ♋ 28 / 21 28} deg.

M D	W D	Remarkable Days Aspects weather &c.		☉ rise	☉ sets	☽'s place	☽ rise	☽ south	☽'s Age
1	7	Lammas-Day; ☌ ♂ ☿	hot	5..0	7..0	♒ 20	8..9	13..15	17
2	D	9th. Sund. past Trin.		5..1	6..59	♓ 4	8..47	14..7	18
3	2	Days 13..56	Sultry	5..2	6..58	17	9..22	14..58	19
4	3	✶ ☉ ♄	weather,	5..3	6..57	♈ 1	9..56	15..49	20
5	4		flying	5..4	6..56	15	10..30	16..40	21
6	5	Transfig. ☿ Stationary		5..5	6..55	♉ 0	11..3	17..30	22
7	6	Days decrease 56 min.		5..6	6..54	14	11..40	18..23	23
8	7		Clouds	5..7	6..53	28	12..21	19..18	24
9	D	10th. Sund. past Trin.		5..8	6..52	♊ 12	13..7	20..15	25
10	2	St Lawrence	with	5..9	6..51	26	13..58	21..13	26
11	3		thunder	5..10	6..50	♋ 10	14..55	22..11	27
12	4	Bulls eye rise 11..59		5..11	6..49	24	15..55	23..8	28
13	5		and	5..12	6..48	♌ 8		23..59	29
14	6	☿ Great. Elong.	rain.	5..13	6..47	21	Sets		☽
15	7		warm	5..14	6..46	♍ 4	7..39	0..50	1
16	D	11th. Sund. past Trin.		5..15	6..45	17	8..12	1..40	2
17	2		wind	5..16	6..44	♎ 0	8..42	2..25	3
18	3	Arcturus Sets 11..25		5..18	6..42	12	9..10	3..7	4
19	4	☌ ♂ ♀	great	5..19	6..41	25	9..38	3..50	5
20	5		dews	5..20	6..40	♏ 7	10..6	4..33	6
21	6	pleiades rise 10..9		5..21	6..39	19	10..36	5..17	7
22	7		Clear	5..22	6..38	♐ 0	11..9	6..2	8
23	D	12th. Sund. past Trin.	☉ enters ♍.	5..23	6..37	12	11..45	6..48	9
24	2	St Bartholomew,	and	5..24	6..36	24	12..25	7..36	10
25	3	☌ ♀ ☿,	warm.	5..26	6..34	♑ 7	13..12	8..27	11
26	4		rain	5..27	6..33	19	14..4	9..20	12
27	5	☌ ☽ ♃	with	5..28	6..32	♒ 2	15..2	10..14	13
28	6	St Augustine	thunder	5..29	6..31	15	16..4	11..8	14
29	7	St John Bap. behead.	followed	5..30	6..30	29	[illegible]	12..3	15
30	D	13th. Sund. past Trin.	by	5..32	6..28	♓ 13	[illegible]	12..55	16
31	2	Days 12..54	cool dews	5..33	6..27	27	7..59	13..47	17

1795 Longitude ♄	1795 Anomally ♄
S ° ′	S ° ′
2 .. 0 .. 50	5 .. 0 .. 10

This eclipse of the ☽ July 31 is ~~visible~~ invisible on this part of the globe but as she is eclipsed near 3° on her North limb at greenwich and many other parts of europe —

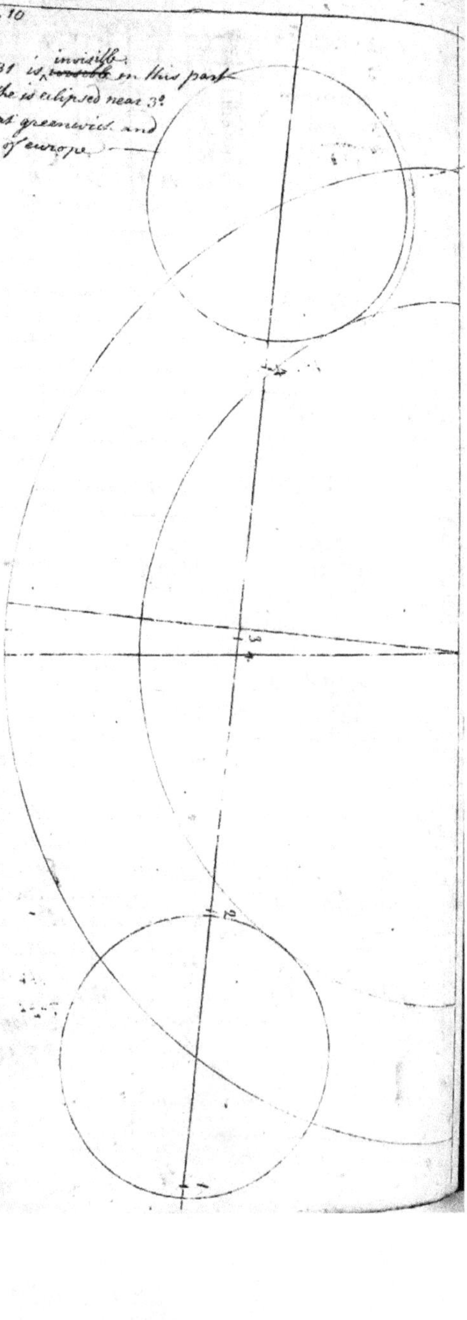

1795 September Ninth Month hath 30 Days

D H M	☊	☉	♄	♃	♂	♀	☿	☽'s
	Planets Places							
Last Q. 5 .. 6 .. 55 aft.		♍	♊	♑	♌	♌	♍	Lat.
New ☽ 13 .. 1 .. 42 morn.								
First Q. 21 .. 4 .. 39 morn.	1	9	13	28	20	27	2	5 S.
Full ○ 28 .. 11 .. 36 morn.	7	15	13	28	24	♍ 5	14	2 S.
~~equation~~ ~~☊~~ Lib:	13	21	14	28	27	12	25	4 N.
☊ { 1 27 / 11 ♋ 27 / 21 26 } deg.	19	27	14	28	♍ 1	20	♎ 6	4 N.
	25	♎ 3	14	28	5	27	15	2 S.

M D	W D	Remarkable Days Aspects weather &c.		☉ rise	☉ sets	☽'s place	☽ ~~rise~~	☽ south	☽'s Age
1	3	Days Decrease 1..52		5..34	6..26	♈ 11	8..35	14..40	18
2	4		very	5..35	6..25	26	9..10	15..33	19
3	5	Dog days end.		5..36	6..24	♉ 10	9..47	16..27	20
4	6		pleasant	5..38	6..22	25	10..26	17..21	21
5	7	□ ☉ ♄	weather	5..39	6..21	♊ 9	11..17	18..17	22
6	D	14th. Sund. past Trin.		5..40	6..20	23	12..1	19..15	23
7	2	□ ♄ ☿.		5..41	6..19	♋ 7	12..55	20..12	24
8	3	Nativity B. V. Mary ☌ ☉ ☿ Occid.		5..43	6..17	21	13..53	21..8	25
9	4		followed	5..44	6..16	♌ 4	14..54	22..2	26
10	5	pleiades rise 8..57	by	5..45	6..15	17	15..56	22..53	27
11	6	Bulls eye rise 10..9	rain,	5..46	6..14	♍ 0	16..58	23..41	28
12	7			5..48	6..12	13	☌	☌	29
13	D	15th. Sund. past Trin.		5..49	6..11	26	sets	0..27	☽
14	2		flying	5..50	6..10	♎ 8	7..18	1..11	2
15	3	Arcturus Sets 9..43		5..52	6..8	21	7..45	1..54	3
16	4		Clouds	5..53	6..7	♏ 3	8..14	2..37	4
17	5	Alphard rise 4..8		5..54	6..6	15	8..43	3..20	5
18	6	Sirius rise 1..52	cool	5..55	6..5	27	9..15	4..4	6
19	7			5..56	6..4	♐ 8	9..49	4..50	7
20	D	16th Sund. past Trin. △ ☉ ♃		5..58	6..2	20	10..28	5..37	8
21	2	St. Matthew	dews,	5..59	6..1	♑ 2	11..11	6..26	9
22	3	☉ enters ♎ Equal Day & Night		6..0	6..0	14	11..59	7..16	10
23	4	♃ Stationary; ☌ ☽ ♃		6..2	5..58	27	12..54	8..9	11
24	5		wind and	6..3	5..57	♒ 10	13..53	9..2	12
25	6	♄ Stationary	rain	6..4	5..56	23	14..58	9..56	13
26	7	St. Cyprian △ ♃ ♀		6..5	5..55	♓ 7	16..6	10..51	14
27	D	17th Sund. past Trin.	followed	6..7	5..53	21		11..44	15
28	2		by	6..8	5..52	♈ 5	rise	12..37	16
29	3	St. Michael	cool	6..9	5..51	20	7..14	13..31	17
30	4	Days 11..38	mornings	6..11	5..49	♉ 5	7..52	14..26	18

True time of full ☉ at Greenwich July 31	31..7..59
Moons Horizontal paralax	0..57..8
Suns Semidiameter	0..15..52
Moons Semidiameter	0..15..30
Semidiameter of the Earths shadow at the Moon	0..41..2[illegible]
Moons true Latitude South Descending	0..50..1[illegible]
Angle of the Moons visible path with the Ecliptic	5..35..[illegible]
Her true horary motion from the sun	0..33..5[illegible]

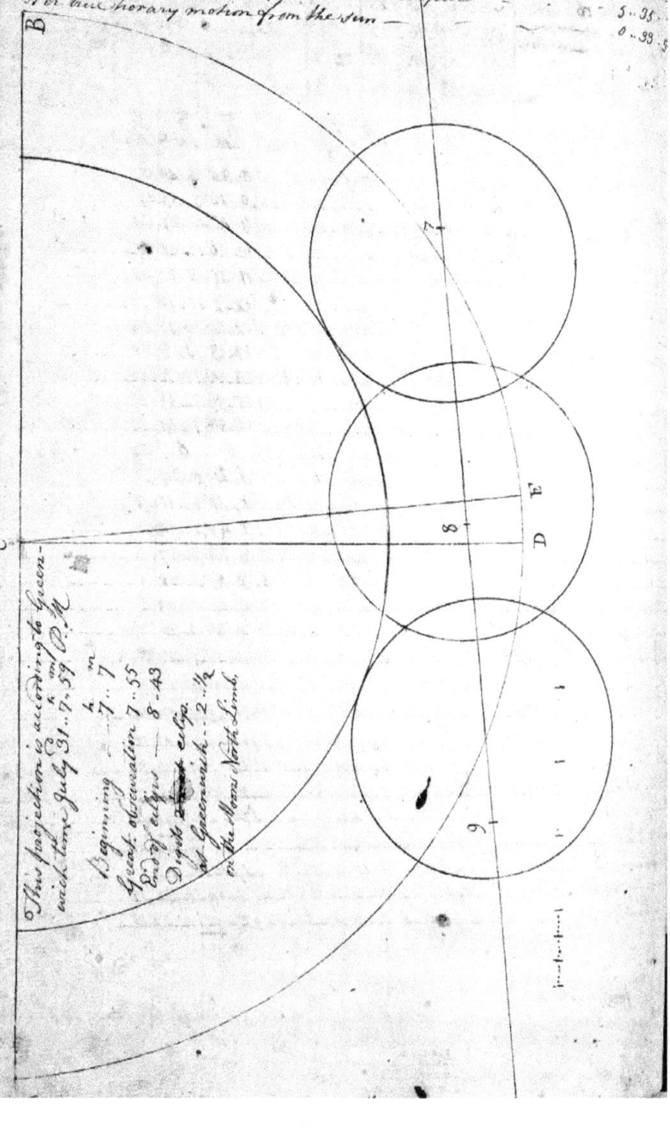

1795 October Tenth Month hath 31 Days

	D	H	M
Last ☾	5	2	8 morn
New ☽	12	5	8 aft.
First ☾	20	19	56 aft.
Full ○	27	8	37 aft.

equation Sub.

☊ { 1 25, 11 ♋ 25, 21 24 } deg.

Planets Places

☽	☉	♄	♃	♂	♀	☿	☽'s
	♎	♊	♑	♍	♎	♎	Lat.
1	8	14	28	9	4	25	5 S.
7	14	14	28	12	12	♏ 4	1 N.
13	20	13	28	16	19	12	5 N.
19	26	13	29	20	27	19	1 N.
25	♏ 2	13	29	24	♏ 4	26	4 S.

M D	W D	Remarkable Days Aspects weather &c.		☉ rise	☉ sets	☽'s place	☽ rise	☽ South	☽ Age
1	5	Days 11..36	Clear	6..12	5..48	♉ 20	8..32	15..23	19
2	6		and	6..13	5..47	♊ 5	9..16	16..20	20
3	7	Pleiades rise 7 34	windy,	6..14	5..46	19	10..5	17..18	21
4	D	18th. Sund. past Trin		6..15	5..45	♋ 4	11..0	18..17	22
5	2		now	6..17	5..43	17	11..58	19..14	23
6	3	Bulls eye rise 8..39	expect	6..18	5..42	♌ 1	12..57	20..7	24
7	4	△ ☉ ♄	rain	6..19	5..41	14	13..57	20..58	25
8	5		followed	6..20	5..40	27	14..59	21..47	26
9	6	Days decrease 3..28	by	6..22	5..38	♍ 10	15..59	22..33	27
10	7		a frost	6..23	5..37	22	16..57	23..16	28
11	D	19th. Sund past Trin.		6..24	5..36	♎ 5		23..59	29
12	2	Days 11..10	flying	6..25	5..35	17	sets	6	☽
13	3		clouds	6..27	5..33	29	6..23	0..42	1
14	4	Procyon rise 11..49		6..28	5..32	♏ 11	6..52	1..25	2
15	5		with	6..29	5..31	23	7..21	2..8	3
16	6	☌ ☉ ♀ Occident.		6..30	5..30	♐ 5	7..54	2..53	4
17	7		wind,	6..32	5..28	17	8..31	3..39	5
18	D	20th. Sund. past Trin. St. Luke		6..33	5..27	29	9..12	4..27	6
19	2		pleasant	6..34	5..26	♑ 11	9..59	5..17	7
20	3	☌ ☽ ♃	and	6..35	5..25	23	10..51	6..8	8
21	4		moderate	6..36	5..24	♒ 5	11..47	6..59	9
22	5	□ ☉ ♃,	weather	6..38	5..22	18	12..47	7..50	10
23	6	☉ enters ♏		6..39	5..21	♓ 1	13..50	8..41	11
24	7	☿ Great. Elong.		6..40	5..20	15	14..58	9..34	12
25	D	21st. Sund. past Trin. Crispin		6..41	5..19	29	16..8	10..27	13
26	2		Clear	6..42	5..18	♈ 14		11..21	14
27	3	Days decrease 4..12	and	6..44	5..16	29	rise	12..16	15
28	4	St. Simon & Jude	cool.	6..45	5..15	♉ 14	6..28	13..13	16
29	5		followed	6..46	5..14	29	7..11	14..12	17
30	6	Pleiades South 1..20	by	6..47	5..13	♊ 14	8..1	15..12	18
31	7	Days 10..24	cold rain	6..48	5..12	29	8..55	16..13	19

Our distilled Spirits is like unto the water of the river of Phrygia which if
sparingly purges the brains and cures madness, but otherwise it infects the brain
and creates madness – See Enticks Dictionary page 458

1795 November eleventh Month hath 30 Days

D H M		Planets Places						
Last Q. 3..0..24 aft.	D	☉	♄	♃	♂	♀	☿	☽'s
New ☽ 11..10..55 morn.		♏	♊	♒	♍	♏	♐	Lat.
First Q. 19..1..30 aft.	1	9	13	0	28	13	1	1 S.
Full ○ 26..6..30 morn. equation Sub.	7	15	12	1	♎ 2	21	1	5 N.
☊ { 1 24	13	21	12	2	5	28	♏ 26	3 N.
11 ♋ 23 } deg.	19	27	11	2	9	♐ 6	18	3 S.
21 23	25	♐ 3	11	3	13	13	16	5 S.

M D	W D	Remarkable Days Aspects weather &c.		☉ rise	☉ sets	☽'s place	☽ rise	☽ South	☽ Age
1	D	22d. Sund. past Trin. All Saints		6..49	5..11	♋ 13	9..53	17..11	20
2	2	Days 10..18	Cold	6..51	5..9	27	10..55	18..8	21
3	3		wind	6..52	5..8	♌ 11	11..57	19..1	22
4	4	☿ Stationary	from	6..53	5..7	24	12..57	19..49	23
5	5		the	6..54	5..6	♍ 7	13..57	20..35	24
6	6	pleiades South 12..52		6..55	5..5	19	14..56	21..19	25
7	7	✱ ♃ ☿	west	6..56	5..4	♎ 2	15..54	22..2	26
8	D	23d. Sund. past Trin.		6..57	5..3	14	16..50	22..43	27
9	2	Sirius rise 10..33	with	6..58	5..2	26	17..47	23..25	28
10	3		rain	6..59	5..1	♏ 8		☌	29
11	4	St. Martin	or	7..0	5..0	20	Sets	0..8	☽
12	5	Days decrease 4..46		7..1	4..59	♐ 2	5..56	0..52	2
13	6		snow	7..2	4..58	14	6..31	1..37	3
14	7	Bulls eye South 1..9		7..3	4..57	25	7..10	2..24	4
15	D	☌ ☉ ☿, Orient. 24th. Sund. past T.		7..4	4..56	♑ 7	7..54	3..13	5
16	2			7..5	4..55	19	8..44	4..3	6
17	3	☌ ☽ ♃	Clear	7..6	4..54	♒ 1	9..38	4..53	7
18	4		and	7..7	4..53	14	10..37	5..44	8
19	5	Days 9..44	Cold	7..8	4..52	27	11..37	6..33	9
20	6	Arcturus rise 3..14		7..8	4..52	♓ 10	12..39	7..22	10
21	7		followed	7..9	4..51	23	13..44	8..11	11
22	D	☉ enters ♐, △ ♄ ♂, 25th. Sund. Sund.		7..10	4..50	♈ 7	14..53	9..2	12
23	2	☿ Stationary,	(past Trin	7..11	4..49	22	16..4	9..55	13
24	3		by	7..12	4..48	♉ 7	17..16	10..49	14
25	4	✱ ♂ ♀	rain	7..12	4..48	22		11..47	15
26	5		or	7..13	4..47	♊ 7	rise	12..48	16
27	6	Algol South 10..41	snow	7..14	4..46	22	6..25	13..50	17
28	7			7..15	4..45	♋ 7	7..33	14..52	18
29	D	Advent Sund.	Cold	7..15	4..45	22	8..37	15..52	19
30	2	Days 9..28	wind	7..16	4..44	♌ 6	9..40	16..48	20

1795 December twelfth Month hath 31 Days

D H M		Planets Places							
	☽	☉	♄	♃	♂	♀	☿	☽'s
Last ☾ 3..2..29 morn.		♐	♊	♒	♎	♐	♏	Lat.
New ☽ 11..6..11 morn.	1	10	10	5	16	21	19	2 N.
First ☽ 19..2..27 morn.	7	16	10	6	20	28	26	5 N.
Full ☉ 25..5..22 aft. equation Sub.	13	22	9	7	24	♑ 6	♐ 4	1 N.
☊ {1 22, 11 ♋ 22, 21 21} deg.	19	28	9	8	27	14	12	5 S.
	25	♑ 4	8	9	♏ 1	21	21	2 S.

M D	W D	Remarkable Days Aspects weather &c.		☉ rise	☉ sets	☽'s place	☽ rise	☽ South	☽ Age
1	3	☍ ☉ ♄	flying	7..16	4..44	♌ 20	10..41	17..38	21
2	4	☿ Great Elong.	clouds	7..17	4..43	♍ 3	11..43	18..26	22
3	5		and	7..18	4..42	16	12..44	19..11	23
4	6	Sirius rise 8..48	wind	7..18	4..42	29	13..41	19..54	24
5	7		with	7..19	4..41	♎ 11	14..38	20..34	25
6	D	2d. Sund. in Advent, Nicholas		7..19	4..41	23	15..35	21..16	26
7	2		rain	7..20	4..40	♏ 5	16..32	21..58	27
8	3	Conception V. Mary	or	7..20	4..40	17	17..28	22..41	28
9	4		snow	7..20	4..40	29	18..24	23..25	29
10	5	pleiades South 10..25		7..21	4..39	♐ 11		☌	30
11	6	Arcturus rise 1..44		7..21	4..39	23	Sets	0..12	☽
12	7		Clear	7..21	4..39	♑ 4	5..43	1..1	2
13	D	3d. Sund. in Advent	and	7..21	4..39	17	6..31	1..50	3
14	2		cold	7..22	4..38	29	7..22	2..39	4
15	3	☌ ☽ ♃	followed	7..22	4..38	♒ 11	8..18	3..28	5
16	4		by	7..22	4..38	23	9..17	4..17	6
17	5	✶ ☉ ♂	snow	7..22	4..38	♓ 6	10..19	5..6	7
18	6	Days decrease 5..28		7..22	4..38	19	11..23	5..55	8
19	7		moderate	7..22	4..38	♈ 3	12..29	6..44	9
20	D	4 Sund. in Advent	Short. day	7..22	4..38	17	13..35	7..32	10
21	2	☉ enters ♑, St. Thomas		7..22	4..38	♉ 1	14..43	8..23	11
22	3	△ ♄ ♃	for	7..22	4..38	15	15..54	9..16	12
23	4	Days 9..16	the	7..22	4..38	♊ 0	17..8	10..14	13
24	5		season	7..22	4..38	15		11..14	14
25	6	Christmas Day		7..22	4..38	♋ 0	rise	12..17	15
26	7	St. Stephen		7..22	4..38	15	6..0	13..19	16
27	D	1st. Sund. past Christmas, St. John		7..22	4..38	♌ 0	7..6	14..19	17
28	2	Innocents.	now	7..21	4..39	14	8..12	15..14	18
29	3		expect	7..21	4..39	28	9..18	16..6	19
30	4		falling	7..21	4..39	♍ 12	10..21	16..54	20
31	5	Silvester	weather	7..20	4..40	25	11..21	17..38	21

1796 January 10th. at 1..15 in the morning eclip ☉ from Node s 5..29..6 °′

According to the Nautical Ephemeris, if the moon changes in the morning of given day, the Succeeding day is the third day of her age but if afternoon the second because it begins at noon, but according to the common ~~reckoning~~ way of reckoning, if the moon changes in the morning of any given day, the Succeeding day is the Second day of her age but if in the afternoon it is allowed to be the first day of her age

♄ Long s ° ′ 2..13..3	Anomal 5..17..22	Node 3..21..34	for the year 1796
☉ 9..10..4	6..1..36		
♃ Long s ° ′ 10..20..49	Anomally s ° ′ 4..9..20	Node s ° ′ 3..8..54	for the year 1796
♂ Long s ° ′ 6..6..54	Anomally s ° ′ 1..4..29	Node s ° ′ 1..18..26	for the year 1796
♀ Long s ° ′ 10..24..22	Anomally s ° ′ 0..16..20	Node s ° ′ 2..14..47	for the Year 1796
☿ Long s ° ′ 8..9..10	Anomally s ° ′ 11..25..3	Node s ° ′ 1..16..7	for the year 1796

Common Notes and Moveable feasts for the year 1796

Dominical Letters	CB
Cycle of the Sun	13
Golden Number	11
Epact	20
Numb. of Direction	6

1796 January ~~First~~ Month hath 31 Days

	d	h	m	
Last ☾	3	1	18	morn
New ☽	10	1	15	morn
First ☽	17	11	2	morn
Full ○	24	5	19	morn.

☊ { 1 — 21; 11 — ♋ 20; 21 — 19 } deg.

Planets Places

☽	☉	♄	♃	♂	♀	☿	☽'
	♑	♊	♒	♏	♒	♑	Lat.
1	11	8	10	5	0	2	5 N.
7	17	7	12	9	9	12	3 N.
13	23	7	14	12	16	22	4 S.
19	29	7	15	15	22	♒ 2	4 S.
25	♒ 6	7	16	19	♓ 0	12	3 N.

M D	W D	Remarkable days Aspects weather &c		☉ rise	☉ set	☽'s place	☽ rise	☽ south	☽'s age
1	6	Circumcision,		7..20	4..40	♎ 7	morn	18..19	22
2	7		windy	7..20	4..40	19	13..25	19..1	23
3	C	1st. Sund. past Chris.		7..20	4..40	♏ 1	14..25	19..44	24
4	2		and	7..19	4..41	13	15..23	20..28	25
5	3		cold,	7..19	[illegible]	25	16..19	21..12	26
6	4	Epiphany		7..18	4..42	♐ 7	17..13	21..58	27
7	5	□ ♂ ♀	rain	7..18	4..42	18	18..6	22..44	28
8	6	Arcturus rise 11..18	or	7..17	4..43	♑ 0	18..57	23..32	29
9	7			7..17	4..43	12	[illegible]..37	☌	30
10	C	☉ eclips invis. 1st. Sund. past Epip		7..16	4..44	24	Sets	0..22	☽
11	2	☌ ☽ ♃		7..15	4..45	♒ 7	6..7	1..12	2
12	3		snow	7..15	4..45	20	7..11	2..2	3
13	4	☌ ☉ ☿ Occident.		7..14	4..46	♓ 3	8..15	2..50	4
14	5		flying	7..13	4..47	16	9..20	3..39	5
15	6	Days increase 18 min		7..13	4..47	♈ 0	10..27	4..28	6
16	7		clouds	7..12	4..48	14	11..36	5..18	7
17	C	2d. Sund. past Epip.		7..11	4..49	28	12..47	6..10	8
18	2		followed	7..10	4..50	♉ 12	13..57	7..3	9
19	3	□ ♃ ♂	by	7..10	4..50	27	15..6	7..57	10
20	4	☉ enter ♒	snow	7..9	4..51	♊ 11	16..11	8..52	11
21	5	Pleiades South 7..20 min		7..8	4..52	25	17..14	9..50	12
22	6		or	7..7	4..53	♋ 10	18..13	10..50	13
23	7	Days 9..48	cold	7..6	4..54	25		11..50	14
24	C	Septuag. Sund.		7..5	4..55	♌ 9	rise	12..48	15
25	2		rain	7..4	4..56	23	6..54	13..42	16
26	3	Sirius South 10..0		7..3	4..57	♍ 7	8..1	14..32	17
27	4			7..2	4..58	20	9..6	15..19	18
28	5		snow	7..1	4..59	♎ 3	10..9	16..4	19
29	6	Day 10 h.	toward	7..0	5..0	16	11..9	16..48	20
30	7		the	6..59	5..1	28	12..7	17..30	21
31	C	Sexagesima Sund.	end	6..58	5..2	♏ 10	13..3	18..12	22

1796, ☉ Long.	Logarithm
January	☉ a ⊗
s ° ′	
1 – 9 .. 11 .. 9	4·99259
7 – 9 .. 17 .. 15	4·99268
13 – 9 .. 23 .. 22	4·99281
19 – 9 .. 29 .. 29	4·99305
25 – 10 .. 5 .. 34	4·99336
February	☉ a ⊕
1 – 10 .. 12 .. 41	4·99383
7 – 10 .. 18 .. 45	4·99430
13 – 10 .. 24 .. 50	4·99483
19 – 11 .. 0 .. 55	4·99532
25 – 11 .. 6 .. 54	4·99606
March	☉ a ⊕
1 – 11 .. 11 .. 55	4·99663
7 – 11 .. 17 .. 55	4·99734
13 – 11 .. 23 .. 54	4·99783
19 – 11 .. 29 .. 50	4·99859
25 – 0 .. 5 .. 50	4·99935

The Elements for an eclipse of the Sun January

True time of New Moon in January 1796 – – – – } d h m 10 : 1 .. 15 A.M.

Semidiameter of the Earths Disc – – – – ° 0. 5[illegible]

Suns distance from nearest Solstice – – 20.

Suns declination South

Moons Latitude North descending

Moons Horary motion from the Sun

Angle of the Moons visible path with Ecliptic – 5.

Suns Semidiameter

Moons Semidiameter

Semidiameter of the penumbra

796 February Second Month hath 29 Days

	h	m	
Last ☾ 1.	5.	20	morn
New ☽ 8.	6.	6	aft.
First ☽ 15.	8.	12	aft.
Full ○ 22.	6.	3	aft.

☊ { 1 ♋ 19, 11 18, 21 18 } deg.

Planets Places

☽	☉	♄	♃	♂	♀	☿	☽'s
	♒	♊	♒	♏	♓	♒	Lat.
1	13	7	18	23	9	23	4 N.
7	19	7	20	26	16	♓ 4	1 S.
13	25	7	21	29	23	11	5 S
19	♓ 1	7	22	♐ 2	♈ 0	17	0 N
25	7	7	23	6	8	15	5 N

M D	W D	Remarkable days Aspects, weather &c.		☉ rise	☉ sets	☽ place	☽ rise	☽ South	☽'s age
1	2	□ ♂ ☿	snow	6..57	5..3	♏ 21	13..58	18..55	23
2	3	purification V. M.		6..56	5..4	♐ 3	14..53	19..41	24
3	4		and	6..55	5..5	15	15..47	20..28	25
4	5	Days increase 56 min.	cold	6..54	5..6	26	16..40	21..16	26
5	6		hard	6..53	5..7	♑ 8	17..28	22..5	27
6	7			6..52	5..8	20	18..12	22..56	28
7	C	Quinqua. Sund. ♃ orient		6..51	5..9	♒ 3	—	23..48	29
8	2	☌ ☽ ♃	weather	6..50	5..10	16	sets	0	☽
9	3	Shrove Tuesday		6..49	5..11	29	5..57	0..38	2
10	4	Ash Wednesday		6..48	5..12	♓ 12	7..6	1..28	3
11	5			6..46	5..14	26	8..14	2..18	4
12	6	Bulls eye set 1..39	windy	6..45	5..15	♈ 10	9..22	3..8	5
13	7	♄ stationary	and	6..44	5..16	24	10..30	3..58	6
14	C	1st. Sund. in Lent Valentine		6..43	5..17	♉ 8	11..38	4..49	7
15	2		cold	6..42	5..18	22	12..45	5..41	8
16	3	Days 10..40		6..40	5..20	♊ 6	13..51	6..35	9
17	4	[illegible]	rain	6..39	5..21	20	14..56	7..33	10
18	5		or	6..38	5..22	♋ 5	16..0	8..35	11
19	6	☉ enter ♓		6..36	5..24	20	16..56	9..37	12
20	7	[illegible]	snow	6..35	5..25	♌ 4	17..43	10..35	13
21	C	2d. Sund. in Lent		6..34	5..26	18	[illegible]	11..32	14
22	2		moderate	6..33	5..27	♍ 2	rise	12..29	15
23	3		weather	6..32	5..28	16	6..43	13..15	16
24	4	St. Matthias		6..31	5..29	29	7..43	13..59	17
25	5	□ ☉ ♄		6..30	5..30	♎ 12	8..43	14..43	18
26	6		toward ~~and~~	6..28	5..32	24	9..43	15..27	19
27	7		the ~~this~~	6..27	5..33	♏ 6	10..42	[illegible]..11	20
28	B	3d. Sund. in Lent	~~month~~	6..26	5..34	18	11..40	[illegible]..55	21
29	2		end	6..25	5..35	♐ 0	12..37	17..40	22

Venus (♀) will be evening Star untill the 7th day of Augt. and then morning Star untill the end of the year.

March

		d h m
1796	New ☽	9 .. 8 .. 7 morn.
	Full ○	23 .. 7 .. 36 morn.

April

1796	New ☽	7 .. 7 .. 15 aft.
	Full ○	21 .. 10 .. 37 aft.

May

1796	New ☽	7 .. 4 .. 2 morn
	Full ○	21 .. 9 .. 56 aft.

June

1796	New ☽	5 .. 11 .. 21 morn.
	Full ○	20 .. 5 .. 21 morn.

July

1796	New ☽	4 .. 6 .. 8 aft.
	Full ○	19 .. 9 .. 2 morn.

August

1796	New ☽	3 .. 1 .. 29 morn.
	Full ○	18 .. 10 .. 18 morn

September

1796	New ☽	1 .. 10 .. 22 morn
	Full ○	16 .. 11 .. 10 aft.
	~~New ☽~~	~~30 .. 9 .. 49 aft~~
~~1796~~	~~New ☽~~	~~30 .. 0 .. 19 aft~~
	~~Full ○~~	~~16 .. 11 .. 10 morn~~

November

1796	~~Full~~	
	New ☽	~~29 .. 5 .. 42~~ morn

To be corrected

October

1796	Full ○	16 .. 11 .. 11 morn
	New ☽	30 .. 0 .. 19 aft

November

1796	Full ○	14 .. 10 .. 25 aft ~~[illegible]~~
	New ☽	29 .. 5 .. 42 morn.

December

1796	Full ○	14 .. 9 .. 19 morn.
	New ☽	29 .. 1 .. 3 morn.

1796 March Third Month hath 31 Days.

	d	h	m	
Last ☾	1	11	32	morn
New ☽	9	8	7	morn
First ☽	16	4	13	morn.
Full ○	23	7	36	morn
Last ☾	31	4	12	aft.

☊ { 1 ♋ 17 ; 11 17 ; 21 16 } deg.

Planets Places							
D	☉	♄	♃	♂	♀	☿	☽'s
	♓	♊	♒	♐	♈	♓	Lat.
1	12	7	25	9	15	12	3 N.
7	18	8	26	11	21	8	3 S.
13	24	8	26	14	28	3	4 S.
19	♈ 0	9	29	17	♉ 6	6	2 N.
25	6	9	♓ 0	19	13	8	5 N

M D	W D	Remarkable days Aspects weather &c.	☉ rise	☉ set	☽'s place	☽ rise	☽ south	☽'s age
1	3	☌ ☉ ☿ Orient St. David	6..24	5..36	♐ 12	13..34	18..26	23
2	4	high	6..23	5..37	23	14..29	19..13	24
3	5	pleiades set 11..56	6..22	5..38	♑ 5	15..23	20..2	25
4	6	winds	6..21	5..39	17	16..13	20..52	26
5	7	with	6..19	5..41	29	16..59	21..42	27
6	B	4th. Sund. Lent. rain,	6..17	5..43	♒ 11	17..41	22..32	28
7	2	☌ ☽ ♃, □ ♄ ☿ or	6..16	5..44	24	18..20	23..22	29
8	3	snow	6..14	5..46	♓ 7		☌	30
9	4	Days increase 1..18	6..13	5..47	21	sets	0..12	☽
10	5	flying	6..12	5..48	♈ 5	6..53	1..2	2
11	6	clouds	6..11	5..49	19	8..2	1..52	3
12	7	Gregory	6..9	5..51	♉ 3	9..11	2..44	4
13	B	5th. Sund. in Lent	6..8	5..52	18	10..20	3..38	5
14	2	moderate	6..7	5..53	♊ 2	11..29	4..34	6
15	3	Days 11..48	6..6	5..54	17	12..38	5..32	7
16	4	weather	6..4	5..56	♋ 1	13..46	6..31	8
17	5	St patrick	6..3	5..57	15	14..50	7..30	9
18	6	cold	6..2	5..58	29	15..46	8..29	10
19	7	☉ enters ♈, ✶ ♀ ☿, Equal day & (night	6..0	6..0	♌ 13	16..32	9..25	11
20	B	Palm Sund.	5..59	6..1	27	17..12	10..19	12
21	2	rain	5..58	6..2	♍ 11	17..49	11..11	13
22	3	Spica ♍ South 1..11	5..57	6..3	24		11..59	14
23	4	and	5..55	6..5	♎ 7	rise	12..45	15
24	5	wind	5..54	6..6	20	7..41	13..30	16
25	6	Good Fryday	5..53	6..7	♏ 3	8..41	14..14	17
26	7	☿ great Elong.	5..52	6..8	15	9..41	14..59	18
27	B	Easter Sund.	5..50	6..10	27	10..40	15..45	19
28	2	Easter Mond.	5..49	6..11	♐ 9	11..38	16..33	20
29	3	Easter Tuesd. pleasant	5..48	6..12	21	12..35	17..21	21
30	4	weather	5..46	6..14	♑ 2	13..30	18..9	22
31	5	Days 12..30	5..45	6..15	14	14..20	18..58	23

1796 ☉ Long. in April				Logarithm ☉ a ⊕
D	s	°	'	
1	0	12	41	5.0003
7	0	18	35	5.0011
13	0	24	26	5.0018
19	1	0	17	5.0026
25	1	6	8	5.0033

April Fourth Month hath 30 Days

	d	h	m	
New ☽	7	7	15	aft.
First ☽	14	0	0	noon
Full ○	21	10	37	aft.
Last ☾	29	11	2	aft.

☊ { 1 ♋ 16, 11 ♋ 15, 21 ♋ 15 } deg.

Planets Places

D	☉	♄	♃	♂	♀	☿	☽'s
	♈	♊	♓	♐	♉	♓	Lat.
1	13	10	2	22	21	15	1 S.
7	19	10	3	24	28	23	5 S.
13	24	11	4	26	♊ 5	♈ 1	1 S.
19	♉ 0	11	6	27	12	11	5 N
25	6	11	7	29	19	22	2 N

M D	W D	Remarkable days Aspects weather &c.		☉ rise	☉ set	☽'s place	☽ rise	☽ south	☽'s age
1	6	Sirius sets 10..53		5..44	6..16	♑ 26	15..6	19..47	24
2	7		Cloudy	5..43	6..17	♒ 8	15..48	20..36	25
3	B	1st. Sund. past East.		5..41	6..19	20	16..28	21..25	26
4	2	St. Ambrose	and	5..40	6..20	♓ 3	17..4	22..14	27
5	3		cool	5..39	6..21	16	17..35	23..3	28
6	4		with rain,	5..38	6..22	29		23..52	29
7	5	♀ sets 9..46		5..36	6..24	♈ 13	sets	☌	☽
8	6		fine	5..35	6..25	..27	7..1	0..41	1
9	7	Days 12..52		5..34	6..26	♉ 12	8..8	1..31	2
10	B	2d. Sund. past East.	pleasant	5..33	6..27	27	9..18	2..25	3
11	2	☌ ☽ ♃		5..32	6..28	♊ 12	10..30	3..23	4
12	3	procyon set 12..20		5..30	6..30	27	11..40	4..25	5
13	4		weather	5..29	6..31	♋ 11	12..45	5..27	6
14	5	Days increase 3..48		5..28	6..32	25	13..43	6..27	7
15	6		flying	5..27	6..33	♌ 9	14..36	7..25	8
16	7		clouds	5..26	6..34	23	15..21	8..20	9
17	B	3d Sund. past East		5..25	6..35	♍ 7	16..0	9..12	10
18	2		with	5..23	6..37	20	16..33	10..4	11
19	3	☉ enter ♉	showers	5..22	6..38	♎ 3	17..4	10..52	12
20	4		of	5..21	6..39	16		11..37	13
21	5	pleiades set 8..57	rain,	5..20	6..40	29	rise	12..21	14
22	6		windy	5..18	6..42	♏ 11	7..40	13..4	15
23	7	St. George		5..17	6..43	23	8..39	13..48	16
24	B	4th Sund. past East	with	5..16	6..44	♐ 5	9..37	14..33	17
25	2	St. Mark		5..15	6..45	17	10..34	15..21	18
26	3		flying	5..14	6..46	29	11..30	16..11	19
27	4	Arietis rise 4..21	clouds,	5..13	6..47	♑ 11	12..24	17..1	20
28	5		and ~~with~~	5..12	6..48	23	13..12	17..51	21
29	6		rain	5..11	6..49	♒ 5	13..54	18..39	22
30	7	Days 13..40		5..10	6..50	17	14..32	19..26	23

776, ⊙ Long. in May	Logarithm ⊙ a ⊕
D S ° '	
1 — 1 .. 11 .. 57	5.0039
7 — 1 .. 17 .. 44	5.0045
13 — 1 23 .. 31	5.0051
19 — 1 .. 29 .. 17	5.0056
25 — 2 .. 5 .. 2	5.0060

1792. May. Fifth Month hath 31 Days

	d	h	m
New ☽	7	4	2 morn
First Qr.	13	8	40 aft.
Full ○	21	1	56 aft.
Last Qr.	29	1	25 aft.

☊ { 1 — 14; 11 ♋ 14; 21 — 13 } Deg.

Planets Places

☽	☉	♄	♃	♂	♀	☿	☽'s
	♉	♊	♓	♐	♊	♉	Lat.
1	12	13	8	29	26	4	4 S.
7	17	14	9	♑ 0	♋ 2	16	4 S.
13	24	15	9	0	8	29	3 N.
19	29	15	10	0	14	♊ 8	5 N.
25	♊ 5	16	11	♐ 29	21	18	1 S.

M D	W D	Remarkable days Aspects weather &c.		☉ rise	☉ sets	☽'s place	☽ rise	☽ south	☽'s age
1	B	Rogation Sund. St. philip & James		5 .. 9	6 .. 51	♒ 29	15 .. 6	20 .. 14	24
2	2	☌ ☽ ♃		5 .. 8	6 .. 52	♓ 12	15 .. 39	21 .. 2	25
3	3	pleiades Sets 8 .. 12		5 - 7	6 .. 53	25	16 .. 11	21 .. 50	26
4	4		Clear	5 .. 5	6 .. 55	♈ 8	16 .. 43	22 - 38	27
5	5	Ascension Day	and	5 .. 4	6 .. 56	22	17 .. 15	23 .. 28	28
6	6	St. John Evang.		5 .. 3	6 .. 57	♉ 6		0	29
7	7		pleasant	5 .. 2	6 .. 58	21	Sets	0 .. 24	☽
8	B	☌ ☉ ☿ Occident. 1st Sund. past As		5 .. 1	6 .. 59	♊ 6	8 .. 26	1 .. 21	2
9	2		expect	5 .. 0	7 .. 0	21	9 .. 36	2 .. 20	3
10	3	♃ rise 1 .. 49		4 .. 59	7 .. 1	♋ 6	10 .. 42	3 .. 22	4
11	4		rain	4 .. 58	7 .. 2	21	11 .. 42	4 .. 24	5
12	5		clear	4 .. 58	7 .. 2	♌ 5	12 .. 39	5 .. 22	6
13	6	♀ Sets 10 .. 34		4 .. 57	7 .. 3	19	13 .. 26	6 .. 17	7
14	7		and	4 .. 56	7 .. 4	♍ 2	14 .. 3	7 .. 7	8
15	B	Whit - Sund.	warm	4 .. 55	7 .. 5	15	14 .. 30	7 .. 55	9
16	2	Whit - Mond.		4 .. 54	7 .. 6	28	14 .. 57	8 .. 40	10
17	3	Whit. Tues.		4 .. 53	7 .. 7	♎ 11	15 .. 25	9 .. 25	11
18	4		flying	4 .. 52	7 .. 8	24	15 .. 54	10 .. 10	12
19	5		clouds	4 .. 52	7 .. 8	♏ 7	16 .. 24	10 .. 55	13
20	6	☉ enter ♊		4 .. 51	7 .. 9	19		11 .. 42	14
21	7		thunder	4 .. 51	7 .. 9	♐ 1	rise	12 .. 30	15
22	B	Trinity Sund.		4 .. 50	7 .. 10	13	8 .. 27	13 .. 18	16
23	2		gust	4 .. 49	7 .. 11	25	9 .. 23	14 .. 6	17
24	3		and	4 .. 48	7 - 12	♑ 7	10 .. 15	14 .. 54	18
25	4	♀ great elong		4 .. 47	7 .. 13	19	11 .. 3	15 .. 42	19
26	5		rain	4 .. 46	7 .. 14	♒ 1	11 .. 47	16 .. 31	20
27	6	procyon Sets 9 - 26		4 .. 46	7 .. 14	13	12 .. 27	17 .. 19	21
28	7		fine	4 .. 45	7 .. 15	25	13 .. 4	18 .. 6	22
29	B	Sund. past Trin. ☌ ☽ ♃		4 .. 44	7 .. 16	♓ 8	13 .. 37	18 .. 53	23
30	2		growing	4 .. 44	7 .. 16	21	14 .. 7	19 .. 39	24
31	3	Days 14 - 34	weather	4 .. 43	7 .. 17	♈ 4	14 .. 37	20 .. 25	25

1796, ☉ Long. in June	Logarithm ☉ a ⊕
D s ° '	
1 — 2..11..46	5.0064
7 — 2..17..30	5.0067
13 — 2..23..14	5.0070
19 — 2..28..57	5.0071
25 — 3..4..40	5.0072

The Elements for an Eclips of the Moon June [1796]

True time of full Moon in June 1796 ——— } D h m 20..5..21 A.M.

Moons Horizontal paralax

Suns Semidiameter ——— 0..5

Moons Semidiameter ——— 0..1

Semediameter of the earths shadow at the ☽ 0..4

Moons Latitud North descending ——— 0..1

Angle of her visable path with the Ecliptic 5..

Her true Horary motion from the Sun ——— 0..2

In the collection of the requisites I find the Sun to be from Ambibazon s 11..18..13..49 ° ' " and the Moon from Catabibazon ~~the same distance~~ viz. s 5..18..13..49 ° ' "

Moons Lat. 61..16 N.D. ' "

It appears to me that the wisest of men at certain times be in an error, for instance Doctor Ferguson informs when the Sun is within 12° of ~~the~~ Node at the time of full, that moon be eclipsed, but I find according to the [me]thod of his projecting a Lunar Eclips there will be none by the above [ele]ments, and yet the Sun is within 11°..46'..11" of the Moons Afcen[ding] Node — But Moons being ~~in~~ in her Apogee prevents the appearance of the Eclips

June Sixth Month hath 30 Days.

		Planets Places						
New ☽ 5 ..11..21 morn.								
First ☽ 12 . 5 ..32 morn.	☽	☉	♄	♃	♂	♀	☿	☽'
Full ○ 20 ..5 ..21 morn		♊	♊	♓	♐	♋	♋	Lat.
Last ☾ 27 ..11 ..41 aft.	1	12	17	12	28	27	4	5 S.
	7	18	18	12	27	♌ 2	12	0 N.
☊ { 1 13; 11 ♋ 12; 21 11 } deg.	13	23	18	13	25	7	16	5 N.
	19	29	19	13	23	12	20	2 N.
	25	♋ 5	20	13	21	16	19	4 S.

M D	W D	Remarkable days Aspects weather &c.		☉ rise	☉ sets	☽'s place	☽ rise	☽ south	☽' age
1	4	□ ☉ ♃		4 .. 13	7 .. 17	♈ 18	15 .. 5	21 .. 14	26
2	5		warm	4 .. 12	7 .. 18	♉ 2	15 .. 41	22 .. 7	27
3	6	Days increase 5 .. 20		4 .. 12	7 .. 18	16	16 .. 21	23 .. 5	28
4	7		winds	4 .. 11	7 .. 19	♊ 1		☌	29
5	B	2d. Sund past Trin		4 .. 11	7 .. 19	16	sets	0 .. 5	☽
6	2	☿ great elong	from	4 .. 11	7 .. 19	♋ 1	8 .. 26	1 .. 5	2
7	3	☌ ☉ ♄ , △ ♃ ☿	the	4 .. 10	7 .. 20	16	9 .. 26	2 .. 5	3
8	4		South	4 .. 10	7 .. 20	♌ 0	10 .. 21	3 .. 5	4
9	5	Arcturus South 8 .. 51		4 .. 10	7 . 20	14	11 .. 7	4 .. 2	5
10	6		rain	4 .. 39	7 . 21	28	11 .. 48	4 .. 56	6
11	7	St. Barnabas	and	4 .. 39	7 . 21	♍ 12	12 .. 24	5 .. 47	7
12	B	3d. Sund past Trin.		4 .. 39	7 .. 21	25	12 .. 58	6 .. 36	8
13	2		wind	4 .. 39	7 .. 21	♎ 8	13 .. 27	7 .. 22	9
14	3	☍ ☉ ♂		4 .. 39	7 .. 21.	21	13 .. 53	8 .. 6	10
15	4		flying	4 .. 38	7 .. 22	♏ 3	14 .. 21	8 .. 49	11
16	5		Clouds	4 .. 38	7 .. 22	15	14 .. 49	9 .. 32	12
17	6	St. Alban		4 .. 38	7 . 22	27	15 .. 21	10 .. 16	13
18	7		with	4 .. 38	7 .. 22	♐ 9	15 .. 55	11 .. 2	14
19	B	4th. Sund. past Trin		4 .. 38	7 .. 22	21		11 .. 50	15
20	2	Longest day	thunder	4 .. 38	7 .. 22	♑ 3	rise	12 .. 39	16
21	3	☉ enter ♋		4 .. 38	7 .. 22	15	8 .. 5	13 .. 29	17
22	4	Days 14 .. 44		4 .. 38	7 .. 22	27	9 .. 37	14 .. 19	18
23	5		gusts .	4 .. 38	7 .. 22	♒ 9	10 .. 20	15 .. 9	19
24	6	St. John Bap.		4 .. 38	7 .. 22	22	10 .. 59	15 .. 59	20
25	7		and	4 .. 38	7 .. 22	♓ 5	11 .. 34	16 .. 47	21
26	B	5th. Sund. past Trin. ☌ ☽ ♃		4 .. 38	7 .. 22	18	12 .. 4	17 .. 32	22
27	2		rain	4 .. 38	7 .. 22	♈ 1	12 .. 32	18 .. 18	23
28	3		ends	4 .. 38	7 .. 22	14	13 .. 2	19 .. 5	24
29	4	St. peter and paul	this	4 .. 39	7 .. 21	27	13 .. 35	19 .. 55	25
30	5	Day decrease 2 min	month	4 .. 39	7 .. 21	♉ 11	14 .. 12	20 .. 48	26

1796 ☉ Long in July D	Logarithm ☉ a ⊕
1—3..10..22	5.0072
7—3..16..5	5.0072
13—3..21..48	5.0070
19—3..27..32	5.0068
25—4..3..16	5.0065

The Elements for the projection of an eclipse of Sun July 4th. 1796

True time of New Moon in July. 1796	d h m 4..6..7 P.M.
Semidiameter of the Earths disc	[illegible]
Suns distance from the nearest Solstice	0..[illegible]
Suns declination North	13..[illegible]
Moons Latitude North Ascending	22..[illegible]
Moons Horary motion from the Sun	0..[illegible]
Angle of the Moons visible path with the Ecliptic	0..[illegible]
Suns Semidiameter	5..[illegible]
Moons Semidiameter	0..[illegible]
Semidiameter of the penumbra	0..[illegible]

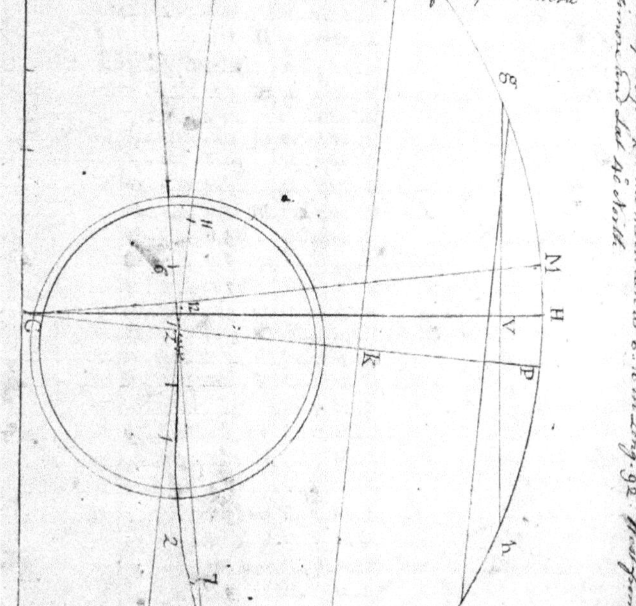

[illegible] Lat. 17..0 N. ☉ is totally and centrally [illegible] totally Eclipsed on the meridian at 6..16 m Long. 92° West from the meridian of Baltimore and Lat 40° North

796 July Seventh Month hath 31 Days

			Planets Places							
	D	☉	♄	♃	♂	♀	☿	☽'s		♂
		♋	♊	♓	♐	♌	♋	Lat.		
New ☽ 4 .. 6 .. 8 aft.	1	10	21	13	19	19	19	4 S.		
First ☽ 11 .. 6 .. 8 aft.	7	16	22	13	18	r 21	15	3 N.		
Full ○ 19 .. 9 .. 2 morn.	13	22	22	13	18	22	12	5 N.		
Last ☾ 27 .. 7 .. 10 morn.	19	28	23	13	18	r 22	13	1 S.		
☊ { 1 ♋ 11 / 11 ♋ 10 / 21 ♋ 10 } deg.	25	♌ 3	24	12	18	19	14	5 S.		

M D	W D	Remarkable days Aspects weather &c.		☉ rise	☉ set	☽'s place	☽ rise	☽ South	☽'s age
1	6	△ ♂ ♀		4 .. 39	7 .. 21	♉ 25	14 .. 52	21 .. 45	27
2	7	Visitation V. Mary		4 .. 40	7 .. 20	♊ 10	15 .. 38	22 .. 45	28
3	B	6th Sund. past Trin.		4 .. 40	7 .. 20	25		23 .. 49	29
4	2	☉ eclip. invis. Tran. St. Martin		4 .. 40	7 .. 20	♋ 10	sets	0	☽
5	3		hot	4 .. 41	7 .. 19	25	8 .. 12	0 .. 53	1
6	4		and	4 .. 41	7 .. 19	♌ 10	9 .. 1	1 .. 51	2
7	5	☌ ☉ ☿ Orient.	sultry,	4 .. 42	7 .. 18	24	9 .. 43	2 .. 45	3
8	6		thunder	4 .. 42	7 .. 18	♍ 8	10 .. 19	3 .. 37	4
9	7		gusts	4 .. 43	7 .. 17	21	10 .. 51	4 .. 26	5
10	B	7th Sund. past Trin.	and	4 .. 43	7 .. 17	♎ 4	11 .. 21	5 .. 12	6
11	2		rain	4 .. 44	7 .. 16	17	11 .. 46	5 .. 54	7
12	3	Spica ♍ Sets 11 .. 14		4 .. 44	7 .. 16	29	12 .. 12	6 .. 36	8
13	4		flying	4 .. 45	7 .. 15	♏ 11	12 .. 40	7 .. 19	9
14	5	Day decrease 14 min.		4 .. 45	7 .. 15	23	13 .. 11	8 .. 3	10
15	6		clouds,	4 .. 46	7 .. 14	♐ 5	13 .. 45	8 .. 49	11
16	7		warm	4 .. 47	7 .. 13	17	14 .. 25	9 .. 39	12
17	B	8th Sund. past Trin.		4 .. 47	7 .. 13	29	15 .. 8	10 .. 29	13
18	2		south	4 .. 48	7 .. 12	♑ 11		11 .. 19	14
19	3	△ ♃ ☿, ♂ Stationary		4 .. 49	7 .. 11	23	rise	12 .. 9	15
20	4	Margaret.		4 .. 49	7 .. 11	♒ 5	8 .. 14	12 .. 59	16
21	5		winds	4 .. 50	7 .. 10	18	8 .. 53	13 .. 49	17
22	6	Magdalene ☉ enter ♌		4 .. 51	7 .. 9	♓ 1	9 .. 31	14 .. 39	18
23	7	☌ ☽ ♃		4 .. 52	7 .. 8	14	10 .. 5	15 .. 27	19
24	B	9th Sund. past Trin.		4 .. 53	7 .. 7	27	10 .. 33	16 .. 13	20
25	2	☿ great elong. St. James		4 .. 54	7 .. 6	♈ 10	11 .. 0	16 .. 58	21
26	3	St. Anne		4 .. 54	7 .. 6	23	11 .. 32	17 .. 46	22
27	4		thunder	4 .. 55	7 .. 5	♉ 7	12 .. 6	18 .. 37	23
28	5	Lyra South 9 .. 59	gusts	4 .. 56	7 .. 4	21	12 .. 42	19 .. 31	24
29	6		and	4 .. 57	7 .. 3	♊ 5	13 .. 23	20 .. 27	25
30	7	Dog days begins	rain	4 .. 58	7 .. 2	19	14 .. 12	21 .. 27	26
31	B	10th Sund. past Trin		4 .. 59	7 .. 1	♋ 4	15 .. 9	22 .. 30	27

1796, ☉ Long in August	Logarithm ☉ a ⊕
D S ° ′	
1 — 4 . 9 . 58	5 . 00615
7 — 4 . 15 . 45	5 . 00579
13 — 4 . 21 . 29	5 . 00531
19 — 4 . 27 . 16	5 . 00476
25 — 5 . 3 . 4	5 . 00417

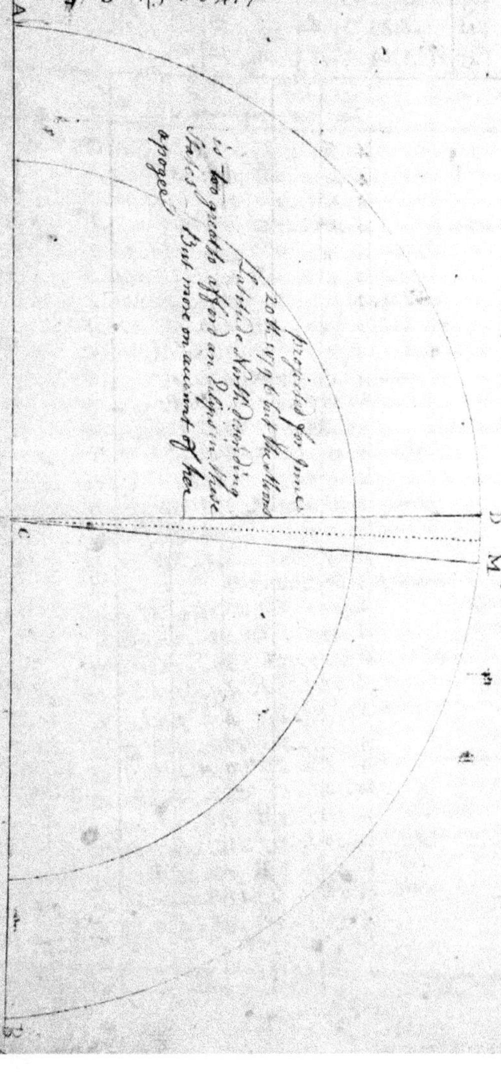

1796 # August Eighth Month hath 31 Days

	D	H	M	
New ☽	3	1	29	morn.
First ☾	10	8	48	morn.
Full ☉	18	10	18	morn.
Last ☾	25	4	7	aft.

☊ { 1 ♋ 9 / 11 ♋ 9 / 21 8 } deg.

☽	☉	♄	♃	♂	♀	☿	☽'s
	♌	♊	♓	♐	♌	♋	Lat.
1	10	24	12	18	17	22	1 N.
7	16	25	11	19	13	♌ 1	5 N.
13	22	25	10	21	9	13	1 N.
19	27	26	10	23	7	25	4 S.
25	♍ 3	26	9	25	5	♍ 8	3 S.

Planets Places

M D	W D	Remarkable days Aspects weather &c.		☉ rise	☉ set	☽'s place	☽ rise	☽ south	☽'s age
1	2	Lammas day		5..0	7..0	♋ 19	16..7	23..30	28
2	3			5..1	6..59	♌ 4		☌	29
3	4	♃ Set 8..14	wind	5..2	6..58	19	Sets	0..30	☽
4	5		and	5..3	6..57	♍ 3	8..15	1..26	2
5	6		rain	5..4	6..56	17	8..52	2..18	3
6	7	Transfig. ☌ ☉		5..5	6..55	♎ 0	9..23	3..6	4
7	B	11 th. Sund past Trin. ♀ Orient		5..6	6..54	13	9..52	3..50	5
8	2		Clear	5..7	6..53	26	10..17	4..34	6
9	3		and	5..8	6..52	♏ 8	10..46	5..18	7
10	4	St. Lawrence		5..9	6..51	20	11..15	6..2	8
11	5		warm,	5..10	6..50	♐ 2	11..44	6..46	9
12	6	Days decrease 1..6		5..11	6..49	14	12..19	7..32	10
13	7		thunder	5..12	6..48	26	12..59	8..20	11
14	B	12th. Sund. past Trin.		5..13	6..47	♑ 7	13..45	9..9	12
15	2		and	5..14	6..46	19	14..36	9..59	13
16	3	Bulls eye rise 11..44		5..15	6..45	♒ 1	15..30	10..49	14
17	4		rain,	5..16	6..44	13		[illegible]..38	15
18	5		great	5..18	6..42	26	rise	12..27	16
19	6	☌ ☽ ♃		5..19	6..41	♓ 9	7..57	13..16	17
20	7		dews	5..20	6..40	22	8..32	14..5	18
21	B	☌ ☉ ☿ Occident. 13th. Sund past Trin.		5..21	6..39	♈ 5	9..3	14..54	19
22	2			5..22	6..38	19	9..34	15..44	20
23	3	☉ enters ♍		5..23	6..37	♉ 3	10..9	16..36	21
24	4	St. Bartholomew		5..24	6..36	17	10..45	17..30	22
25	5		thunder	5..26	6..34	♊ 1	11..24	18..26	23
26	6	Arcturus Sets 10..55	gusts	5..27	6..33	15	12..10	19..24	24
27	7			5..28	6..32	29	13..3	20..24	25
28	B	14th. Sund. past Trin. St. Augustine		5..29	6..31	♋ 14	14..0	21..25	26
29	2	St. John Bap. behead.		5..30	6..30	29	15..5	22..25	27
30	3	~~[illegible]~~ ☍ ☉ ♃ occident	and	5..32	6..28	♌ 14	16..15	23..24	28
31	4	Days 12..54	rain	5..33	6..27	28		☌	29

1796, ☉ Long. in September	Logarithm ☉ a ⊕
D s ° ′	
1 — 5 .. 9 .. 50	5.00342
7 — 5 .. 15 .. 40	5.00273
13 — 5 .. 21 .. 31	5.00201
19 — 5 .. 27 .. 23	5.00126
25 — 6 .. 3 .. 16	5.00050

1796 September Ninth Month hath 30 Days

	D	h	m	
New ☽	1	10	22	morn.
First ☽	8	11	38	aft.
Full ○	16	11	10	aft.
Last ☾	23	10	8	aft.
New ☽	30	9	49	aft.

☊ { 1, 11, 21 } ♋ { 8, 7, 7 } deg.

Planets Places							
D	☉	♄	♃	♂	♀	☿	☽'s
	♍	♊	♓	♐	♌	♍	Lat.
1	10	27	8	28	7	20	5 N.
7	16	27	7	♑ 1	8	29	3 N
13	22	27	6	4	11	♎ 9	3 S.
19	27	28	6	8	14	18	5 S.
25	♎ 3	28	5	11	19	27	2 N.

M D	W D	Remarkable days Aspects weather &c		☉ rise	☉ sets	☽'s place	☽ sets	☽ South	☽'s age
1	5	☍ ♄ ♂	great	5 .. 34	6 .. 26	♍ 12	Sets	0 .. 18	☽
2	6		Dews	5 .. 35	6 .. 25	26	7 .. 27	1 .. 6	2
3	7	Dog days end		5 .. 36	6 .. 24	♎ 9	7 .. 55	1 .. 52	3
4	B	15th Sund past Trin.		5 .. 38	6 .. 22	22	8 .. 23	2 .. 38	4
5	2		flying	5 .. 39	6 .. 21	♏ 5	8 .. 53	3 .. 23	5
6	3	□ ♄ ☿		5 .. 40	6 .. 20	17	9 .. 23	4 .. 6	6
7	4		Clouds	5 .. 41	6 .. 19	29	9 .. 53	4 .. 51	7
8	5	Nativity V. Mary		5 .. 43	6 .. 17	♐ 11	10 .. 26	5 .. 38	8
9	6		and	5 .. 44	6 .. 16	23	11 .. 6	6 .. 26	9
10	7		rain	5 .. 45	6 .. 15	♑ 4	11 .. 49	7 .. 14	10
11	B	16th. Sund. past Trin.		5 .. 46	6 .. 14	16	12 .. 37	8 .. 2	11
12	2			5 .. 48	6 .. 12	28	13 .. 30	8 .. 51	12
13	3	pleiades rise 8. 46		5 .. 49	6 .. 11	♒ 10	14 .. 26	9 .. 40	13
14	4		pleasant	5 .. 50	6 .. 10	22	15 .. 25	10 .. 28	14
15	5	☌ ☽ ♃		5 .. 52	6 .. 8	♓ 4		11 .. 16	15
16	6		weather,	5 .. 53	6 .. 7	17	rise	12 .. 4	16
17	7		followed	5 .. 54	6 .. 6	♈ 0	7 .. 7	12 .. 52	17
18	B	17th. Sund. past Trin.		5 .. 55	6 .. 5	14	7 .. 37	13 .. 40	18
19	2		by	5 .. 56	6 .. 4	28	8 .. 9	14 .. 30	19
20	3	□ ☉ ♄	rain	5 .. 58	6 .. 2	♉ 12	8 .. 42	15 .. 23	20
21	4	St. Matthew		5 .. 59	6 .. 1	26	9 .. 22	16 .. 19	21
22	5	Equal Day & night,		6 .. 0	6 .. 0	♊ 10	10 .. 8	17 .. 19	22
23	6	☉ enters ♎.	cool	6 .. 2	5 .. 58	25	11 .. 2	18 .. 23	23
24	7		Dews	6 .. 3	5 .. 57	♋ 10	12 .. 2	19 .. 26	24
25	B	18th. Sund. past Trin. △ ♄ ☿,		6 .. 4	5 .. 56	25	13 .. 5	20 .. 28	25
26	2	St. Cyprian		6 .. 5	5 .. 55	♌ 9	14 .. 11	21 .. 26	26
27	3		rain	6 .. 7	5 .. 53	23	15 .. 18	22 .. 20	27
28	4		toward	6 .. 8	5 .. 52	♍ 7	16 .. 26	23 .. 10	28
29	5	St. Michael	the	6 .. 9	5 .. 51	21		23 .. 56	29
30	6	Days 11 .. 38	end	6 .. 11	5 .. 49	♎ 5	Sets	[illegible]	☽

1796 ☉ Long in October	Logarithm ☉ a ⊕
D S ° '	
1 — 6 .. 9 .. 11	4 · 99973
7 — 6 .. 15 .. 6	4 · 99897
13 — 6 .. 21 .. 4	4 · 99833
19 — 6 .. 27 .. 2	4 · 99759
25 — 7 .. 3 .. 1	4 · 99686

1796 October Tenth Month hath 31 Days.

D. h. m.
First ☽. 8 .. 6 .. 32 aft.
Full ○ 16 .. 11 .. 11 morn.
Last ☾. 23 .. 6 .. 8 morn.
New ☽ 30 .. 0 .. 19 aft.

☊ { 1 — 6 ; 11 ♋ 6 ; 21 — 5 } Deg.

Planets Places

☽	☉	♄	♃	♂	♀	☿	☽'s
	♎	♊	♓	♑	♌	♏	Lat.
1	9	28	5	15	24	3	5 N.
7	15	28	4	18	29	10	0 N.
13	21	28	1	22	♍ 5	13	5 S.
19	27	28	3	26	11	16	2 S.
25	♏ 3	28	3	♒ 0	17	12	4 N.

M D	W D	Remarkable days Aspects weather &c.		☉ rise	☉ sets	☽'s place	☽ sets	☽ south	☽'s age
1	7	Days decrease 3 .. 8		6 .. 12	5 .. 48	♎ 18	6 .. 33	0 .. 42	1
2	B	19th. Sund. past Trin.		6 .. 13	5 .. 47	♏ 1	7 .. 3	1 .. 28	2
3	2		Cool	6 .. 14	5 .. 46	14	7 .. 33	2 .. 14	3
4	3		dews	6 .. 15	5 .. 45	26	8 .. 4	3 .. 0	4
5	4	♄ Stationary		6 .. 17	5 .. 43	♐ 8	8 .. 37	3 .. 47	5
6	5	✶ ♄ ♀		6 .. 18	5 .. 42	20	9 .. 13	4 .. 34	6
7	6	☿ great elong.	expect	6 .. 19	5 .. 41	♑ 1	9 .. 54	5 .. 21	7
8	7		rain,	6 .. 20	5 .. 40	13	10 .. 40	6 .. 9	8
9	B	20th Sund. past Trin.		6 .. 22	5 .. 38	25	11 .. 32	6 .. 57	9
10	2		white	6 .. 23	5 .. 37	♒ 6	12 .. 27	7 .. 45	10
11	3		frost	6 .. 24	5 .. 36	18	13 .. 25	8 .. 33	11
12	4	☌ ☽ ♃		6 .. 25	5 .. 35	♓ 0	14 .. 26	9 .. 21	12
13	5	♀ rise 2 .. 52		6 .. 27	5 .. 33	13	15 .. 30	10 .. 9	13
14	6		pleasant	6 .. 28	5 .. 32	26	16 .. 36	10 .. 57	14
15	7		weather	6 .. 29	5 .. 31	♈ 9		11 .. 45	15
16	B	21st. Sund. past Trin.		6 .. 30	5 .. 30	23	rise	12 .. 33	16
17	2		flying	6 .. 32	5 .. 28	♉ 7	6 .. 49	13 .. 23	17
18	3	St. Luke	Clouds	6 .. 33	5 .. 27	21	7 .. 24	14 .. 17	18
19	4		wind	6 .. 34	5 .. 26	♊ 5	8 .. 7	15 .. 15	19
20	5	♀ great elong., △ ☉ ♄		6 .. 35	5 .. 25	20	8 .. 56	16 .. 15	20
21	6		and rain	6 .. 36	5 .. 24	♋ 5	9 .. 52	17 .. 17	21
22	7	☉ enters ♏		6 .. 38	5 .. 22	20	10 .. 56	18 .. 19	22
23	B	22d. Sund. past Trin.		6 .. 39	5 .. 21	♌ 4	12 .. 2	19 .. 18	23
24	2		Cool	6 .. 40	5 .. 20	18	13 .. 9	20 .. 13	24
25	3	pleiades rise 6 .. 12	mornings,	6 .. 41	5 .. 19	♍ 2	14 .. 15	21 .. 5	25
26	4		falling	6 .. 42	5 .. 18	16	15 .. 20	21 .. 55	26
27	5			6 .. 44	5 .. 16	♎ 0	16 .. 24	22 .. 42	27
28	6	St. Simon and Jude		6 .. 45	5 .. 15	13	17 .. 27	23 .. 27	28
29	7		weather	6 .. 46	5 .. 14	26		6	29
30	B	☌ ☉ ☿ Orient. 23th. Sund. past Trin		6 .. 47	5 .. 13	♏ 9	Sets	0 .. 12	☽
31	2	Days 10 .. 24		6 .. 48	5 .. 12	22	6 .. 2	0 .. 56	1

1796 ☉ Long. in Novemb.	Logarithm ☉ a ⊕
d s ° '	
1—7-10..1	4.99606
7—7-16..3	4.99542
13—7.22..6	4.99483
19—7..28..11	4.99430
25—8 1..15	4.99383

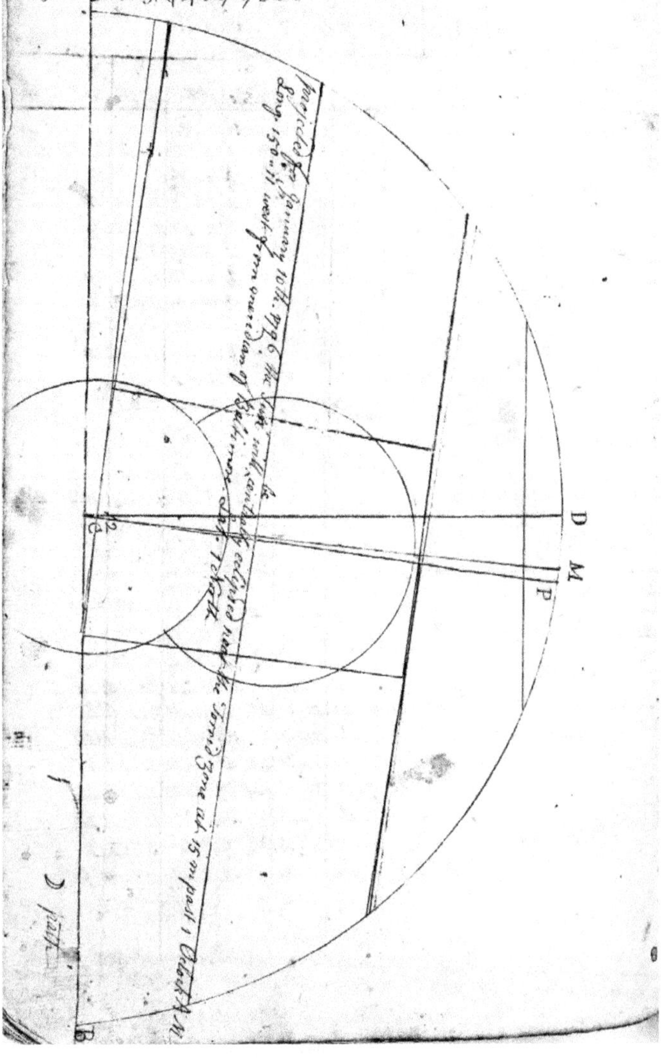

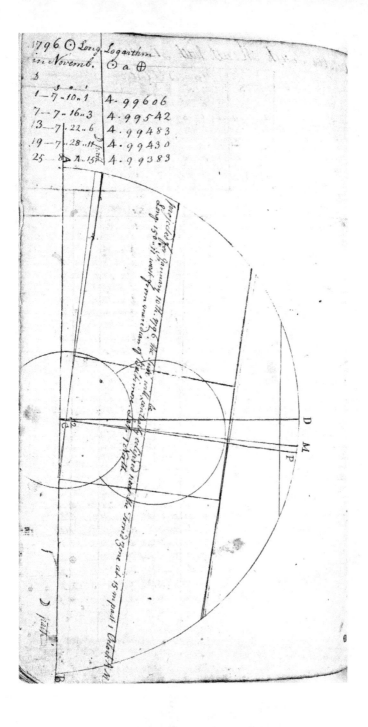

1796 November Eleventh Month hath 30 Days

	d	h	m	
First ☽	7 ..	1 ..	58	aft.
Full ○	14 ..	10 ..	25	aft.
Last ☽	21 ..	4 ..	3	aft.
New ☽	29 ..	5 ..	42	morn.

☊ { 1: 4; 11 ♋ 4; 21: 3 } deg.

Planets Places

D	☉	♄	♃	♂	♀	☿	☽
	♏	♊	♓	♒	♍	♏	Lat.
1	10	27	3	5	24	4	3 N.
7	16	27	3	9	♎ 1	6	3 S.
13	22	27	4	13	8	9	4 S.
19	28	27	4	18	15	13	2 N.
25	♐ 4	26	5	22	22	18	5 N.

M D	W D	Remarkable days Aspects weather &c.		☉ rise	☉ set	☽ place	☽ sets	☽ South	☽ age
1	3	All Saints		6..49	5..11	♐ 4	6..39	1..42	2
2	4	pleiades So. 1..8		6..51	5..9	16	7..18	2..30	3
3	5		windy	6..52	5..8	28	8..1	3..20	4
4	6	□ ♄ ♀	weather,	6..53	5..7	♑ 10	8..47	4..10	5
5	7		rain	6..54	5..6	22	9..36	5..0	6
6	B	24th. Sund. past Trin.		6..55	5..5	♒ 3	10..28	5..47	7
7	2	♀ rise 3..18	or	6..56	5..4	15	11..23	6..33	8
8	3	Sirius rise 10..37		6..57	5..3	27	12..22	7..19	9
9	4	☌ ☽ ♃	snow	6..58	5..2	♓ 9	13..22	8..4	10
10	5	Day Decrease 4..42		6..59	5..1	22	14..22	8..49	11
11	6	St. Martin		7..0	5..0	♈ 5	15..25	9..35	12
12	7		pleasant	7..1	4..59	18	16..31	10..22	13
13	B	25th. Sund. past Trin.		7..2	4..58	♉ 2		11..12	14
14	2		for	7..3	4..57	16	rise	12..5	15
15	3	Bulls eye South 1..5		7..4	4..56	♊ 0	6..0	13..1	16
16	4		the	7..5	4..55	15	6..47	14..1	17
17	5	♃ Sets 12..19		7..6	4..54	♋ 0	7..39	15..4	18
18	6		Season,	7..7	4..53	15	8..42	16..7	19
19	7		flying	7..8	4..52	♌ 0	9..47	17..7	20
20	B	26th. Sund. past Trin.		7..8	4..52	14	10..55	18..4	21
21	2		Clouds	7..9	4..51	28	12..3	18..58	22
22	3	☉ enters ♐		7..10	4..50	♍ 12	13..10	19..48	23
23	4		with	7..11	4..49	26	14..16	20..35	24
24	5	Days decrease 5..8		7..12	4..48	♎ 9	15..19	21..21	25
25	6		wind,	7..12	4..48	22	16..22	22..7	26
26	7		rain	7..13	4..47	♏ 5	17..25	22..53	27
27	B	Advent Sund.		7..14	4..46	18	18..25	23..38	28
28	2	Algol South 10..37	or	7..15	4..45	♐ 0		[illegible]	29
29	3		snow	7..15	4..45	12	Sets	0..23	☽
30	4	Days 9..28		7..16	4..44	24	5..46	1..7	2

1796 ☉ Long in Decemb D	Logarithm ☉ a ⊕
1—8..10..21	4.99342
7—8..16..26	4.99310
13—8..22..33	4.99285
19—8..28..40	4.99268
25—9..4..46	4.99260

Elements for projection of an eclipse of Moon Decem[illegible] 1796

True time of full Moon in December 1796	d h m 14..9..20
Moons Horizontal paralax	° 0..60.[illegible]
Suns Semidiameter	0..16.[illegible]
Moons Semidiameter	0..16.[illegible]
½ Earths Shadow at the Moon	0..44
Moons Latitude South Ascending	0..42
Angle of her visible path with ye eclipt.	5..35
Her true Horary Motion from the Sun	0..34

Elements for projecting an Eclips of Sun December 1796

True time of New Moon in Decemb. 1796 — d h m 29..1..3 A.M.

	° ′ ″
Semidiameter of the Earths disc	0..55..[illegible]
Suns distance from the nearest Solstice	9..[illegible]
Suns declination South	23..11..[illegible]
Moons Latitude South Descending	0..37..[illegible]
Moons Horary motion from the Sun	0..28..[illegible]
Angle of the Moons visible path with the Ecliptic	5..35..[illegible]
Suns Semidiameter	0..16
Moons Semediameter	0..15
Semediameter of the penumbra	0..31

1796 December Twelfth Month hath 31 Days

	d	h	m	
First ☽	7	6	50	morn.
Full ○	14	9	20	morn.
Last ☾	21	2	22	morn.
New ☽	29	1	3	morn.

☊ { 1 ♋ 3 / 11 2 / 21 2 } deg.

Planets Places

☽	☉	♄	♃	♂	♀	☿	☽'s Lat
	♐	♊	♓	♒	♎	♏	
1	10	26	5	26	29	27	0 S.
7	16	25	6	♓ 0	♏ 6	♐ 6	5 S.
13	23	25	7	5	13	15	2 S.
19	29	24	8	9	20	25	5 N
25	♑ 5	24	8	14	28	♑ 4	3 N

M D	W D	Remarkable days Aspects weather &c		☉ rise	☉ sets	☽'s place	☽ sets	☽ South	☽'s age
1	5	△ ♄ ♂		7..16	4..44	♑ 6	6..31	1..55	3
2	6			7..17	4..43	18	7..21	2..45	4
3	7		Cold	7..18	4..42	♒ 0	8..16	3..35	5
4	B	2d. Sund. in Advent		7..18	4..42	12	9..12	4..23	6
5	2		and	7..19	4..41	24	10..9	5..10	7
6	3	Nicholas, ☌ ☽ ♃		7..19	4..41	♓ 6	11..7	5..55	8
7	4	△ ♃ ♀	windy,	7..20	4..40	♓ 18	12..7	6..39	9
8	5	Concep V. Mary		7..20	4..40	♈ 1	13..9	7..23	10
9	6		with	7..20	4..40	♈ 14	14..11	8..8	11
10	7		snow	7..21	4..39	27	15..15	8..55	12
11	B	3d. Sund. in Advent		7..21	4..39	♉ 11	16..23	9..44	13
12	2		or	7..21	4..39	25	17..33	10..37	14
13	3		rain,	7..21	4..39	♊ 9		11..34	15
14	4	☽ eclip invis,		7..22	4..38	24	rise	12..35	16
15	5	☍ ☉ ♄ Occident.		7..22	4..38	♋ 9	6..13	13..38	17
16	6		Clear	7..22	4..38	24	7..18	14..42	18
17	7		and	7..22	4..38	♌ 9	8..27	15..42	19
18	B	4th Sund. in Advent		7..22	4..38	23	9..35	16..38	20
19	2	☌ ♂ ♃	Cold,	7..22	4..38	♍ 7	10..41	17..28	21
20	3	☉ enter ♑		7..22	4..38	21	11..47	18..15	22
21	4	Shortest days		7..22	4..38	♎ 5	12..52	19..1	23
22	5		with	7..22	4..38	18	13..55	19..46	24
23	6	Day 9..16		7..22	4..38	♏ 1	14..57	20..31	25
24	7		rain	7..22	4..38	14	15..59	21..16	26
25	B	Christmas ☌ ☉ ☿ Occident.		7..22	4..38	26	17..0	22..2	27
26	2	St. Stephen		7..22	4..38	♐ 8	17..58	22..48	28
27	3	St. John	or	7..22	4..38	20	18..55	23..35	29
28	4	Innocents		7..21	4..39	♑ 2		☌	30
29	5	☉ eclip. invis		7..21	4..39	♒ 14	sets	0..23	☽.. eclip. 1st
30	6		snow	7..21	4..39	26	5..0	1..12	2
31	7	Silvester		7..20	4..40	♒ 8	5..56	2..2	3

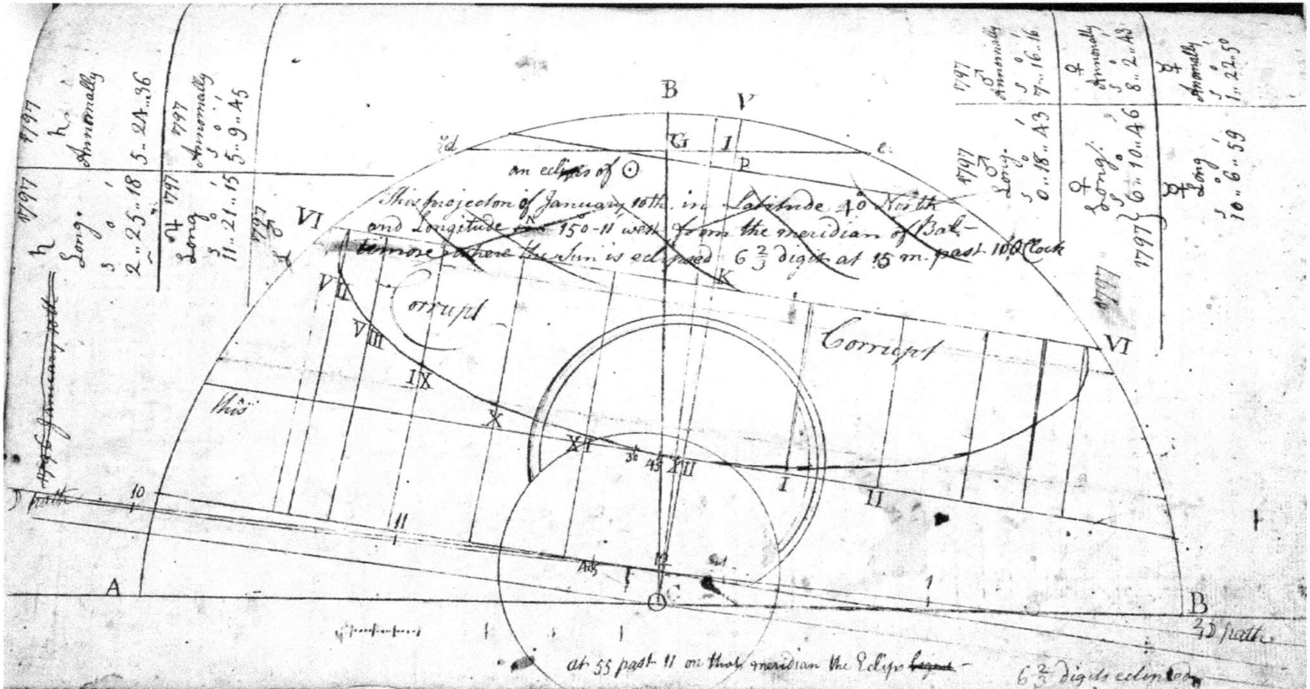

♄ 1797 Long.	♄ 1797 Annomally
s ° ′	
2 .. 25 .. 18	5 .. 24 .. 36

♃ 1797 Long	1797 Annomally
s ° ′	s ° ′
11 .. 21 .. 15	5 .. 9 .. 45

♂ 1797 Long.	♂ 1797 Annomally
s ° ′	s ° ′
0 .. 18 .. 43	7 .. 16 .. 16

♀ 1797 Long.	♀ Annomally
s °	s ° ′
6 .. 10 .. 46	8 .. 2 .. 43

☿ Long	☿ Anomally
s ° ′	s °
10 .. 6 .. 59	1 .. 22 .. 50

1797 January First Month hath 31 Days.

			Planets Places					
First ☽ 5..11..4 aft.	☽	☉	♄	♃	♂	♀	☿	☽'s
Full ○ 12..8..1 aft.		Long.	♊	♓	♓	♐	♑	Lat
Last ☾ 19..6..8 aft.	1	9..11..53	23	10	19	8	16	4 S.
New ☽ 27..8..38 aft	7	9..18..0	23	11	23	15	26	4 S.
	13	9..24..8	22	12	27	21	♒ 6	3 N.
☊ {1 ♋ 1; 11 ♊ 19; 21 ♊ 26} deg.	19	10..0..14	21	13	♈ 2	28	15	5 N
	25	10..6..20	21	14	6	♑ 6	24	1 S.

M D	W D	Remarkable days Aspects weather &c.		☉ rise	☉ sets	☽'s Long.	☽ sets	☽ South	☽'s age
1	A	Circumcision		7..20	4..40	10..20..16	8..8	2..50	4
2	2		high	7..20	4..40	11..2..25	9..8	3..37	5
3	3	☌ ☽ ♃ 11 ... 17.	and	7..20	4..40	11..14..47	10..10	4..22	6
4	4		wind	7..19	4..41	11..27..15	11..13	5..3	7
5	5		snow	7..19	4..41	0..10..0	12..16	5..48	8
6	6	Epiphany		7..18	4..42	0..23..4	13..19	6..33	9
7	7	□ ♄ ♂	or	7..18	4..42	1..6..25	14..22	7..20	10
8	A	1st. Sund past Epip.		7..17	4..43	1..20..14	15..29	8..12	11
9	2	Days increase 10 min.	cold	7..17	4..43	2..4..26	16..37	9..8	12
10	3		rain,	7..16	4..44	2..18..58	17..45	10..8	13
11	4	pleiades South 8..2		7..15	4..45	3..3..47		11..8	14
12	5		clear	7..15	4..45	3..18..46	rise	12..15	15
13	6		and	7..14	4..46	4..3..45	5..56	13..17	16
14	7	☍ ♄ ♀		7..13	4..47	4..18..34	7..9	14..15	17
15	A	2d. Sund. past Epip.		7..13	4..47	5..3..4	8..21	15..9	18
16	2		windy	7..12	4..48	5..17..12	9..31	15..58	19
17	3	Days increase		7..11	4..49	6..0..53	10..37	16..45	20
18	4	Sirius South 10..33		7..10	4..50	6..14..9	11..37	17..28	21
19	5	☉ enters ♒		7..10	4..50	6..27..1	12..37	18..13	22
20	6	♀ rise 5..10		7..9	4..51	7..9..35	13..37	18..58	23
21	7		snow	7..8	4..52	7..21..54	14..37	19..44	24
22	A	3d. Sund. past Epip.		7..7	4..53	8..4..3	15..36	20..3[illegible]	25
23	2		or	7..6	4..54	8..16..4	16..32	21..18	26
24	3		rain	7..5	4..55	8..28..2	17..26	22..9	27
25	4	□ ♂ ♀		7..4	4..56	9..9..58	18..18	22..59	28
26	5		cold	7..3	4..57	9..21..58		23..45	29
27	6	pleiades Set 2..22		7..2	4..58	10..4..3	Sets	6	☽
28	7		and	7..1	4..59	10..16..14	5..50	0..36	1
29	A	4th. Sund. past Epip.		7..0	5..0	10..28..30	6..51	1..22	2
30	2	☌ ☽ ♃	windy	6..59	5..1	11..10..57	7..53	2..6	3
31	3	Days 10..4	snow	6..58	5..2	11..23..31	8..55	2..51	4

A gentleman Sent his Servant with £100 to buy 100 Cattle, with order to
~~to~~ give £5 for each Bullock, 20 Shilling for cows, and one Shilling for
each Sheep; the question is to know what number of each Sort he brought
to his master

Aswer

19	Bullocks at 5£ each	£ 95
1	Cow at 20 S.	1
80	Sheep at 1 S each	4
100	proof	100

Eclipses for 1797

first	June	9	☽
Second	June	24	⊙
Third	Novem.	18	⊙
Fourth	Decemb	3	☽
Fifth	Decemb	18	⊙

Common Notes and moveable feasts for the year. 1797

Dominical Letter	A	Easter Sunday	April	1[illegible]
Cycle of the Sun	14	Ascension Day	May	2[illegible]
Golden Number	12	Whitsunday	June	4
Epact	1	Trinity Sunday	June	11
Number of Direction	26	Advent Sunday	Decemb	3

December 13th 1797 I Dreamed I saw some thing passing by my[illegible]
to and fro, and when I attempted to go ~~the~~ to the door, it would van[illegible]
and reapted it twice or three; at lenght I let in the infernal Spirit
he told me that he had been concerned with a woman by the name of Be[illegible]
Freeman (I never heard the name as I remember) by Some means w[illegible]
into a Skirmish, and I threw him behind the fire and endeavoured [illegible]
him up but all in vain — I know not what become of him but he was
ill formed being — Some part of him in Shape of a man, but ha[illegible]
as a beast, his feet was circular ~~[illegible]~~ or rather globular and did not exceed [illegible]
inch and a half in diameter, but while I held him in the fire he said some[illegible]
respecting he was able to Stand it, but I forget his words

B Banneker

1797 February Second Month hath 28 Days

	☽	☉	♄	♃	♂	♀	☿	☽'s
		Long.	♊	♓	♈	♑	♓	Lat.
First ☽ 4..0..36 aft.	1	10..13..26	22	16	11	14	1	5 S.
Full ○ 11..6..45 morn.	7	10..19..31	21	17	15	22	0	0 S.
Last ☽ 18..9..30 morn.	13	10..25..35	21	19	20	♒ 0	♒ 24	5 N.
New ☽ 26..2..41 aft.	19	11..1..38	21	20	24	7	18	1 N.
☊ { 1, 11, 21 } ♊ { 29, 29, 28 } deg.	25	11..7..40	21	22	28	13	16	4 S.

Planets Places

M D	W D	Remarkable days Aspects weather &c.	☉ rise	☉ set	☽'s Long.	☽ Sets	☽ South	☽'s age
1	4	Days increase 50 min.	6..57	5..3	0..6..18	9..57	3..34	5
2	5	purification V. M.	6..56	5..4	0..19..17	10..59	4..19	6
3	6	Snow	6..55	5..5	1..2..32	12..1	5..5	7
4	7	☿ Stationary or	6..54	5..6	1..16..2	13..6	5..51	8
5	A	5th. Sund. past Epip.	6..53	5..7	1..29..53	14..13	6..48	9
6	2	rain	6..52	5..8	2..14..1	15..23	7..46	10
7	3	moderate	6..51	5..9	2..28..28	16..27	8..48	11
8	4	♀ rise 5-25, △ ☉ ♄	6..50	5..10	3..13..10	17..29	9..52	12
9	5	for	6..49	5..11	3..28..1	18..24	10..54	13
10	6	Days 10..24 the	6..48	5..12	4..12..55		11..56	14
11	7	Season	6..46	5..14	4..27..41	rise	12..53	15
12	A	Septuagesima Sund.	6..45	5..15	5..12..12	7..11	13..47	16
13	2	☌ ☉ ☿ orient.	6..44	5..16	5..26..21	8..17	14..36	17
14	3	Valentine	6..43	5..17	6..10..3	9..22	15..22	18
15	4	wind	6..42	5..18	6..23..20	10..26	16..8	19
16	5	and	6..40	5..20	7..6..11	11..29	16..53	20
17	6	pleiades set 12..57	6..39	5..21	7..18..40	12..29	17..39	21
18	7	☉ enters ♓	6..38	5..22	8..0..53	13..27	18..26	22
19	A	Sexagesima Sund.	6..36	5..24	8..12..52	14..22	19..13	23
20	2	Snow,	6..35	5..25	8..24..40	15..15	20..1	24
21	3	□ ♄ ♃	6..34	5..26	9..6..24	16..4	20..49	25
22	4	flying	6..33	5..27	9..18..13	16..48	21..38	26
23	5		6..32	5..28	10..0..5	17..28	22..26	27
24	6	St. Matthias Clouds,	6..31	5..29	10..12..5	18..4	23..14	28
25	7		6..30	5..30	10..24..16		☌	29
26	A	Quinqua. Sund.	6..28	5..32	11..6..39	Sets	0..2	☽
27	2	☌ ☽ ♃ moderate	6..27	5..33	11..19..14	6..48	0..49	1
28	3	Shrove Tues. weather	6..26	5..34	0..2..5	7..49	1..33	2

Venus (♀) will be morning Star untill the first day of June, and evening Star from that time to the end of the Year.

Five Eclipses for the Year 1797, three of the Sun, and two of the Moon

First of Moon June 9th. at 6 h. 30 m. in the morning, of which a very small portion will be Seen at Baltimore; the moon descends the western horizon a few min. after her eastern limb begins to immerge into the Earths dark shadow — the Moon is 15¼ digits eclipsed 98° west from Baltimore

Second is of the Sun June the 24th. invisible at Baltimore, ☌ at 11 h. 25 m. ☉ is 5¼ digits eclipsed on the Meridian in Long. 9° East from Baltimore and Lat. ~~66°~~ 36 North, in or near the Artic circle. This eclips is not central to any part of the globe — NB the Sun is near 6 digit eclips'd, at

~~Third is of the Sun November the 18th in the morning visible at Baltimore~~

~~Beginning at 7 .. 44 } A.M.~~
~~Middle - - - 9 .. 2~~
~~End - - - 10 .. 20 Digits 9⅔ eclipsed on~~
~~Duration - 2 .. 36 the Suns North Limb~~

Fourth is a total and visible eclips of the Moon December the third and part of the fourth day

	h .. m	
Beginning at - - - - -	9 .. 39	} - - - P.M
Beginning of total darkness - -	10 .. 9	
Middle of the eclips - - - -	11 .. 27	
End of total darkness - - - -	0 .. 45	} 4th day - - A.M
End of the eclips - - - - -	1 .. 15	
Duration of total darkness - - -	2 .. 36	
Duration of this eclips - - - -	3 .. 36	
Digits eclipsed - - - -	20 - -	

Fifth and last is of the Sun Decemb. 18th. invisible at Baltimore, ☌ at the A.M, ☉ is 3⅔ digits eclipsed on his South Limb in Long. 155° 15' East from Baltimore, and Lat 40 South —

1797 March Third Month hath 31 Days

	D	h	m	
First ☽	5	10	18	aft.
Full ○	12	5	33	aft.
Last ☽	20	4	13	morn.
New ☽	28	5	59	morn.

☊			
1	♊	28	deg.
11		27	
21		27	

Planets Places

D	☉ Long.	♄ ♊	♃ ♓	♂ ♉	♀ ♒	☿ ♒	☽ Lat.
1	11..11..39	21	23	1	19	17	5 S.
7	11..17..39	21	24	5	26	21	1 N.
13	11..23..39	21	25	9	♓ 4	26	5 N.
19	11..29..36	21	26	13	11	♓ 3	0 N.
25	0..5..33	22	28	17	19	13	5 S.

M D	W D	Remarkable days Aspects weather &c	☉ rise	☉ sets	☽ Long.	☽ sets	☽ South	☽ age
1	A	Ash wednesday St. David	6..24	5..36	0..15..9	8..51	2..16	3
2	5	cold	6..23	5..37	0..28..27	9..54	3..3	4
3	6	Day increase 2 h.	6..22	5..38	1..11..58	10..58	3..52	5
4	7	wind	6..21	5..39	1..25..41	12..5	4..44	6
5	A	1st. Sund. in Lent	6..19	5..41	2..9..30	13..15	5..42	7
6	2	and	6..17	5..43	2..23..50	14..19	6..42	8
7	3	△ ♄ ☿	6..16	5..44	3..9..14	15..19	7..42	[illegible]
8	4	snow	6..14	5..46	3..22..[illegible]	16..15	8..42	10
9	5	♄ Set 10..39	6..13	5..47	4..7..28	17..2	9..41	11
10	6	moderate	6..12	5..48	4..22..8	17..41	10..39	12
11	7	weather ~~[illegible]~~	6..11	5..49	5..6..44		11..35	13
12	A	2d. Sund. in Lent; Gregory	6..9	5..51	5..21..9	rise	12..30	14
13	2	☿ great elong.	6..8	5..52	6..5..13	7..15	13..20	15
14	3	cold	6..7	5..53	6..18..56	8..20	14..7	16
15	4	rain	6..6	5..54	7..2..14	9..25	14..54	17
16	5	with	6..4	5..56	7..15..8	10..27	15..41	18
17	6	St. patrick,	6..3	5..57	7..27..35	11..29	16..28	19
18	7	wind	6..2	5..58	8..9..46	12..24	17..15	20
19	A	3d. Sund. in Lent. D= Night	6..0	6..0	8..21..40	13..16	18..2	21
20	2	[illegible] [☉ enters ♈	5..59	6..1	9..3..24	14..6	18..52	22
21	3		5..58	6..2	9..15..4	14..55	19..41	23
22	4	Sirius South 6..29	5..57	6..3	9..26..43	15..35	20..30	24
23	5	pleasant	5..55	6..5	10..8..28	16..11	21..18	25
24	6	weather	5..54	6..6	10..20..27	16..47	22..5	26
25	7	Annunciation V. M.	5..53	6..7	11..2..27	17..19	22..51	27
26	A	4th Sund. in Lent	5..52	6..8	11..14..52	17..44	23..36	28
27	2	☌ ☽ ♃	5..50	6..10	11..27..31		☌	29
28	3		5..49	6..11	0..10..31	sets	0..21	☽
29	4	rain	5..48	6..12	0..23..49	7..52	1..7	2
30	5	toward the	5..46	6..14	1..7..25	8..56	1..54	3
31	6	Day 12..30 end	5..45	6..15	1..21..16	10..0	2..43	4

A Table of Declination to the nearest Degree, which is Sufficient for an Annual Ephemeris

D	♈	♉	♊	♋	♌	♍	♎	♏	♐	♑	♒	♓
0	0	12	20	23½	20	12	0	12	20	23½	20	12
1	0	12	20	23½	20	11	0	12	20	23½	20	11
2	0	12	21	23½	20	11	1	12	21	23½	20	11
3	1	13	21	23	20	10	1	13	21	23	20	10
4	2	13	21	23	19	10	2	13	21	23	19	10
5	2	14	21	23	19	10	2	13	21	23	19	10
6	2	14	21	23	19	9	2	14	21	23	19	9
7	3	14	22	23	19	9	3	14	22	23	19	9
8	3	14	22	23	18	9	3	14	22	23	18	9
9	4	14	22	23	18	8	4	15	22	23	18	8
10	4	15	22	23	18	8	4	15	22	23	18	8
11	4	15	22	23	18	7	4	15	22	23	18	7
12	5	15	22	23	17	7	5	15	22	23	17	7
13	5	16	22	23	17	7	5	16	22	23	17	7
14	6	16	23	23	17	6	6	16	23	23	17	6
15	6	16	23	23	16	6	6	16	23	23	16	6
16	6	17	22	23	16	6	6	17	23	23	16	6
17	7	17	23	22	16	5	7	17	23	22	16	5
18	7	17	23	22	15	5	7	17	23	22	15	5
19	7	18	23	22	15	4	7	18	23	22	15	4
20	8	18	23	22	15	4	8	18	23	22	15	4
21	8	18	23	22	15	4	8	18	23	22	15	4
22	9	18	23	22	14	3	9	18	23	22	14	3
23	9	19	23	22	14	3	9	19	23	22	14	3
24	9	19	23	21	14	2	9	19	23	21	14	2
25	10	19	23	21	13	2	10	19	23	21	13	2
26	10	19	23	21	13	2	10	19	23	21	13	2
27	10	20	23	21	13	1	10	20	23½	21	13	1
28	11	20	23½	21	12	1	11	20	23½	21	12	1
29	11	20	23½	20	12	0	11	20	23½	20	12	0
30	12	20	23½	20	12	0	12	20	23½	20	12	0

April Fourth Month hath 30 Days

	D	h	m	
First ☽	4	5	45	morn.
Full ○	11	4	54	morn.
Last ☾	18	10	52	aft.
New ☽	26	6	1[illegible]	aft.

☊			
1	♊	26	deg.
11	♊	26	deg.
21		25	deg.

Planets Places

	☉	♄	♃	♂	♀	☿	☽'s
	Long.	♊	♓	♉	♓	♓	Lat.
1	0..12.27	23	29	22	27	23	2S.
7.	0..18..20	23	♈ 1	26	♈ 5	♈ 3	5N.
13	0..24..13	23	2	♊ 1	12	14	3N.
19	1..0..4	24	4	5	19	26	3S.
25	1..5..55	24	5	9	27	♉ 9	5S.

M D	W D	Remarkable days Aspects weather &c.	☉ rise	☉ set	☽'s Long.	☽ sets	☽ South	☽'s age
1	7	□ ♄ ☿	5..44	6..16	2..5..18	11..4	3..38	5
2	A	5th. Sund. in Lent.	5..43	6..17	2..19..29	12..12	4..38	6
3	2	cool	5..41	6..19	3..3..47	13..15	5..38	7
4	3	St. Ambrose breezes	5..40	6..20	3..18..11	14..13	6..39	8
5	4	from	5..39	6..21	4..2..36	15..5	7..40	9
6	5	Sirius Set 10..38	5..38	6..22	4..17..6	15..50	8..39	10
7	6	the	5..36	6..24	5..1..32	16..28	9..37	11
8	7	west,	5..35	6..25	5..15..52	17..1	10..29	12
9	A	Palm Sund.	5..34	6..26	6..0..3	17..32	11..18	13
10	2	fine	5..33	6..27	6..13..58		12..6	14
11	3	Days 12..56	5..32	6..28	6..27..34	rise	12..54	15
12	4	showers	5..30	6..30	7..10..50	8..24	13..42	16
13	5	of	5..29	6..31	7..23..42	9..27	14..30	17
14	6	Good Fryday	5..28	6..32	8..6..15	10..25	15..18	18
15	7	rain	5..27	6..33	8..18..27	11..20	16..6	19
16	A	Easter-Sund.	5..26	6..34	9..0..23	12..12	16..55	20
17	2	Easter-Mond.	5..25	6..35	9..12..7	12..59	17..44	21
18	3	Easter-Tuesd.	5..23	6..37	9..23..47	13..41	18..33	22
19	4	☉ enters ♉	5..22	6..38	10..5..25	14..19	19..22	23
20	5	pleasant	5..21	6..39	10..17..6	14..53	20..9	24
21	6	Days increase 4..4	5..20	6..40	10..28..54	15..25	20..54	25
22	7	weather	5..18	6..42	11..10..56	15..51	21..38	26
23	A	☌ ☉ ☿ Occident. St. George	5..17	6..43	11..23..16	16..19	22..21	27
24	2	☌ ☽ ♃ (1 Sund. past E.	5..16	6..44	0..5..57	16..47	23..5	28
25	3	St. Mark.	5..15	6..45	0..19..0		23..53	29
26	4	now	5..14	6..46	1..2..28	Set	☌	☽
27	5	Pleiades Set 8..38	5..13	6..47	1..16..16	7..57	0..43	1
28	6	expect	5..12	6..48	2..0..25	8..57	1..32	2
29	7	rain	5..11	6..49	2..14..45	10..4	2..31	3
30	A	2d. Sund. past East.	5..10	6..50	2..29..14	11..8	3..31	4

1797 ~~the D~~ ~~great N.~~ ~~L. Lat.~~

Second eclipse is of the Sun June 24 invisible at Baltimore
& at 11h. 25m A.M, ☉ is 5 1/4 digits eclipsed on the meridian in
9° east from Baltimore and Lat 66 1/2 North, in or near the Artic
N.B. this Eclipse is not central to any part of the Earth

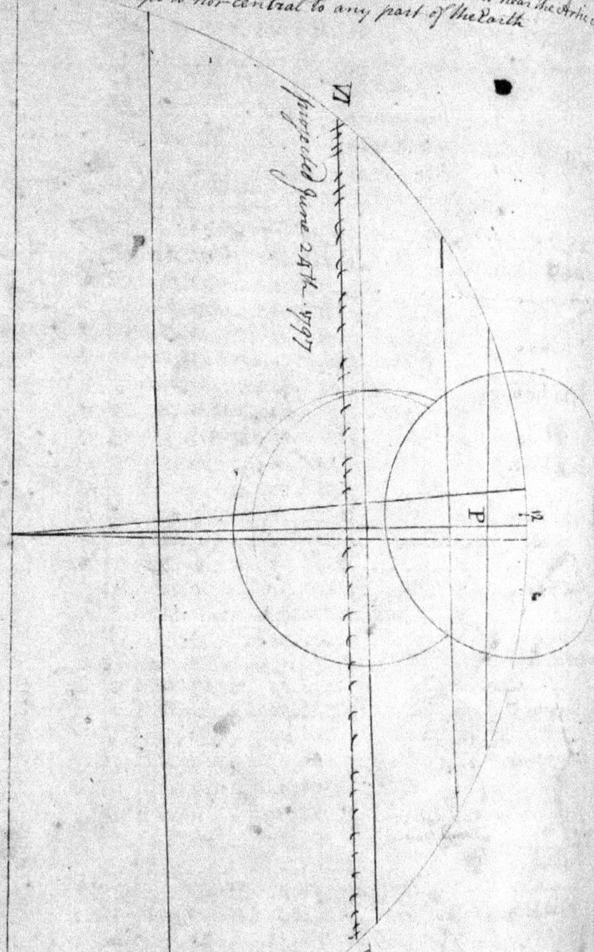

5 1/4 Digits eclipsed

1707 May Fifth Month hath 31 Days.

	d	h	m	
First ☽	3	1	50	aft.
Full ○	10	5	10	aft.
Last ☾	18	4	37	aft.
New ☽	26	3	44	morn.

☊			
1		25	deg.
11	♊	24	deg.
21		24	deg.

Planets Places

☽	☉	♄	♃	♂	♀	☿	☽'s
	Long.	♊	♈	♊	♉	♉	Lat.
1	1..11..45	25	7	13	4	21	2 N.
7	1..17..32	25	8	17	12	♊ 4	5 N.
13	1..23..20	26	10	21	19	13	2 S.
19	1..29..6	27	11	25	27	22	5 S.
25	2..4..52	27	12	29	♊ 4	28	1 S.

M D	W D	Remarkable days, Aspects, weather &c.	☉ rise	☉ set	☽'s Long.	☽ set	☽ South	☽'s age
1	2	philip and James	5..9	6..51	3..13..45	12..9	4..34	5
2	3	pleasant	5..8	6..52	3..28..10	13..5	5..35	6
3	4	Spica ♍ South 10..33	5..7	6..53	4..12..34	13..51	6..36	7
4	5	Showers	5..5	6..55	4..26..56	14..30	7..33	8
5	6	fine	5..4	6..56	5..11..7	15..4	8..25	9
6	7	St John Evang.	5..3	6..57	5..25..15	15..34	9..15	10
7	A	3d. Sund past East.	5..2	6..58	6..9..3	16..2	10..3	11
8	2	growing	5..1	6..59	6..22..43	16..30	10..50	12
9	3	pleiades Set 7..52	5..0	7..0	7..6..6		11..36	13
10	4	weather	4..59	7..1	7..19..43	rise	12..24	14
11	5	Days 14..4	4..58	7..2	8..2..2	8..19	13..14	15
12	6	warm	4..58	7..2	8..14..36	9..16	14..5	16
13	7	and pleasant	4..57	7..3	8..26..46	10..10	14..56	17
14	A	4th Sund. past East;	4..56	7..4	9..8..53	11..0	15..46	18
15	2	Cloudy	4..55	7..5	9..20..44	11..45	16..36	19
16	3	Days increase 4..56	4..54	7..6	10..2..26	12..25	17..24	20
17	4	with rain	4..53	7..7	10..14..7	13..0	18..9	21
18	5	Arcturus South 10..24	4..52	7..8	10..25..52	13..29	18..53	22
19	6	flying	4..52	7..8	11..7..39	13..54	19..35	23
20	7	☉ enters ♊	4..51	7..9	11..19..41	14..18	20..17	24
21	A	Rogation Sund.	4..50	7..10	0..1..58	14..44	20..59	25
22	2	☌☽♃ Clouds	4..49	7..11	0..14..39	15..12	21..43	26
23	3	and	4..48	7..12	0..27..42	15..43	22..31	27
24	4	wind	4..48	7..12	1..11..13	16..19	23..23	28
25	5	☿ great elong, Ascen. day	4..47	7..13	1..25..7		☌	29
26	6	now	4..46	7..14	2..9..23	set	0..19	☽
27	7	expect	4..46	7..14	2..23..58	8..56	1..19	2
28	A	Sund past Ascencion	4..45	7..15	3..8..39	9..56	2..19	3
29	2	rain	4..44	7..16	3..23..24	10..51	3..23	4
30	3	Days 14..32	4..44	7..16	4..8..2	11..40	4..23	5
31	4	Arcturus South 9..32	4..43	7..17	4..22..32	12..23	5..22	6

The Elements for an eclips of the Moon June 9th 1797

~~Mount~~ True time of full Moon in June 1797	D h m 9 .. 6 .. 30
Moons Horizontal parallax	° ′ ″ 0 .. 56 .. 29.
Suns Semidiameter	0 .. 15 .. 56.
Moons Semidiameter	0 .. 15 .. 26.
Semidiameter of ⊕ Shadow at D	0 .. 40 .. 43
Moons true Latitude North Descending	0 .. 19 .. 15
Angle of her visible path with the Ecliptic	5 .. 35 ..
Her true horary motion fr the Sun	29 .. 53

The Elements for an eclips of the Sun June 24th 1797

True time of New Moon in June 1797	24 .. 11 .. 25 r
Semidiameter of the Earths disc	° ′ ″ 1 .. 0 .. 11 r
Suns distance from the nearest Solstice	3 .. 8 .. 42
Suns declination North	23 .. 26 .. 0 r
Moons Latitude North Ascending	0 .. 59 .. 23 r
Moons Horary motion from the Sun	0 .. 34 .. 36 r
Angle of the Moons visible path with the ecliptic	5 .. 35 ..
Suns Semidiameter	0 .. 15 .. 53
Moons Semidiameter	0 .. 16 .. 31
Semidiameter of the penumbra	0 .. 32 .. 24

Eclipses for the Year 1797 for London, five in Numb. three of ~~the~~ Sun and two of the Moon –

The first is of the Moon, June the 9th. at 11h .. 30m in the morning invis London –

Second is a visible eclips of the Sun June 24th. true time of conjunction at 4h .. 25m

Beginning	h m 4 .. 40	P. M
Greatest obscuration	5 .. 30	
End	6 .. 19	Digits eclipsed near 6
Duration	1 .. 39	the Suns North Limb

Third of the Sun visible at London November the 18th at 2h .. 33m P. M.

Beginning	h m 1 .. 34	P. M
Greatest Obscuration	2 .. 50	
The End	4 .. 5	Digits Eclipsed 11 on the
Whole Duration	2 .. 31	Suns North Limb.

Fourth is a visible and total eclips of the Moon Decemb. 4th. 4h .. 24m A

Beginning at	2h .. 36m	Duration of total darkness
Beginning of total darkness	3 .. 34	Duration of this eclips
Middle of the eclips	4 .. 24	Digits eclipsed
End of total darkness	5 .. 14	See right hand page
End of the Eclipse	6 .. 12	5th Eclips

1797 June Sixth Month hath 30 Days

	d	h	m	
First ☽	2	1	8..9	aft.
Full ○	9	6	30	morn.
Last ☽	17	7	0	morn.
New ☽	24	11	25	morn.

☊ { 1 — 23; 11 II 22; 21 — 22 } deg.

Planets Places							
D	☉ Long.	♄ II	♃ ♈	♂ ♋	♀ II	☿ ♋	☽ Lat.
1	2..11..34	28	13	3	12	1	5 N.
7	2..17..18	♋ 0	14	7	20	1	2 N.
13	2..23..2	1	15	11	27	II 28	4 S.
19	2..28..46	1	16	15	♋ 5	25	4 S.
25	3..4..8	2	17	19	12	22	2 N.

M D	W D	Remarkable days Aspects weather &c.	☉ rise	☉ set	☽ Long.	☽ sets	☽ South	☽ age
1	5	☌☉♀ Occident.	4..43	7..17	5..6..48	13..1	6..17	7
2	6	thunder	4..42	7..18	5..20..49	13..33	7..7	8
3	7	gusts and	4..42	7..18	6..4..39	14..1	7..55	9
4	A	Whit-Sund	4..41	7..19	6..18..12	14..28	8..41	10
5	2	Whit-Mond rain,	4..41	7..19	7..1..32	14..56	9..27	11
6	3	Whit-Tuesd	4..41	7..19	7..14..39	15..27	10..13	12
7	4	~~flying~~	4..40	7..20	7..27..33	16..0	11..1	13
8	5		4..40	7..20	8..10..15		11..52	14
9	6	☽ eclip South 5..55	4..40	7..20	8..22..42	rise	12..43	15
10	7	Clouds	4..39	7..21	9..4..58	8..48	13..34	16
11	A	Trinity Sund. Barnabas	4..39	7..21	9..17..5	9..33	14..24	17
12	2		4..39	7..21	9..29..3	10..14	15..14	18
13	3	Spica ♍ set 1..18	4..39	7..21	10..11..0	10..51	16..2	19
14	4	clear	4..39	7..21	10..22..49	11..24	16..48	20
15	5	and warm,	4..38	7..22	11..4..36	11..53	17..30	21
16	6	☌☉☿ Orient.	4..38	7..22	11..16..31	12..16	18..11	22
17	7	St. Alban	4..38	7..22	11..28..36	12..42	18..53	23
18	A	1st. Sund past Trin. ☌☽♃	4..38	7..22	0..10..57	13..11	19..36	24
19	2	thunder &	4..38	7..22	0..23..37	13..42	20..21	25
20	3	Longes day rain	4..38	7..22	1..6..41	14..14	21..9	26
21	4		4..38	7..22	1..20..14	14..48	22..2	27
22	5	☌☉♄ Orient.	4..38	7..22	2..4..8	15..28	23..1	28
23	6		4..38	7..22	2..18..29		☌	29
24	7	Nativity St. John, ☉ eclip	4..38	7..22	3..3..8	set	0..3	☽
25	A	2d. Sund. past Trin	4..38	7..22	3..18..3	8..38	1..5	2
26	2	windy,	4..38	7..22	4..2..56	9..26	2..6	3
27	3	flying	4..38	7..22	4..17..44	10..10	3..5	4
28	4	Clouds.	4..38	7..22	5..2..20	10..50	4..1	5
29	5	St. peter and paul	4..39	7..21	5..16..37	11..24	4..54	6
30	6	rain	4..39	7..21	6..0..35	11..52	5..43	7

Fifth and last Eclipse is of the Sun December 18th at 6 h ..38 m A.M. invisible at London —

[illegible]

at Baltimore; because the Moon, a few minutes after her eastern Limb begins to immerge into the Earths Shadow,

The Moon is 15 ½ digits eclipsed 98 west from Baltimore

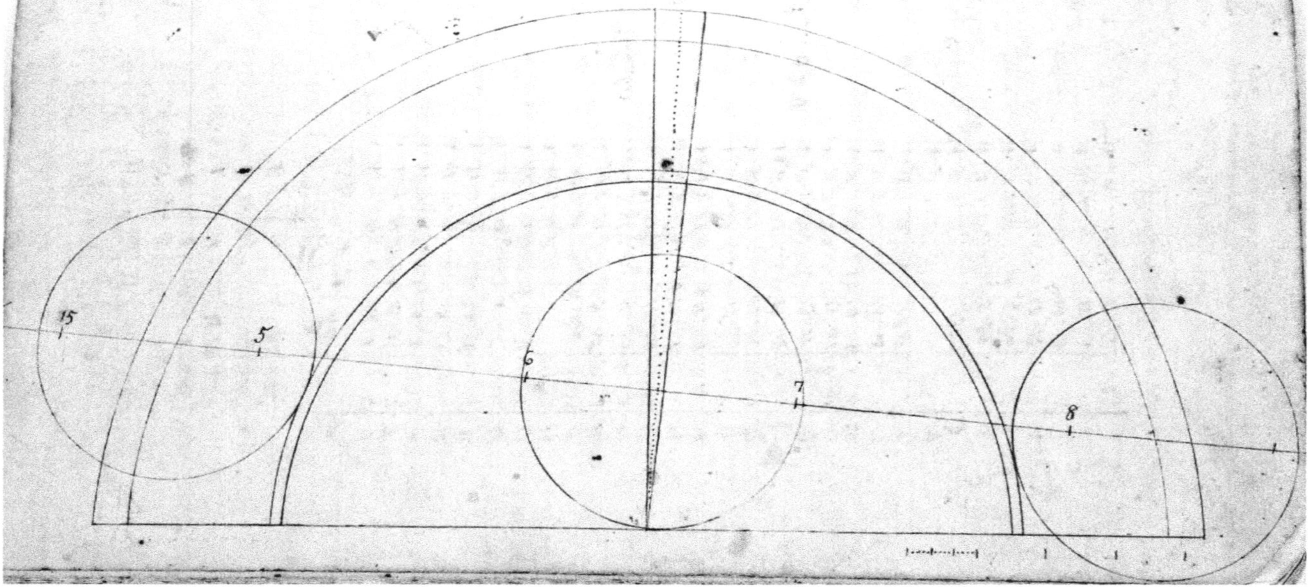

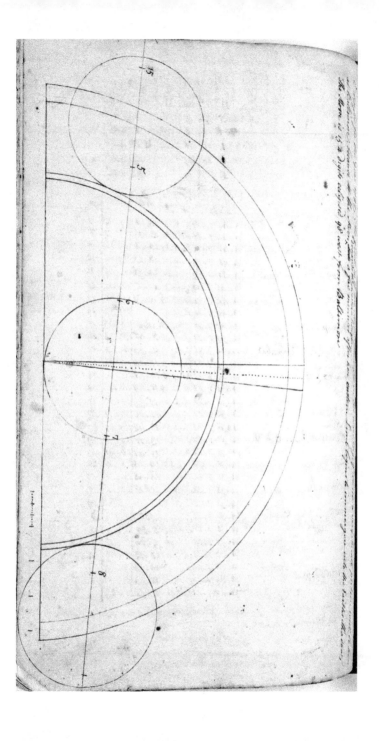

1797. # July Seventh Month hath 31 Days.

	d	h	m	
First ☽	1	3	11	morn.
Full ○	8	9	2	aft.
Last ☽	16	8	8	aft.
New ☽	23	6	19	aft.
First ☽	30	1	57	aft.

☊ { 1, 11, 21 } ♊ { 21, 21, 20 } deg.

Planets Places.							
☽	☉	♄	♃	♂	♀	☿	☽'s
	Long.	♋	♈	♋	♋	♊	Lat.
1	3..10..11	2	18	23	19	22	5 N.
7	3..15..55	3	18	27	26	26	1 S.
13	3..21..39	4	19	♌ 0	♌ 4	♋ 1	5 S.
19	3..27..22	5	19	4	11	10	2 S.
25	4..3..7	5	19	8	19	21	5 N.

M D	W D	Remarkable days Aspects weather &c.	☉ rise	☉ set	☽'s Long.	☽ set	☽ South	☽'s age
1	7	wet.	4..39	7..21	6..14..10	12..20	6..29	8
2	A	3d. Sund past Trin, visitation	4..40	7..20	6..27..30	12..46	7..14	9
3	2	(V. M	4..40	7..20	7..10..32	13..16	8..0	10
4	3	Trans. St. Martin	4..40	7..20	7..23..21	13..51	8..47	11
5	4	harvest	4..41	7..19	8..5..59	14..30	9..36	12
6	5	Days decrease 6 min.	4..41	7..19	8..18..27	15..13	10..27	13
7	6	in	4..42	7..18	9..0..46		11..19	14
8	7	some	4..42	7..18	9..12..59	rise	12..9	15
9	A	4th Sund. past Trin.	4..43	7..17	9..25..6	8..4	12..59	16
10	2	places,	4..43	7..17	10..7..10	8..44	13..49	17
11	3	Days 14..32	4..44	7..16	10..19..9	9..19	14..37	18
12	4	thunder	4..44	7..16	11..1..9	9..49	15..21	19
13	5	☿ great elong [illegible]	4..45	7..15	11..13..12	10..14	16..2	20
14	6	gusts	4..45	7..15	11..25..19	10..39	16..44	21
15	7	and	4..46	7..14	0..7..34	11..4	17..28	22
16	A	5th Sund. past Trin. ☌ ☽ ♃	4..47	7..13	0..20..4	11..32	18..11	23
17	2	rain	4..47	7..13	1..2..50	12..0	18..57	24
18	3	Lyra South 10..39	4..48	7..12	1..15..56	12..34	19..47	25
19	4	Clear	4..49	7..11	1..29..28	13..17	20..42	26
20	5	Margaret and	4..49	7..11	2..13..23	14..10	21..44	27
21	6	warm,	4..50	7..10	2..27..43	15..8	22..47	28
22	7	Magdalen. ☉ enters ♌	4..51	7..9	3..12..24		23..50	29
23	A	6th. Sund. past Trin.	4..52	7..8	3..27..20	sets	☌	☽
24	2	windy,	4..53	7..7	4..12..19	8..5	0..51	1
25	3	St. James △ ♃ ♀	4..54	7..6	4..27..13	8..43	1..49	2
26	4	St. Anne rain	4..54	7..6	5..11..53	9..18	2..43	3
27	5	toward	4..55	7..5	5..26..13	9..50	3..32	4
28	6	the	4..56	7..4	6..10..9	10..19	4..21	5
29	7	end	4..57	7..3	6..23..42	10..46	5..6	6
30	A	7th. Sund. past Trin, Dog	4..58	7..2	7..6..50	11..14	5..52	7
31	2	(days begin	4..59	7..1	7..19..41	11..46	6..39	8

True time of New Moon at London in May 1797 } d h m 26..8..43 A.M

Semidiameter of the Earths disc — — — ° ′ ″ 0..59..8

Suns distance from the nearest Solstice — — — 24..9..0

Suns declination North — — — 21..15..0

Moons Horary motion from the Sun D's Lat. S.A. — — — 1..33..0

Angle of the Moons visible path with the Ecliptic — — — 0..35..44

Suns Semidiameter — — — 5..35..0

Moons Semidiameter — — —

Semidiameter of the penumbra

A Chronological Observation

1796 March 8 Snow, Moon in ♓ her Latitude South.
march 14th Thunder and rain Moon in ♊ her Lat South
16th high wind Moon &c

1797 August Eighth Month hath 31 Days

	☽	☉	♄	♃	♂	♀	☿	☽'s
Full ☉ 7..1..50 aft. (d. h. m.)		Long.	♋	♈	♌	♌	♌	Lat.
Last ☾ 15..[illegible]..17 morn.	1	4..9..49	6	19	12	27	4	2 N.
New ☽ 22..2..26 morn.	7	4..15..33	7	20	16	♍ 5	18	4 S.
First ☾ 29..1..26 morn.	13	4..21..18	8	20	20	12	29	4 S.
☊ { 1, 11, 21 } ♊ { 20, 19, 19 } deg.	19	4..27..5	8	20	24	19	♍ 10	3 N.
	25	5..2..53	9	20	28	27	20	4 N.

M D	W D	Remarkable days Aspects weathers &c		☉ rise	☉ set	☽ Long.	☽ sets	☽ south	☽'s age
1	3	Lammas day		5..0	7..0	8..2..14	12..22	7..29	9
2	4			5..1	6..59	8..14..35	13..3	8..19	10
3	5	♃ South 11..36		5..2	6..58	8..26..49	13..51	9..8	11
4	6		very	5..3	6..57	9..8..56	14..43	9..57	12
5	7	☌ ☉ ☿ Occident.		5..4	6..56	9..21..0	15..37	10..46	13
6	A	8th Sund. past Trin. Transfig.		5..5	6..55	10..3..2		11..35	14
7	2	☌ ☉ ♂ Orient.		5..6	6..54	10..15..7	rise	12..24	15
8	3		warm	5..7	6..53	10..27..12	7..47	13..12	16
9	4		and	5..8	6..52	11..9..22	8..13	13..58	17
10	5	[illegible]. St. Lawrence		5..9	6..51	11..21..38	8..40	14..44	18
11	6		gusty.	5..10	6..50	0..3..59	9..8	15..27	19
12	7	☌ ☽ ♃		5..11	6..49	0..16..31	9..38	16..11	20
13	A	9th Sund. past Trin. △ ♃ ♂		5..12	6..48	0..29..12	10..7	16..56	21
14	2		rain	5..13	6..47	1..12..10	10..38	17..43	22
15	3	Spica ♍ Set 9..1		5..14	6..46	1..25..25	11..12	18..32	23
16	4		and	5..15	6..45	2..8..59	11..56	19..29	24
17	5	Days decrease 1..16		5..16	6..44	2..22..54	12..50	20..31	25
18	6		wind	5..18	6..42	3..7..11	13..54	21..34	26
19	7			5..19	6..41	3..21..48	15..6	22..37	27
20	A	10th Sund. past Trin.		5..20	6..40	4..6..39	16..8	23..39	28
21	2		clear	5..21	6..39	4..21..36		☌	29
22	3	☉ enters ♍		5..22	6..38	5..6..30	Set.	0..37	☽
23	4		great	5..23	6..37	5..21..12	7..53	1..28	2
24	5	St. Bartholomew		5..24	6..36	6..5..35	8..21	2..17	3
25	6		dews	5..26	6..34	6..19..31	8..50	3..5	4
26	7			5..27	6..33	7..3..2	9..21	3..53	5
27	A	11th. Sund. past Trin.		5..28	6..32	7..16..8	9..54	4..41	6
28	2	St. Augustine	thunder	5..29	6..31	7..28..49	10..29	5..29	7
29	3	St. John Bap. beheaded	and	5..30	6..30	8..11..14	11..8	6..18	8
30	4		rain	5..32	6..28	8..23..22	11..52	7..8	9
31	5	Days 12..54		5..33	6..27	9..5..23	12..42	7..59	10

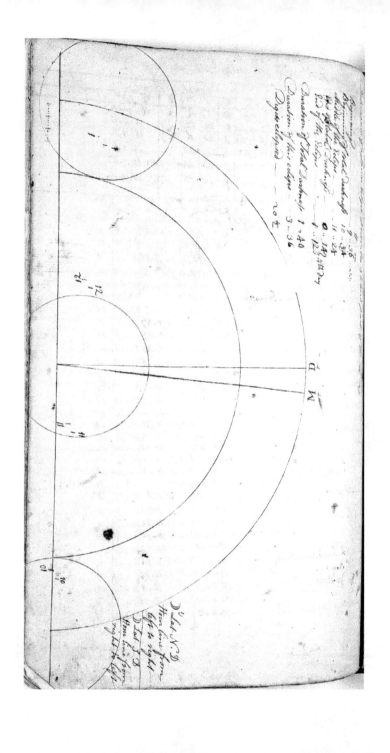

Beginning	9 .. 36
Beginning of total darkness	10 .. 34
Middle of the Eclips	11 .. 24
End of total Darkness	0 .. 14
End of the Eclips	1 .. 12

4th day

Duration of Total Darkness	1 .. 40
Duration of this eclips	3 .. 36
Digits eclipsed	20½

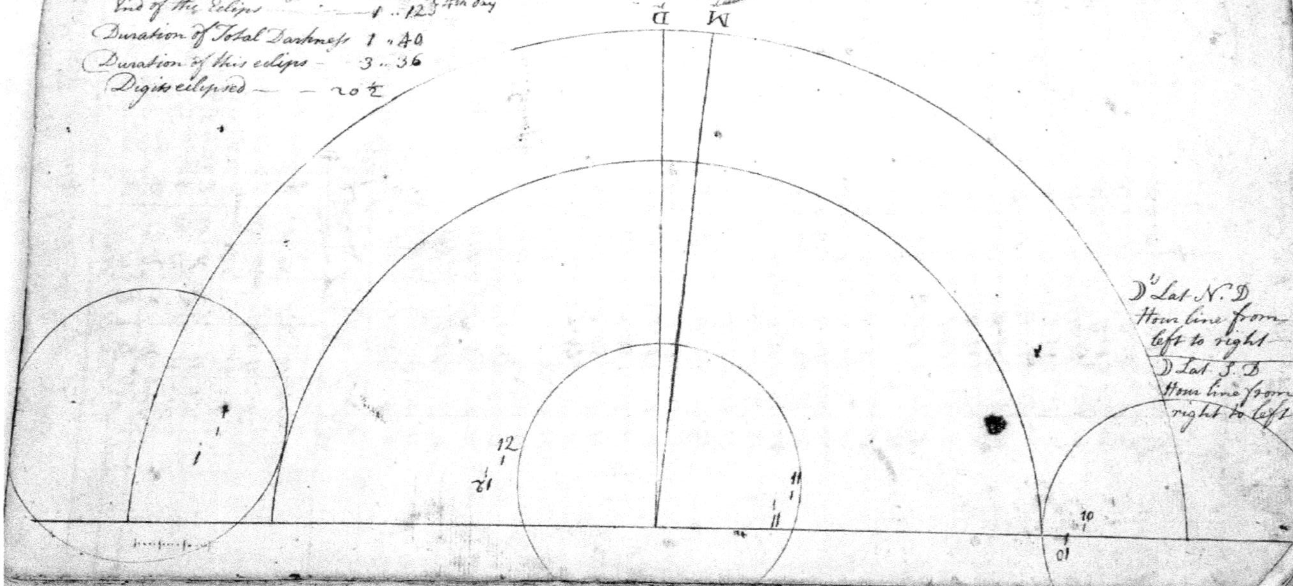

1797 September Ninth Month hath 30 Days

				Planets Places				
Full ○ 6..4..5 morn.		☉	♄	♃	♂	♀	☿	☽'s
Last ☾ 13..4..33 aft.		Long.	♋	♈	♍	♎	♎	Lat.
New ☽ 20..9..49 morn.	1	5..9..39	9	19	2	5	1	3 S.
First ☽ 27..5..40 aft.	7	5..15..29	10	19	6	13	9	5 S.
	13	5..21..20	10	18	10	20	17	0 N.
☊ { 1 — 18 } deg.	19	5..27..11	11	17	14	27	23	5 N.
☊ { 11 II 18 } deg.	25	6..3..4	11	16	17	♏ 5	28	1 N.
☊ { 21 — 17 } deg.								

M D	W D	Remarkable days Aspects weather &c.		☉ rise	☉ set	☽'s Long.	☽ sets	☽ south	☽'s age
1	6	⚹ ☉ ♄	great	5..34	6..26	9..17..16	13..38	8..50	11
2	7		dews,	5..35	6..25	9..29..11	14..37	9..40	12
3	A	12th. Sund. past Trin.	Dog	5..36	6..24	10..11..5	15..37	10..28	13
4	2		(days end	5..38	6..22	10..23..3	16..37	11..15	14
5	3		rain,	5..39	6..21	11..5..11		12..0	15
6	4	pleiades rise 19..11		5..40	6..20	11..17..25	rise	12..43	16
7	5		and	5..41	6..19	11..29..51	7..13	13..25	17
8	6	Nativity V. M.	☌ ☽ ♃	5..43	6..17	0..12..29	7..41	14..10	18
9	7		wind	5..44	6..16	0..25..16	8..11	14..58	19
10	A	13th. Sund. past Trin.		5..45	6..15	1..8..16	8..45	15..48	20
11	2		fine	5..46	6..14	1..21..29	9..23	16..40	21
12	3		pleasant	5..48	6..12	2..4..57	10..6	17..34	22
13	4	☿ great elong, ⚹ ♄ ♂		5..49	6..11	2..18..41	10..55	18..33	23
14	5		weather	5..50	6..10	3..2..39	11..51	19..32	24
15	6		clear	5..52	6..8	3..16..55	12..52	20..31	25
16	7		and	5..53	6..7	4..1..25	14..2	21..30	26
17	A	14th. Sund past Trin.		5..54	6..6	4..16..6	15..18	22..29	27
18	2		cool	5..55	6..5	5..0..54	16..39	23..28	28
19	3	Bulls eye rise 9..41		5..56	6..4	5..15..42		☌	29
20	4		mornings	5..58	6..2	6..0..19	Set	0..20	☽
21	5	St. Matthew		5..59	6..1	6..14..39	6..59	1..8	2
22	6	☉ enters ♎		6..0	6..0	6..28..36	7..27	1..55	3
23	7		Cloudy	6..2	5..58	7..12..7	7..59	2..44	4
24	A	15th. Sund. past Trin.		6..3	5..57	7..25..12	8..35	3..33	5
25	2		with	6..4	5..56	8..7..52	9..15	4..23	6
26	3	St. Cyprian		6..5	5..55	8..20..13	9..59	5..13	7
27	4		showers	6..7	5..53	9..2..14	10..47	6..3	8
28	5		of rain	6..8	5..52	9..14..5	11..39	6..53	9
29	6	St. Michael		6..9	5..51	9..25..51	12..36	7..43	10
30	7	Day 11..38		6..11	5..49	10..7..34	13..40	8..32	11

Delineated for November 18th as appears by the Diagram

To begin at 8 h 4 m

greatest obscuration 9 .. [illegible] } digits 4½ eclipsed on the

End 10 .. 0 } Suns North Limb

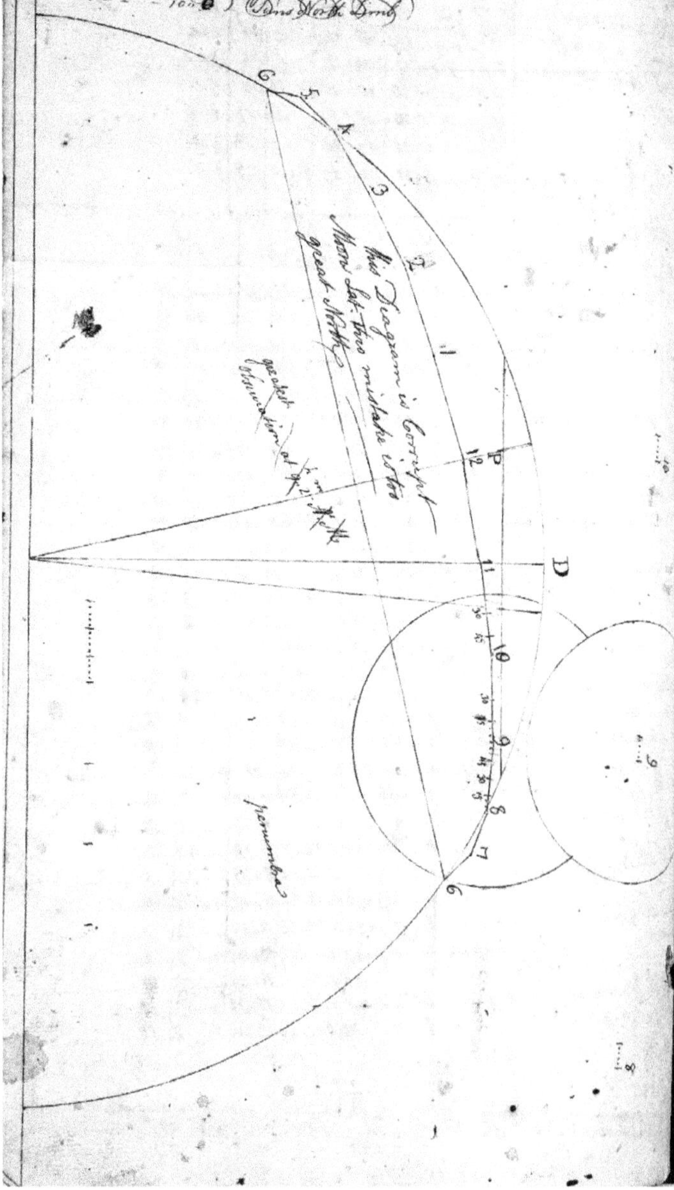

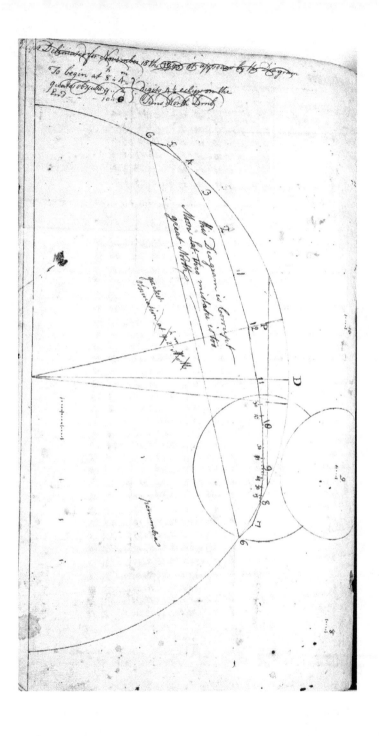

1797 October Tenth Month hath 31 Days

	D	☉	♄	♃	♂	♀	☿	☽'s
				Planets Places				
D h m		Long.	♋	♈	♍	♏	♎	Lat.
Full ○ 5..7..27 aft.	1	6..8..58	11	16	21	12	28	5 S.
Last ☾ 13..0..20 morn.	7	6..14..54	11	15	25	19	28	3 S.
New ☽ 19..8..19 aft.	13	6..20..51	12	14	29	26	21	3 N.
First ☽ 27..0..20 aft.	19	6..26..49	12	13	♎ 3	♐ 3	15	4 N.
☊ {1, 11, 21} ♊ {16, 16, 15} deg.	25	7..2..47	12	12	♎ 7	11	15	2 S.

M D	W D	Remarkable days Aspects weather &c.	☉ rise	☉ set	☽ Long.	☽ Set.	☽ south	☽ age
1	A	16th. Sund. past Trin.	6..12	5..48	10..19..20	14..38	9..19	12
2	2	clear	6..13	5..47	11..1..13	15..35	10..1	13
3	3	♀ Set 7..13	6..14	5..46	11..13..16	16..31	10..44	14
4	4	and	6..15	5..45	11..25..31		11..29	15
5	5	cool,	6..17	5..43	0..8..3	rise	12..15	16
6	6	☌ ☽ ♃	6..18	5..42	0..20..50	6..22	13..1	17
7	7	☍ ☉ ♃ Occident,	6..19	5..41	1..3..51	6..48	13..47	18
8	A	17th. Sund. past Trin.	6..20	5..40	1..17..9	7..21	14..37	19
9	2	now	6..22	5..38	2..0..43	8..2	15..31	20
10	3	pleiades rise 8..8	6..23	5..37	2..14..27	8..52	16..29	21
11	4	expect frost.	6..24	5..36	2..28..24	9..50	17..29	22
12	5	Bulls eye rise 8..17	6..25	5..35	3..12..31	10..52	18..30	23
13	6	☌ ☉ ☿ Orient.	6..27	5..33	3..26..49	11..58	19..29	24
14	7	cloudy	6..28	5..32	4..11..17	13..8	20..26	25
15	A	18th. Sund. past Trin.	6..29	5..31	4..25..47	14..22	21..22	26
16	2	rain	6..30	5..30	5..10..23	15..36	22..16	27
17	3	and	6..32	5..28	5..24..54	16..50	23..10	28
18	4	St. Luke	6..33	5..27	6..9..20		23..57	29
19	5	wind	6..34	5..26	6..23..31	set.	☌	☽
20	6	Days decrease 3..54	6..35	5..25	7..7..23	6..3	0..47	1
21	7		6..36	5..24	7..20..54	6..44	1..37	2
22	A	19th Sund. past Trin.	6..38	5..22	8..4..0	7..26	2..27	3
23	2	clear	6..39	5..21	8..16..42	8..9	3..17	4
24	3	and	6..40	5..20	8..29..2	8..53	4..7	5
25	4	♀ Sets 7..20	6..41	5..19	9..11..5	9..42	4..57	6
26	5	pleasant,	6..42	5..18	9..22..55	10..37	5..46	7
27	6	cool	6..44	5..16	10..4..35	11..36	6..34	8
28	7	St. Simon and Jude	6..45	5..15	10..16..13	12..35	7..20	9
29	A	20th. Sund. past Trin.	6..46	5..14	10..27..52	13..34	8..4	10
30	2	rain	6..47	5..13	11..9..37	14..32	8..47	11
31	3	Days 10..24	6..48	5..12	11..21..34	15..30	9..28	12

Elements for the projection of a Solar Eclips November 18th. 1797

True time of New Moon in November 1797		D H M
		18 .. 9 .. 33 A
Semidiameter of the Earths Disc		0 .. 58 .. 40 r
Suns distance from the nearest Solstice		33 .. 0 .. 0 r
Sun declination South		19 .. 25 .. 0 r
Moons Latitude North descending	60 .. 31 r	~~43 .. 37 .. 06~~
Moon's horary motion from the Sun		0 .. 32 .. 14 r
Angle of the Moons visible path with the Ecliptic		5 .. 35 .. 0 r
Suns Semidiameter		0 .. 16 .. 19 r
Moons Semidiameter		0 .. 16 .. 3 r
Semidiameter of the penumbra		0 .. 32 .. 22

Suns Equated distance from the Moons Ascending Node 5 .. 12 .. 36 .. 5

1797 November Eleventh Month hath 30 Days—

			Planets Places					
d h m	☽	☉	♄	♃	♂	♀	☿	☽'s
Full ○ 4..10..0 morn.		Long.	♋	♈	♎	♐	♎	Lat.
Last ☾ 11..8..5 morn.	1	7..9..48	12	12	11	18	22	5 S.
New ☽ 18..9..33 morn.	7	7..15..50	12	11	15	26	♏ 0	1 N.
First ☽ 26..6..40 morn.	13	7..21..53	11	11	19	♑ 4	9	5 N.
☊ { 1 / 11 / 21 } ♊ { 15 / 14 / 14 } deg.	19	7..27..57	11	10	23	11	19	0 S.
	25	8..4..1	11	10	27	18	28	5 S.

M D	W D	Remarkable days Aspects weather &c.	☉ rise	☉ set	☽ Long.	☽ set	☽ South	☽'s age
1	4	☿ great elong. All Saints	6..49	5..11	0..3..47	16..28	10..10	13
2	5	☌ ☽ ♃,	6..51	5..9	0..16..18	17..26	10..54	14
3	6	hard	6..52	5..8	0..29..10		11..41	15
4	7	frosts,	6..53	5..7	1..12..22	rise	12..31	16
5	A	21st. Sund. past Trin.	6..54	5..6	1..25..52	6..0	13..24	17
6	2	rain	6..55	5..5	2..9..43	6..50	14..20	18
7	3	♀ sets 7..29	6..56	5..4	2..23..46	7..43	15..20	19
8	4	and	6..57	5..3	3..8..0	8..41	16..20	20
9	5	pleiades South 12..36	6..58	5..2	3..22..22	9..45	17..20	21
10	6	wind	6..59	5..1	4..6..46	10..57	18..20	22
11	7	St. Martin	7..0	5..0	4..21..13	12..11	19..18	23
12	A	22d. Sund. past Trin.	7..1	4..59	5..5..37	13..27	20..12	24
13	2	□ ♄ ♃	7..2	4..58	5..20..0	14..37	21..2	25
14	3	Clear	7..3	4..57	6..4..18	15..46	21..51	26
15	4	Bulls eye South 1..3	7..4	4..56	6..18..25	16..53	22..39	27
16	5	and	7..5	4..55	7..2..22	17..57	23..26	28
17	6	Days decrease 4..56	7..6	4..54	7..16..2		☌	29
18	7	cold	7..7	4..53	7..29..25	Set.	0..14	☽
19	A	23d. Sund. past Trin.	7..8	4..52	8..12..29	5..53	1..3	2
20	2	☾ ☍ ♄ ♀	7..8	4..52	8..25..13	6..44	1..55	3
21	3	☉ enter ♐	7..9	4..51	9..7..36	7..36	2..49	4
22	4	Snow	7..10	4..50	9..19..43	8..30	3..40	5
23	5	or	7..11	4..49	10..1..36	9..27	4..28	6
24	6	Days 9..36	7..12	4..48	10..13..19	10..26	5..16	7
25	7	rain	7..12	4..48	10..24..57	11..25	6..0	8
26	A	24th. Sund. past Trin.	7..13	4..47	11..6..36	12..23	6..43	9
27	2	flying	7..14	4..46	11..18..20	13..19	7..24	10
28	3	clouds	7..15	4..45	0..0..13	14..16	8..3	11
29	4	☌ ☽ ♃	7..15	4..45	0..12..21	15..14	8..43	12
30	5	St. Andrew	7..16	4..44	0..24..50	16..13	9..26	13

Elements for the projection of a Lunar Eclips December 3d. 1797

	D .. H .. M
True time of full Moon in December 1797	3 .. 11 .. 24 P.M.
	° .. ′ .. ″
Moon's horizontal parallax	0 .. 58 .. 40
Sun's Semidiameter	0 .. 16 .. 21
D° Ditto	0 .. 16 .. 0
Semidiameter of the Earths shadow at the Moon	0 .. 42 .. 29
Moons Latitude South Ascending	0 .. 5 .. 13
Angle of her visible path with the Ecliptic	5 .. 35 .. 0
Her true horary motion from the Sun	0 .. 32 .. 19

Elements for ~~an~~ the projection of a Solar Eclips December 18th 1797

	D .. H .. M
True time of New Moon in December 1797	18 .. 1 .. 39 [illegible]
	° .. ′ .. ″
Semidiameter of the Earth's disc	0 .. 57 .. 8
Sun's distance from the nearest Solstice	3 .. 0 .. 0
Suns declination South	0 .. 23 .. 26
~~Moon's Latitude South Descending~~	~~+ .. 8 .. 27~~
Moon's horary motion from the Sun	0 .. 30 .. 38
Angle of the Moon's visible path with the Ecliptic	5 .. 35 .. 0
Suns Semidiameter	0 .. 16 .. 22
Moons Semidiameter	0 .. 15 .. 36
Semidiameter of the penumbra	0 .. 31 .. 58

1797

December Twelfth Month hath 31 Days

	d. h. m.
Full ○	3..11..24 aft.
Last ☾	10..6..10 aft.
New ☽	18..1..38 morn.
First ☽	26..2..45 morn.

☊ {1, 11, 21} ♊ {13, 13, 12} deg.

☽	☉	Planets Places ♄	♃	♂	♀	☿	☽'s
	Long.	♋	♈	♏	♑	♐	Lat.
1	8..10..6	10	10	1	25	8	3 S.
7	8..16..10	10	10	5	♒ 2	17	4 N.
13	8..22..17	10	10	8	9	26	4 N.
19	8..28..23	9	10	12	16	♑ 6	3 S.
25	9..4..31	9	11	16	22	16	5 S.

M. D.	W. D.	Remarkable days Aspects weather &c.		☉ rise	☉ set	☽ Long.	☽ Set	☽ south	☽'s age
1	6	□ ♄ ♃		7..16	4..44	1..7..40	17..13	10..12	14
2	7		snow	7..17	4..43	1..20..54		11..2	15
3	A	Advent Sund.		7..18	4..42	2..4..35	rise	11..56	16
4	2		or	7..18	4..42	2..18..34	5..17	12..54	17
5	3	☌ ☉ ☿ Occident.		7..19	4..41	3..2..55	6..20	13..56	18
6	4	Nicholas		7..19	4..41	3..17..25	7..26	15..0	19
7	5		rain	7..20	4..40	4..2..1	8..36	16..2	20
8	6	Conception V. Mary		7..20	4..40	4..16..39	9..50	17..0	21
9	7		clear	7..20	4..40	5..1..9	11..3	17..54	22
10	A	2d. Sund. in Advent		7..21	4..39	5..15..34	12..13	18..44	23
11	2		and	7..21	4..39	5..29..46	13..22	19..33	24
12	3		cold,	7..21	4..39	6..13..50	14..30	20..21	25
13	4	♀ Sets 8..20		7..21	4..39	6..27..40	15..36	21..9	26
14	5		windy	7..22	4..38	7..11..18	16..41	21..58	27
15	6		with	7..22	4..38	7..24..43	17..46	22..48	28
16	7		snow	7..22	4..38	8..7..52	18..50	23..40	29
17	A	3d. Sund. in Advent		7..22	4..38	8..20..47		δ	30
18	2		flying	7..22	4..38	9..3..26	Set.	0..32	☽
19	3		clouds	7..22	4..38	9..15..53	6..6	1..20	2
20	4	Shortest day		7..22	4..38	9..28..4	7..5	2..8	3
21	5	St. Thomas. ☉ enters ♑		7..22	4..38	10..10..3	8..4	2..56	4
22	6		clear and	7..22	4..38	10..21..54	9..3	3..42	5
23	7		windy	7..22	4..38	11..3..38	10..2	4..26	6
24	A	4th. Sund. in Advent		7..22	4..38	11..15..23	11..0	5..8	7
25	2	Christmas Day		7..22	4..38	11..27..13	11..58	5..51	8
26	3	St. Stephen ☌ ☽ ♃		7..22	4..38	0..9..5	12..56	6..31	9
27	4	St. John		7..22	4..38	0..21..14	13..55	7..13	10
28	5	Innocents		7..21	4..39	1..3..40	14..55	7..57	11
29	6		rain or	7..21	4..39	1..16..29	15..56	8..43	12
30	7		snow	7..21	4..39	1..29..43	16..58	9..33	13
31	A	1st. Sund. past Chris. Silvester		7..20	4..40	2..13..22	18..0	10..27	14

1798 Full ☉ Janu^ry 2 - 11 - 33 morn

1798 New ☽ January 16 - 7 - 49 aft } right

Full ☉ ~~February~~ January 31 - 10 - 32 aft. right

New ☽ February 15 - 3 - 3 aft - right

Full ☉ March 2 - 8 - 33 morn

New ☽ March 17 - 9 - 24 morn

Full ☉ March 31 - 5 - 57 aft.

New ☽ April 16 - 1 - 38 morn

Full ☉ April 30 - 3 - 16 morn

New ☽ May 15 - 3 - 7 aft.

Full ☉ May 29 - 1 - 11 aft

New ☽ June 14 - 2 - 1 morn

Full ☉ June 28 - 9 - 31 morn

New ☽ July 13 - 10 - 50 morn

Full ☉ July 27 - 1 - 30 aft.

New ☽ August 11 - 6 - 34 aft

Full ☉ August 26 - 4 - 29 morn.

New ☽ Septemb 10 - 2 - 14 morn.

Full ☉ Septemb. 24 - 9 - 7 aft.

New ☽ October 9 - 10 - 45 morn.

Full ☉ October 24 - 2 - 27 aft

New ☽ Novemb. 7 - 8 - 56 aft.

Full ☉ Novemb 23 - 7 - 28 morn.

New ☽ Decemb 7 - 8 - 51 morn

Full ☉ Decemb 22 - 11 - 9 aft.

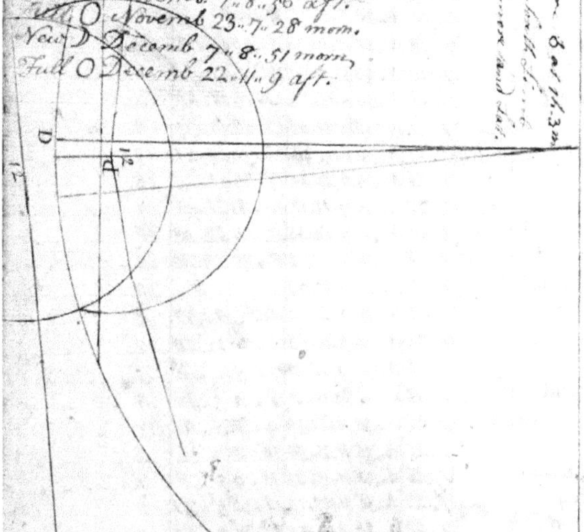

6 This eclipse is invisible at Baltimore ☌ at 1h. 3m A.M ☉ is 3⅔ digits eclipsed on his South Limb in Longitude 155° 15' East from Baltimore and Lat. 40° South

There is an Eclipse of the Sun December the 18th [illegible] visible at Baltimore ☌ at 14. 34m A.M. ☉ is 3⅔ digits eclipsed on his South Limb in Longitude 155° 15' East from Baltimore and Latitude 40° South

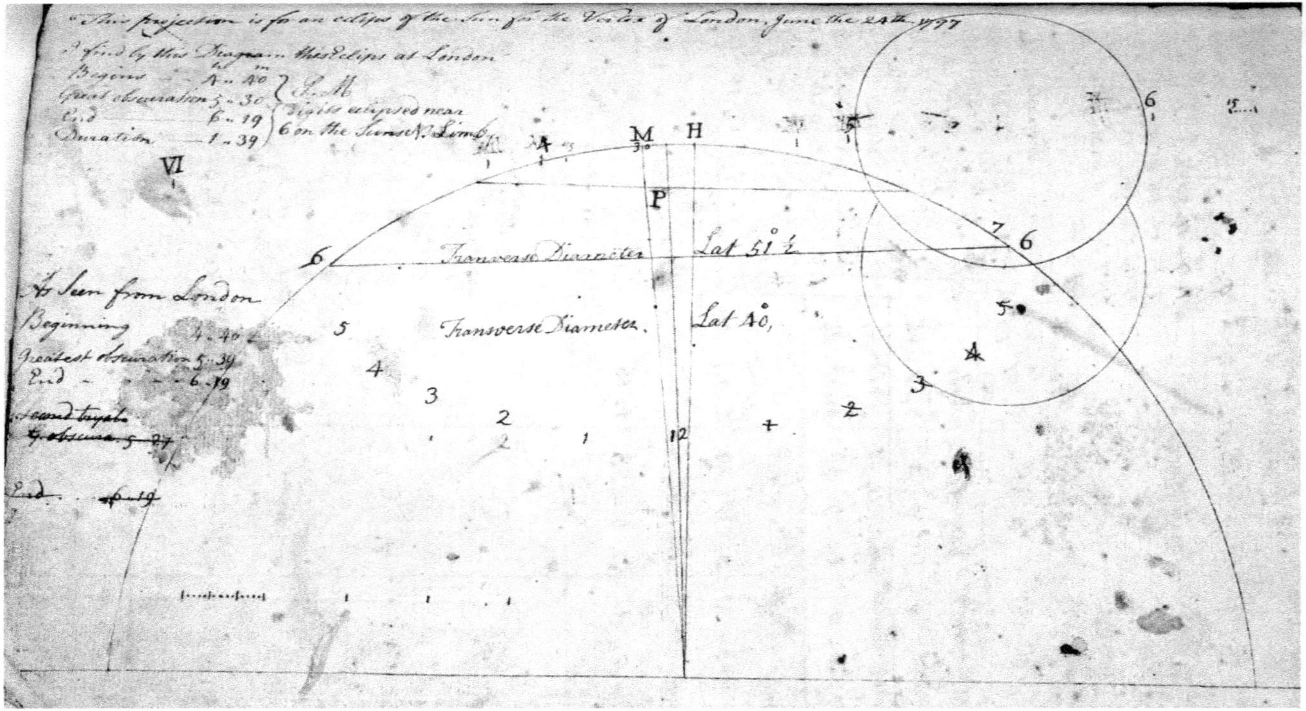
This projection is for an eclipse of the Sun for the Vertex of London, June the 24th 1777
I find by this Diagram this Eclipse at London
Begins — 4 .. 40
Great obscuration 5 .. 30
End — 6 .. 19
Duration — 1 .. 39
P.M
Digits eclipsed near 6 on the Suns N. Limb
VI
M
H
P
Transverse Diameter
Lat 51 ½
Transverse Diameter
Lat 40,
12
As Seen from London
Beginning 4 .. 40
Greatest obscuration 5 .. 39
End — 6 .. 19
End — 6 .. 19

1798	1798	1798
Long. med. ☽	Long. Apog. ☽	Longit ☊
s ° '	s ° '	s ° '
2..19..42	10..24..10	2..11..55
Long. med. ☉	Long. Apog.	
s ° '	s ° '	
9..10..36	3..9..30	
1798 Long. med. ♄	1798 Anomaly ♄	Node ♄
s ° '	s ° '	s ° '
3..7..32	6..6..48	3..21..35
Long. med. ♃	Anomaly ♃	Node
s ° '	s ° '	s ° '
0..21..36	6..10..4	3..8..56
Long. med. ♂	Anomaly ♂	Node
s ° '	s ° '	s ° '
7..0..0	1..27..32	1..18..27
Long. med. ♀	Anomaly ♀	Node
s ° '	s ° '	s ° '
1..25..33	3..17..29	2..14..49
Long. med. ☿	Anomaly ☿	Node
s ° '	s ° '	s ° '
0..0..42	3..16..33	1..16..9

1798	☉ true Long	Anomaly	Log ☉ a ☉ according to May. index
	January		
	s ° '	s ° '	
1	9..11..39	6..2..5	
7	9..17..46	6..8..0	9·9926
13	9..23..54	6..13..55	9·9927
19	10..0..0	6..19..50	9·9928
25	10..6..6	6..25..44	9·9931
			9·9934
	February	Anomal.	Log. ☉ a ☉
1	10..13..11	7..2..38	9·9938
7	10..19..17	7..8..33	9·9943
13	10..25..19	7..14..28	9·9947
19	11..1..23	7..20..23	9·9953
25	11..7..25	7..26..18	9·9955
	☉ Long.	March Anomally	Log. ☉ a ☉
1	11..11..25	8..0..14	9·996
7	11..17..25	8..6..9	9·997
13	11..23..25	8..12..4	9·997
19	11..29..22	8..17..59	9·99
25	0..5..19	8..23..54	9·999
	☉ Long.	April Anomally	Log ☉ a
1	0..12..13	9..0..48	0.000
7	0..18..6	9..6..42	0.001
13	0..23..59	9..12..37	0.0017
19	0..29..50	9..18..32	0.002
25	1..5..41	9..24..27	0.003
	☉ Long.	May Anomally	Log ☉ a
1	1..11..31	10..0..22	0.0037
7	1..17..19	10..6..17	0.004
13	1..23..6	10..12..11	0.004
19	1..28..52	10..18..6	0.005
25	2..4..38	10..24..1	0.005
	☉ Long.	June Anomaly	Log ☉ a
1	2..11..20	11..0..55	0.006
7	2..17..4	11..6..50	0.006
13	2..22..48	11..12..45	0.006
19	2..28..32	11..18..40	0.007
25	3..4..14	11..24..34	0.007

1798 $\odot$ true Long.	Anomaly July	Log $\odot$ a Θ
3..9..59	0..0..29	0.00723
3..15..42	0..6..24	0.00719
3..21..25	0..12..19	0.00708
3..27..9	0..18..14	0.00689
4..2..53	0..24..9	0.00663

$\odot$ Long. 1798	Anomaly August	Log. $\odot$ a Θ
4..9..35	1..1..3	0.00624
4..15..19	1..6..57	0.00583
4..21..4	1..12..52	0.00536
4..26..51	1..18..47	0.00483
5..2..39	1..24..42	0.00424

$\odot$ Long. 1798	Anomaly Septemb.	Log. $\odot$ a Θ
5..9..25	2..1..36	0.00350
1..15..15	2..7..31	0.00283
5..21..6	2..13..26	0.00224
5..26..57	2..19..20	0.00150
6..2..50	2..25..15	0.00075

$\odot$ Long. 1798	Anomaly October	Log. $\odot$ a Θ
6..8..44	3..1..10	9.99999
6..14..40	3..7..5	9.99923
6..20..37	3..13..0	9.99847
6..26..35	3..18..55	9.99772
7..2..33	3..24..49	9.99700

$\odot$ Long. 1798	Anomaly Novemb.	Log. $\odot$ a Θ
7..9..34	4..1..43	9.99620
7..15..36	4..7..38	9.99556
7..21..39	4..13..33	9.99496
7..27..41	4..19..28	9.99451
8..3..46	4..25..23	9.99402

$\odot$ Long. 1798	Anomaly December	Log. $\odot$ a Θ
8..9..51	5..1..18	9.99359
8..15..56	[illegible]..7..12	9.99321
8..22..3	5..13..7	9.99297
8..28..9	5..19..2	9.99278
9..4..17	5..24..57	9.99266

~~1796 John Barton Esq~~
~~July 3 To 1 Book~~

For discovering how many Luminaries ~~Eclipses~~ Eclipses may happen in any year, See a Complete System of Astronomy Vol. 1 page 413 precept 14

To find the time the Moons Southing See Doctrine of the Sphere page 264

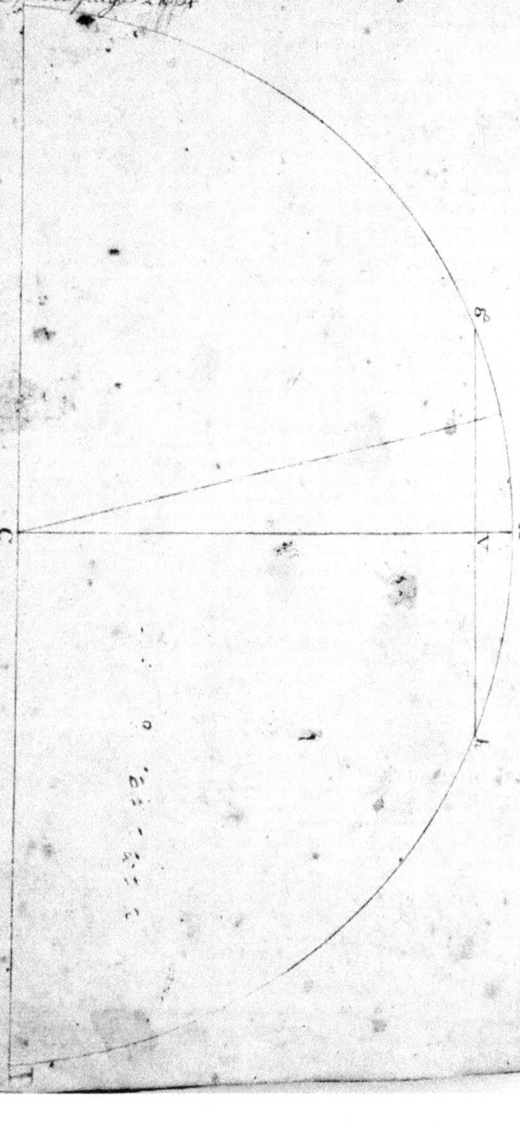

1798 January First Month hath 31 Days.

	d	h	m	
Full ○	2	11	33	morn.
Last ☾	9	6	9	aft.
New ☽	16	7	49	aft.
First ☽	24	9	14	aft.
Full ○	31	10	32	aft.

☊ { 1 ♊ 12, 11 ♊ 11, 21 ♊ 11 } deg.

Planets Places

☽	☉	♄	♃	♂	♀	☿	☽s Lat.
	♑	♋	♈	♏	♒	♑	Lat.
1	12	8	11	20	29	27	1 N.
7	18	7	12	24	♓ 5	♒ 5	5 N.
13	24	7	13	28	11	13	0 S.
19	♒ 0	6	13	♐ 2	16	15	5 S.
25	6	6	14	6	21	10	2 S.

M. D.	W. D.	Remarkable days Aspects weather &c.	☉ rise	☉ set	☽s Long.	☽ Set	☽ South	☽s age
1	2	Circumcision	7..20	4..40	2.27.27		11..29	15
2	3	Snow	7..20	4..40	3.11.48	7..38	12..31	16
3	4	Days increase 4 m.	7..20	4..40	3.26.39	6..19	13..34	17
4	5	or	7..19	4..41	4.11.28	7..32	14..33	18
5	6	cold rain,	7..19	4..41	4.26.18	8..45	15..30	19
6	7	Epiphany	7..18	4..42	5..11..0	9..59	16..23	20
7	G	1st. Sund past Epip. □ ♄ ☿	7..18	4..42	5..25..32	11..7	17..12	21
8	2	clouds	7..17	4..43	6..9..38	12..13	18..0	22
9	3	pleiades South 8..11.	7..17	4..43	6..23..32	13..18	18..47	23
10	4	with	7..16	4..44	7..7..6	14..23	19..37	24
11	5	wind	7..15	4..45	7..20..26	15..28	20..27	25
12	6	♀ Set 8..43	7..15	4..45	8..3..29	16..32	21..17	26
13	7	attended	7..14	4..46	8..16..24	17..29	22..6	27
14	G	2d. Sund past Epip	7..13	4..47	8..29..1	18..23	22..59	28
15	2	with Snow	7..13	4..47	9..11..35		23..52	29
16	3	Sirius South 10..42	7..12	4..48	9..23..55	sets		☽
17	4	moderate	7..11	4..49	10..6..7	5..36	0..43	1
18	5	for	7..10	4..50	10..18..13	6..36	1..28	2
19	6	☉ enters ♒. the	7..10	4..50	11..0..10	7..34	2..12	3
20	7	season	7..9	4..51	11..12..48	8..30	2..54	4
21	G	3d. Sund. past Epip.	7..8	4..52	11..23..59	9..26	3..36	5
22	2	flying clouds	7..7	4..53	0..6..4	10..22	4..17	6
23	3	☌ ☽ ♃ and	7..6	4..54	0..18..15	11..20	4..58	7
24	4	wind	7..5	4..55	1..0..16	12..19	5..39	8
25	5	Convert. St. paul ✱ ☉ ♂	7..4	4..56	1..12..47	13..18	6..22	9
26	6	Snow	7..3	4..57	1..25..36	14..20	7..12	10
27	7	☌ ☉ ☿ Orient	7..2	4..58	2..8..18	15..22	8..6	11
28	G	4th. Sund. past Epip.	7..1	4..59	2..22..26	16..25	9..3	12
29	2	toward	7..0	5..0	3..6..29	17..28	10..5	13
30	3	the end,	6..59	5..1	3..20..48		11..9	14
31	4	Days increase 48 min.	6..58	5..2	4..5..47	rise	12..9	15

Our Shortest day 9..16

Some says, that it is dangerous to let blood in the Dog days, but I questio
it, because that on the 30th Augst. 1796 which was 4 days before the exp
of the Dog days, no harm ensues I bled John Kinney

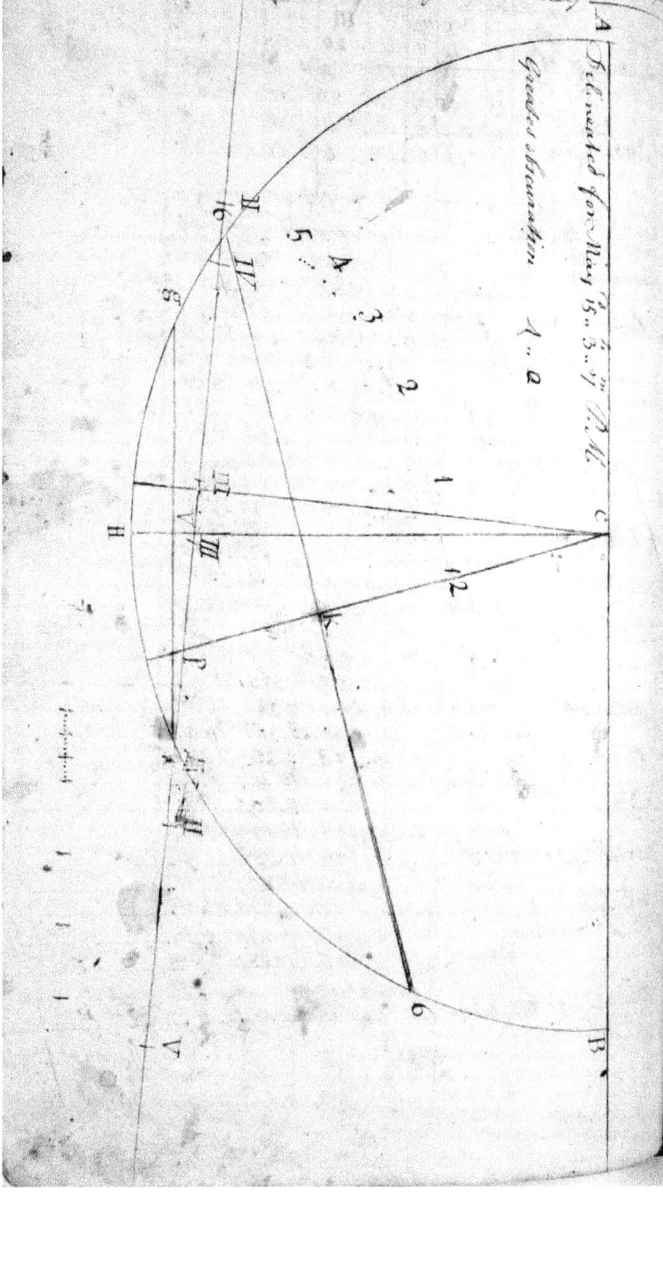

1798 February Second Month hath 28. days

	☽	☉	♄	♃	♂	♀	☿	☽'s
Last ☾ 9 .. 6 .. 13 morn.			Planets Places					
New ☽ .. 15 - 3 - 3 aft.		♒	♋	♈	♐	♓	♒	Lat.
First ☾ 23 - 1 .. 24 aft.	1	13	6	15	11	26	2	5 N.
	7	19	5	16	15	♈ 0	♑ 29	2 N.
☊ { 1 ♊ 10; 11 10; 21 9 } deg.	13	25	5	18	18	3	♒ 0	3 S.
	19	♓ 1	5	19	22	4	5	4 S.
	25	7	5	20	26	5	11	2 N.

M D	W D	Remarkable Days Aspects weather &c.	☉ rise	☉ set	☽'s Long.	☽ rise	☽ South	☽'s age
1	5	Clear	6 .. 57	5 .. 3	4 .. 20 .. 45	6 .. 22	13 .. 9	16
2	6	purification V. Mary	6 .. 56	5 .. 4	5 .. 5 .. 42	7 .. 32	14 .. 4	17
3	7	✶ ☉ ♃	6 .. 55	5 .. 5	5 .. 20 .. 32	8 .. 42	14 .. 55	18
4	G	Septuagesima Sund	6 .. 54	5 .. 6	6 .. 5 .. 5	9 .. 52	15 .. 45	19
5	2	and cold,	6 .. 53	5 .. 7	6 .. 19 .. 22	10 .. 59	16 .. 34	20
6	3	Days 10 .. 16	6 .. 52	5 .. 8	7 .. 3 .. 10	12 .. 6	17 .. 23	21
7	4	Snow	6 .. 51	5 .. 9	7 .. 16 .. 37	13 .. 12	18 .. 12	22
8	5	pleiades Set 1 .. 3	6 .. 50	5 .. 10	7 .. 29 .. 52	14 .. 14	19 .. 3	23
9	6	or rain	6 .. 49	5 .. 11	8 .. 12 .. 40	15 .. 14	19 .. 55	24
10	7		6 .. 48	5 .. 12	8 .. 25 .. 14	16 .. 13	20 .. 48	25
11	G	Sexagesima Sund	6 .. 46	5 .. 14	9 .. 7 .. 34	17 .. 2	21 .. 39	26
12	2	flying	6 .. 45	5 .. 15	9 .. 19 .. 49	17 .. 47	22 .. 28	27
13	3	△ ♃ ♂	6 .. 44	5 .. 16	10 .. 1 .. 59	18 .. 25	23 .. 14	28
14	4	Valentine	6 .. 43	5 .. 17	10 .. 14 .. 5		23 .. 57	29
15	5	Clouds	6 .. 42	5 .. 18	10 .. 26 .. 12	Sets		☽
16	6	days increas 1 .. 24	6 .. 40	5 .. 20	11 .. 8 .. 13	6 .. 10	0 .. 39	1
17	7	Snow	6 .. 39	5 .. 21	11 .. 20 .. 16	7 .. 8	1 .. 21	2
18	G	Quinquagesima Sund.	6 .. 38	5 .. 22	0 .. 2 .. 22	8 .. 6	2 .. 3	3
19	2	☿ great elong ☌ ☽ ♃	6 .. 36	5 .. 24	0 .. 14 .. 34	9 .. 5	2 .. 45	4
20	3	Shrove Tuesd.	6 .. 35	5 .. 25	0 .. 26 .. 51	10 .. 5	3 .. 29	5
21	4	Ash wednesday	6 .. 34	5 .. 26	1 .. 9 .. 19	11 .. 5	4 .. 14	6
22	5	windy with	6 .. 33	5 .. 27	1 .. 21 .. 59	12 .. 7	5 .. 3	7
23	6	△ ☉ ♄	6 .. 32	5 .. 28	2 .. 4 .. 56	13 .. 11	5 .. 56	8
24	7	St. Matthias	6 .. 31	5 .. 29	2 .. 18 .. 13	14 .. 15	6 .. 52	9
25	G	1st Sund. in Lent □ ♄ ♀	6 .. 30	5 .. 30	3 .. 1 .. 51	15 .. 16	7 .. 51	10
26	2	rain	6 .. 28	5 .. 32	3 .. 15 .. 54	16 .. 12	8 .. 51	11
27	3	or Snow	6 .. 27	5 .. 33	4 .. 0 .. 19	17 .. 2	9 .. 51	12
28	4	Days 11 .. 8	6 .. 26	5 .. 34	4 .. 15 .. 2	17 .. 45	10 .. 49	13

Venus (♀) will be evening Star untill the 17th day of March, then morning Star untill the end of the year

True time of New Moon in May, 1798 } D 15 .. H 3 .. M 7 P.M

First Eclipse 1798

But two eclipses at N. Node

Semidiameter of the Earths disc	0 .. 56
Sun's distance from the nearest Solstice	35 ..
Sun's declination North	18 .. 58
Moon's Latitude South Ascend	0 .. 49
Moon's Horary motion from the Sun	0 .. 31
Angle of the Moon's visible path with the Ecliptic	5 .. 35
Sun's Semidiameter	0 .. 16
Moon's Semidiameter	0 .. 15
Semidiameter of the penumbra	0 .. 31

Sun's equated distance from the Moons North Node s 11 .. ° 20 .. ' 32 .. " 11

Second of the Moon May 29th 1 .. 11 P.M Invisible

Third of the Sun November d 7 .. h 8 .. m 46 P.M

	° '
Semidiameter of the Earths disc	0 .. 60
Sun's distance from the nearest Solstice	44
Sun's declination South	16 .. 26
Moon's Latitude North Descending	0 .. 49
Moons Horary Motion from the Sun	0 .. 34
Angle of the Moons visible path with Ecliptic	5 .. 35
Suns Semidiameter	0 .. 16
Moons Semidiameter	0 .. 16
Semidiameter of the penumbra	0 .. 32

Fourth of the Moon
True time of full Moon in November 1798 } 23 .. 7 .. 28 A.M

	° '
Moon's Horizontal paralax	0 .. 55
Suns Semidiameter	0 .. 16
Moons Semidiameter	0 .. 15
Semidiameter of the Earths Shadow at the Moon	0 .. 39
Moons true Latitude North Ascending	0 .. 38
Angle of the Moons visible path with the Ecliptic	5 .. 35
Moons true horary motion from the Sun	0 .. 30

Two eclipses at the South Node

Sun from Node s 6 .. ° 6 .. ' 53

798 March Third Month hath 31 Days

				Planets Places					
d. h. m.	D	☉	♄	♃	♂	♀	☿	☽	
Full ○ 2 . 8 . 23 morn.		♓	♋	♈	♐	♈	♒	Lat.	
Last ☾ 1[illegible] . 2 . 27 aft.	1	11	5	21	29	4	15	5 N.	
New ☽ 17 . 9 . 24 morn.	7	17	5	22	♑ 3	2	27	1 N.	
First ☽ 24 . 11 . 20 aft.	13	23	5	23	7	♓ 29	♓ 10	5 S.	
Full ○ 31 . 5 . 57 aft.	19	29	5	25	10	25	13	4 S.	
☊ {1 ♊ 9, 11 8, 21 8} deg.	25	♈ 5	5	26	14	21	♈ 18	3 N.	

M D	W D	Remarkable days Aspects weather &c	☉ rise	☉ set	☽ Long.	☽ Set	☽ south	☽ age
1	5	St. David	6..24	5..36	4..29..58		11..44	14
2	6	pleiades Set 12..4	6..23	5..37	5..14..59	rise	12..38	15
3	7	Snow,	6..22	5..38	5..29..52	7..30	13..30	16
4	G	2nd. Sund. in Lent	6..21	5..39	6..14..31	8..42	14..22	17
5	2	temperate	6..19	5..41	6..28..45	9..52	15..14	18
6	3	□ ♂ ♀	6..17	5..43	7..12..38	11..0	16..6	19
7	4	♄ Stationary	6..16	5..44	7..26..2	12..5	16..58	20
8	5	Days increase 2..16	6..14	5..46	8..9..1	13..8	17..50	21
9	6	flying	6..13	5..47	8..21..40	14..5	18..42	22
10	7	clouds	6..12	5..48	9..4..29	14..58	19..34	23
11	G	3d. Sund. in Lent	6..11	5..49	9..16..22	15..45	20..24	24
12	2	with	6..9	5..51	9..28..16	16..25	21..12	25
13	3	Bulls eye Set 11..46	6..8	5..52	10..10..14	17..0	21..58	26
14	4	rain	6..7	5..53	10..22..10	17..31	22..42	27
15	5	Days 11..48	6..6	5..54	11..4..8	17..58	23..24	28
16	6	or Snow	6..4	5..56	11..16..9			29
17	7	☌ ☉ ☿ Orient. St. patrick	6..3	5..57	11..28..17	sets	0..6	☽
18	G	4th. Sund. in Lent.	6..2	5..58	0..10..29	7..3	0..49	2
19	2	☌ ☽ ♃	6..1	5..59	0..22..57	8..3	1..32	3
20	3	☉ enter ♈ Equal D. & N.	6..0	6..0	1..5..31	9..3	2..17	4
21	4	temperate	5..59	6..1	1..18..14	10..4	3..4	5
22	5	Arictis Set 9..9	5..58	6..2	2..1..10	11..7	3..55	6
23	6	weather	5..57	6..3	2..14..21	12..10	4..49	7
24	7	△ ☉ ♄	5..55	6..5	2..27..48	13..11	5..46	8
25	G	5th. Sund. in Lent	5..54	6..6	3..11..32	14..8	6..45	9
26	2	(Annunc. N. M.	5..53	6..7	3..25..43	14..58	7..44	10 9..27..13
27	3	cold rain	5..52	6..8	4..9..54	15..45	8..42	11
28	4	Days increase 3..4	5..50	6..10	4..24..9	16..26	[illegible]..39	12
29	5	moderate	5..49	6..11	5..9..18	17..2	10..34	13
30	6	pleiades Set 10..22	5..48	6..12	5..24..12		11..28	14
31	7	Days 12..28	5..46	6..14	6..9..1	rise	12..20	15

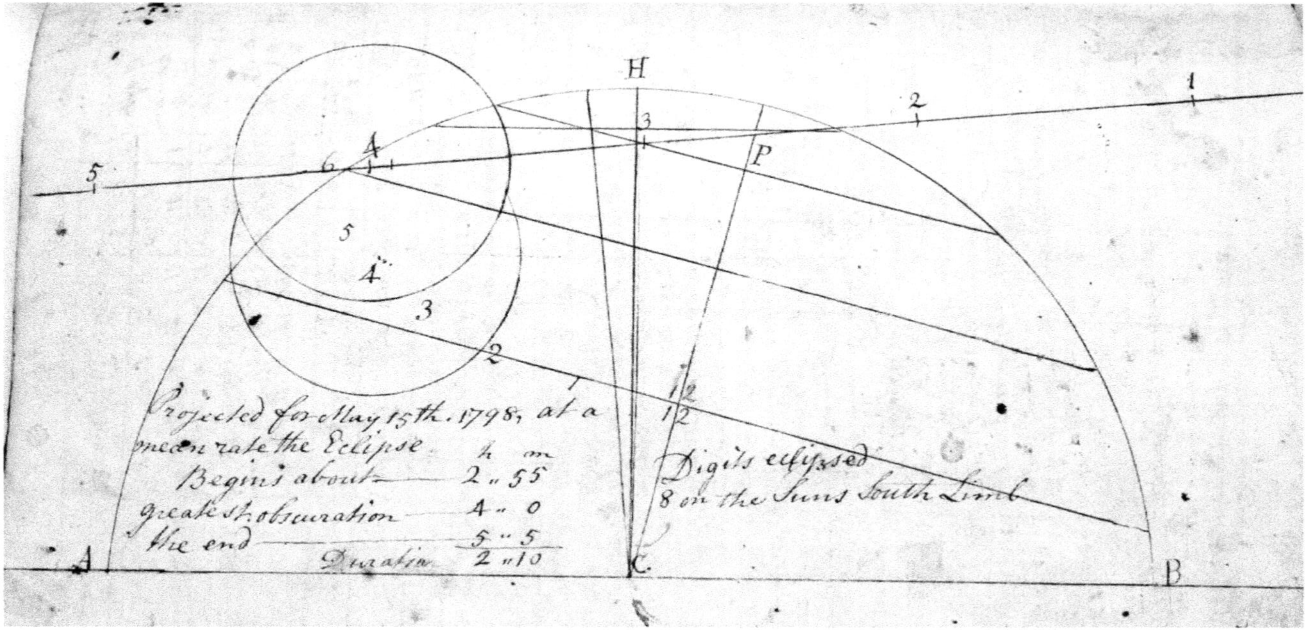
Projected for May 15th. 1798, at a
mean rate the Eclipse h m
Begins about 2 " 55
greatest obscuration 4 " 0
the end 5 " 5
Duration 2 " 10
Digits eclipsed
8 on the Suns South Limb
H
P
A
B
C

April Fourth Month hath 30 Days

	d.	h.	m.	
Last Q.	7	10	0	after.
New ☽	16	1	38	morn.
Full Q.	23	7	22	morn.
Full ☉	30	3	16	morn.

☊ { 1 ♊ 7; 11 7; 21 6 } deg.

Planets Places

☽	☉	♄	♃	♂	♀	☿	☽'s
	♈	♋	♈	♑	♓	♈	Lat.
1	12	5	28	18	19	18	3 N
7	18	6	29	22	18	25	3 S
13	24	6	♉ 1	26	19	♉ 1	5 S
19	♉ 0	7	2	♒ 0	22	13	0 N
25	6	7	4	4	25	24	5 N

M D	W D	Remarkable days Aspects weather &c	☉ rise	☉ set	☽'s Long.	☽ rise	☽ South	☽'s age
1	G	Palm Sund. □ ♂ ☿	5..44	6..16	6..23..37	7..43	13..12	16
2	2	Clear.	5..43	6..17	7..7..54	8..53	14..5	17
3	3	♀ rise 4..47	5..41	6..19	7..21..46	10..1	14..59	18
4	4	St. Ambrose	5..40	6..20	8..5..12	11..7	15..52	19
5	5	and	5..39	6..21	8..18..11	12..7	16..45	20
6	6	Good Fryd.	5..38	6..22	9..0..47	13..1	17..37	21
7	7	pleasant.	5..36	6..24	9..13..2	13..49	18..26	22
8	G	Easter Sund.	5..35	6..25	9..25..4	14..31	19..14	23
9	2	Easter Mond.	5..34	6..26	10..6..56	15..7	20..1	24
10	3	Easter Tuesd.	5..33	6..27	10..18..42	15..39	20..46	25
11	4	April Showers	5..32	6..28	11..0..28	16..8	21..28	26
12	5	brings forth	5..30	6..30	11..12..18	16..34	22..9	27
13	6	☌ ♃ ☿	5..29	6..31	11..24..14	16..59	22..51	28
14	7	May flowers,	5..28	6..32	0..6..20	17..26	23..34	29
15	G	1st. Sund past East.	5..27	6..33	0..18..38			30
16	2	☌ ☽ ♃	5..26	6..34	1..1..11	Sets	0..19	☽
17	3	wind &	5..25	6..35	1..13..57	8..3	1..7	2
18	4	rain,	5..23	6..37	1..26..57	9..7	1..58	3
19	5	□ ☉ ♂	5..22	6..38	2..10..16	10..9	2..52	4
20	6	☉ enter ♉ then	5..21	6..39	2..23..42	11..9	3..48	5
21	7	pleasant again	5..20	6..40	3..7..23	12..7	4..47	6
22	G	2nd. Sund. past East	5..18	6..42	3..21..16	13..1	5..45	7
23	2	☌ ☉ ♃ orient	5..17	6..43	4..5..26	13..51	6..42	8
24	3	pleiades Sets 8..51	5..16	6..44	4..19..44	14..32	7..37	9
25	4	now rain	5..15	6..45	5..4..13	15..4	8..30	10
26	5	Sirius Sets 9..22	5..14	6..46	5..18..50	15..36	9..22	11
27	6	descend	5..13	6..47	6..3..30	16..9	10..14	12
28	7	fields to befriend	5..12	6..48	6..18..9	16..42	11..6	13
29	G	3d. Sund. past East.	5..11	6..49	7..2..36		11..58	14
30	2	Days increase 4..24	5..10	6..50	7..16..48	rise	12..52	15

Common Notes and moveable Feasts for the year 1798

Dominical Letter	G	Easter Sund.	April	8
Cycle of the Sun	15	Ascension Day.	May	17
Golden Number	13	Whitsunday	May	27
Epact	12	Trinity Sund.	June	3
Number of Direction	18	Advent Sund.	December	2

Eclipses for the year 1798 are four in number two of each luminary

First of the Sun May 15 d. 3 h. 7 m. P.M. Invisible at Baltimore, & 3h. 7m P.M. The Sun is central ~~eclipsed~~ eclipsed on the Meridian in Long. 37 ¼ w from the Meridian ~~and~~ of Baltimore and Lat. 49 South

Second of the Moon May 29 d. 1 h. 11 m. P.M. therefore invisible with us

Third of the Sun November 7 d. ~~[illegible] P.M.~~ Invisible at Baltimore & at 8 h. 46 m. the Sun is central and totally Eclipsed on the Meridian in Long 131° west of Baltimore and Lat. 46°. 34 North

~~Fourth and last of the Moon Novemb 23 d. 7 h. 28 m. A.M. Invisible~~

Fourth and last is a visible ~~eclipse~~ eclipse of the Moon November 23 d. 7 h. 28 m. A.M.

Begiming — 6 h. 5 m.

Greatest obscuration — 7. 28

End — 8. 50

Moon Sets in her greatest obscuration

to wit 6½ digits on her South Limb

1795 May Fifth Month hath 31 Days

	d. h. m.
Last ☾	7..3..27 aft.
New ☽	15..3..7 aft.
First ☾	22..3..20 aft.
Full ○	29..1..11 aft.

☋ { ♐ 6 / 11 II 5 / 21 4 } deg.

	☉	♄	♃	♂	♀	☿	☽'s
D.	Long.	♋	♉	♒	♓	II	Lat.
1	1..11..31	8	5	7	29	1	0 N.
7	1..17..19	8	6	11	♈ 3	8	5 S.
13	1..23..6	9	8	14	8	11	3 S.
19	1..28..52	9	9	18	13	11	3 N.
25	2..4..38	10	11	21	19	8	4 N.

M D	W D	Remarkable days Aspects weather &c	☉ rise	☉ set	☽'s Long.	☽ rise	☽ south	☽'s age
1	3	philip & James	5..9	6..51	8..0..38	8..57	13..46	16
2	4	rain	5..8	6..52	8..14..4	10..1	14..43	17
3	5	Spica ♍ South 10..33	5..7	6..53	8..27..4	10..59	15..34	18
4	6	the flowers now	5..5	6..55	9..9..40	11..51	16..28	19
5	7	the fields adorn	5..4	6..56	9..21..57	12..37	17..18	20
6	G	4th. Sund. past East. St. John	5..3	6..57	10..3..54	13..17	18..6	21
7	2	☿ great elong. (evang.	5..2	6..58	10..15..42	13..51	18..50	22
8	3	farmers haste	5..1	6..59	10..27..21	14..19	19..32	23
9	4	Days 14	5..0	7..0	11..9..0	14..43	20..12	24
10	5	to plant ye. corn	4..59	7..1	11..20..42	15..7	20..53	25
11	6	☿ rise 3..9	4..58	7..2	0..2..36	15..31	21..35	26
12	7	rain	4..58	7..2	0..14..35	15..59	22..19	27
13	G	Rogation Sund.	4..57	7..3	0..26..52	16..29	23..5	28
14	2	☌ ☽ ♃	4..56	7..4	1..9..28		23..53	29
15	3	☉ Eclip	4..55	7..5	1..22..21	Sets		☽
16	4	with thunder	4..54	7..6	2..5..23	7..59	0..43	1
17	5	Ascention day	4..53	7..7	2..19..5	8..59	1..36	2
18	6	gusts	4..52	7..8	3..2..51	9..57	2..33	3
19	7	✱ ♄ ♃	4..52	7..8	3..16..50	10..53	3..33	4
20	G	Sund. past Ascen.	4..51	7..9	4..1..1	11..44	4..33	5
21	2	☉ enters II	4..51	7..9	4..15..17	12..28	5..31	6
22	3	Days increase 5..4	4..50	7..10	4..29..41	13..5	6..25	7
23	4	♀ great elong.	4..49	7..11	5..14..6	13..38	7..17	8
24	5	pegasi Markab rise 12..2	4..48	7..12	5..28..35	14..7	8..7	9
25	6	now for rain	4..47	7..13	6..13..2	14..40	8..57	10
26	7	now	4..46	7..14	6..27..22	15..13	9..49	11
27	G	Whitsund. ☌ ☉ ☿ Orient.	4..46	7..14	7..11..36	15..49	10..43	12
28	2	Whit. Mond.	4..45	7..15	7..25..35		11..38	13
29	3	Whit. Tues. ☽ Eclip invis.	4..44	7..16	8..9..17	rise	12..33	14
30	4	clear again	4..44	7..16	8..22..39	8..53	13..29	15
31	5	pegasi Algenib rise 0..56	4..43	7..17	9..5..39	9..46	14..22	16

In the Month of January 1797, on a pleasant day for the Season I observed my honey bees to be out of their hives and Seemed very busy all but one hive, upon examination I found all the bees had evacuated the hive and left not a drop of honey behind them, and on the 9th day of February ensuing, I killed the neighbouring hive of Bees on a Special occation and found a great quantity of honey considering the season, which I immagine the Stronger had violently taken from the weaker and the weaker had persued them to their home resolved to be benefitted by their labour or die in the contest,

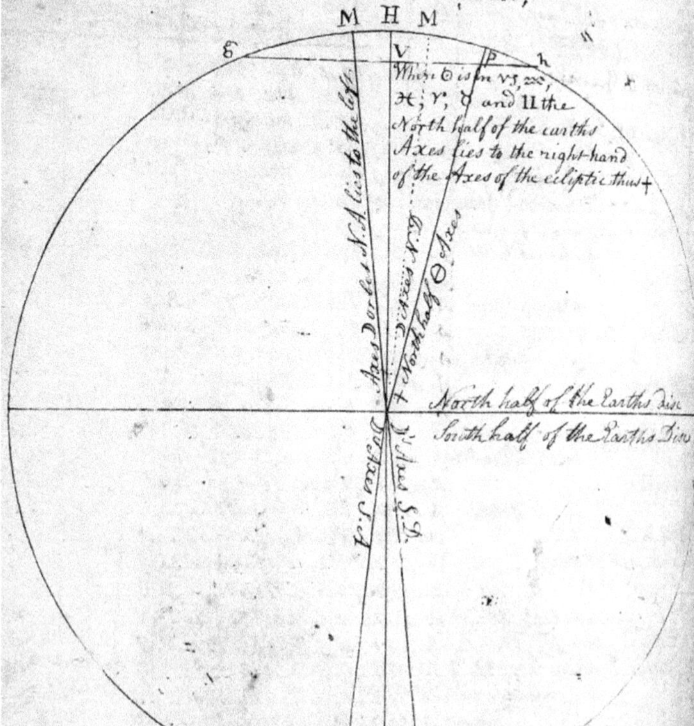

M H M
V
When ☉ is in ♑, ♒, ♓; ♈, ♉ and ♊ the North half of the earths Axes lies to the right hand of the Axes of the ecliptic thus +
North half ☉ Axes
North half of the Earths dia
South half of the Earths Dia
M H M

1798 June Sixth Month hath 30 Days

	☽	☉	♄	♃	♂	♀	☿	☽'s
			Planets Places					
Last ☽ 6d. 6h.. 35m morn.		Long.	♋	♉	♒	♈	♊	Lat.
New ☽ 14.. 2.. 1 morn.	1	2..11..20	11	12	24	26	4	4 S.
First ☽ 20..8..55 aft.	7	2..17..4	12	14	28	♉ 2	2	5 S.
Full ○ 28..0..31 morn.	13	2..22..48	12	15	♓ 0	8	1	1 N.
☊ {1, 11 ♊, 21} {4, 3, 3} deg.	19	2..28..32	13	16	3	14	6	5 N.
	25	3..1..14	14	17	7	21	12	0 S.

M D	W D	Remarkable days Aspects weather &c	☉ rise	☉ set	☽'s Long.	☽ rise	☽ South	☽'s age
1	6	Lyra South 1..37	4..43	7..17	9..18..16	10..33	15..13	17
2	7	warm	4..42	7..18	10..0..35	11..12	16..1	18
3	G	Trinity Sund.	4..42	7..18	10..12..34	11..45	16..45	19
4	2	rain	4..41	7..19	10..24..26	12..14	17..27	20
5	3	Days increase 5..22	4..41	7..19	11..6..5	12..40	18..8	21
6	4	flying clouds	4..41	7..19	11..17..42	13..5	18..49	22
7	5	♀ rise 2..22	4..40	7..20	11..29..20	13..30	19..29	23
8	6	Days 14..40	4..40	7..20	0..11..6	13..56	20..11	24
9	7	windy	4..40	7..20	0..23..3	14..24	20..55	25
10	G	1st Sund past Trin.	4..39	7..21	1..5..19	14..56	21..41	26
11	2	☌ ☽ ♃ St. Barnabas	4..39	7..21	1..17..53	15..32	22..30	27
12	3	like for	4..39	7..21	2..0..50	16..10	23..23	28
13	4	Spica ♍ Sets 1..18	4..39	7..21	2..14..9			29
14	5	rain	4..39	7..21	2..27..52	Sets	0..19	☽
15	6	pegasi Markab rise 10..32	4..38	7..22	3..11..54	8..40	1..17	2
16	7	clear	4..38	7..22	3..26..11	9..32	2..17	3
17	G	2d. Sund. past Trin.	4..38	7..22	4..10..36	10..17	3..15	4
18	2	St. Alban	4..38	7..22	4..25..7	10..55	4..9	5
19	3	☿ great elong	4..38	7..22	5..9..38	11..29	5..1	6
20	4	and warm,	4..38	7..22	5..24..3	12..2	5..53	7
21	5	Longest day ☉ enters ♋	4..38	7..22	6..8..24	12..34	6..45	8
22	6	thunder	4..38	7..22	6..22..40	13..6	7..37	9
23	7	gusts	4..38	7..22	7..6..47	13..41	8..29	10
24	G	3d Sund. past Trin. St. John	4..38	7..22	7..20..42	14..19	9..22	11
25	2	and rain	4..38	7..22	8..4..25	15..1	10..16	12
26	3	pegasi Algenib rise 10..58	4..38	7..22	8..17..52	15..48	11..11	13
27	4	heavy	4..38	7..22	9..1..6		12..5	14
28	5	weather	4..38	7..22	9..14..2	rise	12..58	15
29	6	St. peter & paul	4..39	7..21	9..26..38	9..3	13..48	16
30	7	Days decrease 2 m.	4..39	7..21	10..8..58	9..39	14..36	17

Trigonometry

The Base being given, and the acute ∠ at A, to find the ~~perpendicular~~ hypothenuse
and ~~hypothenuse~~ perpendicular

In this right angled triangle ABG. there is given the Base AB 26 feet, the angle at A 30° to find the length of the hypothenuse.

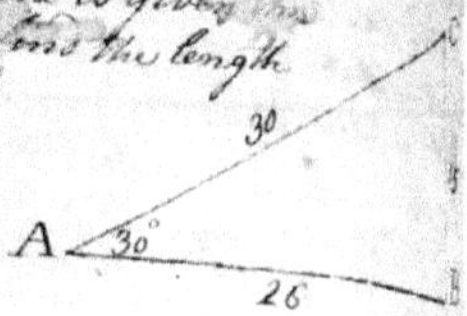

To find the Sine complement
Subtract the given angle at A
from 90°

As Sine complement of the ∠ at A
is to the Logarithm Base 26
So is radius or the Sine of 90°
to the Logarithm of the hypothenuse)
AC = 30 feet

9·93753 Sub
1·41497 add
10·00000 to
11·41497 from
1·47744 = 30 feet ~~hypoth~~ hypothenuse

The hypothenuse being obtained I now seek for the perpendicular
As the Sine of the angle ACB 60°
is to the Logarithm of the base AB 26
So is the Sine of the angle CAB 30
to the Logarithm of the perpendicular CB 15.

9·93753 Sub.
1·41497 add
9·69897 to
11·11394 from
1·17641 = 15

Or this may be performed by projection, Draw a line ~~X~~ at random of sufficient lenght, then lay your protractor on said line, take from thence the [illegible] of 30° at A and draw a line at pleasure for the hypothenuse and let fall a perpendicular on B and that give the lenght of the perpendicular

1798 July Seventh Month hath 31 Days

							Planets Places	
	☽	☉	♄	♃	♂	♀	☿	☽'s
Last ☾ 5..11..35 aft. (d h m)		Long.	♋	♉	♓	♉	♊	Lat.
New ☽ 13..10..50 morn.	1	3..9..59	15	18	8	27	21	5 S.
First ☽ 20..3..1 morn.	7	3..15..42	15	19	10	♊ 4	29	3 S.
Full ○ 27..1..30 aft.	13	3..21..25	16	20	11	11	♋ 13	4 N.
☊ {1 ♊ 2, 11 2, 21 1} deg.	19	3..27..9	17	21	12	18	26	4 N.
	25	4..2..53	18	22	13	25	♌ 8	3 S.

M D	W D	Remarkable days Aspects weather &c.	☉ rise	☉ set	☽'s Long.	☽ rise	☽ South	☽'s age
1	G	4th. Sund. past Trin	4..39	7..21	10..21..4	10..10	15..20	18
2	2	Visitation V. Mary	4..40	7..20	11..2..58	10..37	16..1	19
3	3	expect rain	4..40	7..20	11..14..43	11..2	16..42	20
4	4	Translation, St. Martin	4..40	7..20	11..26..25	11..28	17..23	21
5	5	Farmers go reap	4..41	7..19	0..8..7	11..52	18..3	22
6	6	☌ ☉ ♄ orient.	4..41	7..19	0..19..53	12..19	18..45	23
7	7	God send you	4..42	7..18	1..1..51	12..48	19..30	24
8	G	5th. Sund. past Trin.	4..42	7..18	1..14..2	13..22	20..18	25
9	2	(☌ ☽ ♃	4..43	7..17	1..26..36	13..59	21..8	26
10	3	a good heap	4..43	7..17	2..9..32	14..43	22..2	27
11	4	Lyra South. 11..7	4..44	7..16	2..22..53	15..38	23..2	28
12	5	expect thunder	4..44	7..16	3..6..43			29
13	6	♀ rise 1..53	4..45	7..15	3..20..52	Sets	0..2	☽
14	7	and Showers	4..45	7..15	4..5..21	8..6	0..59	2
15	G	6th. Sund. past Trin.	4..46	7..14	4..20..2	8..45	1..53	3
16	2	to Cherish	4..47	7..13	5..4..46	9..21	2..47	4
17	3	Days 14..26.	4..47	7..13	5..19..26	9..56	3..40	5
18	4	♃ rise 0..25	4..48	7..12	6..3..59	10..30	4..32	6
19	5	the flowers,	4..49	7..11	6..18..20	11..3	5..24	7
20	6	Margaret	4..49	7..11	7..2..25	11..36	6..16	8
21	7	☌ ☉ ☿ Occident.	4..50	7..10	7..16..18	12..11	7..8	9
22	G	7th. Sund. past Trin.	4..51	7..9	7..29..58	12..51	8..2	10
23	2	☉ enters ♌, (Magdelen	4..52	7..8	8..13..21	13..37	8..56	11
24	3	gusty	4..53	7..7	8..26..29	14..27	9..50	12
25	4	St. James	4..54	7..6	9..9..29	15..22	10..45	13
26	5	St. Anne weather	4..54	7..6	9..22..14		11..37	14
27	6		4..55	7..5	10..4..47	rise	12..27	15
28	7	with frequent	4..56	7..4	10..17..8	8..10	13..14	16
29	G	8th. Sund. past Trin. Showers	4..57	7..3	10..29..17	8..37	13..56	17
30	2	Dog days begins of	4..58	7..2	11..11..17	9..3	14..37	18
31	3	Days 14..2 rain	4..59	7..1	11..23..10	9..28	15..18	19

Suppose Ladder 60 feet long be placed in a Street so as to reach a window on one Side 37 feet high, and without moving it at bottom, will reach another on the other side of the Street which is 23 feet high, required the breadth of the

1798 August Eighth Month hath 31 Days

	d	h	m	
Last ☾	2.	4.	3. 24	aft
New ☽	11.	6.	34	aft
First ☾	18.	0.	0	noon
Full ○	26.	4.	29	morn.

☊ { 1 1 / 11 II 0 / 21 0 } deg.

Planets Places

D	☉ Long	♄ ♋	♃ ♉	♂ ♓	♀ ♋	☿ ♌	☽'s Lat.
1	4.4.35	19	23	14	3	22	4 S.
7	4.15.19	19	24	13	10	♍ 2	2 N.
13	4.21.4	20	25	12	17	12	5 N.
19	4.26.51	21	25	11	24	21	1 S.
25	5.2.39	21	26	10	♌ 3	29	5 S.

M D	W D	Remarkable days Aspects weather &c.	☉ rise	☉ set	☽'s Long	☽ rise	☽ South	☽'s age
1	4	Lammas Day	5..0	7..0	0..4..59	9..53	16..0	20
2	5	expect	5..1	6..59	0..16..50	10..19	16..42	21
3	6	Lyra South 9..36	5..2	6..58	0..28..45	10..48	17..26	22
4	7	rain	5..3	6..57	1..10..45	11..20	18..12	23
5	G	9th Sund. past Trin.	5..4	6..56	1..23..2	11..56	19..0	24
6	2	(☌ ☽ ♃	5..5	6..55	2..5..33	12..37	19..52	25
7	3	♀ rise 2..16	5..6	6..54	2..18..31	13..25	20..48	26
8	4	Days decrease 58 min.	5..7	6..53	3..1..53	14..25	21..47	27
9	5	hot	5..8	6..52	3..15..41	15..25	22..46	28
10	6	St. Laurence	5..9	6..51	3..29..55		23..46	29
11	7	and dry,	5..10	6..50	4..14..30	Sets		☽
12	G	10th Sund. past Trin.	5..11	6..49	4..29..16	7..23	0..40	1
13	2	heavy thunder	5..12	6..48	5..14..14	7..55	1..34	2
14	3	Spica ♍ Set 9..5	5..13	6..47	5..29..5	8..27	2..26	3
15	4	wind	5..14	6..46	6..13..46	8..59	3..18	4
16	5	pegasi Markab rise 6..23	5..15	6..45	6..28..7	9..33	4..10	5
17	6	□ ☉ ♃ and rain	5..16	6..44	7..12..11	10..8	5..2	6
18	7	now	5..18	6..42	7..25..54	10..47	5..55	7
19	G	11th Sund. past Trin.	5..19	6..41	8..9..19	11..31	6..49	8
20	2	expect	5..20	6..40	8..22..26	12..19	7..43	9
21	3	pegasi Algenib rise 7..13	5..21	6..39	9..5..20	13..13	8..37	10
22	4	great	5..22	6..38	9..18..0	14..11	9..31	11
23	5	☉ enters ♍	5..23	6..37	10..0..34	15..10	10..21	12
24	6	St. Bartholomew	5..24	6..36	10..12..53	16..9	11..9	13
25	7	Dews	5..26	6..34	10..25..7		11..53	14
26	G	12th Sund. past Trin	5..27	6..33	11..7..17	rise	12..37	15
27	2	rain end	5..28	6..32	11..19..21	7..35	13..21	16
28	3	St. Augustine	5..29	6..31	0..1..22	8..4	14..4	17
29	4	St. John behead.	5..30	6..30	0..13..23	8..32	14..47	18
30	5	the month	5..32	6..28	0..25..23	8..58	15..30	19
31	6	Days 12..54	5..33	6..27	1..7..29	9..25	16..13	20

1798 September : Ninth Month hath 30 Days

			Planets Places					
☽ D. h. m.	☽	☉	♄	♃	♂	♀	☿	☽'s
Last ☾ 3. 3. 43 morn.		Long.	♋	♉	♓	♌	♎	Lat.
New ☽ 10. 2. 14 morn.	1	5. 9. 25	22	26	8	10	7	1. S.
First ☽ 16. 9. 51 aft.	7	5. 15. 15	23	26	6	17	11	5 N.
Full ☉ 24. 9. 7 aft.	13	5. 21. 6	24	26	5	24	12	2 N.
☊ { 1 ♉ 29, 11 28, 21 28 } deg.	19	5. 26. 57	24	26	4	♍ 2	12	4 S.
	25	6. 2. 50	24	26	4	9	7	2 S.

M D	W D	Remarkable Days Aspects weather &c	☉ rise	☉ set	☽'s Long.	☽ rise	☽ South	☽'s age
1	7	☿ great elong. ☌ ☽ ♃	5. 34	6. 26	1. 19. 42	9. 58	17. 1	21
2	G	13th. Sund past Trin.	5. 35	6. 25	2. 2. 6	10. 39	17. 52	22
3	2	Dog days end.	5. 36	6. 24	2. 14. 45	11. 25	18. 46	23
4	3	rain	5. 38	6. 22	2. 27. 45	12. 18	19. 42	24
5	4	Cassiopea South 1. 36	5. 39	6. 21	3. 11. 7	13. 17	20. 40	25
6	5	Days decrease 2. 4	5. 40	6. 20	3. 24. 55	14. 23	21. 39	26
7	6	and wind	5. 41	6. 19	4. 9. 8	15. 33	22. 36	27
8	7	Nativity V. Mary	5. 43	6. 17	4. 23. 38	16. 46	23. 32	28
9	G	14th. Sund. past Trin.	5. 44	6. 16	5. 8. 35			29
10	2	flying	5. 45	6. 15	5. 23. 33	Sets	0. 25	☽
11	3	pleiades rise 8. 53	5. 46	6. 14	6. 8. 30	7. 6	1. 18	2
12	4	clouds	5. 48	6. 12	6. 23. 16	7. 40	2. 11	3
13	5	♀ rise 3. 37	5. 49	6. 11	7. 7. 42	8. 15	3. 4	4
14	6	Days 12. 20	5. 50	6. 10	7. 21. 47	8. 53	3. 57	5
15	7	warm	5. 52	6. 8	8. 5. 31	9. 34	4. 50	6
16	G	15th. Sund. past Trin. ✱ ☉ ♄	5. 53	6. 7	8. 18. 43	10. 20	5. 43	7
17	2	♃ Stationary	5. 54	6. 6	9. 1. 41	11. 12	6. 36	8
18	3	△ ☉ ♃ rain	5. 55	6. 5	9. 14. 17	12. 8	7. 29	9
19	4	and wind,	5. 56	6. 4	9. 26. 45	13. 8	8. 22	10
20	5	pleasant	5. 58	6. 2	10. 9. 0	14. 8	9. 12	11
21	6	St. Matthew	5. 59	6. 1	10. 21. 7	15. 8	9. 58	12
22	7	☉ enters ♎	6. 0	6. 0	11. 3. 42	16. 8	10. 42	13
23	G	16th. Sund. past Trin.	6. 2	5. 58	11. 15. 15		11. 23	14
24	2	weather	6. 3	5. 57	11. 27. 17	rise	12. 5	15
25	3	Bulls eye rise 9. 19	6. 4	5. 56	0. 9. 22	6. 36	12. 48	16
26	4	St. Cyprian	6. 5	5. 55	0. 21. 32	7. 2	13. 31	17
27	5	☌ ☉ ♀ Orient.	6. 7	5. 53	1. 3. 46	7. 31	14. 16	18
28	6	expects rain	6. 8	5. 52	1. 16. 4	8. 5	15. 4	19
29	7	☌ ☽ ♃, St. Michael	6. 9	5. 51	1. 28. 33	8. 43	15. 54	20
30	G	17th. Sund. past Trin.	6. 11	5. 49	2. 11. 11	9. 29	16. 48	21

October Tenth Month hath 31 Days

d h m								
Last ☾ 2..4..28 aft.								
New ☽ 9..10..45 morn.								
First ☽ 16..0..25 aft.								
Full ○ 24..2..27 aft.								

Planet Places

D	☉ Long.	♄ ♋	♃ ♉	♂ ♓	♀ ♍	☿ ♎	☽'s Lat.
1	6..8..44	25	26	3	16	1	2 N.
7	6..14..40	25	26	4	24	♍ 29	5 N.
13	6..20..37	25	25	4	♎ 1	♎ 2	2 S.
19	6..26..35	26	24	6	9	10	5 S.
25	7..2..33	26	24	7	17	20	1 S.

☊ { 1 ♉ 27; 11 27; 21 26 } Deg.

M D	W D	Remarkable days Aspects weather &c.	☉ rise	☉ set	☽'s Long.	☽ rise	☽ south	☽'s age
1	2	Days 11..36 rain,	6..12	5..48	2..24..4	10..20	17..44	22
2	3	take warning	6..13	5..47	3..7..12	11..16	18..40	23
3	4	pleiades South 3..1	6..14	5..46	3..20..38	12..17	19..36	24
4	5	now comes the	6..15	5..45	4..4..27	13..24	20..32	25
5	6	Bulls eye rise 8..43	6..17	5..43	4..18..37	14..35	21..28	26
6	7	cool morning	6..18	5..42	5..3..6	15..46	22..22	27
7	G	18 Sund. past Trin.	6..19	5..41	5..17..52	16..57	23..14	28
8	2	△ ♃ ☿ and like	6..20	5..40	6..2..49			29
9	3	for a frost	6..22	5..38	6..17..46	set	0..4	☽
10	4	Days decrease 3..30	6..23	5..37	7..2..32	6..14	0..57	2
11	5	let not your labour	6..24	5..36	7..17..3	6..53	1..53	3
12	6		6..25	5..35	8..1..8	7..37	2..49	4
13	7	☿ great elong. ✶ ♄ ♃	6..27	5..33	8..14..49	8..24	3..45	5
14	G	19th. Sund past Trin	6..28	5..32	8..28..3	9..16	4..41	6
15	2	be lost	6..29	5..31	9..10..52	10..12	5..35	7
16	3	pleiades South 2..13	6..30	5..30	9..23..23	11..10	6..27	8
17	4	now rain	6..32	5..28	10..5..37	12..9	7..15	9
18	5	St. Luke □ ☉ ♄	6..33	5..27	10..16..49	13..8	8..1	10
19	6	Clear weather	6..34	5..26	10..29..32	14..6	8..45	11
20	7	☌ ♀ ☿ again,	6..35	5..25	11..11..27	15..3	9..27	12
21	G	20th. Sund. past Trin.	6..36	5..24	11..23..22	16..0	10..8	13
22	2	windy	6..38	5..22	0..5..18	16..57	10..50	14
23	3	☉ enters ♏	6..39	5..21	0..17..22		11..32	15
24	4	and cool	6..40	5..20	0..29..32	rise	12..17	16
25	5	morning	6..41	5..19	1..11..54	6..10	13..4	17
26	6	☌ ☽ ♃ and	6..42	5..18	1..24..28	6..47	13..53	18
27	7	evenings	6..44	5..16	2..7..12	7..29	14..46	19
28	G	21st. Sund past Trin.	6..45	5..15	2..20..8	8..18	15..41	20
29	2	St. Simon & Jude	6..46	5..14	3..3..17	9..13	16..37	21
30	3	flying clouds	6..47	5..13	3..16..40	10..13	17..34	22
31	4	Days 10..24 & rain	6..48	5..12	4..0..17	11..17	18..29	23

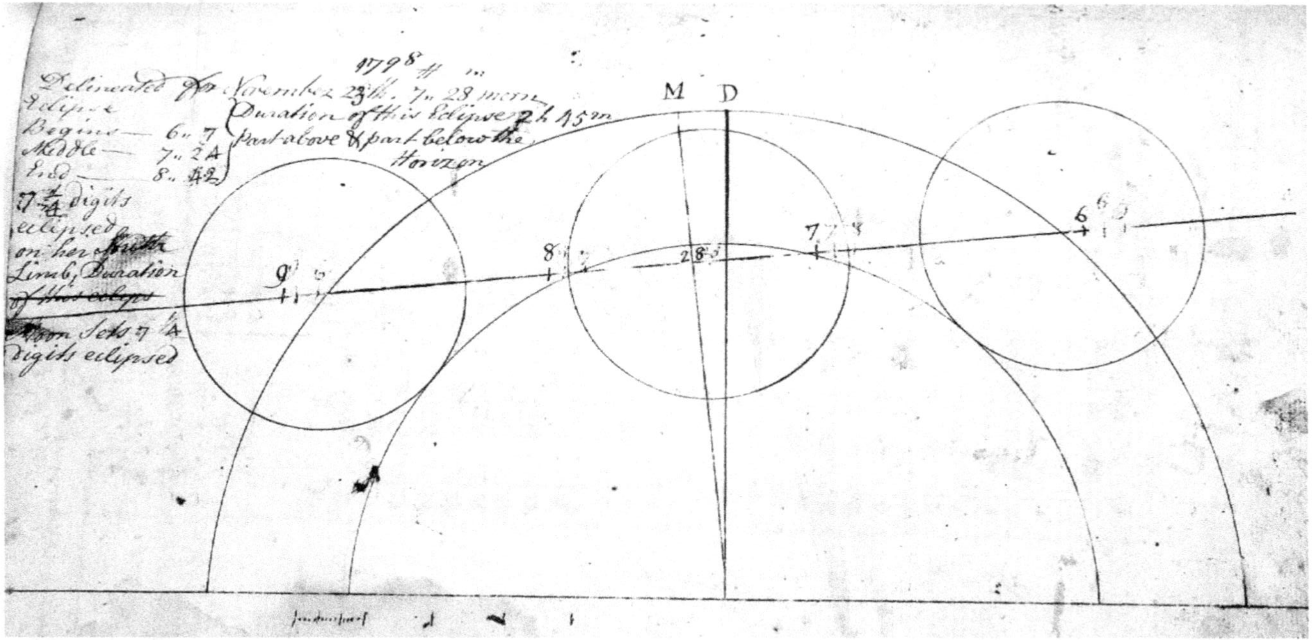
1798 h m
Delineated for November 23th. 7.. 28 morn
Eclipse
Begins — 6.. 7
Middle — 7.. 24
End — 8.. 42
Duration of this Eclipse 2h 15m
Part above & part below the Horizon
7 1/4 digits eclipsed on her North Limb, Duration of this eclipse
Moon Sets 7 1/4 digits eclipsed
M
D
9
8
28
7
6

1798 November Eleventh Month hath 30 Days

	d h m	
Last ☾	1 .. 2 .. 13	morn.
New ☽	7 .. 8 .. 46	aft.
First ☽	15 .. 4 .. 20	morn.
Full ○	23 .. 7 .. 28	morn.
Last ☾	30 .. 0 .. 49	aft.

☊ { 1 ♉ 26 / 11 25 / 21 25 } deg.

Planets Places

☽	☉	♄	♃	♂	♀	☿	☽'s
	Long.	♋	♉	♓	♎	♏	Lat.
1	7 .. 9 .. 34	26	23	10	25	1	5 N.
7	7 .. 15 .. 36	26	22	11	♏ 3	11	1 N.
13	7 .. 21 .. 39	26	21	13	10	21	5 S.
19	7 .. 27 .. 41	26	21	17	18	♐ 0	3 S.
25	8 .. 3 .. 46	26	20	20	25	10	3 N.

M D	W D	Remarkable days Aspects weather &c	☉ rise	☉ set	☽'s Long.	☽ rise	☽ South	☽'s age
1	5	All Saints perhaps	6 .. 49	5 .. 11	4 .. 14 .. 12	12 .. 24	19 .. 24	24
2	6	pleaades South 1 .. 8	6 .. 51	5 .. 9	4 .. 28 .. 22	13 .. 35	20 .. 17	25
3	7	snow or	6 .. 52	5 .. 8	5 .. 12 .. 46	14 .. 47	21 .. 10	26
4	G	22d. Sund. past Trin.	6 .. 53	5 .. 7	5 .. 27 .. 25	15 .. 59	22 .. 3	27
5	2	Days decrease 4 .. 32	6 .. 54	5 .. 6	6 .. 12 .. 9	17 .. 12	22 .. 56	28
6	3	rain	6 .. 55	5 .. 5	6 .. 26 .. 56		23 .. 49	29
7	4	☉ eclip invis.	6 .. 56	5 .. 4	7 .. 11 .. 39	set		☽
8	5	followed	6 .. 57	5 .. 3	7 .. 26 .. 5	5 .. 30	0 .. 42	1
9	6	Sirius rise 10 .. 33	6 .. 58	5 .. 2	8 .. 10 .. 12	6 .. 22	1 .. 38	2
10	7	by	6 .. 59	5 .. 1	8 .. 23 .. 52	7 .. 14	2 .. 35	3
11	G	23d Sund. past Trin.	7 .. 0	5 .. 0	9 .. 7 .. 7	8 .. 8	3 .. 31	4
12	2	♄ Stationary (St. Martin	7 .. 1	4 .. 59	9 .. 19 .. 56	9 .. 4	4 .. 24	5
13	3	☍ ☉ ♃ Occident. frosty	7 .. 2	4 .. 58	10 .. 2 .. 24	10 .. 2	5 .. 14	6
14	4	☌ ☉ ☿ Occident.	7 .. 3	4 .. 57	10 .. 14 .. 29	11 .. 0	6 .. 0	7
15	5	mornings	7 .. 4	4 .. 56	10 .. 26 .. 26	11 .. 58	6 .. 44	8
16	6	Spica ♍ rise 4 .. 26	7 .. 5	4 .. 55	11 .. 8 .. 13	12 .. 55	7 .. 26	9
17	7	rain	7 .. 6	4 .. 54	11 .. 19 .. 56	13 .. 52	8 .. 6	10
18	G	24th. Sund. past Trin.	7 .. 7	4 .. 53	0 .. 1 .. 43	14 .. 47	8 .. 45	11
19	2	or snow	7 .. 8	4 .. 52	0 .. 13 .. 29	15 .. 43	9 .. 26	12
20	3	temperate	7 .. 8	4 .. 52	0 .. 25 .. 27	16 .. 43	10 .. 9	13
21	4	☉ enters ♐	7 .. 9	4 .. 51	1 .. 7 .. 38	17 .. 43	10 .. 53	14
22	5	☌ ☽ ♃,	7 .. 10	4 .. 50	1 .. 20 .. 1		11 .. 42	15
23	6	☽ eclip. vis	7 .. 11	4 .. 49	2 .. 2 .. 43	rise	12 .. 33	16
24	7	[illegible]	7 .. 12	4 .. 48	2 .. 15 .. 39	6 .. 4	13 .. 26	17
25	G	25th. Sund past Trin.	7 .. 12	4 .. 48	2 .. 28 .. 53	6 .. 59	14 .. 24	18
26	2	rain toward	7 .. 13	4 .. 47	3 .. 12 .. 22	7 .. 57	15 .. 20	19
27	3	Day 9 .. 32	7 .. 14	4 .. 46	3 .. 26 .. 3	9 .. 1	16 .. 16	20
28	4	Algol South . 10 .. 37	7 .. 15	4 .. 45	4 .. 9 .. 57	10 .. 8	17 .. 11	21
29	5	the end	7 .. 15	4 .. 45	4 .. 24 .. 1	11 .. 16	18 .. 3	22
30	6	St. Andrew.	7 .. 16	4 .. 44	5 .. 8 .. 17	12 .. 25	18 .. 54	23

B

1798 November 16. Between 8 and 9 O'clock, I saw a bur or so[me]
Condensed particles of the Atmosphere of divers colours gath[ered]
round the moon, and that which was first and nearest to her apparent Center
white, the second of an orange, the third blue, and the fourth was
nearly coloured like unto the rain bow, this small circle was in
breadth, about seven times the moons apparent Diameter

B.B

1798 November 30th, planted 170 pare tree Sprouts

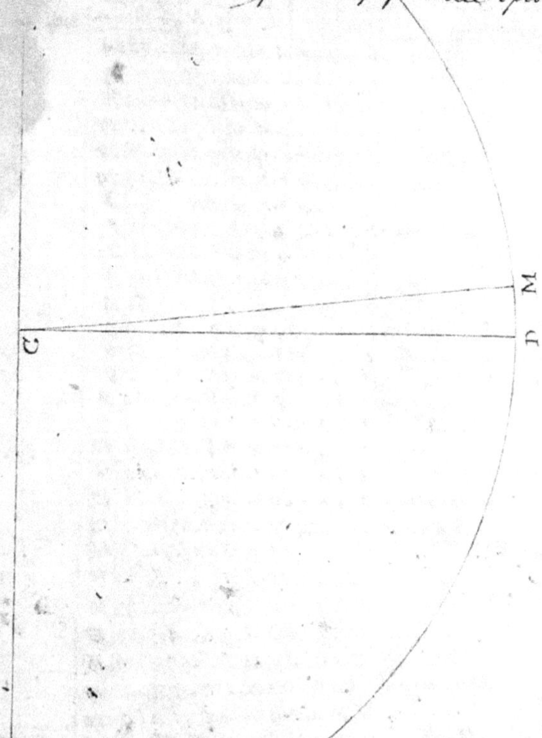

1798 December Twelfth Month hath 31 Days

			Planets Places					
	D	☉	♄	♃	♂	♀	☿	☽'s
New ☽ 7..8..51 morn. (d h m)		Long.	♋	♉	♓	♐	♐	Lat.
First ☽ 15..0..33 morn.	1	8..9..51	26	19	23	3	19	5 N.
Full ○ 22..11..9 aft.	7	8..15..56	25	18	26	10	28	2 S.
Last ☽ 29..9..23 aft.	13	8..22..3	25	18	♈ 0	18	♑ 7	5 S.
☊ {1, 11, 21} ♉ {24, 23, 23} deg.	19	8..28..9	24	17	3	25	16	1 S.
	25	9..4..17	24	17	7	♑ 3	24	5 N.

M D	W D	Remarkable days Aspects weather &c	☉ rise	☉ set	☽'s Long	☽ rise	☽ South	☽'s age
1	7	procyon South 3..0	7..16	4..44	5..22..40	13..34	19..44	24
2	G	Advent Sund.	7..17	4..43	6..7..9	14..48	20..38	25
3	2	Snow	7..18	4..42	6..21..43	16..1	21..32	26
4	3	Day decrease 5..20	7..18	4..42	7..6..36	17..14	22..26	27
5	4	△ ♄ ♂ or rain	7..19	4..41	7..20..44	18..23	23..20	28
6	5	Nicholas	7..19	4..41	8..5..0			29
7	6	hard frosts	7..20	4..40	8..19..0	set	0..14	☽
8	7	Conception V. Mary	7..20	4..40	9..2..38	5..43	1..8	2
9	G	2d. Sund in Advent	7..20	4..40	9..15..52	6..43	2..2	3
10	2	cold and	7..21	4..39	9..28..44	7..43	2..56	4
11	3	pegasi Markab So. 5..40	7..21	4..39	10..11..11	8..43	3..46	5
12	4	windy,	7..21	4..39	10..23..22	9..43	4..32	6
13	5	pegasi Algenib So. 6..39	7..21	4..39	11..5..17	10..41	5..15	7
14	6	Snow or	7..22	4..38	11..16..59	11..38	5..55	8
15	7	rain	7..22	4..38	11..28..37	12..33	6..34	9
16	G	3d. Sund. in Advent	7..22	4..38	0..10..14	13..27	7..13	10
17	2	Sirius South 0..59	7..22	4..38	0..21..58	14..23	7..54	11
18	3	flying	7..22	4..38	1..3..50	15..21	8..37	12
19	4	☌ ☽ ♃ Clouds	7..22	4..38	1..15..55	16..21	9..22	13
20	5	with	7..22	4..38	1..28..20	17..21	10..11	14
21	6	☉ enters ♑ Short day	7..22	4..38	2..11..1		11..3	15
22	7	wind	7..22	4..38	2..24..5	rise	11..58	16
23	G	4th. Sund in Advent	7..22	4..38	3..7..29	5..31	12..55	17
24	2	very cold	7..22	4..38	3..21..18	6..33	13..51	18
25	3	Christmas Day	7..22	4..38	4..5..16	7..38	14..47	19
26	4	St. Stephen	7..22	4..38	4..19..27	8..46	15..41	20
27	5	St. John	7..22	4..38	5..3..48	9..56	16..33	21
28	6	Innocents rain	7..21	4..39	5..18..12	11..6	17..24	22
29	7	or Snow	7..21	4..39	6..2..39	12..17	18..15	23
30	G	1st. Sund. past Chris.	7..21	4..39	6..17..5	13..28	19..6	24
31	2	Silvester.	7..20	4..40	7..1..27	14..39	19..59	25

12 minutes at a moon [illegible] must be added to moons [illegible]

1799

January

		h	m	
New ☽	5	11	13	aft.
Full ○	21	0	52	aft

1799

February

New ☽	4	3	33	aft.
Full ○	20	0	31	morn.

March

New ☽	6	9	6	morn
Full ○	21	10	21	morn

April

New ☽	5	2	45	morn
Full ○	19	6	50	aft.

May

New ☽	4	7	18	aft.
Full ○	19	2	43	morn

June

New ☽	3	3	56	morn.
Full ○	17	4	50	morn.

July

New ☽	2	10	34	aft. r
Full ○	16	8	10	aft. r

August

New ☽	1	9	1	morn r
Full ○	15	7	36	morn r
New ☽	30	6	20	aft. r

September

Full ○	13	9	41	aft. r
New ☽	29	3	13	morn. r

October

Full ○	13	2	20	aft
New ☽	28	0	27	aft.

November

Full ○	12	8	47	morn.
New ☽	26	10	31	aft

December

Full ○	12	3	37	morn.
New ☽	26	9	46	morn

1799	1799	
Long. med. ☉ s ° ′ 9 .. 10 .. 21	Long. Apog. s ° ′ 3 9 31	
Long. med. ☽ s ° ′ 6 .. 29 .. 6	Long. Apog. ☽ 0 .. 4 .. 48	Long. ☊ s ° ′ 1 .. 22 .. 35
Long. med. ♄ s ° ′ 3 .. 19 .. 45	Anomally ♄ s ° ′ 6 .. 19 .. 0	Node ♄ s ° ′ 3 .. 21 .. 35
Long. med. ♃ s ° ′ 1 .. 21 .. 56	Anomolly ♃ s ° ′ 7 .. 10 .. 24	Node ♃ s ° ′ 3 .. 8 .. 57
Long. med. ♂ s ° ′ 1 .. 11 .. 17	Anomally ♂ s ° ′ 8 .. 8 .. 48	Node ♂ s ° ′ 1 .. 18 .. 27
Long. med. ♀ s ° ′ 9 .. 10 .. 20	Anomaly ♀ s ° ′ 11 .. 2 .. 16	Node ♀ s ° ′ 2 .. 14 .. 49
Long. med. ☿ s ° ′ 1 .. 24 .. 25	Anomaly ☿ s ° ′ 5 .. 10 .. 15	Node ☿ s ° ′ 1 .. 16 .. 10

1?99 January First Month hath 31 Days

D. H. M.
New ☽ 5 .. 11 .. 13 aft.
First ☽ 13 .. 9 .. 26 aft.
Full ○ 21 .. 0 .. 52 aft.
Last ☽ 28 .. 5 .. 59 morn.

☊ { 1 / 11 / 21 } ♉ { 23 / 22 / 21 } degr.

Planets Places

☽	☉ Long.	♄ ♋	♃ ♉	♂ ♈	♀ ♑	☿ ♑	☽ Lat
1	9 .. 11 .. 24	23	16	11	12	29	1 N.
7	9 .. 17 .. 31	23	16	14	19	26	5 S.
13	9 .. 23 .. 38	22	16	18	27	19	3 S.
19	9 .. 29 .. 44	22	17	22	♒ 4	16	5 N.
25	10 .. 5 .. 50	21	17	25	12	13	4 N

M D	W D	Remarkable days Aspects weather &c		☉ rise	☉ set	☽'s Long.	☽ rise	☽ South	☽'s age
1	3	Circumcision □ ♂ ♀		7 .. 20	4 .. 40	7 .. 13 .. 48	15 .. 54	20 .. 54	26
2	4	Day increase 4 min		7 .. 20	4 .. 40	7 .. 29 .. 57	17 .. 4	21 .. 51	27
3	5	Sirius South 11 .. 43		7 .. 20	4 .. 40	8 .. 13 .. 56	18 .. 10	22 .. 47	28
4	6		cold	7 .. 19	4 .. 41	8 .. 27 .. 42	19 .. 10	23 .. 42	29
5	7	△ ☉ ♃,	rain	7 .. 19	4 .. 41	9 .. 11 .. 11	[illegible]	☌	☽
6	F	Epiphany	or	7 .. 18	4 .. 42	9 .. 24 .. 22	Set	0 .. 36	1
7	2		Snow	7 .. 18	4 .. 42	10 .. 7 .. 12	6 .. 21	1 .. 28	2
8	3	pleiades South 8 .. 15		7 .. 17	4 .. 43	10 .. 19 .. 43	7 .. 21	2 .. 16	3
9	4		flying	7 .. 17	4 .. 43	11 .. 1 .. 56	8 .. 20	2 .. 58	4
10	5		Clouds	7 .. 16	4 .. 44	11 .. 13 .. 55	9 .. 18	3 .. 38	5
11	6	☌ ☉ ☿ Orient. ☍ ☉ ♄		7 .. 15	4 .. 45	11 .. 25 .. 43	10 .. 15	4 .. 19	6
12	7		with	7 .. 15	4 .. 45	0 .. 7 .. 24	11 .. 12	5 .. 1	7
13	F	Sund. after Epip.		7 .. 14	4 .. 46	0 .. 19 .. 2	12 .. 8	5 .. 43	8
14	2		wind	7 .. 13	4 .. 47	1 .. 0 .. 43	13 .. 4	6 .. 25	9
15	3	☌ ☽ ♃		7 .. 13	4 .. 47	1 .. 12 .. 31	14 .. 0	7 .. 7	10
16	4		and	7 .. 12	4 .. 48	1 .. 24 .. 33	15 .. 0	7 .. 52	11
17	5		Snow	7 .. 11	4 .. 49	2 .. 6 .. 53	15 .. 59	8 .. 40	12
18	6	△ ♃ ☿		7 .. 10	4 .. 50	2 .. 19 .. 34	16 .. 55	9 .. 32	13
19	7	□ ♄ ♂		7 .. 10	4 .. 50	3 .. 2 .. 39	17 .. 49	10 .. 26	14
20	F	Septuagesima Sund. ☉ enters ♒		7 .. 9	4 .. 51	3 .. 16 .. 9		11 .. 23	15
21	2		cold	7 .. 8	4 .. 52	4 .. 0 .. 2	rise	12 .. 20	16
22	3	Bulls eye South 8 .. 4		7 .. 7	4 .. 53	4 .. 14 .. 18	6 .. 15	13 .. 16	17
23	4		westerly	7 .. 6	4 .. 54	4 .. 28 .. 46	7 .. 28	14 .. 11	18
24	5	Spica ♍ rise 11 .. 25		7 .. 5	4 .. 55	5 .. 13 .. 19	8 .. 41	15 .. 5	19
25	6	Convert St paul		7 .. 4	4 .. 56	5 .. 28 .. 3	9 .. 34	15 .. 58	20
26	7	days 9 .. 54		7 .. 3	4 .. 57	6 .. 12 .. 38	11 .. 7	16 .. 48	21
27	F		wind	7 .. 2	4 .. 58	6 .. 27 .. 5	12 .. 16	17 .. 38	22
28	2	pleades Set 2 .. 30 morn.		7 .. 1	4 .. 59	7 .. 11 .. 23	13 .. 24	18 .. 31	23
29	3		rain or	7 .. 0	5 .. 0	7 .. 25 .. 28	14 .. 32	19 .. 28	24
30	4	♃ Set 1 .. 8 mo.		6 .. 59	5 .. 1	8 .. 9 .. 22	15 .. 40	20 .. 26	25
31	5	~~☌ ☉ ☿ Occident~~	Snow	6 .. 58	5 .. 2	8 .. 23 .. 2	16 .. 47	21 .. 24	26

12 minutes must be added to the Moons meridian each in consideration to her ... motion

for by setting ... [illegible]

Venus commenced being Evening Star on the first day of June 1797 and appeared to the naked eye about the 24th July being ~~about~~ about 16° east of the Sun

According to the Nautical Almanac, 1795 the Epact was 9, and the Moons age on the first day of that year was 12 days.

1799							
Days	January Long. ☉ s ° ′	1799 Anomally ☉ s ° ′	Logarithm Dis. ☉ a Θ in hypoth.	Days	July Longit. ☉ s ° ′	1799 Anomal ☉ s ° ′	Logarithm Dis ☉ a Θ
1	9..11..24	6..1..49	4.99264	1	3..9..44	0..0..13	5.00723
7	9..17..31	6..7..44	4.99271	7	3..15..27	0..6..8	5.00719
13	9..23..38	6..13..39	4.99286	13	3..21..10	0..12..3	5.00708
19	9..29..44	6..19..34	4.99310	19	3..26..54	0..17..58	5.00689
25	10..5..50	6..25..28	4.99335	25	4..2..38	0..23..53	5.00663
	February Long. ☉	1799 Anomal. ☉	Logarithm Dis ☉ a Θ		August Long. ☉	1799 Anomal ☉	Logarithm Dis. ☉ a Θ
1	10..12..56	7..2..22	4.99380	1	4..9..20	1..0..47	5.00624
7	10..19..0	7..8..17	4.99426	7	4..15..4	1..6..41	5.00583
13	10..25..4	7..14..12	4.99478	13	4..20..50	1..12..36	5.00536
19	11..1..8	7..20..7	4.99535	19	4..26..36	1..18..31	5.00483
25	11..7..10	7..26..2	4.99598	25	5..2..25	1..24..26	5.00434
	March Long. ☉	1799 Anomal ☉	Logarithm Dis ☉ a Θ		Septemb. Long. ☉	1799 Anomal ☉	Logarithm Dis. ☉ a Θ
1	11..11..10	7..29..58	4.99643	1	5..9..11	2..1..20	5.00361
7	11..17..10	8..5..53	4.99712	7	5..15..1	2..7..15	5.00294
13	11..23..10	8..11..48	4.99785	13	5..20..51	2..13..10	5.00224
19	11..29..7	8..17..43	4.99860	19	5..26..42	2..19..4	5.00150
25	0..5..4	8..23..38	4.99936	25	6..2..35	2..24..59	5.00075
	April Long. ☉ s ° ′	1799 Anomal. ☉ s ° ′	Logarithm Dis. ☉ a Θ		October Long. ☉	1799 Anomal. ☉	Logarithm Dis ☉ a Θ
1	0..11..43	9..0..32	5.00025	1	6..8..29	3..0..54	4.99999
7	0..17..52	9..6..26	5.00088	7	6..14..25	3..6..49	4.99923
13	0..23..44	9..12..21	5.00163	13	6..20..22	3..12..44	4.99847
19	0..29..36	9..18..16	5.00235	19	6..26..20	3..18..39	4.99772
25	1..5..27	9..24..11	5.00306	25	7..2..18	3..24..33	4.99700
	May Long. ☉	1799 Anomal ☉	Logarithm Dis. ☉ a Θ		Novemb. Long. ☉ s ° ′	1799 Anomal ☉	Logarithm Dis. ☉ a Θ
1	1..[illegible]..16	10..0..6	5.00372	1	7..9..18	4..1..27	4.99631
7	1..17..4	10..6..1	5.00434	7	7..15..20	4..7..22	4.99566
13	1..22..51	10..11..55	5.00492	13	7..21..22	4..13..17	4.99506
19	1..28..37	10..17..50	5.00544	19	7..27..26	4..19..12	4.99451
25	2..4..23	10..23..45	5.00590	25	8..3..31	4..25..7	4.99402
	June Long. ☉	1799 Anomal ☉	Logarithm Dis. ☉ a Θ		Decemb. Long. ☉	1799 Anomal ☉	Logarithm Dis ☉ a Θ
[illegible]	[illegible]..5	11..0..39	5.00636	1	8..9..36	5..1..2	4.99359
[illegible]	[illegible]	11..6..34	5.00668	7	8..15..41	5..6..56	4.99324
[illegible]	[illegible]	11..12..29	5.00689	13	8..21..48	5..12..51	4.99297
[illegible]	[illegible]	11..18..24	5.00708	19	8..27..54	5..18..46	4.99278
[illegible]	[illegible]	11..24..18	5.00719	25	9..4..2	5..24..41	4.99268

February Second Month hath 28 Days—

				Planets Places				
	☽	☉	♄	♃	♂	♀	☿	☽
New ☽ 4..3..33 aft. (d h m)		Long.	♋	♉	♈	♒	♑	Lat
First ☽ 12..5..18 aft.	1	10..12..56	21	17	28	21	17	4 S.
Full ○ 20..0..31 morn.	7	10..19..0	20	18	♉ 2	28	24	4 S.
Last ☽ 26..5..8 aft.	13	10..25..4	20	18	7	♓ 6	♒ 1	1 N.
☊ { 1 / 11 / 21 } ♉ { 21 / 20 / 20 } deg	19	11..1..8	20	19	11	13	10	5 N.
	25	11..7..10	19	20	15	21	18	0 N.

M D	W D			☉ rise	☉ set	☽'s Long.	☽ rise	☽ south	☽ age
1	6	☿ great elong. △ ♃ ☿		6..57	5..3	9..6..30	17..43	22..19	27
2	7	purification V. Mary		6..56	5..4	9..19..43	18..31	23..13	28
3	F	Quinqua. Sund.	Cloudy	6..55	5..5	10..2..42		23..58	29
4	2		weather	6..54	5..6	[illegible]..15..26	[illegible]	[illegible]	☽
5	3	Shrove Tuesday	Snow	6..53	5..7	10..27..57	6..3	0..45	1
6	4	Ash wednesday □ ☉ ♃		6..52	5..8	11..10..13	7..2	1..28	2
7	5		pleasant	6..51	5..9	11..22..18	8..1	2..10	3
8	6	Days increase 1..4	for	6..50	5..10	0..4..11	9..0	2..51	4
9	7		the	6..49	5..11	0..15..56	9..57	3..32	5
10	F		Season	6..48	5..12	0..27..43	10..53	4..15	6
11	2	pleiades Set 1..22 mo.		6..46	5..14	1..9..31	11..49	4..59	7
12	3		high	6..45	5..15	1..21..23	12..50	5..47	8
13	4	* ♂ ♀	wind,	6..44	5..16	2..3..26	13..51	6..35	9
14	5	Valentine	rain	6..43	5..17	2..15..45	14..47	7..23	10
15	6	♃ Set 11..59		6..42	5..18	2..28..25	15..41	8..17	11
16	7		or Snow	6..40	5..20	3..11..28	16..35	9..13	12
17	F			6..39	5..21	3..24..58	17..24	10..9	13
18	2	☉ enters ♓		6..38	5..22	4..8..56	18..8	11..5	14
19	3		flying	6..36	5..24	4..23..16		12..1	15
20	4	Spica ♍ South 3..3 mo.		6..35	5..25	5..7..56	rise	12..57	16
21	5		clouds	6..34	5..26	5..22..45	7..29	13..51	17
22	6	* ♄ ♃	with	6..33	5..27	6..7..37	8..39	14..41	18
23	7		rain	6..32	5..28	6..22..23	9..50	15..31	19
24	F	St. Matthias		6..31	5..29	7..6..57	11..0	16..21	20
25	2		winds	6..30	5..30	7..21..15	12..9	17..18	21
26	3	Days increase 1..58	and	6..28	5..32	8..5..14	13..18	18..16	22
27	4		Snow	6..27	5..33	8..18..55	14..35	19..12	23
28	5	pleiades Set 0..16 morn.		6..26	5..34	9..2..17	15..26	20..13	24

Venus (♀) will be evening Star untill the 18th. day of October then morning Star untill the end of the year—

August 27th. 1797. Standing at my door I heard the discharge of a gun, [illegible] 4 or 5 Seconds of time ~~the~~ after the discharge, the Small Shot came rattling [illegible] me, one or two of which Struck the House, which plainly demonstrates that ~~t~~ the Velocity of Sound as much greater than that of a Cannon Bullet

---

1798 February 4th I find in obtaining the Moons Southing we must Confin[e] her to the ecliptic ~~to~~ without regard to her Latitude, otherwise we shall run foul.

Common Notes and moveable feast for Year 1799

			Month	
Dominical letter	F	Easter Sunday	March	24
Cycle of the Sun	16	Ascension Day	May	2
Golden Number	14	Whit. Sunday	May	12
Epact	23	Trinity Sund	May	19
Number of Direction	3	Advent Sunday	Decemb	1

Sunday after Trin. 27

March third Month hath 31 Days

New ☽ 6..9..6 morn.
First ☾ 14..8..43 morn.
Full ○ 21..10..21 morn.
Last ☾ 28..3..32 morn.

☊ {1 / 11 ♉ / 21} {19 / 19 / 18} deg.

☽	☉	♄	♃	♂	♀	☿	☽'s
	Long. s. ° ′	♋	♉	♉	♓	♒	Lat
1	11..11..10	19	20	17	26	25	4 S.
7	11..17..10	19	21	21	♈ 3	♓ 5	4 S.
13	11..23..10	19	22	25	11	15	2 N.
19	11..29..7	19	23	29	18	27	5 N.
25	0..5..4	19	24	♊ 3	25	♈ 8	1 S.

M.D	W.D		☉ rise	☉ set	☽'s Long.	☽ rise	☽ South	☽'s age
1	6	St. David	6..24	5..36	9..15..27	16..39	21..8	25
2	7	♄ South 8..29	6..23	5..37	9..28..24	17..3	22..0	26
3	F	Middle Lent Sund.	6..22	5..38	10..11..6	17..40	22..49	27
4	2	♃ Set 11..16	6..21	5..39	10..23..38	18..11	23..35	28
5	3	rain and	6..19	5..41	11..6..1			29
6	4	wind	6..17	5..43	11..18..15	Set	0..17	☽
7	5	☌ ♃ ♂	6..16	5..44	[illegible]..23	6..58	0..58	2
8	6	flying clouds	6..14	5..46	0..12..24	7..54	1..37	3
9	7	□ ☉ ♄	6..13	5..47	0..24..21	8..5[illegible]	2..18	4
10	F	♄ Stationary	6..12	5..48	1..6..16	9..47	3..0	5
11	2	☌ ☽ ♃	6..11	5..49	1..18..13	10..44	3..45	6
12	3	moderate	6..9	5..51	2..0..14	11..44	4..33	7
13	4	Days 11..44	6..8	5..52	2..12..26	12..[illegible]2	5..23	8
14	5	for the	6..7	5..53	2..24..52	13..39	6..16	9
15	6	Bulls eye Set 11..38	6..6	5..54	3..7..34	14..34	7..11	10
16	7	season	6..4	5..56	3..20..38	15..27	8..8	11
17	F	St. patrick palm Sund.	6..3	5..57	4..4..7	16..12	9..5	12
18	2	rain and	6..2	5..58	4..18..3	16..51	9..59	13
19	3	✱ ☉ ♂ equal Day and Night	6..0	6..0	5..2..24	17..31	10..53	14
20	4	Day increase ☉ enter ♈	5..59	6..1	5..16..59		11..47	15
21	5	wind	5..58	6..2	6..2..0	rise	12..41	16
22	6	☌ ☉ ☿ Occident Good fryday	5..57	6..3	6..16..59	7..44	13..33	17
23	7		5..55	6..5	7..1..54	8..54	14..25	18
24	F	Easter Sund.	5..54	6..6	7..16..33	10..4	15..19	19
25	2	Easter Mond. Annun. V. M.	5..53	6..7	8..0..54	11..14	16..15	20
26	3	Easter Tuesd.	5..52	6..8	8..14..54	12..24	17..13	21
27	4		5..50	6..10	8..28..29	13..26	18..13	22
28	5	Day increase 2..46	5..49	6..11	9..11..41	14..19	19..8	23
29	6	Cold	5..48	6..12	9..24..35	15..12	19..59	24
30	7	rain	5..46	6..14	10..7..14	15..44	20..49	25
31	F	1st Sund. past Easter	5..45	6..15	10..19..42	16..19	21..39	26

April 29th. 1798 Came two Black men with a gun in my inclose and discharg[illegible]
~~the~~ a few perches from door, I being very unwell could not persuge them [illegible]
find who they were.

April Fourth Month hath 30 Days

	d	h	m	
New ☽	5	2	45	morn.
First ☾	12	10	40	aft.
Full ○	19	6	50	aft.
Last ☾	26	5	4	aft.

☊ { 1, 11, 21 } ♉ 18, 17, 17 } deg.

Planets Places

D	☉	♄	♃	♂	♀	☿	☽'s
	Long.	♋	♉	♊	♉	♈	Lat.
1	0..11..43	20	25	7	4	23	5 S.
7	0..17..52	20	27	11	11	♉ 3	0 S.
13	0..23..44	21	29	15	19	13	5 N.
19	0..29..36	21	♊ 0	18	26	17	2 N.
25	1..5..27	21	1	22	♊ 3	22	5 S.

M D	W D			☉ rise	☉ set	☽'s Long.	☽ rise	☽ South	☽'s age
1	2	♃ set 9..59		5..44	6..16	11..1..58	6..[illegible]	22..21	27
2	3	pleiades Set 10..12		5..43	6..17	11..14..10	[illegible]	23..16	28
3	4		expect rain	5..41	6..19	11..26..15	17..[illegible]	23..49	29
4	5	St. Ambrose		5..40	6..20	0..8..18		☌	30
5	6	Bulls eye Set 10..22		5..39	6..21	0..20..22	Set.	0..25	☽
6	7			5..38	6..22	1..2..27	7..45	1..[illegible]	2
7	F	2d Sund. past East.		5..36	6..24	1..14..34	8..44	1..46	3
8	2	☌ ☽ ♃		5..35	6..25	1..26..43	9..43	2..32	4
9	3		pleasant	5..34	6..26	2..9..0	10..41	3..22	5
10	4	□ ☉ ♄		5..33	6..27	2..21..25	11..38	4..16	6
11	5		weather	5..32	6..28	3..4..1	12..34	5..11	7
12	6	Sirius Set 10..16		5..30	6..30	3..16..53	13..25	6..6	8
13	7		flying clouds	5..29	6..31	4..0..4	14..12	7..1	9
14	F	3d Sund. past East.		5..28	6..32	4..13..34	14..56	7..56	10
15	2		wind	5..27	6..33	4..27..27	15..35	8..50	11
16	3	♄ Set 4..16 mor.		5..26	6..34	5..11..45	16..8	9..43	12
17	4		and rain	5..25	6..35	5..26..22	16..41	10..31	13
18	5	Days increase 3..58		5..23	6..37	6..11..15		11..26	14
19	6	♀ Set 8..53		5..22	6..38	6..26..14	rise	12..20	15
20	7	☉ enters ♉		5..21	6..39	7..11..11	8..8	13..16	16
21	F	4th Sund. past East.		5..20	6..40	7..25..55	9..19	14..12	17
22	2		temperate	5..18	6..42	8..10..19	10..29	15..10	18
23	3	Spica ♍ South 11..11		5..17	6..43	8..24..19	11..32	16..[illegible]	19
24	4		weather	5..16	6..44	9..7..54	12..31	17..8	20
25	5	~~Arcturus South 11..53~~		5..15	6..45	9..21..1	13..20	18..[illegible]	21
26	6		rain	5..14	6..46	10..3..48	14..1	18..54	22
27	7	[illegible] Set 11..27		5..13	6..47	10..16..15	14..35	19..39	23
28	F	Rogation Sund.	ends	5..12	6..48	10..28..27	15..5	20..24	24
29	2		this month	5..11	6..49	11..10..29	15..32	21..5	25
30	3	Days 13..40		5..10	6..50	11..22..29	15..57	21..47	26

1799 first Ec[illegible] of the Sun May 4 . 7 . 18 P.M.
Second of the Sun Oct. 28 . 0 . 27 P.M.

Elements for an Eclipse of the ⊙ May. 1799

True time of New Moon in May, 1799	4 . 7 . 18
Semidiameter of the Earth's disc	0 54 . 47
Sun's distance from the nearest Solst	45 . 30
Sun's declination North	16 . 1
Moon's Latitude South Ascending	0 . 6 . 55
Moon's horary motion from the Sun	0 . 27 . 59
Angle of the Moon's visible path with the Ecliptic	5 . 35
Sun's Semidiameter	0 . 16 . 4
Moons Semidiameter	0 . 14 . 58
Semidiameter of the penumbra	0 . 31 . 2
Suns equated distance from ☊	11 . 28 . 40 . 37

Eclipses for the year 1799

First of the Sun on the 4th of May invisible at Baltimore & at 7h 18m P.M. the Sun will be centrally eclipsed on the Meridian at 7h . 29 m P.M in Longitude 111¾ west from Baltimore and Latitude ~~[illegible]~~ 8° . 31 North

Of the Sun october the 28th, invisible at Baltimore & at 0h . 24m P.M the Sun will be totally and centrally eclipsed on the meridian at 0h . 14m P.M in Long. 3° . 30′ west from Baltimore and Lat. 5° . 12′ South

To obtain the Latitude of the above places I took the point where the path of the penumbra center intersected the Earth's axes and the center of the projection in my compass from the line of Sines, the Sector being first set to the radius of the disc, that taken from the Sun's declination being of contrary names leaves the Latitude of the place where the Sun is centrally eclipsed; and the declination greatest

1799 May) Fifth Month hath 31 Days

	☽	☉	♄	♃	♂	♀	☿	☽'s
		Long.	♋	II	II	II	♉	Lat.
New ☽ 4..7..18 aft.	1	1..11..16	21	2	26	11	19	3 S.
First ☾ 11..7..53 morn.	7	1..17..4	21	4	♋ 0	18	17	3 N.
Full ○ 19..2..43 morn.	13	1..22..51	22	5	4	25	14	5 N.
Last ☾ 26..6..4 morn.	19	1..28..37	22	6	7	♋ 2	13	2 S.
☊ {1, 11, 21} ♉ {16, 16, 15} degs.	25	2..4..23	23	8	11	9	13	5 S.

(Column heads of the moon-phase list: d. h. m.; Planets Places)

M D	W D		☉ rise	☉ set	☽'s Long.	☽ rise	☽ south	☽'s age
1	4	philip and James	5..9	6..51	0..4..25	16..20	22..27	27
2	5	Ascension day	5..8	6..52	0..16..20	16..48	23..18	28
3	6	fine	5..7	6..53	0..28..21		23..50	29
4	7	♃ Set 8..34 ☉ eclips invis.	5..5	6..55	1..10..27	Set		☽
5	F	Sund past Ascen.	5..4	6..56	1..22..40	7..41	0..34	1
6	2	☌ ☽ ♃. showers	5..3	6..57	2..5..2	8..34	1..19	2
7	3	☌ ☉ ☿ orient	5..2	6..58	2..17..32	9..32	2..9	3
8	4	of rain	5..1	6..59	3..0..14	10..29	3..4	4
9	5	♀ Set 9..30	5..0	7..0	3..13..5	11..23	4..2	5
10	6	Days increase 4..46	4..59	7..1	3..26..13	12..13	4..58	6
11	7	Clear	4..58	7..2	4..9..34	12..58	5..55	7
12	F	Whit Sunday	4..58	7..2	4..23..13	13..36	6..48	8
13	2	Whit Monday	4..57	7..3	5..7..9	14..11	7..40	9
14	3	Whit. Tuesday	4..56	7..4	5..21..23	14..44	8..31	10
15	4	and warm	4..55	7..5	6..5..54	15..16	9..28	11
16	5	Days 14..12	4..54	7..6	6..20..36	15..48	10..15	12
17	6		4..53	7..7	7..5..30	16..22	11..8	13
18	7	Arcturus South 10..24	4..52	7..8	7..20..22		12..2	14
19	F	Trinity Sund.	4..52	7..8	8..5..4	rise	12..58	15
20	2	rain	4..51	7..9	8..19..35	9..22	13..59	16
21	3	Spica ♍ South 9..22.	4..50	7..10	9..3..31	10..21	14..59	17
22	4	☉ enter II	4..49	7..11	9..17..2	11..15	15..56	18
23	5	Arietis rise 2..40 morn.	4..48	7..12	10..0..9	11..58	16..47	19
24	6	and wind	4..48	7..12	10..12..53	12..37	17..37	20
25	7	♀ Set 9..55	4..47	7..13	10..25..16	13..9	18..24	21
26	F	1 st. Sund. past Trin.	4..46	7..14	11..7..22	13..37	19..17	22
27	2	flying clouds	4..46	7..14	11..19..11	14..1	19..48	23
28	3	♄ Set 10..43	4..45	7..15	0..1..1	14..28	20..27	24
29	4	with rain	4..44	7..16	0..12..47	14..49	21..6	25
30	5	☌ ☉ ♃ orient	4..44	7..16	0..24..35	15..13	21..47	26
31	6	Lyra South 2..1 mor	4..43	7..17	1..6..28	15..41	22..29	27

May 4
1799 I find the Sun will be eclipsed centrally in Lat. So. [illegible]° [illegible]' it appears by adding
that point where the center of penumbra intersects the axes of the disc, to
to the Suns declination, NB the Sector must be set to the radius of the
to obtain this point.
☉ declination North

7°	29'
16	1
23	30

179[illegible] June Sixth Month hath 30 Days

New ☽ 3..9..56 morn.
First ☽ 11..9..26 morn.
Full ○ 17..10..50 morn.
Last ☽ 24..10..14 aft.

☊ { 1 ♉ 15 / 11 ♉ 14 / 21 ♉ 13 } deg.

		Planets Places					
☽	☉	♄	♃	♂	♀	☿	☽'s
	Long.	♋	♊	♋	♋	♉	Lat.
1	2..11..5	23	10	16	17	17	0 N.
7	2..16..50	24	11	19	24	24	5 N.
13	2..22..34	25	12	23	♌ 1	♊ 1	1 N.
19	2..28..18	25	14	27	8	12	5 S.
25	3..4..0	26	15	♌ 1	15	23	3 S.

M D	W D			☉ rise	☉ set	☽'s Long.	☽ rise	☽ South	☽'s age
1	7	☿ great elong.		4..43	7..17	1..18..33	16..11	23..14	28
2	F	2d Sund. past Trin.		4..42	7..18	2..0..45			29
3	2	☌ ☽ ♃		4..42	7..18	2..13..12	Set.	0..4	☽
4	3		rain	4..41	7..19	2..25..54	8..18	0..55	2
5	4	♀ Set. 10..1		4..41	7..19	3..8..50	9..11	1..48	3
6	5		and thunder	4..41	7..19	3..22..2	10..4	2..45	4
7	6	✶ ♀ ☿	☌ ♄ ♀	4..40	7..20	4..5..26	10..50	3..43	5
8	7	☌ ♄ ♀,		4..40	7..20	4..18..54	11..30	4..38	6
9	F	3d Sund. past Trin.		4..40	7..20	5..2..54	12..4	5..30	7
10	2		pleasant	4..39	7..21	5..16..58	12..36	6..19	8
11	3	St. Barnabas 1..7 morn.		4..39	7..21	6..1..15	13..6	7..6	9
12	4		weather	4..39	7..21	6..15..42	13..35	7..55	10
13	5	Lyra South 1..7 morn.		4..39	7..21	7..0..15	14..6	8..47	11
14	6		thunder gusts	4..39	7..21	7..14..54	14..45	9..41	12
15	7	Days increase 5..28		4..38	7..22	7..29..29	15..28	10..39	13
16	F	4th Sund. past Trin		4..38	7..22	8..14..4		11..39	14
17	2	St. Alban		4..38	7..22	8..28..20	rise	12..41	15
18	3		and rain	4..38	7..22	9..12..18	9..5	13..42	16
19	4	Arcturus South 8..13		4..38	7..22	9..25..51	9..55	14..50	17
20	5		very	4..38	7..22	10..9..2	10..35	15..32	18
21	6	☉ enters ♋ Longest Day		4..38	7..22	10..21..46	11..6	16..18	19
22	7		warm	4..38	7..22	11..4..8	11..34	17..0	20
23	F	5th Sund. past Trin.		4..38	7..22	11..16..12	12..1	17..41	21
24	2	St. John	followed by	4..38	7..22	11..28..1	12..22	18..19	22
25	3		thunder	4..38	7..22	0..9..44	12..45	18..58	23
26	4	pegasi Markab rise 9..46		4..38	7..22	0..21..22	13..10	19..37	24
27	5	pegasi Algenib rise 10..50		4..38	7..22	1..3..1	13..35	20..17	25
28	6		and rain	4..38	7..22	1..14..49	14..4	21..0	26
29	7	St. peter and paul		4..39	7..21	1..26..46	14..39	21..56	27
30	F	6th Sund. past Trin. ☌ ☽ ♃,		4..39	7..21	2..8..59	15..24	22..43	28

1799 July Seventh Month hath 31 Days

	d	h	m	
New ☽	2..	10..	34	aft.
First ☽	9..	10..	17	aft.
Full ○	16..	8..	10	aft.
Last ☽	24..	3..	22	aft.

☊ { 1 ♉ 13 / 11 ♉ 12 / 21 12 } deg.

Planets Places.

☽	☉ Long.	♄ ♋	♃ ♊	♂ ♌	♀ ♌	☿ ♋	☽'s Lat.
1	3..9..44	27	16	4	22	6	3 N.
7	3..15..27	28	18	8	29	19	5 N.
13	3..21..10	28	19	12	♍ 5	♌ 0	2 S.
19	3..26..54	29	20	16	12	12	5 S.
25	4..2..38	♌ 0	21	20 [illegible]	[illegible]	23	0.

Years of Christ	Moons Long. s ° '	Moons Anom. s ° '	Moons Node s ° '
1806	1..15..9	3..25..32	9..7..8
1807	5..27..21	6..27..4	8..17..48
1808	10..3..55	9..22..59	7..28..29
1809	2..26..29	1..4..46	7..9..6
1810	7..5..52	4..3..29	6..19..46
1811	11..15..15	7..2..12	6..0..27
1812	3..24..38	10..0..55	5..11..7
1813	7..17..12	1..12..42	4..21..44
1814	0..26..35	4..11..26	4..2..24
1815	5..5..58	7..10..9	3..13..5
1816	9..15..21	10..8..52	2..23..45
1817	2..7..55	1..20..39	2..4..22
1818	6..17..18	4..19..22	1..15..2
1819	10..26..41	7..18..6	0..25..42
1820	3..19..4	10..16..49	0..6..23

☽ age: 29, ☽, 1, 2, 3, 4, 5, 6, 7, 8, 9, 10, 11, 12, 13, 14, 15, 16, 17, 18, 19, 20, 21, 22, 23, 24, 25

28	F	10th Sund. past Trin. ☌ ☽ ♃,	4..56	7..4	[illegible]	[illegible]	21..23	26
29	2	and rain	4..57	7..3	2..29..55	14..51	22..16	27
30	3	Dog days begin.	4..58	7..2	3..12..43	15..52	23..15	28
31	4	Days 14..2	4..59	7..1	3..25..56		☌	29

Cia The long/marks are barrels Cyder for BB

IIII			
3	$	for Barton & Jamson	

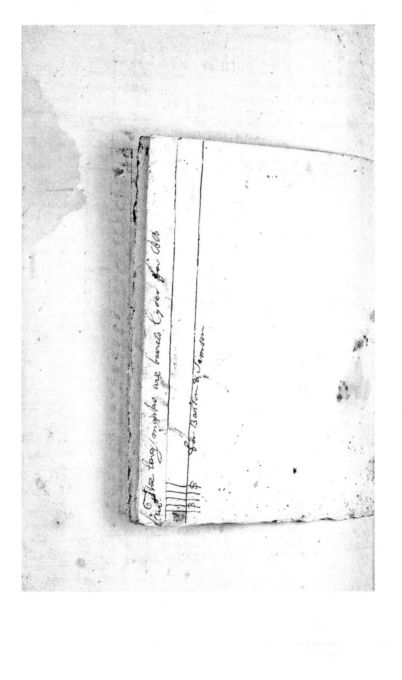

1799 July Seventh Month hath 31 Days

New ☽ 2..10..34 aft.
First ☾ 9..10..17 aft.
Full ○ 16..8..10 aft.
Last ☾ 24..3..22 aft.

(d. h. m.)

☊ { 1 ♉ 13, 11 ♉ 12, 21 12 } deg.

Planets Places.

D	☉ Long.	♄ ♋	♃ ♊	♂ ♌	♀ ♌	☿ ♋	☽'s Lat.
1	3..9..44	27	16	4	22	6	3 N.
7	3..15..27	28	18	8	29	19	5 N.
13	3..21..10	28	19	12	♍ 5	♌ 0	2 S.
19	3..26..54	29	20	16	12	12	5 S.
25	4..2..38	♌ 0	21	20	18	23	0.

M D	W D		☉ rise	☉ set	☽'s Long.	☽ rise	☽ South	☽'s age
1	2	♀ Set 9..45	4..39	7..21	2..22..26		23..36	29
2	3	Visitation V. Mary	4..40	7..20	3..4..16	Set	☌	☽
3	4	thunder gusts	4..40	7..20	3..17..22	8..2	0..32	1
4	5	Translation St. Martin	4..40	7..20	4..0..48	8..49	1..26	2
5	6	☌ ☉ ☿ Occident.	4..41	7..19	4..14..31	9..30	2..22	3
6	7	and rain	4..41	7..19	4..28..26	10..8	3..15	4
7	F	7th Sund. past Trin	4..42	7..18	5..12..29	10..42	4..[illegible]	5
8	2	hot	4..42	7..18	5..26..48	11..10	4..55	6
9	3	Lyra South..11..18	4..43	7..17	6..11..10	11..42	5..42	7
10	4	and Sultry	4..43	7..17	6..25..36	12..12	6..32	8
11	5	Spica ♍ Set 11..18	4..44	7..16	7..10..2	12..46	7..26	9
12	6		4..44	7..16	7..24..30	13..26	8..21	10
13	7	Days decrease 14 min	4..45	7..15	8..8..53	14..12	9..19	11
14	F	8th. Sund. past Trin	4..45	7..15	8..23..10	15..9	10..20	12
15	2	wind and	4..46	7..14	9..7..13		11..21	13
16	3	pegasi Markab rise 8..24	4..47	7..13	9..21..1	rise	12..20	14
17	4	rain	4..47	7..13	10..4..29	8..22	13..15	15
18	5	pegasi Algenib. rise 9..24	4..48	7..12	10..17..36	8..58	14..4	16
19	6	flying	4..49	7..11	11..0..22	9..31	14..50	17
20	7	Margaret clouds	4..49	7..11	11..12..46	9..59	15..35	18
21	F	9th. Sund. past Trin	4..50	7..10	11..24..53	10..22	16..17	19
22	2	Magdelene ☉ enters ♌	4..51	7..9	0..6..45	10..43	16..53	20
23	3	with thunder	4..52	7..8	0..18..27	11..8	17..32	21
24	4	gusts	4..53	7..7	1..0..4	11..33	18..12	22
25	5	St. James	4..54	7..6	1..11..41	12..2	18..54	23
26	6	St. Anne	4..54	7..6	1..23..25	12..33	19..40	24
27	7	wind	4..55	7..5	2..5..17	13..15	20..30	25
28	F	10th Sund. past Trin ☌ ☽ ♃,	4..56	7..4	2..17..26	13..58	21..21	26
29	2	and rain	4..57	7..3	2..29..55	14..51	22..16	27
30	3	Dog days begin.	4..58	7..2	3..12..43	15..52	23..15	28
31	4	Days 14..2	4..59	7..1	3..25..56		☌	29

1799 August Eighth Month hath 31 Days—

New ☽	d 1 .. h 9 .. m 1 morn.
First ☽	8 .. 3 .. 51 morn.
Full ○	15 .. 7 .. 36 morn.
Last ☽	23 .. 6 .. 30 morn.
New ☽	30 .. 6 .. 20 aft.
☊ {1, 11, 21} ☋	{11, 11, 10} deg.

Planets Places

☽	☉	♄	♃	♂	♀	☿	☽s
	Long.	♌	♊	♌	♍	♍	Lat.
1	4 .. 9 .. 20	1	23	24	25	3	5 N.
7	4 .. 15 .. 4	2	24	28	♎ 1	11	0 N.
13	4 .. 20 .. 50	2	25	♍ 2	7	18	5 S.
19	4 .. 26 .. 36	3	26	5	12	22	2 S.
25	5 .. 2 .. 25	4	27	9	17	27	4 N.

M D	W D	Remarkable days aspects weather &c.	☉ rise	☉ set	☽s Long.	☽ Set	☽ South	☽s age
1	5	Lammas Day	5 .. 0	7 .. 0	4 .. 9 .. [illegible]	Set	0 .. 10	☽
2	6	Days decrease 46 min.	5 .. 1	6 .. 59	4 .. 23 .. 27	7 .. 49	1 .. 1	2
3	7	expect rain,	5 .. 2	6 .. 58	5 .. 7 .. 40	8 .. 24	1 .. 53	3
4	F	11th. Sund. past Trin.	5 .. 3	6 .. 57	5 .. 21 .. 40	8 .. 58	2 .. 45	4
5	2	hot	5 .. 4	6 .. 56	6 .. 6 .. 33	9 .. 31	3 .. 37	5
6	3	and sultry	5 .. 5	6 .. 55	6 .. 21 .. 3	10 .. 3	4 .. 29	6
7	4	♀ Set. 8 .. 55	5 .. 6	6 .. 54	7 .. 5 .. 32	10 .. 34	5 .. 21	7
8	5	with	5 .. 7	6 .. 53	7 .. 19 .. 56	11 .. 10	6 .. 13	8
9	6	thunder	5 .. 8	6 .. 52	8 .. 4 .. 14	11 .. 52	7 .. 7	9
10	7	St. Lawrence	5 .. 9	6 .. 51	8 .. 18 .. 24	12 .. 43	8 .. 6	10
11	F	12th. Sund. past Trin.	5 .. 10	6 .. 50	9 .. 2 .. 20	13 .. 43	9 .. 8	11
12	2	and	5 .. 11	6 .. 49	9 .. 16 .. 8	14 .. 46	10 .. 8	12
13	3	♀ great elong. ☿ great elong	5 .. 12	6 .. 48	9 .. 29 .. 40	15 .. 54	11 .. 5	13
14	4	rain	5 .. 13	6 .. 47	10 .. 12 .. 59		11 .. 57	14
15	5	Lyra South 8 .. 50	5 .. 14	6 .. 46	10 .. 26 .. 0	rise	12 .. 45	15
16	6	Spica ♍ Set. 8 .. 57	5 .. 15	6 .. 45	11 .. 8 .. 41	7 .. 59	13 .. 32	16
17	7	great	5 .. 16	6 .. 44	11 .. 21 .. 8	8 .. 26	14 .. 13	17
18	F	13th. Sund. past Trin	5 .. 18	6 .. 42	0 .. 3 .. 19	8 .. 51	14 .. 54	18
19	2	dews	5 .. 19	6 .. 41	0 .. 15 .. 16	9 .. 15	15 .. 33	19
20	3	pegasi Markab South 0 .. 56 morn	5 .. 20	6 .. 40	0 .. 27 .. 2	9 .. 39	16 .. 13	20
21	4	warm	5 .. 21	6 .. 39	1 .. 8 .. 46	10 .. 4	16 .. 55	21
22	5	wind	5 .. 22	6 .. 38	1 .. 20 .. 27	10 .. 36	17 .. 39	22
23	6	☉ enters ♍	5 .. 23	6 .. 37	2 .. 2 .. 11	11 .. 12	18 .. 27	23
24	7	St. Bartholomew	5 .. 24	6 .. 36	2 .. 14 .. 7	11 .. 54	19 .. 17	24
25	F	14th. Sund. past Trin. ☌ ☽ ♃,	5 .. 26	6 .. 34	2 .. 26 .. 10	12 .. 48	20 .. 11	25
26	2	followed	5 .. 27	6 .. 33	3 .. 8 .. 37	13 .. 45	21 .. 8	26
27	3	by	5 .. 28	6 .. 32	3 .. 21 .. 26	14 .. 45	22 .. 3	27
28	4	St. Augustine	5 .. 29	6 .. 31	4 .. 4 .. 39	15 .. 51	22 .. 58	28
29	5	St. John behead.	5 .. 30	6 .. 30	4 .. 18 .. 19		23 .. 52	29
30	6	rain	5 .. 32	6 .. 28	5 .. 2 .. 21	Set.	☌	☽
31	7	Days 12 .. 54	5 .. 33	6 .. 27	5 .. 16 .. 46	7 .. 13	0 .. 44	1

1799 September Ninth Month hath 30 Days

	☽	☉	♄	♃	♂	♀	☿	☽'s
d h m			Planets Places					
First ☾ 2. 6.. 0.. 0 noon		Long.	♌	♊	♍	♎	♍	Lat
Full ○ 13.. 9.. 41 aft.	1	5.. 9.. 11	5	28	14	22	26	3 N.
Last ☾ 21.. 11.. 13 aft.	7	5.. 15.. 1	5	29	18	26	21	4 S.
New ☽ 29.. 3.. 13 morn	13	5.. 20.. 51	6	29	21	29	16	4 S.
☊ {1, 11, 21} ♉ {10, 9, 9} deg.	19	5.. 26.. 42	7	♋ 0	25	♏ 1	15	2 N.
	25	6.. 2.. 35	7	1	29	2	15	5 N.

M D	W D	Remarkable days aspects weather &c.	☉ rise	☉ set	☽'s Long.	☽ Set	☽ South	☽'s age
1	F	15th Sund. past Trin.	5.. 34	6.. 26	6.. 1.. 23	7.. 43	1.. 32	2
2	2	rain	5.. 35	6.. 25	6.. 16.. 9	8.. 13	2.. 21	3
3	3	Dog days end.	5.. 36	6.. 24	7.. 0.. 52	8.. 44	3.. 13	4
4	4	and	5.. 38	6.. 22	7.. 15.. 27	9.. 22	4.. 7	5
5	5	♃ rise 11.. 35	5.. 39	6.. 21	7.. 29.. 53	10.. 5	5.. 4	6
6	6	wind	5.. 40	6.. 20	8.. 14.. 4	10.. 54	6.. 3	7
7	7	♀ Set 7.. 57	5.. 41	6.. 19	8.. 28.. 0	11.. 51	7.. 4	8
8	F	16th Sund. past Trin. Nativity	5.. 43	6.. 17	9.. 11.. 42	12.. 54	8.. 5	9
9	2	V. Mary	5.. 44	6.. 16	9.. 25.. 11	13.. 59	9.. 2	10
10	3	pleasant	5.. 45	6.. 15	10.. 8.. 26	15.. 4	9.. 55	11
11	4	☌ ☉ ☿ Orient.	5.. 46	6.. 14	10.. 21.. 28	16.. 5	10.. 45	12
12	5	and temperate,	5.. 48	6.. 12	11.. 4.. 16		11.. 32	13
13	6	△ ♃ ♀, ☌ ☉ ♂	5.. 49	6.. 11	11.. 16.. 52	rise	12.. 16	14
14	7	cool rain	5.. 50	6.. 10	11.. 29.. 16	6.. 45	12.. 57	15
15	F	17th Sund past Trin.	5.. 52	6.. 8	0.. 11.. 29	7.. 11	13.. 36	16
16	2	Days decrease 2.. 30	5.. 53	6.. 7	0.. 23.. 32	7.. 35	14.. 18	17
17	3	great	5.. 54	6.. 6	1.. 5.. 27	8.. 0	15.. 0	18
18	4	[illegible] Occident	5.. 55	6.. 5	1.. 17.. 17	8.. 32	15.. 44	19
19	5	pegasi Markab South 11.. 8	5.. 56	6.. 4	1.. 29.. 6	9.. 8	16.. 31	20
20	6	Dews	5.. 58	6.. 2	2.. 10.. 59	9.. 50	17.. 21	21
21	7	St. Matthew	5.. 59	6.. 1	2.. 22.. 57	10.. 39	18.. 14	22
22	F	18th Sund. past Trin. = day & night	6.. 0	6.. 0	3.. 5.. 10	11.. 33	19.. 8	23
23	2	☉ ent. ♎	6.. 2	5.. 58	3.. 17.. 36	12.. 32	20.. 3	24
24	3	pleiades rise 8.. 6	6.. 3	5.. 57	4.. 0.. 26	13.. 34	20.. 57	25
25	4	followed	6.. 4	5.. 56	4.. 13.. 38	14.. 39	21.. 51	26
26	5	St. Cyprian	6.. 5	5.. 55	4.. 27.. 18	15.. 47	22.. 44	27
27	6	Bulls eye rise 9.. 12	6.. 7	5.. 53	5.. 11.. 23	16.. 58	23.. 37	28
28	7	by rain	6.. 8	5.. 52	5.. 25.. 51		6	29
29	F	19th Sund. past Trin. St. Michael	6.. 9	5.. 51	6.. 10.. 38	set.	0.. 28	☽
30	2	Days 11.. 38	6.. 11	5.. 49	6.. 25.. 31	6.. 50	1.. 12	2

True time of New Moon in October 1799 } d h m 28..0..24

	° ′ ″
Semidiameter of the Earth's disc	0..60..45
Sun's distance from nearest Solstice	55..0..0
Sun's declination South	13..12..0
Moon's Latitude North descending	0..7..30
Moon's horary motion from the Sun	0..35..6
Angle Moon's visible path with Ecliptic	5..35..0
Sun's semidiameter	0..16..13
Moon's Semidiameter	0..16..39
Semidiameter of the penumbra	0 32..52

Suns Equated dis. from ☊ s ° ′ ″ 5..28..35..39

1799 October Tenth Month hath 31 Days

	d	h	m	
First ☽	5	8	27	aft.
Full ○	13	2	20	aft.
Last ☽	21	2	49	aft.
New ☽	28	0	24	aft.

☊ { 1 ♉ 8 / 11 ♉ 8 / 21 ♉ 7 } deg.

Planets Places

D	☉	♄	♃	♂	♀	☿	☽'s
	Long.	♌	♋	♎	♏	♍	Lat
1	6..8..29	8	1	3	1	23	0 S.
7	6..14..25	8	1	7	0	♎ 1	5 S.
13	6..20..22	9	1	11	♎ 27	12	2 S.
19	6..26..20	9	1	15	23	22	4 N.
25	7..2..18	9	1	19	20	♏ 2	4 N.

M D	W D		☉ rise	☉ set	☽'s Long.	☽ set	☽ south	☽'s age
1	3	✱☉♄, △♃♀	6..12	5..48	7..10..26	7..26	2..6	3
2	4	♃ Stationary	6..13	5..47	7..25..10	8..8	3..3	4
3	5	♀ set 6..34	6..14	5..46	8..9..39	8..54	4..1	5
4	6	Days decrease 3..14	6..15	5..45	8..23..50	9..50	5..2	6
5	7	expect rain	6..17	5..43	9..7..40	10..52	6..3	7
6	F	20th. Sund. past Trin	6..18	5..42	9..21..11	11..55	7..2	8
7	2	□♃☿	6..19	5..41	10..4..22	13..1	7..56	9
8	3	✱♄♂	6..20	5..40	10..17..19	14..3	8..47	10
9	4	white frost	6..22	5..38	11..0..4	15..6	9..36	11
10	5	♃ rise 10..36	6..23	5..37	11..12..36	16..8	10..20	12
11	6	pleiades South 2..31 morn.	6..24	5..36	11..25..0	17..8	11..2	13
12	7	cool	6..25	5..35	0..7..18		11..43	14
13	F	21st Sund. past Trin.	6..27	5..33	0..19..29	rise	12..24	15
14	2	Bulls eye rise 8..10	6..28	5..32	1..1..32	6..15	13..6	16
15	3	morning	6..29	5..31	1..13..35	6..45	13..49	17
16	4	♀ retrograde	6..30	5..30	1..25..36	7..17	14..36	18
17	5	rain	6..32	5..28	2..7..37	7..54	15..25	19
18	6	St. Luke	6..33	5..27	2..19..42	8..41	16..16	20
19	7	☌♀☿, ☌☽♃,	6..34	5..26	3..1..52	9..34	17..11	21
20	F	22nd. Sund. past Trin	6..35	5..25	3..14..13	10..30	18..5	22
21	2	pegasi Algenib South. 10..18	6..36	5..24	3..26..48	11..31	18..58	23
22	3	frosts	6..38	5..22	4..9..40	12..35	19..50	24
23	4	☉ enters ♏	6..39	5..21	4..22..55	13..42	20..42	25
24	5	△☉♃	6..40	5..20	5..6..33	14..50	21..33	26
25	6	☌☉☿ Occident.	6..41	5..19	5..20..38	15..57	22..22	27
26	7	cold	6..42	5..18	6..5..5	17..7	23..12	28
27	F	23d Sund. past Trin.	6..44	5..16	6..19..50		0	29
28	2	St. Simon & Jude ☉ eclip. invis.	6..45	5..15	7..4..48	set	0..5	☽
29	3	rain	6..46	5..14	7..19..47	6..8	0..59	1
30	4	Pegasi Markab South. 8..26	6..47	5..13	8..4..39	6..51	1..54	2
31	5	Days 10..24	6..48	5..12	8..19..12	7..44	2..55	3

1798 Dec.r 29	} Jonathan Ellicott Elias Ellicott and John Ellicott in acct with Benjamin Banneker	
	by Cash Receiv'd of them ~~[illegible]~~ in poor pay	
1799	~~To Cash paid for [illegible]~~	£0.1.10½
January 12	} by an Almanac	
January 15	by pork to value of	0.2.11
	previous to the above Dec.r 22 1798	0.3.4
	By 9½ lb pork at 6d per lb }	
Feb. 27	by 1 Bushel of Corn	0.4.9
March 8	by 5 yards Sheeting at 4/ per yd	0.4.6
	by 6 Skeins thread at 1d	1.0.0
	by 7¼ lb pork at 9	0.0.6
	by ½ gallon Molasses at 5.4	0.5.5½
March 19	by a Bushel of Corn	0.2.8
		2.4.0
April 1	by 7¼ lb pork at 9d per lb	0.4.6
	half pound Tobacco at 2 s per lb	0.5.5¼
April 6	by a Bushel of Corn	0.1.0
April 13	by 7½ lb pork at 9 d per lb	0.4.6
		0.5.7½
	½ gallon molasses at 5/4 per gal	0.2.8
April 30	by 6 lb pork at 13 d per lb	3.7.9
	½ gallon molasses at 5/4 per gallon	0.6.6
May 6	by a Bushel of Corn	0.2.8
		0.5.0
May 17	by 4½ lb pork at 1 s per lb	4.1.11
		0.4.6
	by ½ gallon molasses at 5.4 per gal	0.2.8
May 31	by 6½ lb pork at 1 s per lb	0.6.6
June 1	by ½ Bushel of Corn at 5 s per Bu	0.2.6
		0.5.6
June 12	by a Bushel Do at 5/6	0.1.0
July 1	By a paper of Ink powder	0.5.0
July 12	By a Bushel of Corn at 5 s	5.9.7
		0.3.6
Augt. 9	By 1¾ nankeen at 2 s per yd	0.3.3
	1½ yards Muslin at 2/2	0.1.4½
	Twist thread and moulds	0.3.3
	pork	0.7.6
	a pair of Stokings	6.8.5½
Cash of George Ellicott £0.12.0		
Augt 13	By ¼ lb Gun powder	0.7.6
Sept.r	paid the taylor for making my jasket	0.8.3
Sept. 21	By 9 lb pork at 11d per lb	0.2.8½
		7.6.11½
19	By ¼ lb powder and 1 lb Shot	
~~[illegible]~~ 6	~~By 6 lb pork~~	
Nov.r	Dec.r 4 Receᵈ of Elias Ellicott 4 dollars	1.10.0
		8.16.1½
Nov. 9	the value of	3.0.10½
		12.0.0

the above is the Second payment

1799 November Eleventh Month hath 30 Days

First ☽ 4..7..40 morn
Full ☉ 12..8..47 morn
Last ☽ 20..3..8 morn.
New ☽ 26..10..31 aft.

☊ {1, 11, 21} ♉ {6, 6, 5} deg.

Planets Places							
D	☉	♄	♃	♂	♀	☿	☽'s
	Long.	♌	♋	♎	♎	♏	Lat.
1	7..9..18	10	1	23	17	14	4 S.
7	7..15.20	10	1	♏ 27	17	23	4 S.
13	7..21.22	10	0	♏ 1	17	♐ 2	2 N.
19	7..27.26	10	0	5	20	11	5 N.
25	8..3..31	10	♊ 29	9	22	20	1 S.

M D	W D			☉ rise	☉ set	☽'s Long	☽ Lat	☽ south	☽'s age
1	6	All Saints		6..49	5..11	9..3..26	8..46	3..57	4
2	7		high wind	6..51	5..9	9..17..15	9..51	4..58	5
3	F	24th Sund. past Trin.		6..52	5..8	10..0..38	10..56	5..55	6
4	2		and rain	6..53	5..7	10..13..41	11..58	6..46	7
5	3	pleiades South 0..52 mor.		6..54	5..6	10..26..10	13..[illegible]	7..31	9
6	4		Clear and	6..55	5..5	11..8..53	14..42	8..9	10
7	5	Days decrease 4..36		6..56	5..4	0..23..43	15..38	8..47	11
8	6		cold.	6..57	5..40	1..5..35	16..33	9..29	12
9	7		now	6..58	5..40	1..17..30	17..27	10..14	13
10	F	25th Sund. past Trin.		6..59	5..1	1..29..30	18..21	11..0	14
11	2	St. Martin.		7..0	5..0	2..11..39		11..50	15
12	3		expect snow	7..1	4..59	1..23..58	rise	12..43	16
13	4	Sirius rise 10..17		7..2	4..58	2..2..27	6..2	13..37	17
14	5		or cold	7..3	4..57	2..15..9	7..3	14..33	18
15	6	☌ ☽ ♃		7..4	4..56	2..28..10	8..5	15..26	19
16	7		rain	7..5	4..55	3..10..37	8..7	16..16	20
17	F	26th Sund. past		7..6	4..54	3..23..7	9..41	17..5	21
18	2		windy	7..7	4..53	4..5..52	10..24	17..53	22
19	3	♃ South 8..27		7..8	4..52	4..18..52	11..26	18..38	23
20	4		weather	7..8	4..52	5..2..27	12..30	19..27	24
21	5	☉ enters ♐		7..9	4..51	5..16..8	13..37	20..9	25
22	6		foggy	7..10	4..50	6..0..9	14..47	20..59	26
23	7		clouds	7..11	4..49	6..14..32	15..57	21..49	26
24	F	27th Sund. past Trin.		7..12	4..48	6..29..12	17..7	22..42	27
25	2		cold	7..12	4..48	7..14..4		23..39	28
26	3	pegasi Markab South 8..45		7..13	4..47	7..29..2	set.	☌	☽
27	4		rain	7..14	4..46	8..13..53	5..28	0..39	1
28	5	pegasi Algenib South 7..45		7..15	4..45	8..28..29	5..26	1..39	2
29	6		or snow	7..15	4..45	9..12..44	7..29	2..40	3
30	7	St. Andrew		7..16	4..44	9..26..31	8..37	3..40	4

On the night of December 25th 1797

Dreamed I had a fawn or young deer, whose hair was white and like unto a young lambs wool, and all parts about it beautiful to behold, then I said to myself I will set my little captive at his Liberty but I will first clip the tips of his ears that I may know him if ever I should see him again then taking a pair of Shears and cut off the tip of one ear, and he cryed like unto a child with the pain which greeved me very much also, then I did not attempt to cut the other but was very sorry for that I had done I set him at liberty and he ran a considerable distance then stopt & looked back for me, I advanced toward him and he come and met me and he took a lock of wool from my garment and wiped the blood of the wound which I had made on him (which realy affected me) I took him in my arms and brought him home and held him on my knees, he asked the woman if she had any bread she answered in the affirmative, and gave him some, which the began to eat then asked for milk in a cup, [illegible] the dog has got the cup with milk in it under the house but there is milk in the cupboard

My Dream left me — B Banneker

1798 March 6th [illegible] in garden Nursery some young pare trees, [illegible] the [illegible] Bushel of Corn in the same row 15 red kind grew near the old pare

Jar April 13	by 7 ½ lb pork a 9 d [illegible]
	½ gallon molasses a 5/4 ⅌ ga[illegible]
April 30	by 6 lb pork a 13 d [illegible]
	½ gallon molasses a 5/[illegible]
May 6	by a Bushel of Corn
May 17	by 4 ½ lb pork a 1 S [illegible]
	by ½ gallon molasses a[illegible]
May 31	by 6 ½ lb pork a 1 S [illegible]
June 1	by ½ Bushel of Corn
June 12	by a Bushel D° a[illegible]
July 1	By a paper of Ink p[illegible]
July 12	By a Bushel of C[illegible]
Augt. 9	By 1 ¾ nank[illegible]
	1 ½ yards M[illegible]
	Twist thre[illegible]
	pork [illegible]
	a pair[illegible]

Cash of George [illegible]
£ or 12

Augt. 13	By[illegible]
Sept.	pd[illegible]
Sept. 21	[illegible]
[illegible] 19	
Nov[illegible]	
N[illegible]	

Banneker

January

1805

2 27
8 22
6 5
2 25
[illegible] 21
5

1799 December Twelfth Month hath 31 Days

	d	h	m	
First ☾	3	11	49	aft.
Full ○	12	3	37	morn.
Last ☾	19	3	31	aft.
New ☽	26	9	46	morn.

☊ { 1, 11, 21 } ♉ { 5, 4, 4 } deg.

Planets Places

☽	⊙ Long.	♄ ♌	♃ ♊	♂ ♏	♀ ♎	☿ ♐	☽'s Lat.
1	8..9..36	10	29	14	26	28	5 S.
7	8..15..41	10	28	18	♏ 1	♑ 6	1 S.
13	8..21..48	10	27	22	6	11	4 N.
19	8..27..54	9	26	26	11	16	3 N.
25	9..4..2	9	25	♐ 0	17	6	4 S.

M D	W D		⊙ rise	⊙ set	☽'s Long.	☽ Set	☽ South	☽'s age
1	F	Advent Sund.	7..16	4..44	10..9..59	9..44	4..35	5
2	2	Days decrease 5..18	7..17	4..43	10..22..56	10..48	5..24	6
3	3	rain	7..18	4..42	11..5..34	11..50	[illegible]..9	7
4	4	Bulls eye South 11..40	7..18	4..42	11..17..50	12..49	6..51	8
5	5	or snow	7..19	4..41	11..29..56	13..46	7..31	9
6	6	Nicolas	7..19	4..41	0..11..53	14..42	8..9	10
7	7	☿ great elong.	7..20	4..40	0..23..43	15..38	8..47	11
8	F	2nd. Sund. in Advent. conception	7..20	4..40	1..5..35	16..33	9..29	12
9	2	(V. Mary	7..20	4..40	1..17..30	17..27	10..14	13
10	3	♃ South 0..46 morn.	7..21	4..39	1..29..30	18..21	11..0	14
11	4	very	7..21	4..39	2..11..39		11..50	15
12	5	☌ ☽ ♃	7..21	4..39	2..23..58	rise	12..43	16
13	6	pegasi Markab South 5..31	7..21	4..39	3..6..27	6..2	13..37	17
14	7	cold	7..22	4..38	3..19..9	7..3	14..33	18
15	F	3d. Sund. in Advent	7..22	4..38	4..2..3	8..5	15..26	19
16	2	pegasi Algenib south 6..26	7..22	4..38	4..15..9	9..7	16..16	20
17	3	wind	7..22	4..38	4..28..29	10..11	17..5	21
18	4	☍ ⊙ ♃ ~~Occident~~	7..22	4..38	5..12..3	11..16	17..53	22
19	5	and rain	7..22	4..38	5..25..50	12..22	18..38	23
20	6		7..22	4..38	6..9..56	13..29	19..27	24
21	7	⊙ enter ♑ Shortest day	7..22	4..38	6..24..13	14..37	20..18	25
22	F	4th Sund. in Advent.	7..22	4..38	7..8..49	15..50	21..12	26
23	2	or	7..22	4..38	7..23..30	17..5	22..10	27
24	3	snow,	7..22	4..38	8..8..16	18..20	23..13	28
25	4	Christmas Day	7..22	4..38	8..23..0		☌	29
26	5	St. Stephen	7..22	4..38	9..7..30	Set.	0..16	☽
27	6	St. John	7..22	4..38	9..21..44	6..7	1..14	2
28	7	Innocents	7..21	4..39	10..5..35	7..16	2..11	3
29	F	1st. Sund. past Chris.	7..21	4..39	10..19..0	8..23	3..4	4
30	2	cold rain	7..21	4..39	11..2..0	9..25	3..52	5
31	3	Silvester	7..20	4..40	11..14..35	10..26	4..34	6

1800

January

Full ○ 10.. 9.. 17 aft. (h m)
~~New ☽ 24..10..23 aft.~~

February

Full ○ 9..6..56 aftn.
New ☽ 23..6..29 aftn

March — correct

Full ○ 10..1..21 morn.
New ☽ 24..3..40 morn.

April — correct

Full ○ 8..11..26 morn
New ☽ 22..7..36 aft.

May — correct

Full ○ 7..7..38 aft.
New ☽ 22..11..31 morn

June — correct

Full ○ 6..2..49 morn.
Right New ☽ 21..2..44 morn

July

Full ○ 6..9..53 morn
New ☽ 21..4..49 aft.

August

Full ○ 4..7..56 morn.
New ☽ 19..7..33 aft.

September

Full ○ 3..3..58 morn
New ☽ 18..5..12 aft.

October

Full ○ 2..6..45 morn.
New ☽ 17..5..56 aft.

November

Full ○ 1..8..39 morn
New ☽ 16..2..24 aft.

December

Full ○ 1[illegible]..5..5 morn
New ☽ 15..2..56 aft. — 15..1..44 morn. by lay.
Full ○ 30..0..42 aft

1800	1800	1800
Long. med. ☉ (s ° ') 9..10..7	Long. Apog. (s ° ') 3..9..33	
Long. med. ☽ (s ° ') 11..8..28	Long. Apog. (s ° ') 1..15..28	Long ☊ (s ° ') 1..3..14
Long. med. ♄ (s ° ') 4..1..56	Anomaly ♄ (s ° ') 7..1..10	Long ☊ (s ° ') 3..21..35
Long. med. ♃ (s ° ') 2..22..12	Anomaly ♃ (s ° ') 8..10..38	Node (s ° ') 3..8..57
Long. med. ♂ (s ° ') 7..22..3	Anomaly ♂ (s ° ') 2..19..33	Node (s ° ') 1..18..28
Long. med. ♀ (s ° ') 4..23..32	Anomaly ♀ (s ° ') 6..15..26	Node (s ° ') 2..14..50
Long. med. ☿ (s ° ') 3..13..2	Anomaly ☿ (s ° ') 6..29..51	Node (s ° ') 1..16..11

1800 January First Month hath 31 Days

			Planets Places					
	☽	☉	♄	♃	♂	♀	☿	☽'s
		Long.	♌	♊	♐	♏	♑	Lat.
First ☽. 2..6..10 aft.	1	9..11..9	8	24	4	24	1	3 S.
Full ☉ 10..10..57 aft.	7	9..17..6	8	23	8	♐ 4	1	3 N.
Last ☽. 18..0..30 mor.	13	9..23..23	8	23	12	7	0	5 N.
New ☽ 24..7..23 aft.	19	9..29..30	8	22	16	13	6	1 S.
☊ { ♉ 3 3 2 } deg.	25	10..5..35	7	22	21	20	12	5 S.

M. D	W. D	Remarkable days Aspects weather &c.		☉ rise	☉ set	☽'s Long.	☽ Set	☽ South	☽'s age
1	4	Circumcision		7..20	4..40	11..26..33	11..17	5..8	7
2	5		Cold	7..20	4..40	0..8..44	12..15	5..50	8
3	6	Days increase 4 min.		7..20	4..40	0..20..47	13..13	6..33	9
4	7		rain	7..19	4..41	1..2..40	14..10	7..16	10
5	E	2nd Sund. past Chris		7..19	4..41	1..14..31	15..6	7..59	11
6	2	Epiphany		7..18	4..42	1..26..25	16..3	8..44	12
7	3	△♄♂	or	7..18	4..42	2..8..19	17..0	9..32	13
8	4	☌☽♃		7..17	4..43	2..20..15	17..57	10..22	14
9	5		Snow,	7..17	4..43	3..2..23		11..12	15
10	6	Sirius South 11..8		7..16	4..44	3..14..43	rise	12..2	16
11	7		for	7..15	4..45	3..27..2	5..49	12..52	17
12	E	1st Sund. past Epip		7..15	4..45	4..10..17	6..51	13..42	18
13	2		ought	7..14	4..46	4..23..32	7..56	14..32	19
14	3	pleiades South 7..49		7..13	4..47	5..7..17	9..3	15..22	20
15	4		I know,	7..13	4..47	5..21..0	10..13	16..13	21
16	5	days 9..36 min		7..12	4..48	6..5..19	11..23	17..4	22
17	6		wind	7..11	4..49	6..19..38	12..35	17..56	23
18	7		blows	7..10	4..50	7..4..18	13..48	18..51	24
19	E	2d Sunday past past Epip		7..10	4..50	7..18..57	15..5	19..50	25
20	2	☉ enter ♒		7..9	4..51	8..3..36	16..16	20..49	26
21	3		high,	7..8	4..52	8..18..15	17..23	21..48	27
22	4	♀ rise 4 h 4 mom.		7..7	4..53	9..2..32	18..22	22..47	28
23	5		the	7..6	4..54	9..16..48		23..46	29
24	6		Clouds	7..5	4..55	10..0..28	Sets	☌	☽
25	7	☿ great elong. Convert. St. paul		7..4	4..56	10..14..9	5..52	0..40	1
26	E	3d Sund. past Epip		7..3	4..57	10..27..16	6..53	1..26	2
27	2	☌♂♀		7..2	4..58	11..10..16	7..54	2..11	3
28	3		doth	7..1	4..59	11..22..37	8..55	2..55	4
29	4	Bulls eye South 7..49		7..0	5..0	0..5..4	9..56	3..38	5
30	5		fly,	6..59	5..1	0..17..6	10..56	4..20	6
31	6	days increase 48 min.		6..58	5..2	0..29..9	11..53	5..2	7
						1..11..2			

True time New ☽ January 1800
January 24-7-23 proved by their Longitudes

See page 38

Mean New Moon in March 1800 ☉ ☽ h m is 25..0..22 according[…]
24..0..23 Greenwich

D	1800 January Long. ☉	1800 Logarithm ☉ a ⊖	D	But I think July 1800 Long. ☉	it on the Log. ☉ a ⊖
1	9..11..9	4.99259	1	3..10..27	5.00728
7	9..17..6	4.99264	7	3..16..10	5.00723
13	9..23..23	4.99278	13	3..21..54	5.00710
19	9..29..30	4.99300	19	3..27..37	5.00690
25	10..5..35	4.99331	25	4..3..21	5.00663
D	February	Logarithm		August	Logarithm
1	10..12..41	4.99375	1	4..10..4	5.00625
7	10..18..47	4.99421	7	4..15..49	5.00587
13	10..24..51	4.99474	13	4..21..34	5.00539
19	11..0..54	4.99532	19	4..27..21	5.00486
25	11..6..57	4.99595	25	5..3..9	5.00427
D	March	Logarithm		Septemb.	Logarithm
1	11..11..56	4.99651	1	5..9..55	5.00353
7	11..17..56	4.99722	7	5..15..45	5.00284
13	11..23..55	4.99796	13	5..21..36	5.00213
19	11..29..52	4.99859	19	5..27..28	5.00139
25	0..5..49	4.99935	25	6..3..20	5.00063
D	April	Logarithm	D	October	Logarithm
1	0..12..43	5.000252	1	6..9..14	4.99986
7	0..18..37	5.00101	7	6..15..10	4.99909
13	0..24..29	5.00176	13	6..21..7	4.99846
19	1..0..20	5.00249	19	6..27..5	4.99771
25	1..6..11	5.00319	25	7..3..4	4.99698
	May	Logarithm	D	Novemb.	Logarithm
1	1..12..0	5.00385	1	7..10..4	4.99618
7	1..17..48	5.00447	7	7..16..6	4.99553
13	1..23..35	5.00504	13	7..22..9	4.99493
19	1..29..21	5.00556	19	7..28..13	4.99438
25	2..5..8	5.00594	25	8..4..17	4.99390
	June	Logarithm	D	Decemb.	Logarithm
1	2..11..50	5.00640	1	8..10..22	4.99352
7	2..17..34	5.00673	7	8..16..27	4.99315
13	2..23..18	5.00698	13	8..22..34	4.99288
19	2..29..2	5.00715	19	8..28..41	4.99273
25	3..4..45	5.00726	25	9..4..48	4.99261

February Second Month hath 29 Days

	☽	h	m	
First ☽	1	3	20	aft.
Full ☉	9	2	40	aft.
Last ☽	16	1	6	aft.
New ☽	23	9	35	morn.

☊ 1 ♉ 2 } deg.
11 1
21 0

Planets Places

D	☉ Long.	♄ ♌	♃ ♊	♂ ♐	♀ ♐	☿ ♑	☽ Lat.
1	10..12..41	6	21	26	28	21	1 N.
7	10..18..47	5	21	♑	♑ 5	♒ 0	5 N.
13	10..24..51	5	21	5	12	9	2 N.
19	11..0..54	4	21	9	19	19	5 S.
25	11..6..57	4	22	13	27	28	2 S.

M. D	W. D	Remarkable days aspects weather &c.	☉ rise	☉ Set	☽ Long.	☽ Sets	☽ South	☽ age
1	7	days 10..6	6..57	5..3	1..11..2	12..50	5..45	8
2	E	4th Sund. past Epip	6..56	5..4	1..22..53	13..47	6..30	9
3	2	(purification V. M.	6..55	5..5	2..4..43	14..44	7..17	10
4	3	☌ ☽ ♃	6..54	5..6	2..16..43	15..40	8..5	11
5	4	now	6..53	5..7	2..28..42	16..31	8..54	12
6	5	pleiades Set. 1..41 mor.	6..52	5..8	3..11..4	17..19	9..44	13
7	6	Snow	6..51	5..9	3..23..26	18..6	10..35	14
8	7	△ ☉ ♃	6..50	5..10	4..6..20		11..27	15
9	E	Septuagesima Sund.	6..49	5..11	4..19..13	rise	12..19	16
10	2	or rain,	6..48	5..12	5..2..46	6..49	13..11	17
11	3	days increase 1..12	6..46	5..14	5..16..[illegible]	7..58	14..3	18
12	4	now	6..45	5..15	6..0..30	9..7	14..55	19
13	5	♀ rise 4..31 mo.	6..44	5..16	6..14..42	10..17	15..47	20
14	6	Valentine	6..43	5..17	6..29..18	11..29	16..39	21
15	7	clear	6..42	5..18	7..13..53	12..46	17..38	22
16	E	♃ Set. 2..48 morn.	6..40	5..20	7..28..34	14..0	18..37	23
17	2	again,	6..39	5..21	8..13..14	15..7	19..36	24
18	3	boreas	6..38	5..22	8..27..26	16..13	20..36	25
19	4	☉ enter ♓	6..36	5..24	9..12..4	17..9	21..34	26
20	5	triumph	6..35	5..25	9..25..55	17..56	22..29	27
21	6	Spica MR South 2..59 morn.	6..34	5..26	10..9..45	18..36	23..20	28
22	7	with	6..33	5..27	10..22..57		[illegible]	29
23	E	Quinqua. Sund.	6..32	5..28	11..6..9	Set.	0..8	☽
24	2	St. Matthias	6..31	5..29	11..18..45	6..50	0..51	2
25	3	Shrove Tuesd.	6..30	5..30	0..1..20	7..46	1..34	3
26	4	Ash wednesday	6..28	5..32	0..13..28	8..43	2..16	4
27	5	cold	6..27	5..33	0..25..35	9..42	2..58	5
28	6	Days 11..8 wings	6..26	5..34	1..7..28	10..41	3..41	6
			~~6..25~~	~~5..35~~	~~1..19..22~~	[illegible]	~~4..26~~	

(♀) will be morning Star until the Sixth day of August, then evening Star until the End of the Year

1800 This Year ~~I Shall~~ in obtaining the planets places I Shall keep by the old Stile with the addition of 12 days according to the method prescribed by Doct.r Ferguson, but I had like to forgot the Sun and Moon had only 11 day added to the old Stile ~~till near the end of the year~~

Common Notes and moveable feasts for the Year 1800.

Dominical Letter	E	Easter Sunday	April	13
Cycles of the Sun	17	Ascension Day	May	22
Golden Number	15	Whit Sunday	June	1
Epact	4	Trinity Sunday	June	8
Number of Direction	23	Advent Sunday	Novemb.	30

1800 # March Third Month hath 31 Days

			Planets Places					
	☽	☉	♄	♃	♂	♀	☿	☽
		Long	♌	♊	♑	♒	♓	Lat.
First Q. 3 d. 0 h. 20 m. aftn.	1	11..10.56	4	22	17	2	8	3 N.
Full ○ 11..3..0. morn	7	11..16.56	4	22	21	9	20	5 N.
Last Q. 17..8..0 aft.	13	11.22.55	3	22	25	16	♈ 2	1 S.
New ☽ 25..2..0 morn	19	11.28.52	3	23	29	24	13	5 S
☊ {1 ♉ 0; 11 ♈ 29; 21 29}	25	0..4..49	3	24	♒	♓ 2	23	1 S

M D	W D	Remarkable days Aspects weather &c		☉ rise	☉ set	☽ Long	☽ Set	☽ south	☽ age
1	7	St. David		6..25	5..35	1..19.22	11..41	4..26	7
2	E	1st. Sund. in Lent.		6..24	5..36	2..1..12	12..38	5..13	8
3	2		ready	6..23	5..37	2..13..8	13..32	6..1	9
4	3	☌☽♃		6..22	5..38	2..25..4	14..26	6..51	10
5	4		to freeze	6..21	5..39	3..7..18	15..17	7..42	11
6	5		all	6..19	5..41	3..19..33	16..4	8..33	12
7	6	☌☉☿ Occident		6..17	5..43	4..2..16	16..47	9..24	13
8	7		freezing	6..16	5..44	4..15..0	17..23	10..15	14
9	E	2nd. Sund. in Lent		6..14	5..46	4..28.13	17..59	11..6	15
10	2		thing	6..13	5..47	5..11..55		11..57	16
11	3	♃ Sets 1..26 morn.		6..12	5..48	5..25.36	rise	12..48	17
12	4		this	6..11	5..49	6..9..54	8..9	13..40	18
13	5	□☉♃		6..9	5..51	6..24..11	9..15	14..32	19
14	6		month	6..8	5..52	7..8..50	10..30	15..26	20
15	7		called	6..7	5..53	7..23..29	11..43	16..23	21
16	E	3d. Sund. in Lent.		6..6	5..54	8..8..8	12..55	17..24	22
17	2	St. partrick		6..4	5..56	8..22..48	14..1	18..26	23
18	3		March	6..3	5..57	9..7..6	15..2	19..27	24
19	4	*☉♂		6..2	5..58	9..21..25	15..56	20..25	25
20	5	☉ enters ♈		6..1	5..59	10..5..8	16..37	21..18	26
21	6	Equal Day & Night.		6..0	6..0	10..18..50	17..12	22..8	27
22	7		the	5..59	6..1	11..1..53	17..45	22..55	28
23	E	4th Sund. in Lent		5..58	6..2	11..14..56	18..12	23..40	29
24	2	□☉♄		5..57	6..3	11..27..24		☌	30
25	3	Annunciation V. M.		5..55	6..5	0..9..52	Set	0..23	☽
26	4		Body	5..54	6..6	0..21..56	7..46	1..3	2
27	5	Bulls eye Set 10..55		5..53	6..7	1..4..0	8..42	1..45	3
28	6		doth	5..52	6..8	1..15..52	9..41	2..29	4
29	7		Search	5..50	6..10	1..27..48	10..38	3..15	5
30	E	5th Sund. in Lent		5..49	6..11	2..9..36	11..35	4..4	6
31	2	☌☽♃		5..48	6..12	2..21..29	12..29	4..54	7
				5..46	6..14	3..3..36		5..45	

Elements for an Eclipse of the Sun April 23d. 1800

True time of New Moon in April 1800	D. h. m 23.. 6... 10 P.M.
Semidiameter of the Earth's disc	° ′ ″ 0..54..56
Sun distance from nearest Solstice	56..31 –
Suns declination, North	12 50
Moon's latitude North Ascending	0. 32 –
Moon horary motion from the Sun –	0..30..31
Angle of the Moon's visible path with the ecliptic	- - - 5 35
Sun's Semidiameter	0.. 16.. 8
Moon's Semidiameter	0.. 14.. 59
Semidiameter of the penumbra	0.. 31.. 7

Eclipses for the year 1800

First of the Moon April the 9th. about 33 min. past the noon of our day therefore invisible on this Side the globe

Second of the Sun April 23d. ~~invisible at the City of Washington~~ & at 6h. after noon, the Sun will be ~~[illegible]~~ centrally eclipsed on the Meridian in Long. 84° west and Lat 52° 50′ North

Third of the Moon October 2nd about 2h. 37 min. after noon invisible

Fourth of the Sun October the 18th. invisible at the City of Washington & at 6h. the Sun will be centrally and totally eclipsed on the meridian in Long. ~~[illegible]~~ ~~the City of Washington 97° 57 east and Lat.~~ 95° east and Lat 47° 57 South –
NB the Sun is about 6 digits eclipsed at Greenwich

1800 April Fourth Month hath 30 Days

	D.	h.	m.	
First Q.	2	5	56	mor.
Full ○	9	0	33	aftn.
Last Q.	16	3	36	morn.
New ☽	23	6	24	aft.
First Q.	30	7	42	aft.

☊ { 1 ♈ 28; 11 ♈ 28; 21 ♈ 27 }

Planets Places

☽	☉	♄ ♌	♃ ♊	♂ ♒	♀ ♓	☿ ♉	☽'s Lat.
1	0..11..43	3	25	8	10	2	5 N.
7	0..17..37	3	25	16	17	2	2 S.
13	0..23..29	3	25	20	24	3	5 S.
19	0..29..22	3	26	24	♈ 1	♈ 14	3 S.
25	1..5..11	3	28	27	9	26	3 N.

M D	W D	Remarkable days Aspects weather &c.		☉ rise	☉ Set	☽'s Long.	☽ Rise	☽ South	☽'s age
1	3	Pleiades Set 10.14		5..46	6..14	3..3..36	13..20	5..45	8
2	4	♀ great elong.	now	5..44	6..16	3..15..44	14..11	6..36	9
3	5	Bulls eye Set 10..29		5..43	6..17	3..28..11	14..53	7..26	10
4	6	St. Ambrose		5..41	6..19	4..10..51	15..31	8..16	11
5	7		expect	5..40	6..20	4..23..54	16..6	9..6	12
6	E	Palm Sund.		5..39	6..21	5..7..15	16..38	9..55	13
7	2	♄ Stationary		5..38	6..22	5..20..56	17..9	10..44	14
8	3	days increase 3..32		5..36	6..24	6..4..56	[illegible]	11..35	15
9	4		rain	5..35	6..25	6..19..15	rise	12..27	16
10	5			5..34	6..26	7..3..45	8..19	13..22	17
11	6	Good friday		5..33	6..27	7..18..24	9..32	14..20	18
12	7		now	5..32	6..28	8..3..6	10..47	15..20	19
13	E	Easter Sund. □ ♄ ☿		5..30	6..30	8..17..47	11..58	16..21	20
14	2	Easter Mond.		5..29	6..31	9..2..20	13..0	17..23	21
15	3	Easter Tuesd.		5..28	6..32	9..16..39	13..54	18..23	22
16	4		clear again	5..27	6..33	10..0..42	14..42	19..19	23
17	5	Sirius Set 9..58		5..26	6..34	10..14..25	15..22	20..10	24
18	6		April	5..25	6..35	10..27..49	15..51	20..58	25
19	7		Showers	5..23	6..37	11..10..54	16..20	21..44	26
20	E	☌ ☉ ☿ orient 1st. Sund. past Eas.		5..22	6..38	11..23..39	16..45	22..26	27
21	2	(☉ enter ♉		5..21	6..39	0..6..8	17..15	23..10	28
22	3	Spica ♍ South 11..14		5..20	6..40	0..18..27	[illegible]	23..54	29
23	4	☉ eclip		5..18	6..42	1..0..26	Set.	☌	☽
24	5	Procyon Set 11..39		5..17	6..43	1..12..22	7..42	0..38	1
25	6		is the	5..16	6..44	1..24..13	8..41	1..22	2
26	7		Advent	5..15	6..45	2..6..4	9..37	2..6	3
27	E	2nd. Sund. past East.		5..14	6..46	2..17..56	10..31	2..53	4
28	2	☌ ☽ ♃		5..13	6..47	2..29..54	11..21	3..43	5
29	3		of	5..12	6..48	3..12..0	12..9	4..34	6
30	4	Days 13..38		5..11	6..49	3..24..19	12..53	5..26	7
				~~5..10~~	~~6..50~~	~~4..6..53~~	.	~~6..47~~	

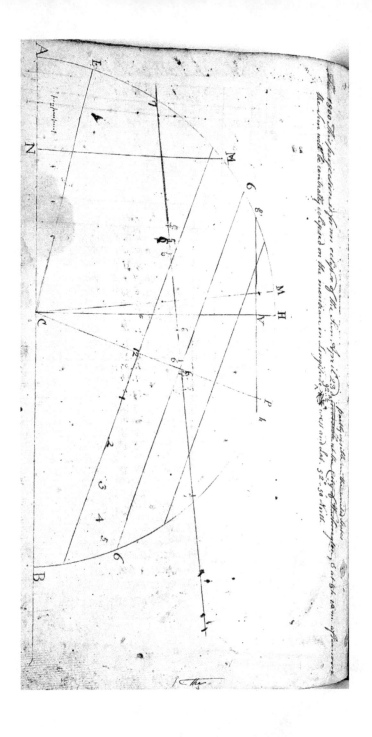

1800 This projection is for an eclipse of the Sun April 23 d. ~~invisible~~ partly visible in the united States ~~at the City of Washington~~, & at 6h. 16m. afternoon the Sun will be centrally eclipsed on the meridian in Longitude 92° ... west and Lat. 52°-50' North.

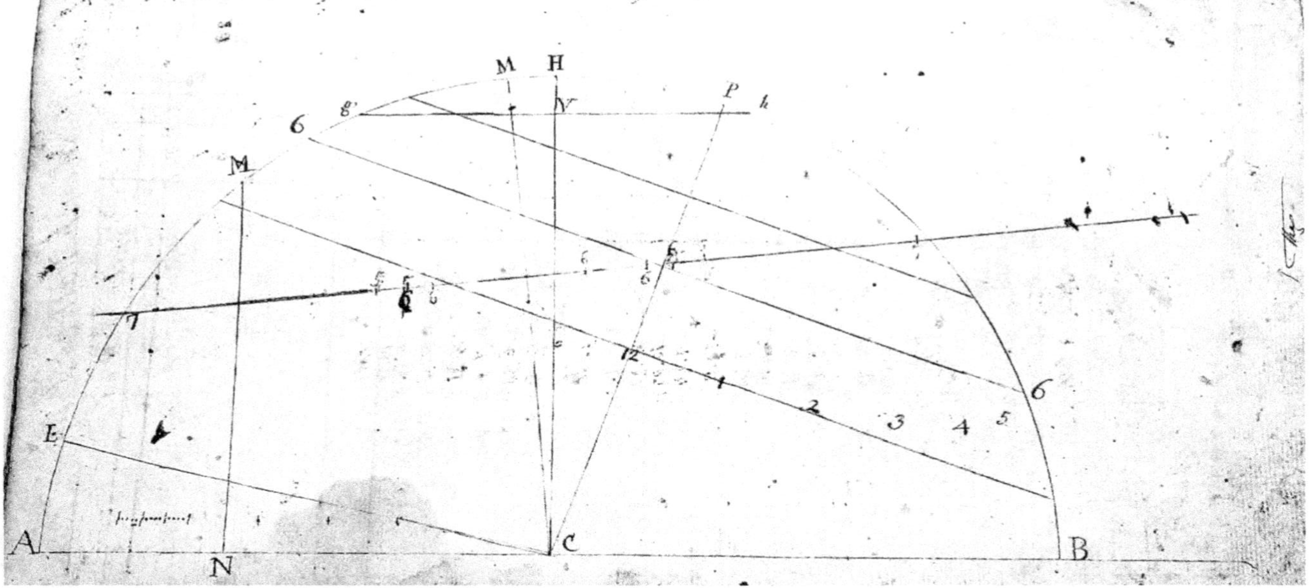

May Fifth Month hath 31 Days

~~First ☽ 1..8..10 aft~~
Full ○ 8..8..51 aft.
Last ☾ 15..2..48 aft.
New ☽ 23..9..23 morn
~~First~~ ☽ 31..6..38 morn.

☊ { 1 ♈ 27; 11 ♈ 26; 21 ♈ 26 } deg.

Planets Places

D	☉ Long	♄ ♌	♃ ♊	♂ ♓	♀ ♈	☿ ♈	☽ Lat.
1	1..11..2	4	29	1	16	23	5 N.
7	1..16..50	4	♋	5	23	25	1 S.
13	1..22..37	4	1	10	♉ 0	28	5 S.
19	1..28..23	5	2	14	8	♉ 4	0 N.
25	2..4..10	5	4	18	16	11	5 N

M D	W D	Remarkable days Aspects weather &c:		☉ rise	☉ set	☽ Long.	☽ Set	☽ South	☽ age
1	5	Philip and James		5..10	6..50	4..6..53	13..33	6..17	8
2	6	♀ rise 4..11 morn		5..9	6..51	4..19..43	14..9	7..6	9
3	7		May	5..8	6..52	5..2..54	14..41	7..54	10
4	E	3d Sund. past East		5..7	6..53	5..16..23	15..13	8..41	11
5	2		flowers	5..5	6..54	6..0..12	15..45	9..31	12
6	3	days increase 4..36		5..4	6..56	6..14..21	16..15	10..23	13
7	4		the	5..3	6..57	6..28..45		11..16	14
8	5	Arcturus South 11..3		5..2	6..58	7..13..20	rise	12..12	15
9	6	Spica ♍ South 10..9		5..1	6..59	7..28..2	8..34	13..11	16
10	7		clouds	5..0	7..0	8..12..44	9..44	14..13	17
11	E	4th. Sund. past East.		4..59	7..1	8..27..21	10..52	15..15	18
12	2		darkens	4..58	7..2	9..11..49	11..51	16..16	19
13	3		now	4..58	7..2	9..26..1	12..40	17..13	20
14	4	☿ great elong.		4..57	7..3	10..9..55	13..22	18..7	21
15	5		the	4..56	7..4	10..23..31	13..56	18..56	22
16	6	Arietis rise 3..8 morn.		4..55	7..5	11..6..45	14..24	19..41	23
17	7		sky,	4..54	7..6	11..19..40	14..50	20..25	24
18	E	Rogation Sund.		4..53	7..7	0..2..19	15..13	21..8	25
19	2		now	4..52	7..8	0..14..41	15..43	21..51	26
20	3		rain	4..52	7..8	0..26..51	16..13	22..35	27
21	4	☉ enter ♊		4..51	7..9	1..8..49	16..40	23..20	28
22	5	Ascent. Day		4..51	7..9	1..20..44		S	29
23	6		descends	4..50	7..10	2..2..33	Set	0..5	D.
24	7		from	4..49	7..11	2..14..24	8..25	0..50	2
25	E	Sund. past Ascent.		4..48	7..12	2..26..19	9..13	1..38	3
26	2	☌ ☽ ♃		4..47	7..13	3..8..20	10..3	2..28	4
27	3		on	4..46	7..14	3..20..32	10..49	3..18	5
28	4	Days 14..28		4..46	7..14	4..2..56	11..31	4..8	6
29	5		high	4..45	7..15	[illegible]..15..38	12..5	4..57	7
30	6	Days increase 5..16		4..44	7..16	4..28..38	12..39	5..46	8
31	7	Lyra South 2..1 morn.		4..44	7..16	5..11..56	13..10	6..34	9
~~31~~				~~4..43~~	~~7..17~~	~~5..25..55~~		~~7..22~~	

~~June 1st 6..4..33~~

The first great Locust year that I can Remember was 1749.
I was then about Seventeen years of age when thousands of them came and
was creeping up the trees and bushes, I then immagined they came
to eat and destroy the fruit ~~Earth~~ of the Earth, and would occation a
famine in the Land, I therefore began to kill and destroy them, but
I soon saw that my labour was in vain, therefore gave over my pretension
Again in the year 1766 which is Seventeen year after their first appearance
to me, they made a Second, and appeared to me to be full as numerous as
as the first. I then being about thirty four year of age I had more Sense
than to endeavour to destroy them, knowing that they was not so pernicious to the fruit of the Earth as I did immagine they would be
Again in the year 1783 which was Seventeen years Since their ~~last~~ Second
appearance to me they made their third and they may be expected again
in they year 1800 which is Seventeen Since their third appearance to me
So that if I may venture so to express it, their periodical return is Seventeen years, but they like the Comets make but a Short stay with us
The female has a Sting in her tail as Sharp and hard as a thorn with which
She perforates the branches of the trees and in them holes lays eggs, the
branch soon dies and fall, then the egg by some Occult ~~occation~~ cause immerges
a great depth into the earth and there continues for the Space
of Seventeen years as aforesaid
I like to forgot to inform that if their lives are Short B. Banneker
they are merry, they begin to Sing or make a noise from
the first they come out of Earth till they die, the hindermost part rots off
and it does not appear to be any pain to them for they Still continue
on Singing till they die

1800 June Sixth Month hath 30 Days

~~Full ☉ 7..0..40 morn~~
Full ☉ 7..0..49 morn.
Last ☾ 14..0..36 aft.
New ☽ 22..4..12 morn.
First ☾ 29..5-30 aft.

☊ { 1 ♈ 25 / 11 25 / 21 24 } deg.

Planets Places								
☽	☉	♄	♃	♂	♀	☿	☽'s	From the Tables
	Long.	♌	♋	♓	♉	♉	Lat.	this full moon is
1	2..10..52	6	6	24	24	22	1 N.	June 7..2..49 Mor
7	2..16..36	7	7	28	♊ 1	♊ 3	5 S.	and new moon
13	2..22..20	7	8	♈ 2	8	16	2 S.	is 22..2..44 mor
19	2..28..4	8	9	6	15	29	4 N.	
25	3..3..47	8	11	10	23	♋ 12	4 N.	

M D	W D	Remarkable days aspects weather &c.		☉ rise	☉ set	☽'s Long.	☽ set	☽ South	☽'s age
1	E	Whit-Sund ✱ ♂ ♀		4..43	7..17	5..25..35	13..41	7..22	10
2	2	Whit Mond.		4..43	7..17	6..9..33	14..12	8..13	11
3	3	Whit Tuesd.		4..42	7..18	6..23..48	14..45	9..4	12
4	4		now come	4..42	7..18	7..8..17	15..22	9..58	13
5	5		rain	4..41	7..19	7..22..56	16..0	10..55	14
6	6		to cheer	4..41	7..19	8..7..39		11..57	15
7	7		the earth	4..41	7..19	8..22..19	rise	12..59	16
8	E	Trinity Sund		4..40	7..20	9..6..54	9..36	14..1	17
9	2		with	4..40	7..20	9..21..12	10..30	14..59	18
10	3		heavy	4..40	7..20	10..5..19	11..13	15..54	19
11	4	St. Barnabas		4..39	7..21	10..19..6	11..49	16..45	20
12	5		thunder	4..39	7..21	11..2..31	12..18	17..32	21
13	6		from	4..39	7..21	11..15..37	12..49	18..17	22
14	7		its birth,	4..39	7..21	11..28..21	13..15	19..0	23
15	E	1st Sund. past Trin		4..39	7..21	0..10..56	13..42	19..43	24
16	2		first	4..38	7..22	0..23..12	14..7	20..26	25
17	3	St. Alban		4..38	7..22	1..5..15	14..33	21..9	26
18	4		flying high	4..38	7..22	1..17..13	15..7	21..55	27
19	5		next	4..38	7..22	1..29..4	15..44	22..43	28
20	6	☌ ☉ ☿ occident		4..38	7..22	2..10..55	16..24	23..31	29
21	7	Longest days ☉ enters ♋		4..38	7..22	2..22..46		☌	30
22	E	2nd Sund past Trin ☌ ☽ ♃		4..38	7..22	3..4..43	set.	0..20	☽
23	2		falling	4..38	7..22	3..16..49	8..40	1..9	2
24	3	St. John	low	4..38	7..22	3..29..6	9..23	1..58	3
25	4		to make the	4..38	7..22	4..11..38	9..59	2..47	4
26	5	Spica South 0..9 morn		4..38	7..22	4..24..27	10..36	3..36	5
27	6		herbs and	4..38	7..22	5..7..35	11..8	4..25	6
28	7		plants to grow	4..38	7..22	5..21..3	11..39	5..14	7
29	E	3d Sund. past Trin. St. peter & paul.		4..38	7..22	6..4..50	12..8	6..3	8
30	2	Day 14..42		4..39	7..21	6..18..56	12..40	6..52	9
				~~4..39~~	~~7..21~~	~~7..3..47~~		~~7..42~~	

~~July 1 7..17..53~~

1800 April 23d Sun eclipsed ~~about~~ 10 min. past 6 O'clock afternoon, by projection it begins some minute befor the true Conjunction and Sun Sets before the greatest obscuration So it is partly visible in the united States

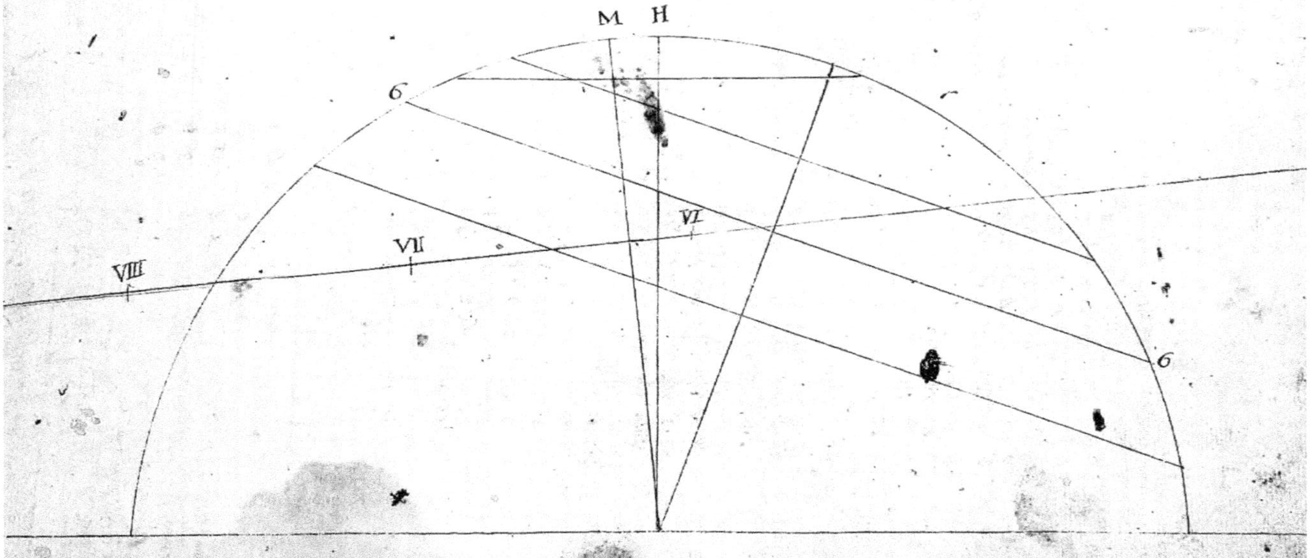

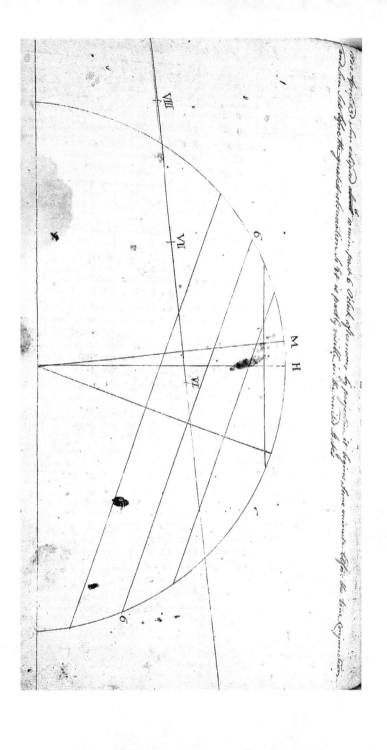

1800 July Seventh Month hath 31 Days

	☽	☉	Planets Places ♄	♃	♂	♀	☿	☽'s
		Long.	♌	♋	♈	♋	♋	Lat.
Full ☉ 6 . 7 .. 46 morn.	1	3 .. 9 .. 30	9	12	14	♋ 0	24	2 S.
Last ☾ 13 .. 2 .. 54 aft.	7	3 .. 15 .. 13	10	13	18	8	♌ 5	5 S.
New ☽ 21 .. 6 .. 24 aft.	13	3 .. 20 .. 57	10	15	22	15	15	1 N.
First ☾ 29 .. 11 .. 36 morn.	19	3 .. 26 .. 40	11	16	25	23	22	5 N.
☊ { 1 ♈ 24; 11 ♈ 23; 21 ♈ 22 } deg.	25	4 .. 2 .. 21	12	17	28	♌ 0	♍ 0	2 N.

M D	W D	Remarkable Days Aspects weather &c	☉ rise	☉ Set	☽ Long.	☽ Set	☽ South	☽'s age
1	3	~~days decrease 2 min~~	4 .. 39	7 .. 21	7 .. 3 .. 17	13 .. 9	7 .. 42	10
2	4	Visitation V. M.	4 .. 39	7 .. 21	7 .. 17 .. 53	13 .. 48	8 .. 36	11
3	5	the farmer	4 .. 40	7 .. 20	8 .. 2 .. 34	14 .. 34	9 .. 37	12
4	6	Translation St. Martin	4 .. 40	7 .. 20	8 .. 17 .. 16	15 .. 27	10 .. 38	13
5	7	says I	4 .. 40	7 .. 20	9 .. 1 .. 55		11 .. 42	14
6	E	4th Sund. past Trin.	4 .. 41	7 .. 19	9 .. 16 .. 22	rise	12 .. 43	15
7	2	hope	4 .. 41	7 .. 19	10 .. 0 .. 37	9 .. 1	13 .. 38	16
8	3	Lyra South 11 .. 19	4 .. 42	7 .. 18	10 .. 14 .. 33	9 .. 40	14 .. 32	17
9	4	no rain,	4 .. 42	7 .. 18	10 .. 28 .. 10	10 .. 14	15 .. 21	18
10	5	Spica ♍ Set 11 .. 23	4 .. 43	7 .. 17	11 .. 11 .. 28	10 .. 42	16 .. 6	19
11	6	will come	4 .. 43	7 .. 17	11 .. 24 .. 25	11 .. 9	16 .. 50	20
12	7	till I	4 .. 44	7 .. 16	0 .. 7 .. 5	11 .. 36	17 .. 33	21
13	E	5th Sund. past Trin. ☌ ♃ ♀	4 .. 44	7 .. 16	0 .. 19 .. 29	12 .. 4	18 .. 16	22
14	2	secure	4 .. 45	7 .. 15	1 .. 1 .. 40	12 .. 31	19 .. 0	23
15	3	Arcturus Set 1 .. 41 morn.	4 .. 45	7 .. 15	1 .. 13 .. 40	13 .. 1	19 .. 45	24
16	4	my	4 .. 46	7 .. 14	1 .. 25 .. 34	13 .. 36	20 .. 31	25
17	5	grain,	4 .. 47	7 .. 13	2 .. 7 .. 24	14 .. 13	21 .. 20	26
18	6	□ ☉ ♂	4 .. 47	7 .. 13	2 .. 19 .. 14	14 .. 59	22 .. 10	27
19	7	now	4 .. 48	7 .. 12	3 .. 1 .. 9	15 .. 47	23 .. 0	28
20	E	6th Sund. past Trin. ☌ ☽ ♃	4 .. 49	7 .. 11	3 .. 13 .. 9		23 .. 50	29
21	2	(Margaret	4 .. 49	7 .. 11	3 .. 25 .. 20	Set	☌	☽
22	3	Magdelene	4 .. 50	7 .. 10	4 .. 7 .. 44	7 .. 55	0 .. 40	1
23	4	☉ enters ♌	4 .. 51	7 .. 9	4 .. 20 .. 22	8 .. 33	1 .. 29	2
24	5	come rain	4 .. 52	7 .. 8	5 .. 3 .. 20	9 .. 2	2 .. 15	3
25	6	St. James	4 .. 52	7 .. 8	5 .. 16 .. 35	9 .. 31	3 .. 1	4
26	7	☿ great elong. St. Anne	4 .. 53	7 .. 7	6 .. 0 .. 23	10 .. 0	3 .. 47	5
27	E	7th Sund. past Trin.	4 .. 54	7 .. 6	6 .. 14 .. 13	10 .. 29	4 .. 37	6
28	2	from	4 .. 55	7 .. 5	6 .. 28 .. 22	11 .. 2	5 .. 28	7
29	3	the cloud,	4 .. 56	7 .. 4	7 .. 12 .. 51	11 .. 38	6 .. 22	8
30	4	Dog days begin	4 .. 57	7 .. 3	7 .. 27 .. 29	12 .. 22	7 .. 21	9
31	5	Days decrease 42 min.	4 .. 58	7 .. 2	8 .. 12 .. 11	13 .. 14	8 .. 21	10
			4 .. 59	7 .. 1	8 .. 26 .. 53		9 .. 2	

Aug 3 [illegible] 5

Evil Communication Corrupts good manners, I hope to live to hear that, Good Communication Corrects bad manners —

A very melting Sermon being preached one day which caused all the Congregation to weep but one man, which attracted the notice of the people after Sermon, a curious inquirer demanded his reason for not weeping as well as the rest of the congregation, he pertinently replied I do not belong to the parish

1799 New Moon May 4th, ☌ at 7h. 18m. P.M, by Calculation ☉ Long. greater than ☽ by 17′ — May 19th full Moon at 2h. 43m. A.M, ☽ Long. greater than ☉ by 1°.. 6′ as appears by Calculation

1800 New Moon May 23d. ☌ at 9h. 23m. A.M, ☉ Long 2.. 2.. 10
☽ Long 2.. 1 .. 15
☉ greatest 55

1800 August Eighth Month hath 31 Days

	d	h	m	
Full ☉	4	4	0	aft.
Last ☾	12	7	16	morn.
New ☽	20	8	28	morn.
First ☽	27	6	0	morn.

☊ { 1 ♈ 22 / 11 ♈ 21 / 21 ♈ 21 } deg.

Planets Places

☽	☉ Long.	♄ ♌	♃ ♋	♂ ♉	♀ ♌	☿ ♍	☽'s Lat.
1	4..9..7	13	19	3	8	7	5 S.
7	4..14..52	14	20	6	16	9	2 S.
13	4..20..37	14	21	9	23	11	4 N.
19	4..26..24	15	22	12	♍ 1	7	4 N.
25	5..2..11	15	24	15	8	3	3 S.

M D	W D	Remarkable days Aspects weather &c.		☉ rise	☉ Set	☽ Long.	☽ Set	☽ South	☽'s age
1	6	Lammas-Day		4..59	7..1	8..26..33	14..14	9..25	11
2	7		with	5..0	7..0	9..11..28	15..6	10..27	12
3	E	8th. Sund. past Trin.		5..1	6..59	9..25..51		11..25	13
4	2		thunder	5..2	6..58	10..9..56	rise	12..20	14
5	3	Lyra South 9..28		5..3	6..57	10..23..44	8..11	13..11	15
6	4	☌ ☉ ♀ Occident		5..4	6..56	11..7..12	8..41	13..59	16
7	5	Days 13..50 ent		5..5	6..55	11..20..21	9..10	14..44	17
8	6	Days decrease 56 min.		5..6	6..54	0..3..10	9..37	15..28	18
9	7		Sounding	5..7	6..53	0..15..42	10..3	16..12	19
10	E	9th. Sund. past Trin. St. Lawrence		5..8	6..52	0..28..0	10..30	16..56	20
11	2		Sharp &	5..9	6..51	1..10..5	11..1	17..41	21
12	3	Spica ♍ Set 9..12		5..10	6..50	1..22..3	11..37	18..28	22
13	4		cloud,	5..11	6..49	2..3..55	12..17	19..16	23
14	5	Arcturus Set 11..40		5..12	6..48	2..15..45	13..0	20..5	24
15	6		very warm	5..13	6..47	2..27..37	13..45	20..55	25
16	7		Clear	5..14	6..46	3..9..36	14..35	21..46	26
17	E	10th. Sund. past Trin. ☌ ☽ ♃		5..15	6..45	3..21..37	15..28	22..35	27
18	2		and	5..16	6..44	4..3..53	16..28	23..23	28
19	3		dry,	5..18	6..42	4..16..24		6 [illegible]	29
20	4	Days 13..22		5..19	6..41	4..29..10	Set.	0..10	☽
21	5		with Silver	5..20	6..40	5..12..16	7..32	0..[illegible]	2
22	6		dews	5..21	6..39	5..25..42	8..2	1..43	3
23	7	☉ enters ♍		5..22	6..38	6..9..27	8..30	2..31	4
24	E	11th Sund. past Trin, St. Bartholomew		5..23	6..37	6..23..32	9..3	3..22	5
25	2		from	5..24	6..36	7..7..56	9..39	4..15	6
26	3	☌ ☉ ☿ orient		5..26	6..34	7..22..19	10..20	5..11	7
27	4		clear	5..27	6..33	8..7..6	11..4	6..11	8
28	5	St. Augustine		5..28	6..32	8..21..48	12..5	7..16	9
29	6	St. John behead.		5..29	6..31	9..6..23	13..8	8..19	10
30	7		Sky	5..30	6..30	9..20..57	14..12	9..19	11
31	E	12th Sund. past Trin		5..32	6..28	10..5..18	15..21	10..16	12
				5..33	6..27	10..19..[illegible] 11..2..5[illegible]		11..9	

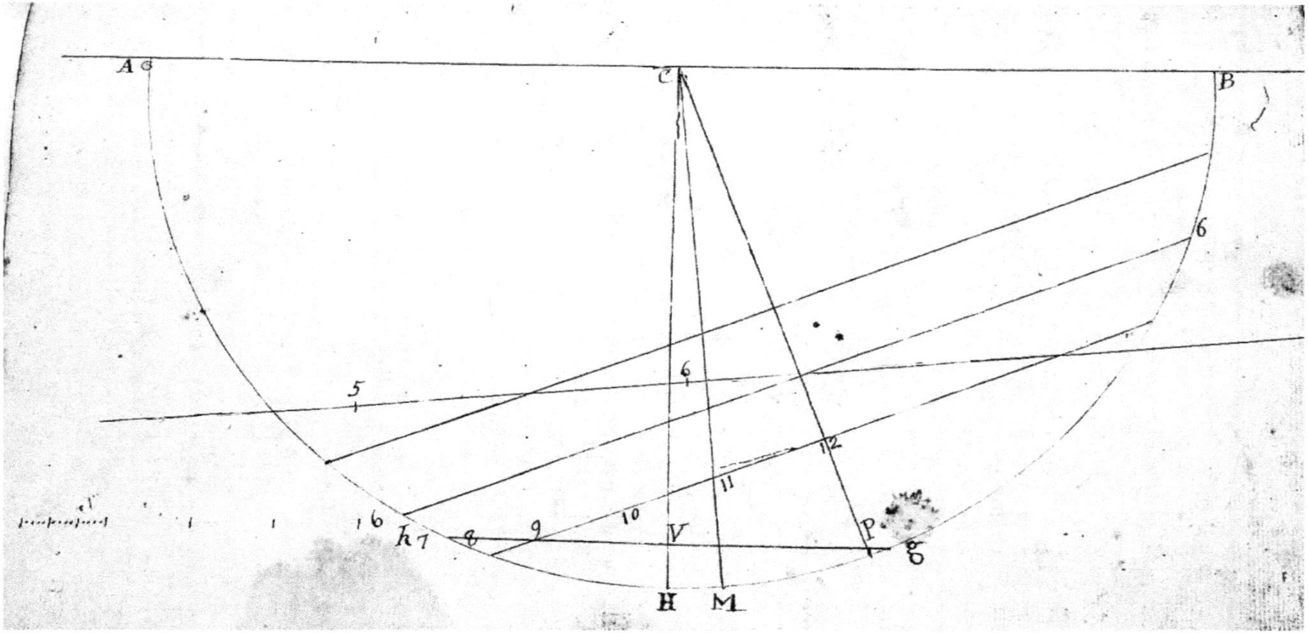

A
C
B
6
5
6
12
11
10
16
h7
8
9
V
P
g
H
M

1800 September Ninth Month hath 30 Days

d h m							
Full ○ 3..10..14 morn							
Last ☾ 10..7..18 morn							
New ☽ 18..8..16 aft							
First ☽ 25..1..52 aft							
☊ {1, 11, 21} ♈ {20, 20, 19} deg.							

Planets Places

☽	☉	♄	♃	♂	♀	☿	☽'s
	Long.	♌	♋	♉	♍	♌	Lat.
1	5..8..57	16	25	18	16	28	4 S.
7	5..14..47	17	26	20	24	♍ 1	3 N
13	5..20..38	18	27	22	♎ 1	4	5 N
19	5..26..30	18	29	23	9	14	0 S
25	6..2..21	19	♌	23	16	24	5 S

M D	W D	Remarkable days aspects weather &c.	☉ rise	☉ set	☽ Long.	☽ set	☽ South	☽'s age
1	2	Bulls eye ris 10..45	5..33	6..27	10..19..12	16..29	11..9	13
2	3	Showers	5..34	6..26	11..2..51		11..59	14
3	4	Dog days end	5..35	6..25	11..16..20	rise	12..46	15
4	5	now	5..36	6..24	11..29..10	7..42	13..30	16
5	6	Days 12..44	5..38	6..22	0..11..52	8..9	14..14	17
6	7	may	5..39	6..21	0..24..16	8..39	14..58	18
7	E	13th Sund. past Trin.	5..40	6..20	1..6..29	9..6	15..42	19
8	2	Nativity V. Mary	5..41	6..19	1..18..31	9..37	16..28	20
9	3	descend	5..43	6..17	2..0..25	10..18	17..17	21
10	4	pegasi Markab South 11..39	5..44	6..16	2..12..15	10..59	18..6	22
11	5	the	5..45	6..15	2..24..6	11..44	18..55	23
12	6	pegasi Algenib South 0..41 mo.	5..46	6..14	3..5..59	12..34	19..45	24
13	7	vegetable	5..48	6..12	3..17..59	13..28	20..35	25
14	E	14 Sund. past Trin. ☌ ☽ ♃	5..49	6..11	4..0..8	14..26	21..25	26
15	2	□ ☉ ♂	5..50	6..10	4..12..30	15..24	22..13	27
16	3	to	5..52	6..8	4..25..7	16..27	23..0	28
17	4	befriend,	5..53	6..7	5..8..2		23..47	29
18	5	pleiades rise 8..28	5..54	6..6	5..21..16	set	☌	☽
19	6	now rain	5..55	6..5	6..4..51	6..39	0..34	1
20	7		5..56	6..4	6..18..45	7..10	1..22	2
21	E	15 Sund. past Trin St. Matthew	5..58	6..2	7..2..56	7..40	2..13	3
22	2	now cool,	5..59	6..1	7..17..24	8..20	3..8	4
23	3	☉ enters ♎ equal Day & Night	6..0	6..0	8..2..1	9..4	4..7	5
24	4	just as the	6..2	5..58	8..16..43	9..59	5..10	6
25	5	mighty	6..3	5..57	9..1..25	11..2	6..15	7
26	6	St. Cyprian	6..4	5..56	9..16..1	12..6	7..17	8
27	7	powers,	6..5	5..55	10..0..25	13..15	8..14	9
28	E	16th Sund. past Trin.	6..7	5..53	10..14..33	14..26	9..10	10
29	2	St. Michael	6..8	5..52	10..28..24	15..32	10..1	11
30	3	Days decrease 3..2 rule	6..9	5..51	11..11..53	16..36	10..48	12

Elements for an Eclipse of the Sun October 18th. 1800

True time of New Moon in October 1800		d h m 18.. 6.. 0 A.M
Moon's horizontal paralax		° ' " 0.. 59.. 41
Sun's distance from the nearest Solstice		65.. 0.. 0
Suns declination South		9.. 57.. 0
Moon's Latitude South descending		0.. 36.. 39
Moon's horary motion from the Sun		0.. 36.. 00
Angle of the Moon's visible path with the Ecliptic		5.. 35.. 0
Sun's Semidiameter		0.. 16.. 11
Moon's Semidiameter		0.. 16.. 9
Semidiameter of the penumbra		0.. 32.. 20

Wind may be lulled, by the explosions of a vigorous Cannonade See Hamilton Moore's practical Navigator. page 241

---

2 Kings Chap 23. verse 11, And he took away the horses that the kings of Judah had given to the Sun —

---

2 Samuel 12. 31 And he brought away the people that were therein, and put them under Saws, and under harrows of iron, and under axes of iron, and made them pass through the brick-kiln

1801 Long. med ☉ s ° '	1801 Long. Apog s ° '	1801 Long. med ☽ s ° '	1801 Long. Apog s
9.. 9.. 52	3.. 9.. 34	3.. 17.. 52	2.. 26.. 8
Long. med. ♄ s ° '	Anomaly ♄ s ° '	Node ♄ s ° '	
4.. 14.. 12	7.. 13.. 24	3.. 21.. 35	
Long. med ♃ s ° '	Anomaly ♃ s ° '	Node ♃ s ° '	
3.. 22.. 38	9.. 11.. 3	3.. 8.. 58	
Long. med ♂ s ° '	Anomaly ♂ s ° '	Node ♂ s ° '	
2.. 3.. 51	9.. 1.. 20	1.. 18.. 29	
Long. med ♀ s ° '	Anomaly ♀ s ° '	Node ♀	
0.. 9.. 55	2.. 1.. 49	2.. 14.. 50	
Long. med. ☿ s ° '	Anomaly ☿ s ° '	Node ☿ s ° '	
5.. 11.. 31	8.. 27.. 39	1.. 16.. 12	

1800 October Tenth Month hath 31 Days

Full ○ 2 2..37 aft.
Last ☾ 10..4..36 aft.
New ☽ 18..6..9 morn.
First ☾ 24..19..37 aft.
Full ○ 31..7..38 morn.

☊ { 1, 11, 21 } ♈ { 19, 18, 18 } deg.

Planets Places

☽	☉ Long.	♄ ♌	♃ ♌	♂ ♉	♀ ♎	☿ ♎	☽'s Lat.
1	6..8..15	20	1	23	24	4	4 S.
7	6..14..11	20	1	22	♏ 1	15	5 N.
13	6..20..8	21	2	21	9	25	4 N.
19	6..26..6	22	3	21	16	♏ 5	3 S.
25	7..2..5	22	3	19	24	15	4 S.

M D	W D	Remarkable days Aspects weather &c.		☉ rise	☉ set	☽ Long.	☽ set	☽ South	☽'s age
1	4	Bulls eye rise 8..57		6..11	5..49	11..25..4		11..33	13
2	5	☽ eclip. invis	expect.	6..12	5..48	0..7..55	rise	12..20	14
3	6	Days decrease 3..10		6..13	5..47	0..20..29	6..48	13..3	15
4	7		rain	6..14	5..46	1..2..49	7..15	13..48	16
5	E	17th. Sund. past Trin.		6..15	5..45	1..14..55	7..50	14..34	17
6	2		an	6..17	5..43	1..26..53	8..22	15..21	18
7	3		early	6..18	5..42	2..8..45	9..2	16..9	19
8	4	☌ ☉ ☿, occident		6..19	5..41	2..20..36	9..48	16..59	20
9	5		frost;	6..20	5..40	3..2..27	10..36	17..49	21
10	6		Save	6..22	5..38	3..14..22	11..27	18..38	22
11	7	☌ ☽ ♃		6..23	5..37	3..26..27	12..23	19..26	23
12	E	18th. Sund. past Trin.		6..24	5..36	4..8..40	13..23	20..14	24
13	2		your	6..25	5..35	4..21..10	14..23	21..2	25
14	3		crop	6..27	5..33	5..3..55	15..28	21..50	26
15	4	pleiades rise 6..50		6..28	5..32	5..16..58	16..33	22..38	27
16	5		before	6..29	5..31	6..0..22	17..39	23..27	28
17	6		it is	6..30	5..30	6..14..5		☌	29
18	7	St. Luke ☉ eclip. invis.		6..32	5..28	6..28..7	Sets	0..17	☽
19	E	19th Sund. past Trin.		6..33	5..27	7..12..25	6..22	1..7	2
20	2		lost;	6..34	5..26	7..26..57	7..3	2..2	3
21	3		heavy clouds	6..35	5..25	8..11..38	7..56	3..3	4
22	4		hazy	6..36	5..24	8..26..20	8..55	4..6	5
23	5	☉ enters ♏		6..38	5..22	9..11..0	9..58	5..9	6
24	6		rain	6..39	5..21	9..25..31	11..8	6..11	7
25	7		high	6..40	5..20	10..9..49	12..16	7..7	8
26	E	20th. Sund. past Trin.		6..41	5..19	10..23..50	13..24	8..0	9
27	2			6..42	5..18	11..7..31	14..30	8..49	10
28	3	St. Simon and Jude	wind	6..44	5..16	11..20..52	15..34	9..35	11
29	4			6..45	5..15	0..3..53	16..39	10..20	12
30	5		clear	6..46	5..14	0..16..38	17..40	11..4	13
31	6	Days 10..26	again	6..47	5..13	0..29..0		11..48	14
				~~6..48~~	~~5..12~~	~~1..11..17~~		~~12..34~~	
						1..~~23..20~~			

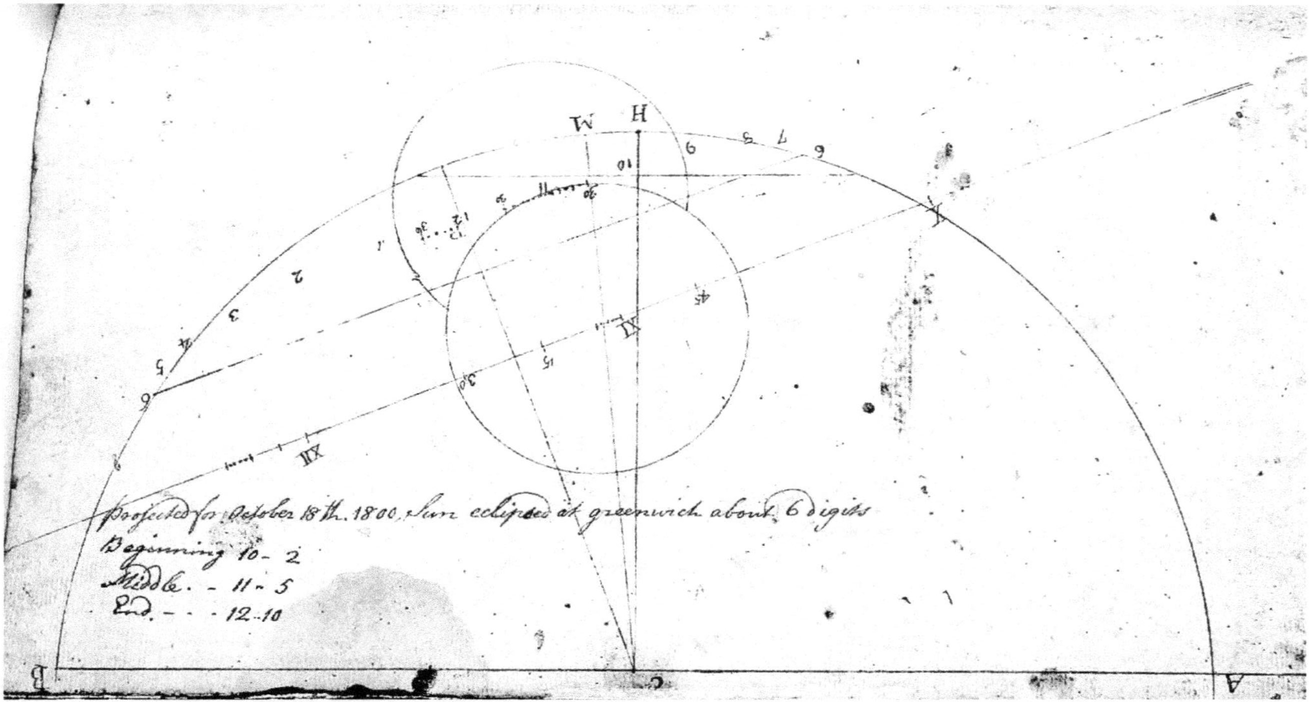
Projected for October 18th. 1800, Sun eclipsed at greenwich about 6 digits
Beginning 10 - 2
Middle - 11 - 5
End - - - 12 - 10
H
A
B
C

1800 November: Eleventh Month hath 30 Days:

	☽	☉	♄	♃	♂	♀	☿	☽'s
			Planets Places					
Full ☽ 1..7..38 morn		Long.	♌	♌	♉	♐	♏	Lat.
Last ☾ 9..0..20 aft.	1	7..9..4	23	3	17	2	25	3 N.
New ☽ 16..4..18 aft.	7	7..15..6	23	4	15	10	♐ 4	5 N.
First ☽ 23..8..28 morn	13	7..21..9	23	4	13	17	12	1 S.
~~Full ☽ 30..3..38 morn.~~	19	7..27..13	23	4	10	25	19	5 S.
☊ {1: 17; 11 ♈ 17; 21: 16} deg.	25	8..3..17	24	4	9	♑ 2	26	0 S.

M. D.	W. D.	Remarkable days Aspects weather &c		☉ rise	☉ set	☽ Long.	☽ rise	☽ south	☽'s age
1	7	All Saints △ ♃ ♀		6..48	5..12	1..11..17	rise	12..34	15
2	E	21st. Sund. past Trin.		6..49	5..11	1..23..20	6..24	13..21	16
3	2		rain	6..51	5..9	2..5..15	7..5	14..9	17
4	3		or	6..52	5..8	2..17..7	7..47	14..58	18
5	4		snow,	6..53	5..7	2..28..56	8..34	15..47	19
6	5		which	6..54	5..6	3..10..51	9..26	16..37	20
7	6	☍ ☉ ♂		6..55	5..5	3..22..50	10..19	17..26	21
8	7	☌ ☽ ♃		6..56	5..4	4..4..58	11..17	18..13	22
9	E	22d Sund. past Trin.		6..57	5..3	4..17..17	12..17	19..0	23
10	2		of	6..58	5..2	4..29..52	13..17	19..46	24
11	3	St. Martin		6..59	5..1	5..12..45	14..17	20..32	25
12	4		the	7..0	5..0	5..25..57	15..23	21..19	26
13	5		two	7..1	4..59	6..9..29	16..33	22..9	27
14	6		I don't	7..2	4..58	6..23..21	17..43	23..0	28
15	7	□ ☉ ♄	know	7..3	4..57	7..7..31		23..55	29
16	E	23d. Sund. past Trin.		7..4	4..56	7..21..59	Set.	☌	☽
17	2	△ ♄ ♀		7..5	4..55	8..6..33	5..44	0..51	1
18	3		Some	7..6	4..54	8..21..16	6..40	1..51	2
19	4		clouds	7..7	4..53	9..5..58	7..43	2..54	3
20	5		flies	7..8	4..52	9..20..34	8..49	3..56	4
21	6		high	7..8	4..52	10..4..59	9..59	4..54	5
22	7	☉ enters ♐		7..9	4..51	10..19..9	11..8	5..48	6
23	E	24th. Sund. past Trin.		7..10	4..50	11..3..2	12..16	6..38	7
24	2		Some	7..11	4..49	11..16..34	13..21	7..26	8
25	3		low	7..12	4..48	11..29..47	14..23	8..11	9
26	4	☿ great elong		7..12	4..48	0..12..42	15..25	8..56	10
27	5								
28	6		now the	7..13	4..47	0..25..16	16..26	9..40	11
29	7		wind begins	7..14	4..46	1..7..37	17..25	10..25	12
30	E	Advent Sund.	to blow	7..15	4..45	1..19..45	18..24	11..10	13
30				7..15	4..45	2..1..43		11..57	14
				~~7..16~~	~~4..44~~	~~2..13..36~~		~~12..46~~	
						~~2..25..27~~			

Projected for an eclipse of the Sun October 18th 1800, the Sun will be eclipsed about 6 digits on his ~~South~~ North limb as seen from Greenwich, Ferguson's keeping of all visible eclipses at London says nothing of this, so that the mistake may be in me.

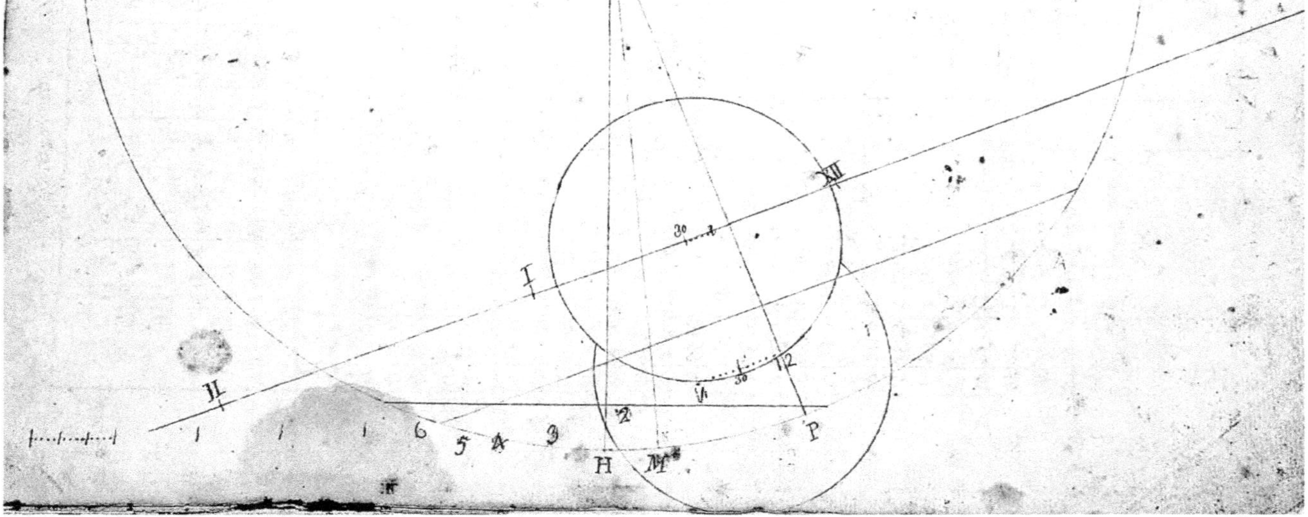

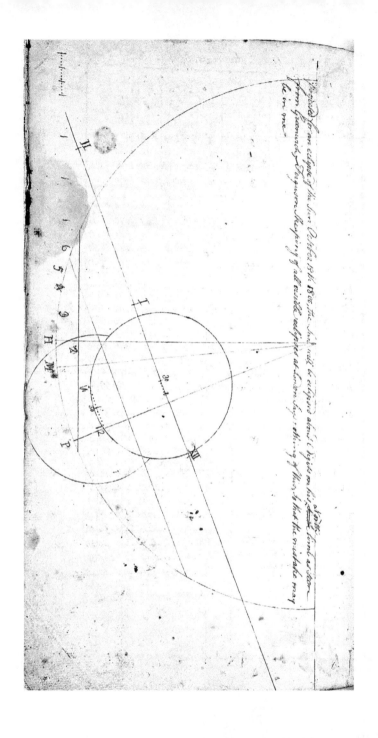

1800 December Twelfth Month hath 31 Days

Full ○ 1..3..42 morn.
Last ☾ 9..3..48 morn.
New ☽ 16..1..8 morn
First ☽ 22..9..51 aft
Full ○ 30..0..42 morn

☊ {1 ♈ 15, 11 15, 21 14} deg.

Planets Places

☽	☉ Long.	♄ ♌	♃ ♌	♂ ♉	♀ ♑	☿ ♐	☽'s Lat.
1	8..9..28	24	4	8	10	26	5 N.
7	8..15..28	24	4	8	17	25	3 N.
13	8..21..35	24	4	8	25	18	4 S.
19	8..27..42	23	3	8	♒ 2	12	4 S.
25	9..3..49	23	2	9	10	13	3 N.

M D	W D	Remarkable days Aspects weather &c		☉ rise	☉ set	☽ Long.	☽ rise	☽ South	☽'s age
				7..16	4..44	2..13..36	rise	12..46	15
1	2	Bulls eye South 11..53	winter	7..16	4..44	2..25..27	6..25	13..36	16
2	3			7..17	4..43	3..7..17	7..14	14..25	17
3	4	days decrease 5..18	weather	7..18	4..42	3..19..12	8..6	15..13	18
4	5			7..18	4..42	4..1..15	9..0	15..59	19
5	6	☌ ☽ ♃		7..19	4..41	4..13..29	9..57	16..45	20
6	7	Nicholas		7..19	4..41	4..25..56	10..58	17..31	21
7	E	2nd Sund. in Advent		7..20	4..40	5..8..39	12..1	18..17	22
8	2	Conception V. M.	gather	7..20	4..40	5..21..39	13..5	19..3	23
9	3		your fire	7..20	4..40	6..5..0	14..9	19..50	24
10	4		wood	7..21	4..39	6..18..41	15..17	20..41	25
11	5			7..21	4..39	7..2..42	16..28	21..34	26
12	6	☌ ☉ ☿ Orient.	together	7..21	4..39	7..17..0	17..42	22..30	27
13	7			7..21	4..39	8..1..30	18..58	23..31	28
14	E	3d Sund. Advent		7..22	4..38	8..16..11		☌	29
15	2	△ ☉ ♄	now we	7..22	4..38	9..0..52	sets	0..34	☽
16	3			7..22	4..38	9..15..34	6..23	1..34	2
17	4	pegasi Markab South 5..14	may	7..22	4..38	10..0..7	7..33	2..32	3
18	5			7..22	4..38	10..14..25	8..42	3..28	4
19	6	pegasi Alginib South 6..13	expect	7..22	4..38	10..28..27	9..51	4..18	5
20	7			7..22	4..38	11..12..10	10..57	5..7	6
21	E	4th Sund in Advent		7..22	4..38	11..25..34	12..3	5..53	7
22	2	☉ enters ♑	a Snow	7..22	4..38	0..8..38	13..5	6..38	8
23	3		it is the	7..22	4..38	0..21..24	14..5	7..22	9
24	4			7..22	4..38	1..3..52	15..4	8..7	10
25	5	Christmas Day		7..22	4..38	1..16..5	16..3	8..52	11
26	6	St. Stephen		7..22	4..38	1..28..10	17..1	9..39	12
27	7	St. John		7..22	4..38	2..10..5	17..58	10..27	13
28	E	1st. Sund past Chris. Innocents	season all men	7..21	4..39	2..21..57		11..15	14
29	2		may know	7..21	4..39	3..3..48	rise	12..4	15
30	3			7..21	4..39	3..15..40	5..41	12..52	16
31	4	Silvester		~~7..20~~	~~4..40~~	~~3..27..38~~		~~13..39~~	
						4..9..48			

1800 Ellicott & Co. Cr

January 20	By a pair of Stockens
22	By 6 1/2 yards Rushia Drilling a 3/9 ℘ yd
February 7	By 4 yard Ticklenburg at 2/6 ℘ yd
	By 1/2 lb Soap
February 17	By paying Samuel pairpoint
March 29	By 4 1/2 yard Russia Sheeting at 3/9 ℘ yd
	By 3 1/2 yards Irish Linnen a 4 S ℘ yd
	By 8 Skeins thread
April 16	By Cash Received
May 17	By Cash of George Ellicott
May 2[illegible]	By paying the Sheriff
July 1	By Cash of G. Ellicott
	By a peck of Salt
Novr 11	By Cash a Dollar
Novr 22	By 1 1/4 yd Coating a 8 S ℘ yd
	By 1 1/2 yard flannel at 3/6 ℘ yd
	By 1/4 yard Linnen a 2/8 ℘ yd
	By thread
	By a pair of Shoes
	The above acct Settled to November 10th 1800 — Cash

£ s (right-hand column, top to bottom): 0 5 · 1 4 · 0 10 · 0 0 · 0 3 · 2 4 · 0 16 · 0 14 · 0 0 · 0 11 · 4 7 · 0 7 · 0 8 · 0 – · 0 1 · 5 7 · 0 7 · 5 14 · 0 10 · 0 5 · 0 0 · 0 0 · 0 11 · 7 2 · 4 17 · 12 0

1801 ~~Third Pay~~ the above is the Second payment

Janry 31	By 2 1/2 yards Rusia Sheeting a 3/9 ℘ yd
	By 3 1/2 do white Linnen at 3/9 ℘ yd
	By thread
April 1	By a pair of Shoes at a dollar & Quarter
May 9	By a Razor at
June 13	By 8 pounds of pork at 1 S ℘ lb
June 18	By 1/2 Bushel Corn a 6/6 ℘ Bus
July 17	By paying the Sheriff
July 20	By half Bushel of Corn
Augt 6	By half Bushel Do
Augt 13	By 6 1/2 yards Camblet at 3/6 ℘ yd
	By 2 yards brown holland at 3 S ℘ yd
	Silk twist and ~~moulds and Buckram and~~ thread
	Buckram and moulds
	By 4 1/2 lb pork at 1 S ℘ lb
Sept 2	By 2 1/2 Dollars & 1/2 Bushel Corn
Oct 19	By a Razor at 1/2 dollar
	By paying the Taylor for making a Coat
Novr 2	By 2 1/2 yard Corduroy at 8/8 ℘ yd
	dozen Buttons
	3/4 yard Rushia duck a 2/10 ℘ yd
Nov. 28	Cash Received ~~of them~~

£ s (right-hand column, top to bottom): 0 9 · 0 13 · 0 0 · 0 9 · 1 12 · 0 4 · 0 8 · 0 3 · 0 4 · 2 11 · 0 3 · 0 3 · 1 2 · 0 6 · 0 1 · 0 0 · 0 4 · 4 13 · 1 2 · 0 3 · 0 16 · 1 1 · 0 1 · 0 2 · 8 1 · 3 18 · 12 0

the above is the third payment

1801 January First Month hath 31 Days

	D	h	m	
Last ☾	7	5	37	aft.
New ☽	14	10	2	morn
First ☽	21	2	24	aft.
Full ○	29	6	30	aft.

☊ { 1 ♈ 14, 11 13, 21 13 } deg.

☽	☉	♄	♃	♂	♀	☿	☽'s
	Long.	♌	♎	♉	♒	♐	Lat.
1	9..10..53	23	2	12	17	18	5 N.
7	9..17..0	23	1	13	25	26	0 S.
13	9..23..8	22	0	14	♓ 2	♑ 4	5 S.
19	9..29..14	22	0	17	9	13	1 S.
25	10..5..20	21	♍ 29	19	16	21	5 N.

M D	W D		☉ rise	☉ set	☽'s Long.	☽ rise	☽ South	☽'s age
1	5	Circumcision ☿ great elong ☌ ☽ ♃	7..20	4..40	3..27..39	6..38	13..41	17
2	6		7..20	4..40	4..9..45	7..36	14..27	18
3	7		7..20	4..40	4..22..4	8..36	15..12	19
4	D	2nd. Sund. past Chris.	7..19	4..41	5..4..38	9..36	15..57	20
5	2		7..19	4..41	5..17..29	10..37	16..42	21
6	3	Epiphany	7..18	4..42	6..0..40	11..42	17..30	22
7	4		7..18	4..42	6..14..9	12..50	18..18	23
8	5		7..17	4..43	6..27..58	13..59	19..9	24
9	6		7..17	4..43	7..12..7	15..8	20..4	25
10	7		7..16	4..44	7..26..31	16..26	21..3	26
11	D	1st. Sund past Epip.	7..15	4..45	8..11..6	17..36	22..5	27
12	2		7..15	4..45	8..25..49	18..43	23..8	28
13	3		7..14	4..46	9..10..31		☌	29
14	4		7..13	4..47	9..25..8	Set.	6..8	☽
15	5		7..13	4..47	10..9..35	6..12	1..3	2
16	6		7..12	4..48	10..23..47	7..21	1..57	3
17	7		7..11	4..49	11..7..41	8..27	2..46	4
18	D	2nd. Sund past Epip.	7..10	4..50	11..21..17	9..33	3..34	5
19	2		7..10	4..50	0..4..31	10..38	4..19	6
20	3	☉ enter ♒	7..9	4..51	0..17..26	11..40	5..4	7
21	4		7..8	4..52	1..0..4	12..41	5..49	8
22	5		7..7	4..53	1..12..26	13..41	6..35	9
23	6		7..6	4..54	1..24..35	14..41	7..22	10
24	7		7..5	4..55	2..6..34	15..41	8..10	11
25	D	3d. Sund past Epip, Covert St. paul	7..4	4..56	2..18..29	16..34	8..59	12
26	2		7..3	4..57	3..0..18	17..25	9..48	13
27	3		7..2	4..58	3..12..9	18..11	10..36	14
28	4	☌ ☽ ♃	7..1	4..59	3..24..3		11..24	15
29	5		7..0	5..0	4..6..6	rise	12..12	16
30	6		6..59	5..1	4..18..17	6..18	12..58	17
31	7		6..58	5..2	5..0..42	7..17	13..43	18

D	1801 January Long ☉	1801 Logarithm ☉ a Θ	1801 July Long ☉	1801 Logarithm ☉ a Θ
	s ° ′		s ° ′	
1	9..10..53	4.99259	3..9..15	5.00728
7	9..17..0	4.99264	3..14..59	5.00724
13	9..23..8	4.99278	3..20..42	5.00713
19	9..29..14	4.99300	3..26..26	5.00698
25	10..5..20	4.99331	4..2..10	5.00673
	February Long ☉	**Logarithm ☉ a Θ**	**August Long ☉**	**Logarithm ☉ a Θ**
	s ° ′		s ° ′	
1	10..12..26	4.99375	4..8..32	5.00634
7	10..18..30	4.99421	4..14..36	5.00594
13	10..24..35	4.99474	4..20..22	5.00548
19	11..0..39	4.99532	4..26..8	5.00495
25	11..6..40	4.99590	5..1..56	5.00437
	March Long ☉	**Logarithm ☉ a Θ**	**Septemb. Long ☉**	**Logarithm ☉ a Θ**
	s ° ′		s ° ′	
1	11..10..40	4.99629	5..8..42	5.00364
7	11..16..40	4.99698	5..14..32	5.00296
13	11..22..40	4.99771	5..20..22	5.00225
19	11..28..38	4.99846	5..26..13	5.00151
25	0..4..35	4.99922	6..2..6	5.00076
	April Long ☉	**Logarithm ☉ a Θ**	**October Long ☉**	**Logarithm ☉ a Θ**
	s °			
1	0..11..30	5.00012	6..8..0	5.00012
7	0..17..23	5.00088	6..13..56	4.99935
13	0..23..15	5.00165	6..19..53	4.99859
19	0..29..6	5.00237	6..25..52	4.99746
25	1..4..58	5.00308	7..1..49	4.99710
	May Long ☉	**Logarithm ☉ a Θ**	**Novemb. Long ☉**	**Logarithm ☉ a Θ**
	s ° ′			
1	1..10..47	5.00374	7..8..49	4.99629
7	1..16..36	5.00427	7..14..51	4.99563
13	1..22..23	5.00486	7..20..53	4.99502
19	1..28..10	5.00539	7..26..57	4.99447
25	2..3..55	5.00587	8..3..2	4.99398
	June Long ☉	**Logarithm ☉ a Θ**	**December Long ☉**	**Logarithm ☉ a ☉**
1	[illegible]..10..38	5.00634	8..9..7	4.99355
[illegible]	[illegible]..16..22	5.00668	8..15..10	4.99325
[illegible]	[illegible]..22..6	5.00694	8..21..17	4.99296
[illegible]	[illegible]..27..50	5.00713	8..27..23	4.99275
[illegible]	[illegible]..3..23	5.00724	9..3..31	4.99263

February Second Month hath 28 Days

☽	h	m	
Last Q	6	6..0	morn
New ☽	12	8..58	aft.
First Q	20	7..8	morn
Full ○	28	0..34	aft.

1	♈	12	deg.
11		12	
21		11	

☽	☉ Long.	♄ ♌	♃ ♋	♂ ♉	♀ ♓	☿ ♒	☽ Lat.
1	10.12.26	21	28	22	21	3	2 N.
7	10.18..30	21	27	25	♈ 1	13	4 S.
13	10..24..35	20	27	28	8	23	3 S.
19	11..0..39	20	26	♊ 0	15	♓ 4	1 N.
25	11..6..40	19	26	3	22	15	5 N.

M D	W D		☉ rise	☉ set	☽'s Long.	☽ rise	☽ South	☽'s age
1	D	Septuagesima Sund.	6..57	5..3	5..13..24	8..16	14..28	19
2	2		6..56	5..4	5..26..23	9..19	15..14	20
3	3		6..55	5..5	6..9..42	10..26	16..1	21
4	4		6..54	5..6	6..23..20	11..34	16..51	22
5	5		6..53	5..7	7..7..19	12..45	17..45	23
6	6		6..52	5..8	7..21..35	13..58	18..43	24
7	7		6..51	5..9	8..6..4	15..11	19..44	25
8	D		6..50	5..10	8..20..43	16..22	20..47	26
9	2		6..49	5..11	9..5..25	17..24	21..49	27
10	3		6..48	5..12	9..20..6	18..20	22..49	28
11	4		6..46	5..14	10..4..41		23..46	29
12	5		6..45	5..15	10..19..1	set	☌	☽
13	6	☌ ☉ ☿ Occident	6..44	5..16	11..3..5	6..17	0..39	1
14	7	Valentine	6..43	5..17	11..16..51	7..20	1..25	2
15	D	Quinqua. Sund.	6..42	5..18	0..0..17	8..23	2..11	3
16	2		6..40	5..20	0..13..22	9..25	2..56	4
17	3	Shrove Tuesday	6..39	5..21	0..26..9	10..27	3..41	5
18	4	Ashwednesday	6..38	5..22	1..8..40	11..29	4..27	6
19	5	☉ enter ♓	6..36	5..24	1..20..56	12..29	5..13	7
20	6		6..35	5..25	2..3..1	13..25	6..1	8
21	7		6..34	5..26	2..14..57	14..25	6..50	9
22	D	1st Sund in Lent.	6..33	5..27	2..26..49	15..14	7..39	10
23	2		6..32	5..28	3..8..40	16..3	8..28	11
24	3	St Matthias	6..31	5..29	3..20..31	16..49	9..18	12
25	4		6..30	5..30	4..2..28	17..29	10..6	13
26	5		6..28	5..32	4..14..31	18..1	10..53	14
27	6		6..27	5..33	4..26..52		11..38	15
28	7		6..26	5..34	5..9..23	rise	12..23	16
					5..22..12			

A, B, and C, discoursing about their ages, Says A, if from double the sursolid root of B's age, double the biquadrate root of C's age be taken the remainder will be equal to the Sursolid root of my age, Says B, the Square root of my age is equal to one fourth part of A's, and says C, the Square root of my age is one more than the Square root of B's, Required their Several ages—

A's	Age	32	The Sursolid root of which is 2
B's		64	The Cube of root of which is 4
C's		81	The biquadrate root of which is 3

Eclipses for the year 1801 are Six in Number—

First of the Sun March 14. 7^h. 30^m

It appears by the Schome the Sun will rise Eclipsed, the greatest obscuration will about 7 O'clock, when the Sun will be 8 digets eclipsed—

To find the Latitude of the moon in the Sysygy, first find the true place of the Node, which being Subtracted from the true place of the Sun, leaves the Suns distance from the Node which is the Argument of Latitude at the time of Conjunction, but in the time of opposition we must add Six Signs to the Sun's distance from the Node, which gives the Moon's distance from the Same Node, and is the Argument of her Latitude at that time—

March Third Month hath 31 Days.

	D	h	m	
Last ☾	7	2	0	aftern.
New ☽	14	7	42	morn.
First ☽	22	5	3	morn
Full ○	30	3	62	morn

☊ { 1 ♈ 11, 11 ♈ 10, 21 ♈ 10 } deg.

☽	☉ Long.	♄ ♌	♃ ♋	♂ ♊	♀ ♈	☿ ♓	☽ Lat.
1	11.19.40	19	25	6	26	23	2 N.
7	11.16.40	18	25	9	♉ 2	♈ 2	5 S.
13	11.22.40	18	25	12	9	11	2 S.
19	11.28.38	18	25	15	15	11	4 N.
25	0.4.35	17	25	19	21	12	4 N.

M.D.	W.D.		☉ rise	☉ Set	☽ Long.	☽ rise	☽ South	☽ age
	D	2nd. Sund. in Lent. St. David.	6..25	5..35	5..22..12	6..59	13..9	17
	2		6..24	5..36	6..5..21	8..3	13..56	18
	3		6..23	5..37	6..18..49	9..8	14..44	19
	4		6..22	5..38	7..2..37	10..20	15..37	20
	5		6..21	5..39	7..16..42	11..32	16..33	21
	6		6..19	5..41	8..1..5	12..44	17..33	22
	7		6..17	5..43	8..15..39	13..56	18..35	23
	D	3d. Sund. in Lent	6..16	5..44	9..0..20	15..3	19..38	24
	2		6..14	5..46	9..15..3	16..3	20..40	25
	3		6..13	5..47	9..29..41	16..49	21..38	26
	4		6..12	5..48	10..14..9	17..33	22..33	27
	5		6..11	5..49	10..28..23	18..5	23..24	28
	6	☌ ☽ ☿	6..9	5..51	11..12..20		☌	29
	7	♀ great elong	6..8	5..52	11..25..57	set	0..12	☽
	D	4th. Sund in Lent	6..7	5..53	0..9..13	7..11	0..58	2
	2		6..6	5..54	0..22..9	8..13	1..42	3
	3	St. Patrick	6..4	5..56	1..4..50	9..14	2..26	4
	4		6..3	5..57	1..17..14	10..13	3..13	5
	5		6..2	5..58	1..29..25	11..12	4..1	6
	6		6..1	5..59	2..11..24	12..9	4..50	7
	7	☉ enter ♈ = day & night	6..0	6..0	2..23..19	13..3	5..40	8
22	D	5th. Sund. Lent	5..59	6..1	3..5..9	13..53	6..30	9
	2		5..58	6..2	3..17..0	14..40	7..21	10
	3		5..57	6..3	3..28..54	15..22	8..8	11
	4	☿ great elong. Annunci V.M.	5..55	6..5	4..10..55	15..58	8..35	12
	5		5..54	6..6	4..23..5	16..29	9..41	13
	6		5..53	6..7	5..5..28	17..0	10..26	14
	7		5..52	6..8	5..18..8	17..28	11..11	15
29	D	Palm Sund.	5..50	6..10	6..1..5		11..58	16
	2		5..49	6..11	6..14..22	rise	12..45	17
	3		5..48	6..12	6..27..59	8..13	13..35	18
					7..11..55			

Common Notes and moveable Feasts for the Year 1801

Dominical Letter	D	Easter Sunday	April
Cycle of the Sun	18	Ascension day	
Golden Number	16	Whitsunday	
Epact	15	Trinity Sunday	d
Number of Direction	15	Advent sunday	
		Sund. after Trinity 25	

Eclipses visible for the year 1801 are Six in Number

First of the Sun March 14 d 7 h 56 m A. M.

It appears by projection the Sun will rise eclipsed, the greatest obscuration will be about 7 O'clock, when the Sun will be about 8½ Digits eclipsed on his ~~North~~ South Limb.

Second is a total and visible eclipse of the Moon March 30 d .. 2 h .. 34 m

	h m	
Beginning	1 .. 22	A. M.
Beginning of total Darkness	2 .. 20	
Middle of the eclipse	3 .. 06	
End of total Darkness	3 .. 52	
End of the eclipse	4 .. 48	Moon eclipsed 22 1/3 Digits
Duration	3 .. 24	

Third of the Sun April 12 d .. 8 h .. 10 m P. M invisible at Baltimore

---

Fourth of the Sun September 8 d .. 2 h .. 55 m A. M. invisible at Baltimore

---

Fifth is a total and visible eclipse of the Moon 21 st. and part of the 22 day of September

	H M	
Beginning 21 day	10 .. 40	P. M.
Beginning of total darkness	11 .. 6	
Middle of the eclipse 22 day	0 .. 17	
End of total darkness	1 .. 27	A. M.
End of the eclipse	1 .. 52	Digits eclipsed 21
Duration of the eclipse	3 .. 12	

Sixth and last is of the Sun October 7 d .. 5 h .. 36 m P. M invisible at Baltimore —

That eclipse of the Sun on the 14th. day of March 1801

	h m	
Beginning	6 .. 21	A. M.
Great obscuration	7 .. 23	
The end	8 .. 25	

1801 April Fourth Month hath 30 Days

	☽	h	m	
Last ☾	5	10	48	aft.
New ☽	12	9	24	aft.
First ☽	20	9	22	aft.
Full ○	28	10	52	aft.

☊ {1 ♈ 9, 11 ♈ 9, 21 ♈ 8} deg.

☽	☉	♄	♃	♂	♀	☿	☽'s
	Long.	♌	♋	♊	♉	♈	Lat.
1	0..11..30	17	25	22	27	8	3 S.
7	0..17..23	17	25	26	♊ 1	5	5 S.
13	0..23..15	17	25	29	6	3	2 N.
19	0..29..6	17	26	♋ 3	9	5	5 N.
25	1..4..58	17	26	6	12	8	1 N.

M D	W D		☉ rise	☉ set	☽ Long.	☽ rise	☽ South	☽'s age
1	4		5..46	6..14	7..11..55	9..22	14..30	19
2	5		5..44	6..16	7..26..9	10..35	15..28	20
3	6	Good Fryday	5..43	6..17	8..10..35	11..48	16..29	21
4	7	St. Ambrose	5..41	6..19	8..25..16	12..55	17..32	22
5	D	Ester Sund.	5..40	6..20	9..9..58	13..58	18..35	23
6	2	Easter Mond.	5..39	6..21	9..24..40	14..50	19..35	24
7	3	Easter Tuesd.	5..38	6..22	10..9..14	15..34	20..31	25
8	4		5..36	6..24	10..23..36	16..12	21..24	26
9	5		5..35	6..25	11..7..42	16..44	22..13	27
10	6		5..34	6..26	11..21..29	17..15	23..2	28
11	7		5..33	6..27	0..4..58		23..48	29
12	D	1st Sund. past East.	5..32	6..28	0..18..7	set.	☌	☽
13	2		5..30	6..30	1..0..55	7..14	0..33	1
14	3		5..29	6..31	1..13..27	8..13	1..17	2
15	4		5..28	6..32	1..25..45	9..12	2..4	3
16	5		5..27	6..33	2..7..51	10..12	2..53	4
17	6		5..26	6..34	2..19..47	11..5	3..42	5
18	7		5..25	6..35	3..1..39	11..57	4..32	6
19	D	2nd Sund. past East.	5..23	6..37	3..13..31	12..45	5..22	7
20	2	☉ enters ♉	5..22	6..38	3..25..20	13..25	6..10	8
21	3		5..21	6..39	4..7..18	14..5	6..58	9
22	4		5..20	6..40	4..19..22	14..36	7..43	10
23	5		5..18	6..42	5..1..39	15..6	8..28	11
24	6		5..17	6..43	5..14..10	15..33	9..13	12
25	7	☿ great elong	5..16	6..44	5..26..56	16..0	9..57	13
26	D	3d. Sund. past East.	5..15	6..45	6..10..2	16..31	10..44	14
27	2		5..14	6..46	6..23..27		11..33	15
28	3		5..13	6..47	7..7..14	rise	12..25	16
29	4		5..12	6..48	7..21..17	8..25	13..22	17
30	5		5..11	6..49	8..5..38	9..37	14..22	18
					8..20..11			

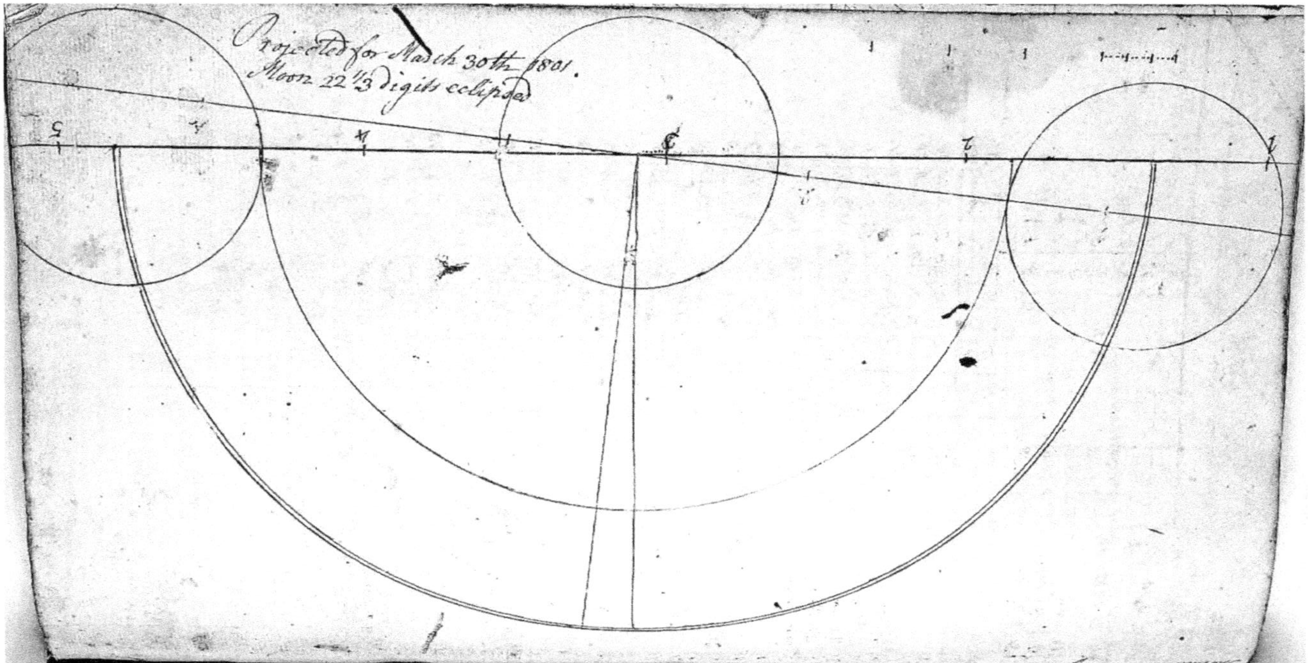
Projected for March 30th 1801.
Moon 22 1/3 digits eclipsed

1801 May Fifth Month hath 31 Days

	D	H	M	
Last ☾	5	4	0	morn.
New ☽	12	10	39	morn.
First ☽	20	2	26	aft.
Full ○	27	10	6	aft

☊ { 1 ♈ 8 ; 11 7 ; 21 6 } deg.

☽	☉	♄	♃	♂	♀	☿	☽
	Long.	♌	♋	♋	♊	♈	Lat.
1	1..10..47	17	27	10	13	15	5 S.
7	1..16..36	17	28	13	14	22	2 S.
13	1..22..23	17	29	17	12	♉ 1	4 N.
19	1..28..10	18	♌ 0	19	10	12	4 N.
25	2..3..55	18	0	21	6	23	2 S.

M D	W D		☉ rise	☉ set	☽ Long.	☽ rise	☽ south	☽ age
1	6	Phillip and James	5..10	6..50	8..20..11	10..45	15..22	19
2	7		5..9	6..51	9..4..52	11..51	16..28	20
3	D	4th. Sund. past East.	5..8	6..52	9..19..35	12..48	17..29	21
4	2		5..7	6..53	10..4..12	13..34	18..27	22
5	3		5..5	6..55	10..18..44	14..12	19..20	23
6	4		5..4	6..56	11..3..0	14..45	20..11	24
7	5		5..3	6..57	11..16..58	15..16	20..59	25
8	6		5..2	6..58	0..0..37	15..47	21..47	26
9	7		5..1	6..59	0..13..55	16..13	22..33	27
10	D	Rogation Sund.	5..0	7..0	0..26..56	16..45	23..19	28
11	2		4..59	7..1	1..9..37		6	29
12	3		4..58	7..2	1..22..2	Set	0..6	☽
13	4		4..58	7..2	2..4..14	8..5	0..50	2
14	5	Ascencion Day	4..57	7..3	2..16..14	9..2	1..39	3
15	6		4..56	7..4	2..28..10	9..55	2..30	4
16	7		4..55	7..5	3..10..0	10..42	3..19	5
17	D	Sund. past Ascen.	4..54	7..6	3..21..51	11..27	4..8	6
18	2		4..53	7..7	4..3..45	12..2	4..55	7
19	3		4..52	7..8	4..15..44	12..36	5..40	8
20	4		4..52	7..8	4..27..54	13..6	6..25	9
21	5		4..51	7..9	5..10..14	13..35	7..10	10
22	6		4..51	7..9	5..22..53	14..4	7..55	11
23	7		4..50	7..10	6..5..47	14..33	8..43	12
24	D	Whit-Sund.	4..49	7..11	6..19..2	15..2	9..27	13
25	2	Whit. Mond.	4..48	7..12	7..2..37	15..32	10..17	14
26	3	Whit. Tuesd..	4..47	7..13	7..16..30	—	11..10	15
27	4	☌ ☉ ♀ orient.	4..46	7..14	8..0..43	rise	12..9	16
28	5		4..46	7..14	8..15..10	8..34	13..11	17
29	6		4..45	7..15	8..29..48	9..38	14..13	18
30	7		4..44	7..16	9..14..30	10..32	15..15	19
31	D	Trinity Sund.	4..44	7..16	9..29..11	11..25	16..14	20
					10..13..47			

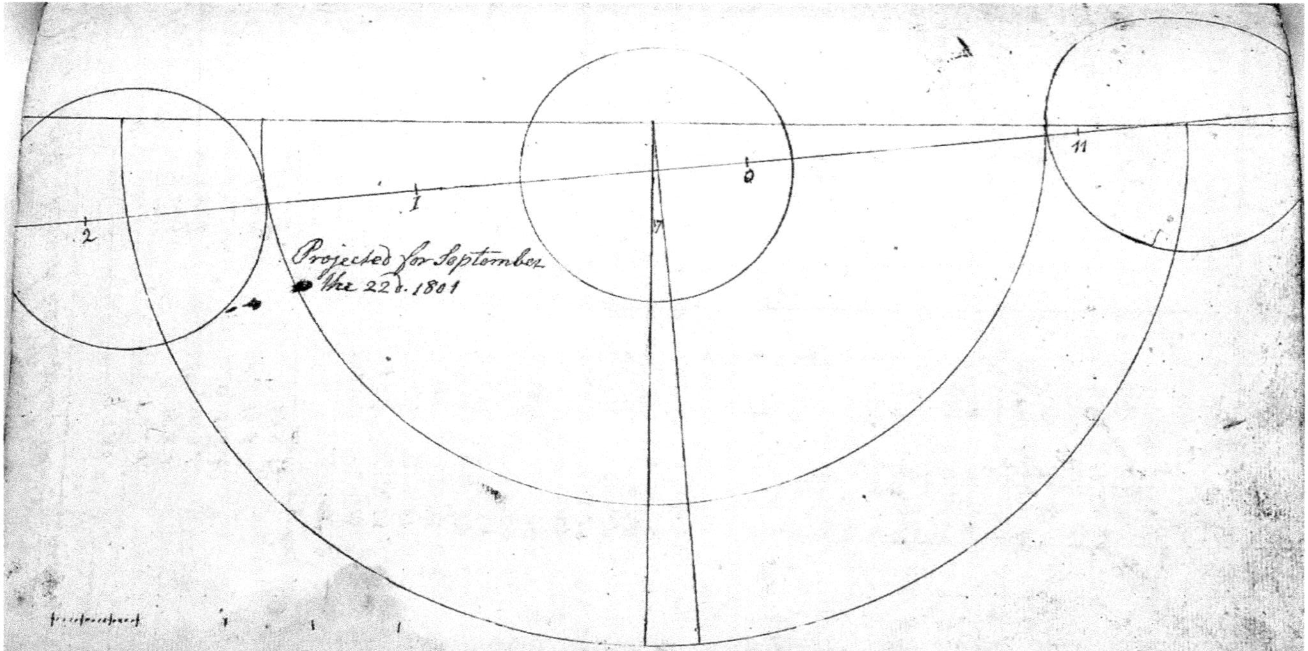
Projected for September
the 22d. 1801
2
1
0
11
17

1801 June Sixth Month hath 30 Days

	d	h	m	
Last ☾	3..	0..	28	aft.
New ☽	11..	3..	14	morn.
First ☽	19..	7..	34	morn.
Full ○	26..	2..	18	aft.

☊ { 1, 11 ♈, 21 } { 6m, 5, 5 } deg.

☽	☉ Long.	♄ ♌	♃ ♌	♂ ♋	♀ ♊	☿ ♊	☽'s Lat.
1	2..10..38	19	2	26	2	8	4 S.
7.	2.16.22	19	3	♌ 2	0	21	3 N.
13	2..22..6	20	4	6	♉ 27	♋ 4	5 N.
19	2..27..50	20	5	9	28	14	0 N.
25	3..3..32	21	6	13	28	25	5 S.

M D	W D		☉ rise	☉ Set	☽ Long.	☽ rise	☽ South	☽ age
1	2	1st Sund. past Trin.	4..43	7..17	10..13..47	12..9	17..9	21
2	3		4..43	7..17	10..28..11	12..43	18..2	22
3	4		4..42	7..18	11..12..20	13..15	18..51	23
4	5		4..42	7..18	11..26..8	13..46	19..39	24
5	6		4..41	7..19	0..9..39	14..13	20..26	25
6	7		4..41	7..19	0..22..50	14..40	21..11	26
7	D	2nd. Sund past Trin.	4..41	7..19	1..5..40	15..11	21..59	27
8	2		4..40	7..20	1..18..15	15..47	22..47	28
9	3		4..40	7..20	2..0..34	16..24	23..35	29
10	4		4..40	7..20	2..12..41		☌	30
11	5	St. Barnabas	4..39	7..21	2..24..38	Set	0..23	☽
12	6		4..39	7..21	3..6..30	8..34	1..11	2
13	7		4..39	7..21	3..18..21	9..17	1..58	3
14	D	3d. Sund. past Trin.	4..39	7..21	4..0..11	9..57	2..46	4
15	2		4..39	7..21	4..12..8	10..32	3..32	5
16	3		4..38	7..22	4..24..12	11..5	4..17	6
17	4		4..38	7..22	5..6..26	11..30	4..59	7
18	5		4..38	7..22	5..18..55	11..57	5..44	8
19	6		4..38	7..22	6..1..40	12..26	6..29	9
20	7		4..38	7..22	6..14..44	12..55	7..15	10
21	D	4th. Sund. past Trin.	4..38	7..22	6..28..7	13..25	8..3	11
22	2		4..38	7..22	7..11..51	14..3	8..55	12
23	3		4..38	7..22	7..25..53	14..45	9..52	13
24	4		4..38	7..22	8..10..11	15..32	10..51	14
25	5		4..38	7..22	8..24..44		11..54	15
26	6		4..38	7..22	9..9..25	rise	12..56	16
27	7		4..38	7..22	9..24..7	9..10	13..55	17
28	D	5th Sund past Trin.	4..38	7..22	10..8..47	9..56	14..53	18
29	2		4..39	7..21	10..23..18	10..35	15..47	19
30	3		4..39	7..21	11..7..36	11..8	16..37	20
					11..21..35			

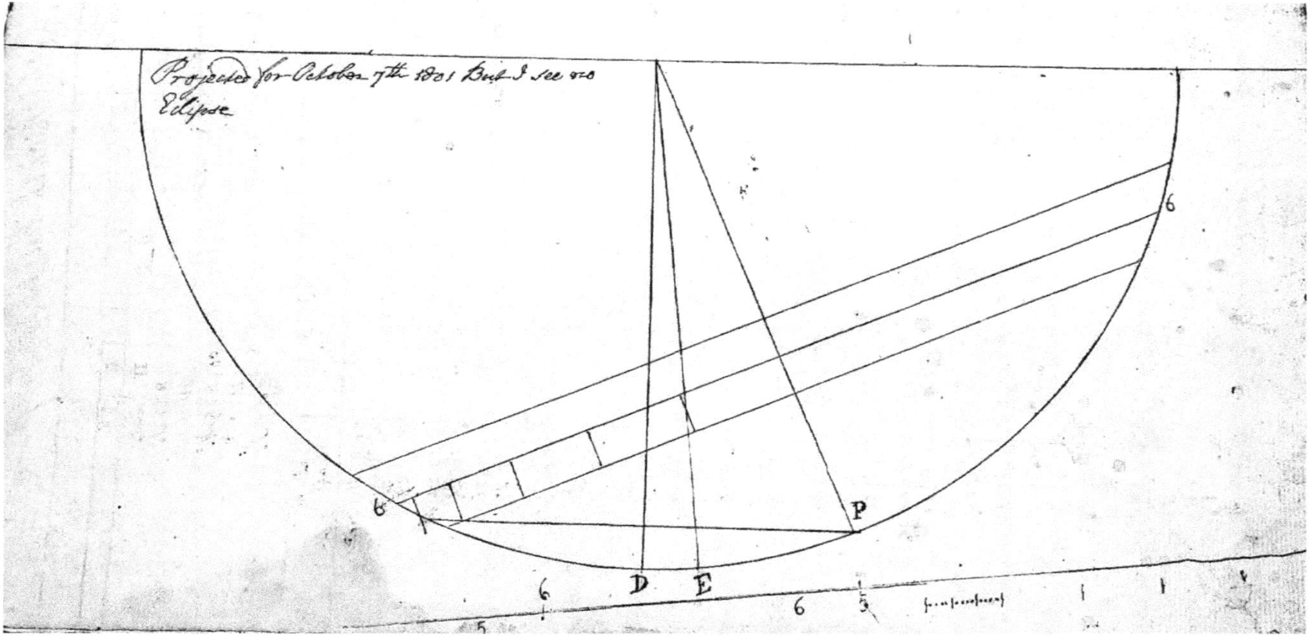
Projected for October 7th 1801 But I see no
Eclipse
6
6
P
D
E
6
6
5
5

1801 July Seventh Month hath 31 Days.

	D	H	M	
Last Q.	2	9	44	aft.
New ☽	10	5	54	aft.
First Q.	18	8	32	morn.
Full ○	25	8	52	morn.

☊ { 1 ♈ 4 / 11 ♈ 4 / 21 ♈ 3 } deg

D	☉ Long.	♄ ♌	♃ ♌	♂ ♌	♀ ♊	☿ ♌	☽'s Lat.
1	3. 9. 15	21	7	16	2	4	1 S.
7	3. 14. 59	22	9	20	5	10	5 N.
13	3. 20. 42	23	10	24	9	17	3 N.
19	3. 26. 26	23	11	28	13	♍ 4	3 S.
25	4. 2. 10	24	13	♍ 2	18	21	4 S.

M D	W D		☉ rise	☉ set	☽ Long.	☽ [illegible]	☽ South	☽ age
1	4	☿ great elong.	4. 39	7. 21	11. 21. 35	11. 36	17. 26	21
2	5		4. 39	7. 21	0. 5. 17	12. 5	18. 12	22
3	6		4. 40	7. 20	0. 18. 37	12. 35	18. 59	23
4	7		4. 40	7. 20	1. 1. 39	13. 5	19. 46	24
5	D		4. 40	7. 20	1. 14. 22	13. 38	20. 34	25
6	2		4. 41	7. 19	1. 26. 49	14. 13	21. 24	26
7	3		4. 41	7. 19	2. 9. 3	14. 54	22. 13	27
8	4		4. 42	7. 18	2. 21. 5	15. 39	23. 2	29
9	5		4. 42	7. 18	3. 3. 1		23. 50	30
10	6		4. 43	7. 17	3. 14. 52	set	☌	☽
11	7		4. 43	7. 17	3. 26. 42	7. 50	0. 35	1
12	D		4. 44	7. 16	4. 8. 34	8. 23	1. 20	2
13	2		4. 44	7. 16	4. 20. 33	8. 56	2. 5	3
14	3		4. 45	7. 15	5. 2. 42	9. 26	2. 50	4
15	4		4. 45	7. 15	5. 15. 2	9. 55	3. 35	5
16	5		4. 46	7. 14	5. 27. 38	10. 22	4. 19	6
17	6		4. 47	7. 13	6. 10. 31	10. 50	5. 3	7
18	7		4. 47	7. 13	6. 23. 43	11. 19	5. 50	8
19	D		4. 48	7. 12	7. 7. 16	11. 52	6. 40	9
20	2		4. 49	7. 11	7. 21. 7	12. 31	7. 34	10
21	3		4. 49	7. 11	8. 5. 19	13. 18	8. 33	11
22	4		4. 50	7. 10	8. 19. 44	14. 12	9. 35	12
23	5		4. 51	7. 9	9. 4. 20	15. 15	10. 38	13
24	6		4. 52	7. 8	9. 19. 2		11. 39	14
25	7		4. 52	7. 8	10. 3. 45	rise	12. 38	15
26	D		4. 53	7. 7	10. 18. 21	8. 26	13. 34	16
27	2		4. 54	7. 6	11. 2. 45	9. 0	14. 26	17
28	3		4. 55	7. 5	11. 16. 56	9. 33	15. 16	18
29	4		4. 56	7. 4	0. 0. 49	10. 3	16. 3	19
30	5		4. 57	7. 3	0. 14. 20	10. 30	16. 50	20
31	6		4. 58	7. 2	0. 27. 33	10. 59	17. 37	21
					1. 10. 25			

1801 August Eighth Month hath 31 Days

D h m	☽	☉	♄	♃	♂	♀	☿	☽s
Last ☾ 1..8..56 morn.		Long.	♌	♌	♍	♊	♌	Lat
New ☽ 9..11..8 morn.	1	4..8..52	25	14	6	23	18	3 N.
First ☾ 17..1..24 morn.	7	4..14..36	26	15	9	29	13	5 N.
Full ○ 23..4..12 aft.	13	4..20..22	26	17	15	♋ 5	8	0 S.
Last ☾ 30..10..8 aft.	19	4..26..8	27	18	20	11	11	5 S.
☊ {1, 11, 21} ♈ {3, 2, 2} deg.	25	5..1..56	28	19	25	17	14	4 S.

M D	W D		☉ rise	☉ set	☽s Long	☽ rise	☽ south	☽ age
1	7	♀ great elong.	4..59	7..1	1..10..25	11..33	18..25	22
2	D		5..0	7..0	1..23..1	12..7	19..14	23
3	2		5..1	6..59	2..5..22	12..49	20..4	24
4	3		5..2	6..58	2..17..30	13..31	20..54	25
5	4		5..3	6..57	2..29..29	14..19	21..44	26
6	5	☍	5..4	6..56	3..11..20	15..9	22..32	27
7	6		5..5	6..55	3..23..11	16..1	23..20	28
8	7		5..6	6..54	4..5..2		8	29
9	D		5..7	6..53	4..16..58	set	0..6	☽
10	2		5..8	6..52	4..29..1	7..29	0..48	1
11	3		5..9	6..51	5..11..13	7..54	1..30	2
12	4		5..10	6..50	5..23..41	8..22	2..13	3
13	5		5..11	6..40	6..6..24	8..51	2..58	4
14	6		5..12	6..48	6..19..25	9..20	3..44	5
15	7		5..13	6..47	7..2..47	9..50	4..33	6
16	D		5..14	6..46	7..16..28	10..26	5..26	7
17	2		5..15	6..45	8..0..29	11..12	6..23	8
18	3		5..16	6..44	8..14..46	12..0	7..23	9
19	4		5..18	6..42	8..29..17	13..0	8..25	10
20	5		5..19	6..41	9..13..56	14..5	9..28	11
21	6		5..20	6..40	9..28..39	15..17	10..28	12
22	7		5..21	6..39	10..13..21		11..26	13
23	D		5..22	6..38	10..27..52	rise	12..21	14
24	2		5..23	6..37	11..12..11	7..35	13..11	15
25	3		5..24	6..36	11..26..12	8..7	14..0	16
26	4	☿ great elong.	5..26	6..34	0..9..56	8..34	14..47	17
27	5		5..27	6..33	0..23..20	9..4	15..35	18
28	6		5..28	6..32	1..6..24	9..35	16..23	19
29	7		5..29	6..31	1..19..10	10..10	17..13	20
30	D		5..30	6..30	2..1..37	10..48	18..3	21
31	2		5..32	6..28	2..13..51	11..30	18..53	22
					2..25..55			

1801 September Ninth Month hath 30 Days.

	☽	h	m	
New ☽	8	2	55	morn.
First ☾	15	8	5	morn.
Full ○	22	1	[illegible]	morn.
Last ☾	29	3	26	aft.

☊ {1, 11, 21} ♈ {1, 0, 0} deg.

☽	☉ Long.	♄	♃	♂	♀	☿	☽'s Lat.
		♌	♌	♍	♋	♌	
1	5.8.42	29	21	27	24	23	5 N.
7	5.14.32	29	22	29	♌ 2	♍ 4	2 N.
13	5.20.22	♍ 0	23	♎ 3	8	16	4 S.
19	5.26.13	1	25	7	15	26	3 S.
25	6.2.6	2	26	11	25	♎ 7	4 N.

M D	W D		☉ rise	☉ set	☽'s Long.	☽ rise	☽ south	☽'s age
1	3		5.33	6.27	2.25.55	12.20	19.43	23
2	4		5.34	6.26	3.7.51	13.10	20.33	24
3	5		5.35	6.25	3.19.43	14.2	21.21	25
4	6		5.36	6.24	4.1.33	14.57	22.8	26
5	7		5.38	6.22	4.13.25	15.53	22.53	27
6	D		5.39	6.21	4.25.22	16.52	23.37	28
7	2		5.40	6.20	5.7.29		[illegible]	29
8	3		5.41	6.19	5.19.45	set.	0.20	☽
9	4		5.43	6.17	6.2.23	6.58	1.1	2
10	5		5.44	6.16	6.15.14	7.26	1.46	3
11	6		5.45	6.15	6.28.24	7.55	2.33	4
12	7		5.40	6.14	7.11.54	8.31	3.23	5
13	D		5.48	6.12	7.25.43	9.13	4.20	6
14	2		5.49	6.11	8.9.52	9.59	5.18	7
15	3		5.50	6.10	8.24.17	10.56	6.19	8
16	4		5.52	6.8	9.8.51	11.59	7.22	9
17	5		5.53	6.7	9.23.34	13.9	8.24	10
18	6		5.54	6.6	10.8.16	14.20	9.23	11
19	7		5.55	6.5	10.22.53	15.31	10.19	12
20	D		5.56	6.4	11.7.21	16.40	11.11	13
21	2		5.58	6.2	11.21.33		12.1	14
22	3		5.59	6.1	0.5.27	rise	12.50	15
23	4		6.0	6.0	0.19.1	7.14	13.38	16
24	5		6.2	5.58	1.2.16	7.45	14.26	17
25	6		6.3	5.57	1.15.10	8.19	15.15	18
26	7		6.4	5.56	1.27.48	8.54	16.5	19
27	D		6.5	5.55	2.10.11	9.37	16.56	20
28	2		6.7	5.53	2.22.19	10.24	17.47	21
29	3		6.8	5.52	3.4.19	11.13	18.36	22
30	4		6.9	5.51	3.16.12	12.2	19.25	23
					3.28.3			

1801 October Tenth Month hath 31 Days

	D	h	m	
New ☽	7	5	36	aft.
First Q.	14	4	43	aft.
Full ☉	21	11	36	morn
Last Q.	29	10	52	morn

☊ { 1, 11 ♓, 21 } 29, 29, 28 } deg.

☽	☉	♄	♃	♂	♀	☿	☽
	Long.	♍	♌	♎	♍	♎	Lat.
1	6..8..0	2	27	15	4	17	5 N.
7	6..13..56	3	28	19	9	27	1 S.
13	6..19..53	4	29	23	13	♏ 6	5 S.
19	6..25..52	4	♍ 0	27	21	15	0 N.
25	7..1..49	5	1	♏ 0	28	23	5 N.

M D	W D		☉ rise	☉ set	☽ Long.	☽ rise	☽ south	☽'s age
1	5		6..11	5..49	3..28..3	12..58	20..13	24
2	6		6..12	5..48	4..9..54	13..55	20..58	25
3	7		6..13	5..47	4..21..48	14..54	21..42	26
4	D		6..14	5..46	5..3..50	15..52	22..26	27
5	2		6..15	5..45	5..16..1	16..49	23..9	28
6	3		6..17	5..43	5..28..26		23..52	29
7	4		6..18	5..42	6..11..7	set	☌	☽
8	5		6..19	5..41	6..24..8	6..5	0..36	1
9	6		6..20	5..40	7..7..27	6..37	1..25	2
10	7		6..22	5..38	7..21..5	7..13	2..16	3
11	D		6..23	5..37	8..5..4	8..0	3..15	4
12	2		6..24	5..36	8..19..20	8..52	4..15	5
13	3		6..25	5..35	9..3..49	9..54	5..17	6
14	4		6..27	5..33	9..18..29	11..0	6..19	7
15	5		6..28	5..32	10..3..11	12..8	7..19	8
16	6		6..29	5..31	10..17..52	13..20	8..15	9
17	7		6..30	5..30	11..2..25	14..32	9..10	10
18	D		6..32	5..28	11..16..46	15..44	10..1	11
19	2		6..33	5..27	0..0..50	16..50	10..50	12
20	3		6..34	5..26	0..14..35		11..39	13
21	4		6..35	5..25	0..28..2	rise	12..27	14
22	5		6..36	5..24	1..11..7	6..24	13..16	15
23	6		6..38	5..22	1..23..54	6..58	14..5	16
24	7		6..39	5..21	2..6..24	7..41	14..56	17
25	D		6..40	5..20	2..18..41	8..24	15..47	18
26	2		6..41	5..19	3..0..45	9..12	16..37	19
27	3		6..42	5..18	3..12..41	10..3	17..26	20
28	4		6..44	5..16	3..24..33	10..58	18..13	21
29	5		6..45	5..15	4..6..23	10..52	18..59	22
30	6		6..46	5..14	4..18..15	12..49	19..43	23
31	7		6..47	5..13	5..0..12	13..46	20..26	24
					5..12..18			

It is said and generally believed that when the Moon is Changing that she is in conjunction with the Sun viz. in the same Sign, the same degree and minute with him, likewise when the Moon is full that she is ~~direct~~ in direct opposition to the Sun being in the opposite Sign, degre and minute to him, but it will not be the case, ~~tho~~ in Calculations tho made by the best of Calculators

I have taken all the fulls and new Moons ~~out~~ from the Nautical Almanac for the year 1781 and have given the difference at each time in motion

	d	h	m	difference ☉ and ☽ ° ′	
January full Moon	9	21	4	1 .. 46	☉ greatest
January new Moon	24	0	11	0 .. 1	
February full Moon	8	8	28	0 .. 58	☉ greatest
February New Moon	22	17	55	0 .. 1	
March full Moon	9	18	32	0 .. 20	
March New Moon	24	12	7	0 .. 12	☽ greatest
April full Moon	8	3	41	0 .. 28	☉ greatest
April new Moon	23	5	21	0 .. 12	☽ greatest
May full Moon	7	12	18	1 .. 22	☉ greatest
May New Moon	22	20	21	0 .. 9	☉ greatest
June full Moon	5	20	53	1 .. 49	☉ greatest
June New Moon	21	8	34	0 .. 21	☉ greatest
July full Moon	5	6	18	0 .. 14	☉ greatest
July New Moon	20	18	33	1 .. 15	☉ greatest
August full Moon	3	17	31	0 .. 31	☉ greatest
August New Moon	19	3	20	0 .. 21	☉ greatest
Septemb full Moon	2	7	25	0 .. 0	
Septemb New Moon	17	11	58	1 .. 25	☉ greatest
October full Moon	2	0	2	0 .. 2	☽ greatest
October new Moon	16	21	9	2 .. 44	☉ greatest 2 .. 44
October full Moon	31	18	29	0 .. 20	☽ greatest
Novemb new Moon	15	7	12	0 .. 52	☉ greatest
November full Moon	30	12	55	0 .. 2	☽ greatest
Decemb new Moon	14	18	15	1 .. 50	☉ greatest
Decemb full Moon	30	5	54	0 .. 9	☉ greatest

1801 November. Eleventh Month hath 30 Days

	d. h. m	D	☉	♄	♃	♂	♀	☿	☽'s
New ☽	6. 6.. 38 morn.		Long.	♍	♍	♏	♎	♐	Lat.
First ☾	12. 11.. 4 morn.	1	7. 8..49	5	2	4	6	2	1 N.
Full ○	20. 1..50 morn.	7	7.14..51	6.	3	8	14	6	4 S.
Last ☾	28. 6..56 morn.	13	7.20..53	6	4	13	21	11	3 S.
☊ {1, 11, 21} ♓	28, 27, 27 deg.	19	7.26..57	7	4	18	29	7	4 N.
		25	8.. 3..2	7	5	23	♏ 6	3	4 S.

M D	W D		☉ rise	☉ set	☽ Long.	☽ rise	☽ South	☽'s age
1	D		6..48	5..12	5..12..18	14..45	21..9	25
2	2		6..49	5..11	5..24..37	15..46	21..53	26
3	3		6..51	5..9	6..7..8	16..48	22..38	27
4	4		6..52	5..8	6..19..57	17..52	23..25	28
5	5		6..53	5..7	7..3..6		☌	29
6	6		6..54	5..6	7..16..34	set.	0..13	☽
7	7		6..55	5..5	8..0..22	5..55	1..6	2
8	D		6..56	5..4	8..14..27	6..41	2..4	3
9	2		6..57	5..3	8..28..50	7..42	3..6	4
10	3		6..58	5..2	9..13..24	8..45	4..8	5
11	4		6..59	5..1	9..28..6	9..54	5..9	6
12	5		7..0	5..0	10..12..48	11..5	6..5	7
13	6		7..1	4..59	10..27..27	12..16	7..1	8
14	7		7..2	4..58	11..11..55	13..28	7..53	9
15	D		7..3	4..57	11..26..9	14..37	8..43	10
16	2		7..4	4..56	0..10..5	15..45	9..32	11
17	3		7..5	4..55	0..23..42	16..51	10..20	12
18	4		7..6	4..54	1..6..58	17..55	11..7	13
19	5		7..7	4..53	1..19..56		11..57	14
20	6		7..8	4..52	2..2..35	rise	12..47	15
21	7		7..8	4..52	2..14..58	6..14	13..37	16
22	D		7..9	4..51	2..27..8	7..4	14..27	17
23	2		7..10	4..50	3..9..9	7..54	15..17	18
24	3		7..11	4..49	3..21..8	8..45	16..4	19
25	4	☌ ☉ ☿	7..12	4..48	4..2..54	9..38	16..51	20
26	5		7..12	4..48	4..14..44	10..37	17..35	21
27	6		7..13	4..47	4..26..38	11..36	18..18	22
28	7		7..14	4..46	5..8..39	12..34	19..1	23
29	D	Advent Sund.	7..15	4..45	5..20..49	13..30	19..43	24
30	2		7..15	4..45	6..3..13	14..30	20..27	25
					6..15..53			

This projection was laid down for an Eclipse of Moon September 11th 1802

	h m	
Beginning	5 .. 26	P. M
The middle	6 .. 44	
The end	8 .. 6	
Duaration	2 .. 40	

Digits Eclipsed 9 ½ from the ~~Earth~~ north side the Earths Shadow

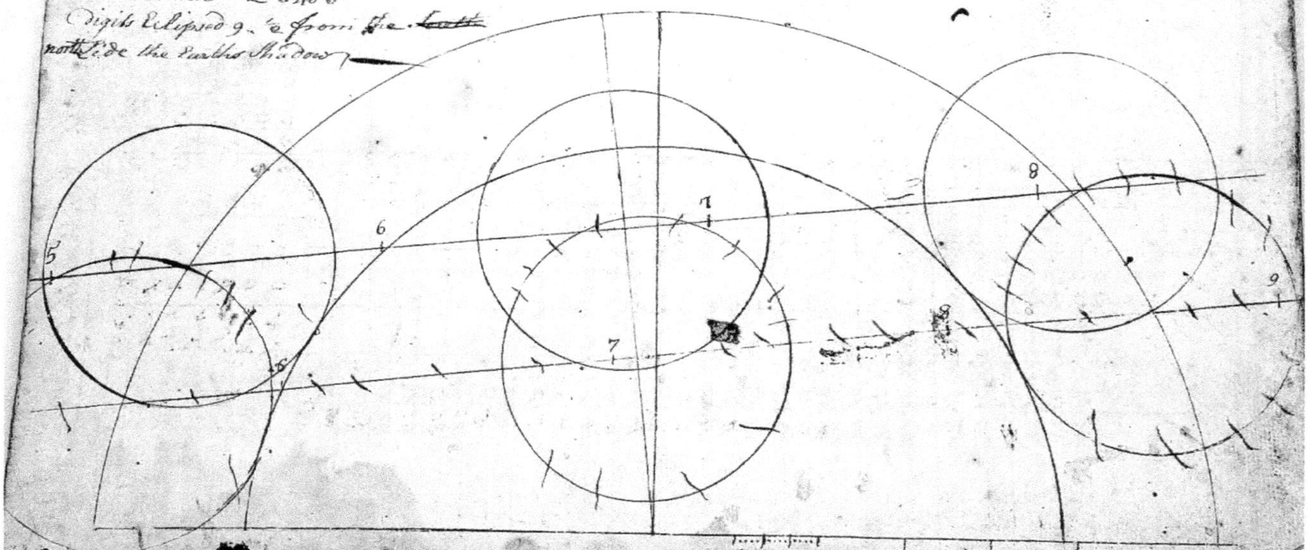

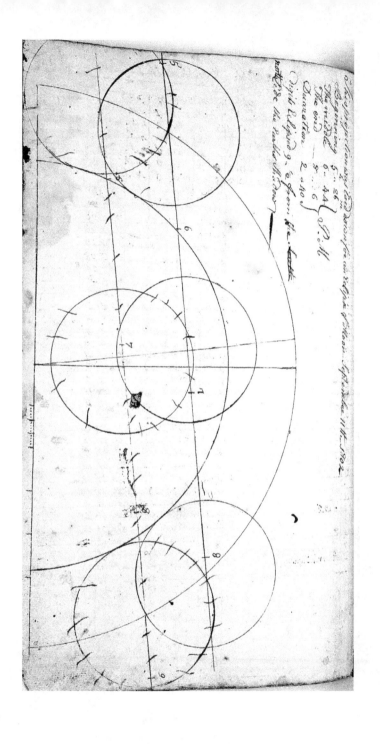

1801 December Twelfth Month hath 31 Days

☊	D	☉	♄	♃	♂	♀	☿	☽'s
New ☽ 5..6..51 morn.		Long	♍	♍	♏	♏	♏	Lat.
First ☾ 12..9..50 morn.	1	8..9..7	7	5	27	14	26	2 S.
Full ○ 19..7..42 aft.	7	8..15..10	7	5	♐ 1	21	28	5 S.
Last ☾ 28..0..10 morn.	13	8..21..17	7	6	5	29	♐ 0	1 N.
☊ {1 ♓ 26, 11 ♓ 26, 21 25} deg.	19	8..27..23	7	6	10	♐ 6	8	5 N.
	25	9..3..31	7	6	14	14	15	2 N.

M D	W D		☉ rise	☉ set	☽ Long.	☽ rise	☽ South	☽'s age
1	3		7..16	4..44	6..15..53	15..31	21..12	26
2	4		7..16	4..44	6..28..50	16..38	22..1	27
3	5		7..17	4..43	7..12..7	17..45	22..52	28
4	6		7..18	4..42	7..25..43		23..49	29
5	7		7..18	4..42	8..9..40	set	6	☽
6	D		7..19	4..41	8..23..54	5..22	0..45	
7	2		7..19	4..41	9..8..24	6..22	1..45	
8	3		7..20	4..40	9..23..2	7..28	2..47	
9	4		7..20	4..40	10..7..43	8..40	3..46	
10	5		7..20	4..40	10..22..25	9..[illegible]	4..41	
11	6		7..21	4..39	11..6..58	11..3	5..34	
12	7		7..21	4..39	11..21..22	12..13	6..26	
13	D		7..21	4..39	0..5..27	13..22	7..15	
14	2		7..21	4..39	0..19..14	14..29	8..3	
15	3		7..22	4..38	1..2..43	15..35	8..51	
16	4		7..22	4..38	1..15..51	16..39	9..39	
17	5		7..22	4..38	1..28..40	17..40	10..29	
18	6		7..22	4..38	2..11..12		11..19	
19	7		7..22	4..38	2..23..29	rise	12..9	
20	D		7..22	4..38	3..5..34	5..36	12..59	
21	2		7..22	4..38	3..17..31	6..30	13..48	
22	3		7..22	4..38	3..29..24	7..23	14..34	
23	4		7..22	4..38	4..11..13	8..17	15..18	
24	5		7..22	4..38	4..23..9	9..13	16..1	
25	6		7..22	4..38	5..5..3	10..10	16..44	
26	7		7..22	4..38	5..17..7	11..10	17..27	
27	D		7..22	4..38	5..29..23	12..11	18..8	
28	2		7..22	4..38	6..11..54	13..13	18..54	
29	3		7..21	4..39	6..24..41	14..16	19..40	
30	4		7..21	4..39	7..7..47	15..20	20..30	
31	5		7..21	4..39	7..21..13	16..28	21..25	
				1802	8..4..59			

Radical D March	Mean New Moon in March			Sun's mean Anomaly			Moon's mean Anomaly			Sun's Dist. from ☊		
	D	H	M	s	°	'	s	°	'	s	°	'
1802	9	7	10	8	1	10	6	20	29	0	9	29
1803	22	10	33	8	20	4	6	3	10	0	28	44

Common Notes and moveable Feasts for the Year 1802

Dominical Letter	C
Cycle of the Sun	19
Golden Number	17
Epact	26
Number of Direction	28

Eclipses for the Year 1802

First of the Sun March the third about midnight therefore invisible on this side of the globe

Second of the Moon March the 19th about Sunrise, moon sets a very small digit eclipsed on her North north Limb

Third of the moon September [illegible] is a visible Eclipse of the Moon September 11th

	h	m
Begining	5	32
Beginning of total darkness	6	6
Middle of Eclipse middle	7	6
End of total Darkness	8	2
End of Eclipse	8	36

P. M. [illegible] 15 digits eclipsed from the south of Earth's shadow

	h	m
Duration	3	4

1802 January first Month hath 31 Days

	d	h	m	
New ☽	4	4	34	morn
First ☽	10	9	42	aft
Full ○	18	4	56	aft
Last ☽	26	4	38	aft

☽	☉ Long.
1	9..10..39
7	9..16..47
13	9..22..54
19	9..29..0
25	10..5..6

☊ { 1 ♓ 25 / 11 ♓ 24 / 21 – 24 } deg.

M D	W D	Remarkable Days Aspects weather &c	☉ rise	☉ set	☽ Long.	☽ rise	☽ South	☽ age
1	6		7..20	4..40	8..4..59	17..36	22..21	27
2	7		7..20	4..40	8..19..3	18..45	23..22	28
3	C		7..20	4..40	9..3..23		♂	☽
4	2		7..19	4..41	9..17..56	set	0..24	1
5	3		7..19	4..41	10..2..38	6..8	1..19	2
6	4		7..18	4..42	10..17..22	7..18	2..14	3
7	5		7..18	4..42	11..2..0	8..32	3..10	4
8	6		7..17	4..43	11..16..30	9..44	4..3	5
9	7		7..17	4..43	0..0..44	10..52	4..52	6
10	C		7..16	4..44	0..14..43	12..1	5..41	7
11	2		7..15	4..45	0..28..21	13..7	6..29	8
12	3		7..15	4..45	1..11..40	14..11	7..18	9
13	4		7..14	4..46	1..24..41	15..14	8..7	10
14	5		7..13	4..47	2..7..21	16..17	8..58	11
15	6	Days increase 18 min	7..13	4..47	2..19..46	17..12	9..49	12
16	7		7..12	4..48	3..1..57	18..5	10..40	13
17	C		7..11	4..49	3..13..59		11..29	14
18	2		7..10	4..50	3..25..54	rise	12..17	15
19	3		7..10	4..50	4..7..44	5..59	13..2	16
20	4		7..9	4..51	4..19..35	6..54	13..46	17
21	5		7..8	4..52	5..1..28	7..50	14..29	18
22	6		7..7	4..53	5..13..28	8..47	15..11	19
23	7		7..6	4..54	5..25..37	9..46	15..53	20
24	C		7..5	4..55	6..8..0	10..47	16..37	21
25	2		7..4	4..56	6..20..38	11..50	17..23	22
26	3		7..3	4..57	7..3..32	12..55	18..10	23
27	4		7..2	4..58	7..16..27	14..3	19..[illegible]	24
28	5		7..1	4..59	8..0..21	15..11	20..0	25
29	6		7..0	5..0	8..14..18	16..22	20..59	26
30	7	days increase 46 m.	6..59	5..1	8..28..28	17..26	22..1	27
31	C		6..58	5..2	9..12..56	18..25	23..2	28

In the year 1795, according to the Nautical Almanac the ~~the~~ ~~Change~~ Moon was full that year in the month February —— 3..12.32

But according to Doc. Leadbetter the moon was full —— 3..9..44

By the Nautical Almanac New Moon in February —— 19..1..5

By Leadbetter's method New Moon in February —— 19..3..1

1795 By the Nautical Almanac Full Moon in ~~February~~ March 5..5..

By Leadbetter's method Full Moon in March —— 5..2..4

1795 By the Nautical Almanac New moon in March —— 20..11..

By Leadbetter's method New moon in ~~March~~ March 20..13..

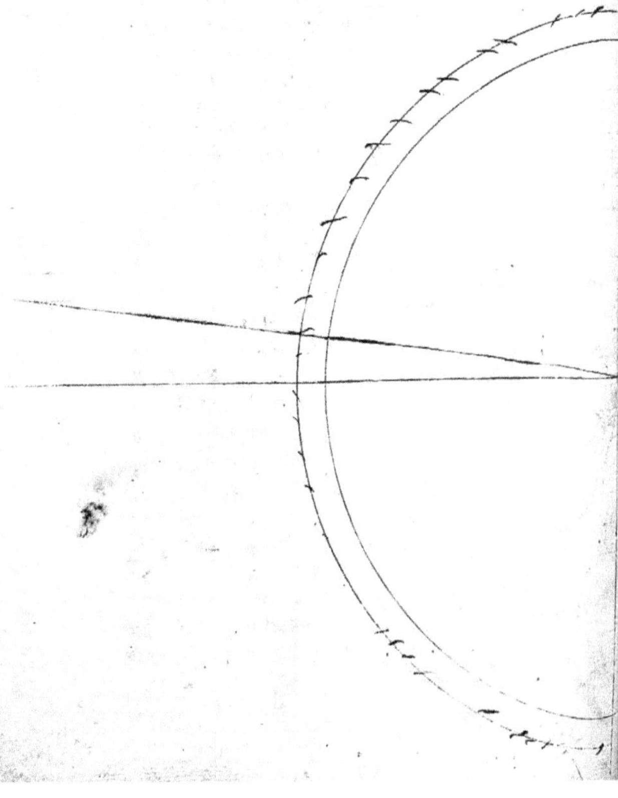

1802 February Second Month hath 28 Days —

	d	h	m	
New ☽	2	1	40	aft.
First ☾	9	11	20	morn.
Full ○	17	0	58	aft.
Last ☾	25	4	41	morn.

☽	☉ Long.
1	10..12..12
7	10..18..16
13	10..24..20
19	11..0..23
25	11..6..26

☉ 1, 11, 21 ♓ 23, 23, 22 deg.

M D	W D		☉ rise	☉ set	☽ Long.	☽ rise	☽ South
1	2		6..57	5..3	9..27..33		23..57
2	3		6..56	5..4	10..12..14	set	☌
3	4		6..55	5..5	10..26..58	6..6	0..51
4	5		6..54	5..6	11..11..32	7..21	1..45
5	6		6..53	5..7	11..25..56	8..29	2..36
6	7		6..52	5..8	0..10..5	9..37	3..27
7	C		6..51	5..9	0..23..54	10..45	4..17
8	2		6..50	5..10	1..7..24	11..53	5..7
9	3		6..49	5..11	1..20..34	13..0	5..57
10	4		6..48	5..12	2..3..25	14..2	6..47
11	5		6..46	5..14	2..16..0	14..57	7..38
12	6		6..45	5..15	2..28..18	15..54	8..29
13	7		6..44	5..16	3..10..24	16..42	9..19
14	C	Septuages. Sund.	6..43	5..17	3..22..22	17..26	10..7
15	2		6..42	5..18	4..4..14	18..1	10..54
16	3		6..40	5..20	4..16..4		11..39
17	4		6..39	5..21	4..27..56	rise	12..22
18	5		6..38	5..22	5..9..53	6..37	13..4
19	6		6..36	5..24	5..21..56	7..37	13..46
20	7		6..35	5..25	6..4..11	8..37	14..29
21	C		6..34	5..26	6..16..42	9..38	15..14
22	2		6..33	5..27	6..29..24	10..39	16..1
23	3		6..32	5..28	7..12..29	11..43	16..51
24	4		6..31	5..29	7..25..52	12..53	17..46
25	5		6..30	5..30	8..9..36	14..4	18..45
26	6		6..28	5..32	8..23..38	15..10	19..47
27	7		6..27	5..33	9..7..57	16..11	20..48
28	C	Quinqua Sund.	6..26	5..34	9..22..29	17..7	21..48

1801	Articles Rec'd of Ellicott & Co. for the fourth payment	
Decemb. 23	7 3/4 lb pork a 1 S per lb	
	paid the taylor for making my Breeches	£0..7..
January 15	10 1/2 lb pork at 8d. per lb —	
1802	1/2 gallon molases at 5/6 per gal.	0..7..
February 2	A pair of Shoes at —	0..2..
March 3	7 3/4 lb pork a 11d. per lb	0..1[illegible]
March 29	7 1/2 lb pork a 9d per lb	0..7..
	A Small water pail 18d	0..5..
April 15	A fine hat a 4 dollars =	0..1[illegible]
		2..2..
	7 3/4 lb pork a 11d per lb	1..10..
	1/2 Bushel of Corn —	0..6..
April 28	8 lb pork a 8d. per lb	0..2..
	1/2 Bushel Corn a 2/6	0..5..
		0..8..
		4..9..
May 10	11 lb pork at 1 S per lb	0..11..
	~~a pound of~~ 1/2 pound Candles & a pound Soap	0..1..
May 20	a gun lock at —	0..9..
	1/2 Bushel corn 2/6 and 1/2 gal molases 2/3	0..4..
		5..16..
June 23	paid the Sheriff —	0..4..
June 26	3 1/4 yds Irish linnen a 4 S per yd	0..13..
	3 1/2 yds linnen ~~at~~ 2/6 per yd	0..8..
	thread and Buttons	0..0..
July	1/2 Bushel of corn, a	0..2..
July 8	Cash to pay for a Book - 3 Dollars =	1..2..
	Cash Receiv'd said day 1 Dollar. =	0..7..
		8..1[illegible]
Aug.t 4	a padlock 2 S. 1/4 lb powder 16 1/2 d. [illegible] shot 9d.	0..[illegible]
	8 lb pork a 10d. per lb, 2 lb Soap a 6d.	0..7..
Sep.t 13	1/2 Bushel Corn a 5 S per Bush	0..2..
Oc.t 26	a pair of Shoes at —	0..11..
		10..[illegible]
Nov. 16	Cash Receiv'd —	1..18..
		12..0..
1802	Articles Receiv'd of Ellicott & Co. for fifth payment	
Nov.r 16	3 1/2 yds Cloth at 10 S. per yd.	£1..15..[illegible]
	[illegible]	
January 10	paid Jacob Thomas [illegible]	0..[illegible]
	[illegible]	
1803 March 22	[illegible]	
	A pair Stockings 10[illegible]	
	[illegible]	
[illegible]	[illegible] gallon [illegible] 2/3 a pen knife 1/6	
April 19	Cash of John Ellicott	0..7..
May 19	paid the Sheriff	0..4..
[illegible]	[illegible]	

March Third Month hath 31 Days

h m	☽	☉ Long.
.11.58 aft.		
..4.52 morn.		
9 5..24 morn.	1	11.10.26
6..8..9 morn.	7	11.16.26
21 } deg.	13	11.22.26
21	19	11.28.24
20	25	0..4.21

	☉ rise	☉ set	☽ Long.	☽ rise	☽ South
	6..25	5..35	10..7..10	17..53	22.46
ve Tuesd.	6..24	5..36	10.21.53		23.40
wednesd.	6..23	5..37	11..6..32	Set	δ
	6..22	5..38	11..21..3	6..20	0..33
	6..21	5..39	0..5..20	7..29	1..22
	6..19	5..41	0..19..21	8..38	2..11
	6..17	5..43	1..3..2	9..45	3..0
	6..16	5..44	1..16..22	10..50	3..50
	6..14	5..46	1..29..24	11..51	4..40
	6..13	5..4?	2..12..5	12..51	5..32
	6..12	5..48	2..24..34	13..48	6..25
	6..11	5..49	3..6..47	14..40	7..17
	6..9	5..51	3..18..49	15..25	8..6
	6..8	5..52	4..0..45	16..5	8..54
	6..7	5..53	4..12..35	16..39	9..39
	6..6	5..54	4..24..25	17..11	10..23
	6..4	5..56	5..6..18	17..37	11..6
	6..3	5..57	5..18..17		11..48
	6..2	5..58	6..0..26	rise	12..30
	6..1	5..59	6..12..46	7..32	1?..15
	6..0	6..0	6..25..23	8..35	14..1
	5..59	6..1	7..8..15	9..38	14..50
	5..58	6..2	7..21..28	10..45	15..42
	5..57	6..3	8..5..0	11..57	16..42
	5..55	6..5	8..18..54	13..5	17..42
	5..54	6..6	9..3..4	14..5	18..42
	5..53	6..7	9..17..28	15..1	19..42
	5..52	6..8	10..2..5	15..53	20..42
	5..50	6..10	10..16..47	16..34	21..38
	5..49	6..11	11..1..29	17..10	22..32
	5..48	6..12	11..16..6	17..43	23..23

1801	Articles Reced of Ellicott & Co. for the fourth p[illegible]
Decemb. 23	7 3/4 lb pork a 1 S ~~p lb~~
	paid the taylor for making my Breeches
January 15	10 1/2 lb pork at 8 d. p lb
1802	1/2 gallon molasses at 5/6 p gal.
February 2	A pair of Shoes at
March 3	7 3/4 lb pork a 11 d. p lb
March 29	7 1/2 lb pork a 9 d p lb
	A small water pail 1 S d
April 15	A fine hat a 4 dollars
	7 1/4 lb pork a 11 d. p lb
	1/2 Bushel of corn
April 28	8 lb pork a 8 d. p lb
	1/2 Bushel corn a 2/6
May 10	11 lb pork at 1 S p lb
	~~a pound at~~ 1/2 pound Candles & a pound Soa[illegible]
May 20	a gun lock at
	1/2 Bushel corn 2/6 and 1/2 gal molasses
June 23	paid the Sheriff
June 26	3 1/4 yd Irish linnen a 4 S p yd
	3 1/2 yds linnen at 2/6 p yd
	thread and Buttons
July	1/2 Bushel of corn, a
July 8	Cash to pay for a Book - 3 Dollars
	Cash Receiv'd said day 1 Dollar
Aug 4	a padlock 2 S. 3/4 lb powder 16 1/2 d. p[illegible] shot 9 d.
	8 lb pork a 10 d. p lb, 1/2 lb Soap a 6 d.
Sept. 13	1/2 Bushel Corn a 5 S p Bush.
Oct. 26	a pair of Shoes at
Nov. 16	Cash Receiv'd
1802	Articles Receiv'd of Ellicott & Co. for fifth pa[illegible]
Nov. 16	3 1/2 yds Cloth at 10 S. p yd
	[illegible] great Coat
January 10	paid Jacob Thomas
	A pair of Shoes
March 22	[illegible] at 3/6. A yard Linnen [illegible]
	A pair Stockings 10. A pair [illegible]
	[illegible] powder 1/2 A comb [illegible]
[illegible]	[illegible] 2/3 a pen knife 1/6
April 19	Cash of John Ellicott
May 19	paid the Sheriff
[illegible]	[illegible]

1802 March Third Month hath 31 Days

	h	m	
New ☽ 3	11	58	aft.
First ☽ 11	4	52	morn.
Full ○ 19	5	24	morn.
Last ☽ 26	8	9	morn.

☊		♓	
1		21	deg.
11		21	deg.
21		20	deg.

☽	☉ Long.
1	11.10.26
7	11.16.26
13	11.22.26
19	11.28.24
25	0.4.21

M D	W D		☉ rise	☉ set	☽ Long.	☽ rise	☽ South
1	2		6..25	5..35	10..7.10	17..53	22.46
2	3	Shrove Tuesd.	6..24	5..36	10..21.53		23.40
3	4	Ash wednesd.	6..23	5..37	11..6..32	Set	☌
4	5		6..22	5..38	11..21..3	6..20	0..33
5	6		6..21	5..39	0..5..20	7..29	1..22
6	7		6..19	5..41	0..19..21	8..38	2..11
7	C		6..17	5..43	1..3..2	9..45	3..0
8	2		6..16	5..44	1..16..22	10..50	3..50
9	3		6..14	5..46	1..29..24	11..51	4..40
10	4		6..13	5..48	2..12..5	12..51	5..32
11	5		6..12	5..48	2..24.34	13..48	6..25
12	6		6..11	5..49	3..6..47	14..40	7..17
13	7		6..9	5..51	3..18..49	15..25	8..6
14	C		6..8	5..52	4..0..45	16..5	8..54
15	2		6..7	5..53	4..12..35	16..39	9..39
16	3		6..6	5..54	4..24..25	17..11	10..23
17	4		6..4	5..56	5..6..18	17..37	11..6
18	5		6..3	5..57	5..18..17		11..48
19	6		6..2	5..58	6..0..26	rise	12..30
20	7		6..1	5..59	6..12..46	7..32	13..15
21	C		6..0	6..0	6..25..23	8..35	14..1
22	2		5..59	6..1	7..8..15	9..38	14..50
23	3		5..58	6..2	7..21..28	10..45	15..42
24	4		5..57	6..3	8..5..0	11..57	16..42
25	5		5..55	6..5	8..18..54	13..5	17..42
26	6		5..54	6..6	9..3..4	14..5	18..42
27	7		5..53	6..7	9..17..28	15..1	19..42
28	C		5..52	6..8	10..2..5	15..53	20..42
29	2		5..50	6..10	10..16..47	16..34	21..38
30	3		5..49	6..11	11..1..29	17..10	22..32
31	4		5..48	6..12	11..16..6	17..43	23..23

New and Full moons for the Year 1781 by the Nautical Almanac and by a method prescribed by Mr. Leadbetter

By the Almanac			according to Leadbetter		
January	○	9..21..4	January	○	9..23..27 Right
January	☽	24..0..11	January	☽	23..22..8 R
February	○	8..8..28	Feb.	○	8..12..12
February	☽	22..17..55	Feb.	☽	22..16..50
March	○	9..18..32	March	○	9..17..54
March	☽	24..12..7	March	☽	24..11..52
April	○	8..3..41	April	○	8..3..0
April	☽	23..5..21	April	☽	23..5..36
May	○	7..12..18	May	○	7..11..4
May	☽	22..20..21	May	☽	22..21..50
June	○	5..20..53	June	○	5..16..4
June	☽	21..8..34	June	☽	21..11..34
July	○	5..6..18	July	○	5..3..58
July	☽	20..18..33	July	☽	20..21..50
August	○	3..17..31	Augt	○	3..15..2
August	☽	19..3..20	Augt	☽	18..23..40
Septem	○	2..7..25	Septem	○	2..6..22
Septemb	☽	17..11..58	Septem	☽	17..16..38 *
October	○	2..0..2	October	○	1..23..44
October	☽	16..21..9	October	☽	16..21..0
October	○	31..18..29	Octobe	○	31..19..6
Novemb	☽	15..7..12	Novem	☽	15..7..2
Novemb	○	30..12..55	Novem	○	30..13..4
Decemb	☽	14..18..15	Decem	☽	14..17..6
December	○	30..5..54	Decem	○	30..8..40

Eclipses for the Year 1802

First of the Sun March the third about midnight therefore invisible

Second a very small eclipse of the Moon March 19th about Sunrise, Moon Sets Eclipsed about 1 degt ~~[illegible]~~ on her limb.

Third is a visible eclipse of the Moon the 11th day of Setember

	h m	
Beging of the eclipse	5..32	P. M.
Beginning of total darkness	6..6	
Middle of the eclipse	7..6	Digits eclipsed 15 from the South of the Earth's shadow
End of total darkness	8..2	
End of the eclipse	8..36	
Duration	3..4	

NB. through mistake I have omitted an invisible eclipse of the Sun August the 28..0..52 (h m) morning

1802 May Fifth Month hath 31 Days

	d	h	m	
New ☽	1	5	30	aft
First Q	9	0	41	aft
Full ☉	16	11	42	morn
Last Q	24	6	35	morn
New ☽	31	4	58	morn

☊ { 1, 11, 21 } ♓ { 19, 18, 18 } deg.

D	☉ Long.
1	1..10.33
7	1..16.22
13	1..22..9
19	1..27..50
25	2..3..41

M D	W D	Remarkable days Aspects weather &c	☉ rise	☉ set	☽ Long.	☽ set	☽ south
1	7		5..10	6..50	1..7..39	set	♂
2	C		5..9	6..51	1..21..4	7..43	0..40
3	2		5..8	6..52	2..4..9	8..47	1..32
4	3		5..7	6..53	2..16..52	9..47	2..24
5	4		5..5	6..55	2..29..21	10..41	3..16
6	5		5..4	6..56	3..11..36	11..30	4..7
7	6		5..3	6..57	3..23..39	12..11	4..56
8	7		5..2	6..58	4..5..36	12..52	5..45
9	C		5..1	6..59	4..17..26	13..26	6..30
10	2		5..0	7..0	4..29..16	13..55	7..12
11	3		4..59	7..1	5..11..8	14..21	7..54
12	4		4..58	7..2	5..23..7	14..46	8..36
13	5		4..58	7..2	6..5..14	15..11	9..18
14	6		4..57	7..3	6..17..33	15..36	10..2
15	7		4..56	7..4	7..0..8		10..49
16	C		4..55	7..5	7..12..58	rise	11..37
17	2		4..54	7..6	7..26..9	7..37	12..30
18	3		4..53	7..7	8..9..40	8..44	13..25
19	4		4..52	7..8	8..23..29	9..49	14..2[illegible]
20	5		4..52	7..8	9..7..38	10..49	15..2[illegible]
21	6		4..51	7..9	9..22..1	11..45	16..[illegible]
22	7		4..51	7..9	10..6..38	12..31	17..[illegible]
23	C	Rogation Sund.	4..50	7..10	10..21..19	13..12	18..[illegible]
24	2		4..49	7..11	11..6..1	13..44	19..[illegible]
25	3		4..48	7..12	11..20..40	14..16	[illegible]
26	4		4..47	7..13	0..5..6	14..48	[illegible]
27	5	Ascent Day	4..46	7..14	0..19..8	15..19	21..43
28	6		4..46	7..14	1..3..11	15..50	22..35
29	7		4..45	7..15	1..16..46	16..25	23..26
30	C		4..44	7..16	2..0..1	[illegible]	
31	2		4..44	7..16	2..12..55	set	0..19

		South
May	23	18..20
	24	19..13
	25	20..3
	26	20..53
	27	21..43
	28	22..35
	29	23..26

Andrew McKey – Fre.^k Co Verginia
Samuel Lais Fiatte C. Pennsylvania
Sol. Shepherd – Frederick Co Meriland

1801 Sep.^t 21 Sun's place ^s 5 .. ^o 28 .. ^' 11 } full ☉ ^d 22 .. ^h 1 .. ^m 4
Moon's place 11 .. 21 .. 33 }

By Subtracting the North Node of the Moon from the true place of the Sun, we gain the Sun's distance from the Same Node

1803 Long. med. ☉	1803 Long. Apog ☉	1803 Long. med ☽	1803 Long. Apog.
s ° '	s ° '	s ° '	s ° '
9 .. 9 .. 24	3 .. 9 .. 36	0 .. 6 .. 38	5 .. 17 .. 28

Articles Rec.^d of Elliott for fifth Payment

1803 May 20	To 2½ [illegible] white [illegible] Sheeting a [illegible]	[illegible]
	2 yards [illegible] [illegible]	[illegible]
	7¾ lb pork at 10 [illegible]	0..6.[illegible]
June	paid Nanny Hall	[illegible]
June 18	7¼ lb pork at 10^d p. lb	0..6.3
	½ gallon molasses 2/3 a pound Soap 1 S	0..6.[illegible]
July 9	8½ lb bacon [illegible] 8/6 – paper & thread 10 [illegible]	0..3.3
	A Handkerchief	0..9.[illegible]
		0..5.[illegible]
		2..18..[illegible]
July 13	1 pound of Tobacco [illegible] a dose of Castor oil 18	0..3.[illegible]
July 22	Cash [illegible] [illegible] gallon molasses 2/3	0..[illegible]
August	7 9½ lb pork at 11 [illegible]	0..7.[illegible]
		3..19..[illegible]
15 Sep.^t 7	7 lb pork at 11 [illegible]	[illegible]
	½ gallon [illegible]	[illegible]
[illegible] 1	8 lb pork a 11 [illegible]	[illegible]
	½ [illegible] powder 2/6 – 2 lb Shot [illegible]	0..4.[illegible]
	5 lb pork at 11 [illegible]	[illegible]
	½ lb [illegible]	[illegible]
	[illegible]	0..3..[illegible]
		5..9..8
Nov [illegible]	An Ink Stand	0..3..[illegible]
Nov 11	½ lb Tobacco	0..0..11
	Cash of Geore Elliott	1..3..9
		5..17..[illegible]
	Nov. 14 Received	6..2..6
		12 0 [illegible]

1787 true time of New Moon in Ma[illegible] [illegible] H M [illegible]..59 { Sun's Long 11..28..56
Moons Long 11..27..52

Full Moon preceding the new 4.13..48 { ☉ Long 11..13..27
☽ Long 5..14..06

1802 June Sixth Month hath 30 Days—

First ☽ 8..7..20 morn
Full ☉ 15..9..11 aft.
Last ☽ 22..0..34 aft.
New ☽ 29..6..16 aft.

☊ { 1 ♓ 47 } deg
11 16
21 16

☽	☉ Long.
1	2..16..24
7	2..16..8
13	2..21..52
19	2..27..36
25	3..3..19

M D	W D		☉ rise	☉ set	☽ Long	☽ set	☽ South
			4..43	7..17	2..25..32	8..32	1..9
1	3		4..43	7..17	3..7..54	9..22	1..59
2	4		4..42	7..18	3..20..4	10..8	2..49
3	5		4..42	7..18	4..2..2	10..48	3..37
4	6		4..41	7..19	4..13..57	11..22	4..22
5	7		4..41	7..19	4..25..47	11..51	5..6
6	C	Whit Sund.	4..41	7..19	5..7..37	12..20	5..49
7	2	Whit Mond.	4..40	7..20	5..19..33	12..44	6..31
8	3	Whit Tuesd.	4..40	7..20	6..1..33	13..8	7..11
9	4		4..40	7..20	6..13..45	13..34	7..54
10	5		4..39	7..21	6..26..11	14..6	8..39
11	6		4..39	7..21	7..8..52	14..39	9..25
12	7		4..39	7..21	7..21..53	15..16	10..16
13	C		4..39	7..21	8..5..11		11..12
14	2		4..39	7..21	8..18..50	rise	12..10
15	3		4..38	7..22	9..2..50	8..33	13..[illegible]
16	4		4..38	7..22	9..17..5	9..29	14..10
17	5		4..38	7..22	10..1..37	10..19	15..8
18	6		4..38	7..22	10..16..14	11..0	16..4
19	7		4..38	7..22	11..0..57	11..36	16..58
20	C		4..38	7..22	11..15..36	12..10	17..[illegible]
21	2		4..38	7..22	0..0..11	12..42	[illegible]..49
22	3		4..38	7..22	0..14..31	13..14	[illegible]..31
23	4		4..38	7..22	0..28..35	13..48	[illegible]..21
24	5		4..38	7..22	1..12..21	14..25	[illegible]
25	6		4..38	7..22	1..25..46	15..3	22..[illegible]
26	7		4..38	7..22	2..8..52	15..42	22..[illegible]
27	C		4..38	7..22	2..21..39		23..[illegible]
28	2		4..39	7..21	3..4..9	Set	[illegible]
29	3		4..39	7..21	3..16..25	8..[illegible]	[illegible]
30	4						

June ☽ rise
21 17..50
22 18..42
23 19..34
24 20..26
25 21..18
26 22..10
27 23..1
28 23..51
29 8
30 0..42

This projection is for May 8d 1h 0m morning 1762 a back tryal to see how my present method will agree with the former this eclipse has the same appearance as that of ~~Doct~~ Doctor Ferguson but defference in time, Ferguson's time of opposition of Sun & Moon

	d	h	m	s	
	8	3	50	50	A.M.
	8	1	0	0	
		2	50	50	

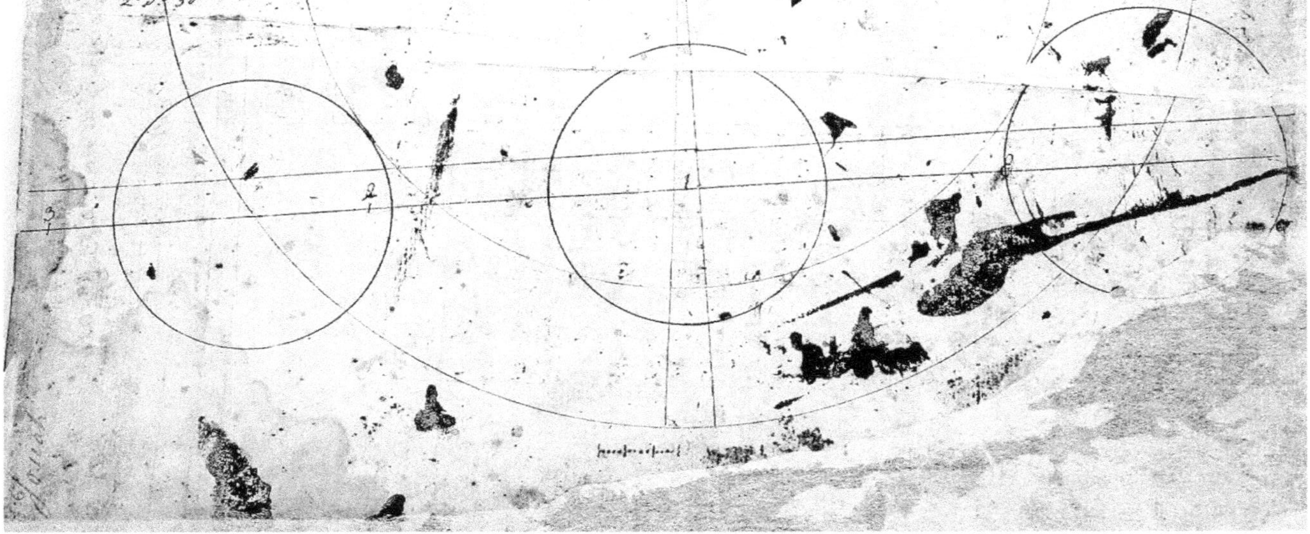

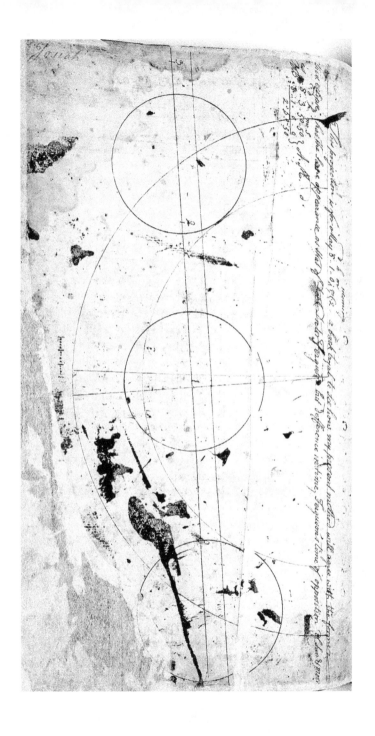

1802 July Seventh Month 31 Days

	d h m
First ☽	7..9..6 aft.
Full ○	15..4..34 morn.
Last ☽	21..7..25 aft.
New ☽	29..9..36 morn.

☊ { 1 ♓ 15 ; 11 ♓ 14 ; 21 14 } deg

☽	☉ Long.
1	3..9..3
7	3..14..46
13	3..20..39
19	3..26..13
25	4..1..57

M D	W D	☉ rise	☉ set	☽ Long.	☽ set	☽ South
1	5	4..39	7..21	3..28..29	8..41	1..26
2	6	4..39	7..21	4..10..26	9..15	2..12
3	7	4..40	7..20	4..22..17	9..44	2..56
4	C	4..40	7..20	5..4..7	10..13	3..39
5	2	4..40	7..20	5..15..59	10..41	4..21
6	3	4..41	7..19	5..27..56	11..8	5..2
7	4	4..41	7..19	6..10..3	11..32	5..45
8	5	4..42	7..18	6..22..20	11..57	6..28
9	6	4..42	7..18	7..4..52	12..29	7..14
10	7	4..43	7..17	7..17..42	13..2	8..2
11	[illegible]	4..43	7..17	8..0..50	13..43	8..54
12	2	4..44	7..16	8..14..19	14..28	9..51
13	3	4..44	7..16	8..28..6	15..24	10..49
14	4	4..45	7..15	9..12..13		11..49
15	5	4..45	7..15	9..26..35	rise	12..48
16	6	4..46	7..14	10..11..10	8..50	13..47
17	7	4..47	7..13	10..25..52	9..24	14..42
18	C	4..47	7..13	11..10..34	9..58	15..34
19	2	4..48	7..12	11..25..12	10..32	16..25
20	3	4..49	7..11	0..9..40	11..6	17..17
21	4	4..49	7..11	0..23..54	11..40	18..9
22	5	4..50	7..10	1..7..50	12..14	19..0
23	6	4..51	7..9	1..21..26	12..50	19..53
24	7	4..52	7..8	2..4..43	13..31	20..46
25	C	4..52	7..8	2..17..39	14..16	21..39
26	2	4..53	7..7	3..0..19	15..3	22..31
27	3	4..54	7..6	3..12..42	15..53	23..21
28	4	4..55	7..5	3..24..53		δ
29	5	4..56	7..4	4..6..54	set	0..10
30	6	4..57	7..3	4..18..47	7..42	0..50
31	7	4..58	7..2	5..0..40	8..11	1..33

April 24th. 1802 Being weary holing for corn I
laid down on my bed and fell into a deep Sleep and
dreamed I had a Child in my arms and was viewing
the back part of it's head where it ~~sore~~ had been sore, and
I found it was healed with a hole through the Skin
and Scull bone and came out at forehead, that I could
see very distinctly through the childs head the hole being
large enough to receive an ordinary finger—
I called some woman to see the strange sight, and she
put her Spectacles on and saw it, and asked me if I had
previously lanced that place in the childs head, I
answered in the affirmative
N.B. the Child was well
as any other

On the night of the 27th November 1802 my house was vio-
lent broke open and Several articles taken out

1802 August Eighth Month hath 31 Days.

	d	h	m	
First ☽	6	3	42	aft.
Full ○	13	10	51	morn.
Last ☽	20	5	30	morn.
New ☽	28	0	52	morn.

☊ { 1 / 11 / 21 } ♓ { 13 / 13 / 12 } deg.

D	⊙ Long.
1	4.8.38
7	4.14.23
13	4.20.8
19	4.25.55
25	5.1.42

M D	W D		⊙ rise	⊙ set	☽ Long.	☽ Set	☽ South
1	C		4..59	7..1	5.12.28	8..38	2..14
2	2		5..0	7..0	5.24.22	9..4	2..57
3	3		5..1	6..59	6.6.28	9..31	3..38
4	4		5..2	6..58	6.18.33	9..57	4..21
5	5		5..3	6..57	7.0.58	10..25	5..6
6	6		5..4	6..56	7.13.39	10..57	5..53
7	7		5..5	6..55	7.26.35	11..34	6..45
8	C		5..6	6..54	8.9.51	12..22	7..41
9	2		5..7	6..53	8.23.28	13..15	8..38
10	3		5..8	6..52	9.7.26	14..14	9..37
11	4		5..9	6..51	9.21.40	15..18	10..37
12	5		5..10	6..50	10.6.8		11..36
13	6		5..11	6..49	10.20.46	rise	12..32
14	7		5..12	6..48	11.5.29	8..0	13.26
15	C		5..13	6..47	11.20.11	8..31	14..18
16	2		5..14	6..46	0.4.45	9..2	15..10
17	3		5..15	6..45	0.19.7	9..36	16..2
18	4		5..16	6..44	1.3.12	10..19	16..54
19	5		5..18	6..42	1.17.0	10..46	17..46
20	6		5..19	6..41	2.0.28	11..28	18..39
21	7		5..20	6..40	2.13.35	12..10	19..33
22	C		5..21	6..39	2.26.25	13..2	20..26
23	2		5..22	6..38	3.8.55	13..54	21..17
24	3		5..23	6..37	3.21.14	14..48	22..7
25	4		5..24	6..36	4.3.19	15..43	22..54
26	5		5..26	6..34	4.15.16	16..42	23..38
27	6		5..27	6..33	4.27..8		6
28	7		5..28	6..32	5.8.58	Set	0..20
29	C		5..29	6..31	5.20.50	7..13	1..0
30	2		5..30	6..30	6.2.46	7..37	1..40
31	3		5..32	6..28	6.14.53	8..2	2..22

Sun's mean Anomaly at the time of mean New Moon in March according to the ~~mode~~ ancient and modern method of obtaining his Anomaly

	Mean New Moon in March			Ancient Ano.			Modern Ano.		
	D	H	M	S	°	'	S	°	'
1787	18	14	10	8	17	22	8	17	13
1788	6	22	59	8	6	38	8	6	29
1789	25	20	31	8	25	0	8	24	52
1790	15	5	20	8	14	16	8	14	7
1791	4	14	9	8	3	32	8	3	22
1792	22	11	41	8	21	54	8	21	45
1793	11	20	30	8	11	10	8	11	1
1794	30	18	3	8	29	32	8	29	22
1795	20	2	51	8	18	48	8	18	37
1796	8	11	40	8	8	4	8	7	55
1797	27	9	12	8	26	26	8	26	17
1798	16	18	1	8	15	42	8	15	32
1799	6	2	50	8	4	58	8	4	49
1800	25	0	22	8	23	20	8	23	11

Moon's mean Anomaly at the same time

	S	°	'	S	°	'
1787	3	21	22	3	21	24
1788	2	1	10	2	1	13
1789	1	6	48	1	6	49
1790	11	16	36	11	16	39
1791	9	26	24	9	26	27
1792	9	2	1	9	2	5
1793	7	11	49	7	11	51
1794	6	17	26	6	17	30
1795	4	27	14	4	27	17
1796	3	7	2	3	7	5
1797	2	12	39	2	12	36
1798	0	22	27	0	22	29
1799	11	2	16	11	2	18
1800	10	7	53	10	7	55

1802 September Ninth Month hath 30 Days

	d	h	m	
First ☽	5	0	22	aft.
Full ○	11	6	47	aft.
Last ☾	18	7	1	morn.
New ☽	26	[illegible]	0	aft.

Co { 1 ♓ 12 ; 11 ♓ 11 ; 21 ♓ 11 } deg.

☽	☉ Long.
1	5..8..28
7	5..14..19
13	5..20..9
19	5..26..0
25	6..1.52

M D	W D	☉ rise	☉ set	☽ Long.	☽ set	☽ South
		5..33	6..27	6..27..7	8..32	3..6
1	4	5..34	6..26	7..9..38	9..2	3..53
2	5	5..35	6..25	7..22..26	9..39	4..42
3	6	5..36	6..24	8..5..31	10..20	5..35
4	7	5..38	6..22	8..18..58	11..9	6..32
5	C	5..39	6..21	9..2..43	12..10	7..33
6	2	5..40	6..20	9..16..49	13..15	8..34
7	3	5..41	6..19	10..1..9	14..21	9..32
8	4	5..43	6..17	10..15..42	15..34	10..30
9	5	5..44	6..16	11..0..25		11..24
10	6	5..45	6..15	11..15..7	rise	12..16
11	7	5..46	6..14	11..29..45	7..8	13..8
12	C	5..48	6..12	0..14..14	7..40	14..0
13	2	5..49	6..11	0..28..29	8..14	14..52
14	3	5..50	6..10	1..12..28	8..53	15..45
15	4	5..52	6..8	1..26..6	9..32	16..39
16	5	5..53	6..7	2..9..25	10..15	17..34
17	6	5..54	6..6	2..22..24	11..5	18..28
18	7	5..55	6..5	3..5..5	11..56	19..19
19	C	5..56	6..4	3..17..31	12..51	20..10
20	2	5..58	6..2	3..29..42	13..47	20..58
21	3	5..59	6..1	4..11..44	14..44	21..44
22	4	6..0	6..0	4..23..38	15..39	22..27
23	5	6..2	5..58	5..5..28	16..34	23..8
24	6	6..3	5..57	5..17..19		23..49
25	7	6..4	5..56	5..29..12	Set	ʒ
26	C	6..5	5..55	6..11..12	6..17	0..30
27	2	6..7	5..53	6..23..21	6..40	1..11
28	3	6..8	5..52	7..5..44	7..9	1..57
29	4	6..9	5..51	7..18..22	7..44	2..44
30	5					

1803 Febr 2nd in the morning part of the day there
arose a very dark cloud followed by snow and hail and a flash of light-
ning and loud thunder crack, and then the storm abated
untill after noon, when another cloud arose the same
point viz. North west, with a beautiful shower of
~~[illegible]~~ of snow but what beautifyed the snow
was the brightness of the Sun which was near setting
at that time, I looked for the rain bow or rather snow
bow, but I think the snow was of too dense a nature to exhibit the representation of the bow in the cloud
NB the above was followed by very cold weather a few days

Mean New Moon in March 1804, with the Sun and Moon's mean Anomalies Greenwich time

Mean New Moon in March	Sun's mean Anomaly	Moon's mean Anomaly	
	1804		
D H M	S ° '	S ° '	We must observe
11 .. 0 .. 22	8 .. 9 .. 30	4 .. 12 .. 54	to subtract 77 degrees nation or 5h. 8.m.
	1805		to reduce it to the
29 .. 21 .. 55	8 .. 27 .. 42	3 .. 18 .. 34	Meridian of the city of Washington

1802 October Tenth Month hath 31 Days

		☽	☉ Long.
First ☾ 4..9..46 morn		1	6..7..42
Full ☉ 11..1..10 morn		7	6..13..43
Last ☾ 18..9..24 morn		13	6..19..39
New ☽ 26..1..24 aft.		19	6..25..37
☊ { 1 10 / 11 ♓ 10 / 21 9 } deg.		25	7..1..35

M D	W D		☉ rise	☉ set	☽ Long.	☽ set	☽ South
			6..11	5..49	8..1..17	8..25	3..36
1	6		6..12	5..48	8..14..32	9..8	4..31
2	7		6..13	5..47	8..28..7	10..4	5..29
3	C		6..14	5..46	9..12..2	11..6	6..29
4	2		6..15	5..45	9..26..14	12..14	7..29
5	3		6..17	5..43	10..10..41	13..23	8..26
6	4		6..18	5..42	10..25..18	14..35	9..21
7	5		6..19	5..41	11..10..1	15..47	10..14
8	6		6..20	5..40	11..24..43	17..0	11..7
9	7		6..22	5..38	0..9..18		11..59
10	C		6..23	5..37	0..23..43	rise	12..50
11	[illegible]		6..24	5..36	1..7..50	6..56	13..44
12	3		6..25	5..35	1..21..39	7..35	14..38
13	4		6..27	5..33	2..5..9	8..17	15..32
14	5		6..28	5..32	2..18..19	9..3	16..26
15	6		6..29	5..31	3..1..10	9..55	17..20
16	7		6..30	5..30	3..13..52	10..48	18..11
17	C		6..32	5..28	3..26..3	11..42	19..0
18	2		6..33	5..27	4..8..8	12..37	19..46
19	3		6..34	5..26	4..20..6	13..33	20..31
20	4		6..35	5..25	5..1..59	14..30	21..14
21	5		6..36	5..24	5..13..49	15..29	21..55
22	6		6..38	5..22	5..25..41	16..28	22..36
23	7		6..39	5..21	6..7..36	17..27	23..17
24	C		6..40	5..20	6..19..40		23..58
25	2		6..41	5..19	7..1..55	set	..8..
26	3		6..42	5..18	7..14..23	5..48	0..44
27	4		6..44	5..16	7..27..9	6..23	1..34
28	5		6..45	5..15	8..10..13	7..8	2..27
29	6		6..46	5..14	8..23..37	7..58	3..21
30	7		6..47	5..13	9..7..20	8..58	4..21
31	C						

The days of year reckoned from the beginning of January

Days	January	February	March	April	May	June	July
1	1	32	60	91	121	152	182
2	2	33	61	92	122	153	183
3	3	34	62	93	123	154	184
4	4	35	63	94	124	155	185
5	5	36	64	95	125	156	186
6	6	37	65	96	126	157	187
7	7	38	66	97	127	158	188
8	8	39	67	98	128	159	189
9	9	40	68	99	129	160	190
10	10	41	69	100		161	191
11	11	42	70	101	130	162	192
12	12	43	71	102	131	163	193
13	13	44	72	103	132	164	194
14	14	45	73	104	133	165	195
15	15	46	74	105	134	166	196
16	16	47	75	106	135	167	197
17	17	48	76	107	136	168	198
18	18	49	77	108	137	169	199
19	19	50	78	109	138	170	200
20	20	51	79	110	139	171	201
21	21	52	80	111	140	172	202
22	22	53	81	112	141	173	203
23	23	54	82	113	142	174	204
24	24	55	83	114	143	175	205
25	25	56	84	115	144	176	206
26	26	57	85	116	145	177	207
27	27	58	86	117	146	178	208
28	28	59	87	118	147	179	209
29	29		88	119	148 149	180 181	210 211
30	30		89	120	150		212
31	31		90		151		

1802 November Eleventh Month hath 30 Days

	D.	h.	m.	
First ☽	2.	2. 6..	20	aft.
Full ○	9..	4..	8	morn
Last ☽	17..	2..	0	morn
New ☽	25.	7..	40	morn

☊ { 1, 11, 21 } ♓ { 8, 8, 7 } deg.

	☉ Long.
1	7-8.35
7	7..14.37
13	7.20.39
19	7.26.43
25	8.2.46

M. D.	W. D.		☉ rise	☉ set	☽ Long.	☽ set	☽ South
1	2		6..40	5.12	9..21..23	10..2	5..21
2	3		6..49	5..11	10..5.43	11..13	6..20
3	4		6..51	5..9	10.20..15	12..24	7..16
4	5		6..52	5..8	11.4..59	13..36	8..10
5	6		6..53	5-7	11..19.53	14..50	9..3
6	7		6..54	5-6	0..4.17	16..1	9..54
7	C		6..55	5..5	0..18.48	17..10	10..46
8	2		6..56	5..4	1..3..5		11..38
9	3		6..57	5..3	1..17..7	rise	12..31
10	4		6..58	5..2	2..0..47	6..15	13..26
11	5		6..59	5..1	2..14..8	6..58	14..21
12	6		7..0	5..0	2..27..8	7..49	15..15
13	7		7..1	4..59	3..9..51	8..43	16..6
14	C		7..2	4..58	3..22..19	9..37	16..56
15	2		7..3	4..57	4..4.31	10..34	17..43
16	3		7..4	4..56	4.16.34	11..31	18.27
17	4		7..5	4..55	4.28.28	12..29	19..10
18	5		7..6	4..54	5.10.20	13..27	19.50
19	6		7..7	4..53	5..22..9	14..25	20.30
20	7		7..8	4..52	6..4..2	15..23	21.12
21	C		7..8	4..52	6..16..2	16..21	21..54
22	2		7..9	4..51	6..28..9	17..19	22.39
23	3		7..10	4..50	7..10.31	18..19	23.27
24	4		7..11	4..49	7..23.6		δ
25	5		7..12	4..48	8..6..0	set	0..15
26	6		7..12	4..48	8..19..13	5..45	1..8.
27	7		7..13	4..47	9..2.45	6..43	2..6
28	C		7..14	4..46	9..16.38	7..46	3..5
29	2		7..15	4..45	10..0.48	8..52	4..3
30	3		7..15	4..45	10.15..14	10..3	4.59

	Mean D			☉ Anomaly			D Anomaly			Node		
	d	h	m	s	°	′	s	°	′	s	°	′
1800	~~24~~ 19	14		8	23	20	10	7	53	11	3	58
1801	12	4	3	8	12	36	8	17	41	11	12	1
1802	3	12	52	8	1	52	5	27	29	11	20	4
1803	22	10	26	8	20	47	6	3	6	0	28	~~47~~
1804	10	19	14	8	9	30	4	12	54	1	6	46

~~the above Table is Reduced to our Meridian~~

1805	29	16	47	8	27	52	3	18	31	2	15	29
1806	19	1	36	8	17	8	1	28	19	2	23	32
~~1801~~	~~2~~	~~9~~	~~11~~	~~8~~	~~12~~	~~36~~	~~8~~	~~17~~	~~41~~			
~~1802~~	~~21~~	~~6~~	~~44~~	~~9~~	~~0~~	~~58~~	~~7~~	~~23~~	~~18~~			
~~1803~~	~~28~~	~~13~~	~~6~~	~~9~~	~~8~~	~~36~~	~~5~~	~~8~~	~~33~~			

Adapted to the meridian of Baltimore

We must add 5h. 8m. to time in Table to make it correspond with the time at ~~Green~~ greenwich

1804 D Long 4 .. 29 .. 16 | 6 .. 28 .. 14

1804 mean New D March 9 .. 19 .. 15 | 8 .. 9 .. 20 | 4 .. 12 .. 54 adapted to the meridian of the city of Washington

adapted to the City of Washington

1803 mean New D March 21 .. 15 .. 34 Greenwich time

	D mean Long	Apog	
1804	4 .. 16 .. 5	6 .. 28 .. 7	Adapted to our Long

the former ... tion of ...

Month hath 31 Days

Lunations				D	Long
First Q	2..4..23	morn.		1	8..8..51
Full O	9..0..	morn.		7	8..14..57
Last Q	16..10..54	aft.		13	8..21..3
New D	24..7..33	aft.		19	8..27..10
First Q	31..1..6	aft.		25	9..3..17

{1, 11, 21} ♓ {7, 6, 6} deg.

M D	W D		☉ rise	☉ set	☽ Long.	☽ set	☽ south
1	4		7..16	4..44	10..29..52	11..14	5..54
2	5		7..16	4..44	11..14..33	12..26	6..46
3	6		7..17	4..43	11..29..15	13..37	7..37
4	7		7..18	4..42	0..13..51	14..48	8..28
5	C		7..18	4..42	0..28..16	15..58	9..20
6	2		7..19	4..41	1..12..27	17..8	10..12
7	3		7..19	4..41	1..26..18	18..13	11..6
8	4		7..20	4..40	2..9..51		12..2
9	5		7..20	4..40	2..23..2	rise	12..57
10	6		7..20	4..40	3..5..54	6..26	13..49
11	7		7..21	4..39	3..18..29	7..21	14..40
12	C		7..21	4..39	4..0..50	8..18	15..29
13	2		7..21	4..39	4..12..59	9..15	16..13
14	3		7..21	4..39	4..24..57	10..12	16..56
15	4		7..22	4..38	5..6..50	11..9	17..38
16	5		7..22	4..38	5..18..39	12..6	18..18
17	6		7..22	4..38	6..0..31	13..3	18..59
18	7		7..22	4..38	6..12..25	14..0	19..41
19	C		7..22	4..38	6..24..28	14..57	20..23
20	2		7..22	4..38	7..6..42	15..57	21..9
21	3		7..22	4..38	7..19..10	17..1	21..58
22	4		7..22	4..38	8..1..53	18..6	22..51
23	5		7..22	4..38	8..14..54		23..47
24	6		7..22	4..38	8..28..17	set	[illegible]
25	7		7..22	4..38	9..11..58	5..20	0..43
26	C		7..22	4..38	9..25..58	6..24	1..39
27	2		7..22	4..38	10..10..17	7..32	2..35
28	3		7..22	4..38	10..24..48	8..45	3..30
29	4		7..21	4..39	11..9..28	9..57	4..23
30	5		7..21	4..39	11..24..11	11..8	5..15
31	6		7..21	4..39	0..8..51	12..18	6..5
					0..23..23		

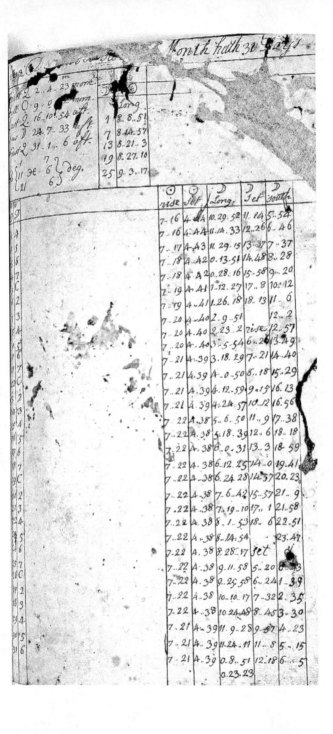

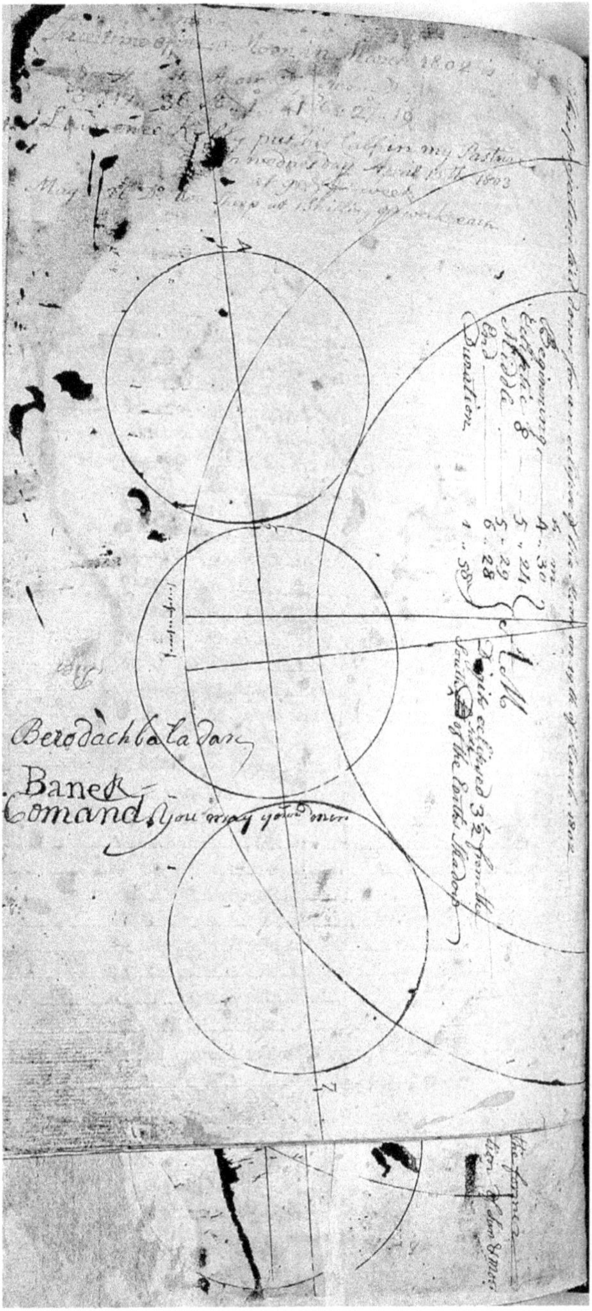
This projection laid down for an eclipse of the Moon on 19th of March 1802
Beginning — 4 . 30
Ecliptic — 5 . 24
Middle — 5 . 29
End — 6 . 28
Duration — 1 . 58
A M
Digits eclipsed 3½ from the South side of the Earths Shadow
Berodachbaladan
Baneker
Comand you may your men
Lawrence put his Calf in my Pasture
May 1803
the forme
tion of Sun & Moo

Years of Christ	Moon's Long. s	°	′	Moon's Anom. s	°	′	Moon's Node s	°	′
1806	1	15	9	3	25	32	9	7	8
1807	5	27	21	6	27	4	8	17	48
1808	10	3	55	9	22	59	7	28	29
1809	2	26	29	1	4	46	7	9	6
1810	7	5	52	4	3	29	6	19	46
1811	11	15	15	7	2	12	6	0	27
1812	3	24	38	10	0	55	5	11	7
1813	7	17	12	1	12	42	4	21	44
1814	0	26	35	4	11	26	4	2	24
1815	5	5	58	7	10	9	3	13	5
1816	9	15	21	10	8	52	2	23	45
1817	2	7	55	1	20	39	2	4	22
1818	6	17	18	4	19	22	1	15	2
1819	10	26	41	7	18	6	0	25	42
1820	3	19	4	10	16	49	0	6	23

Aug. The long marks are barrels Cyder for BB

|||||| B | $ Dr Barton & Jemson

A Note About the Authors

Daniel Alexander Payne Murray (1852–1925) was an author, politician and historian who was one of the first Black men to work for the Library of Congress. Born to formerly enslaved parents, Murray got his start at nine years old working with his brother in the U.S. Senate Restaurant. Catching the attention of Senator Timothy Howe and the Librarian of Congress Ainsworth Rand Spofford, Murray began working part-time at the Library of Congress in 1871. Within ten years he rose to assistant librarian and over the course of his forty-one year career at the library, Murray began to compile books and pamphlets by Black authors, growing to what is now known as the "Daniel A. P. Murray Pamphlet Collection." Seen as an authority on African American concern, Daniel Alexander Payne Murray was an important contributor and collector of Black history.

Will W. Allen is believed to have been a data collector or historian.

A Note from the Publisher

Spanning many genres, from non-fiction essays to literature classics to children's books and lyric poetry, Mint Edition books showcase the master works of our time in a modern new package. The text is freshly typeset, is clean and easy to read, and features a new note about the author in each volume. Many books also include exclusive new introductory material. Every book boasts a striking new cover, which makes it as appropriate for collecting as it is for gift giving. Mint Edition books are only printed when a reader orders them, so natural resources are not wasted. We're proud that our books are never manufactured in excess and exist only in the exact quantity they need to be read and enjoyed.

Printed in the USA
CPSIA information can be obtained
at www.ICGtesting.com
JSHW022004221123
52507JS00009B/5

9 798888 970140